Economic Analysis of Substance Use and Abuse

The Experience of Developed Countries and Lessons for Developing Countries

ACADEMIA STUDIES IN ASIAN ECONOMIES

General Editor: Sheng-Cheng Hu, *Director, Institute of Economics, Academia Sinica, Taiwan*

Titles in the series include:

Economic Efficiency and Productivity Growth in the Asia-Pacific Region
Edited by Tsu-Tan Fu, Cliff J. Huang and C.A. Knox Lovell

Food Security in Asia
Economics and Policies
Edited by Wen S. Chern, Colin A. Carter and Shun-Yi Shei

Economic Analysis of Substance Use and Abuse: The Experience of Developed Countries and Lessons for Developing Countries
Edited by Michael Grossman and Chee-Ruey Hsieh

The Economics of Health Care in Asia-Pacific Countries
Edited by Teh-Wei Hu and Chee-Ruey Hsieh

Economic Analysis of Substance Use and Abuse

The Experience of Developed Countries and Lessons for Developing Countries

Edited by

Michael Grossman

Distinguished Professor of Economics, City University of New York Graduate School and University Center and Director, Health Economics Program, National Bureau of Economic Research, New York, USA

and

Chee-Ruey Hsieh

Research Fellow, The Institute of Economics, Academia Sinica, Taipei, Taiwan, ROC

ACADEMIA STUDIES IN ASIAN ECONOMIES

Edward Elgar

Cheltenham, UK • Northampton, MA, USA

Published by
Edward Elgar Publishing Limited
Glensanda House
Montpellier Parade
Cheltenham
Glos GL50 1UA
UK

Edward Elgar Publishing, Inc.
136 West Street
Suite 202
Northampton
Massachusetts 01060
USA

A catalogue record for this book
is available from the British Library

Library of Congress Cataloguing in Publication Data

The economic analysis of substance use and abuse : the experience of developed countries and lessons for developing countries / edited by Michael Grossman, Chee-Ruey Hsieh.

p. cm. — (Academia studies in Asian economies)

Includes bibliographical references and index.

1. Substance abuse—Economic aspects—United States. 2. Substance abuse—Economic aspects—Cross-cultural studies. 3. Drug abuse—Economic aspects—United States. 4. Alcoholism—Economic aspects—United States. 5. Drug abuse—Economic aspects—Cross-cultural studies. 6. Alcoholism—Economic aspects—Cross-cultural studies. 7. Substance abuse—Economic aspects—Developing countries. I. Title: Experience of developed countries and lessons for developing countries. II. Grossman, Michael, 1942– III. Hsieh, Chee-Ruey. IV. Series.

HV4999.2 .E253 2001
338.4'336229—dc21 00–067344

ISBN 1–84064–625–X
Printed and bound in Great Britain by MPG Books Ltd, Bodmin, Cornwall

Contents

Contributors

David M. Bishai Assistant Professor, Department of Population and Family Health Sciences, Johns Hopkins University School of Hygiene and Public Health, Baltimore, MD, USA.

Frank J. Chaloupka Professor, Department of Economics, University of Illinois at Chicago, IL, USA, and Research Associate, National Bureau of Economic Research, New York, USA.

Likwang Chen Assistant Investigator, Division of Health Policy Research, National Health Research Institutes, Taipei, Taiwan.

Paul Contoyannis Research Fellow, Department of Economics and Related Studies, University of York, Heslington, York, UK.

Matthew Farrelly Senior Economist, Center for Economic Research, Research Triangle Institute, Research Triangle Park, NC, USA.

Michael T. French Associate Professor, Health Services Research Center, Department of Epidemiology and Public Health, and Department of Economics, University of Miami, FL, USA.

Tsu-tan Fu Research Fellow, Institute of Economics, Academia Sinica, Taipei, Taiwan.

Michael Grossman Distinguished Professor of Economics, City University of New York Graduate School and University Center and Director, Health Economics Program, National Bureau of Economic Research, New York, USA.

Alphonse G. Holtmann Professor, Department of Economics, University of Miami, FL, USA.

Chee-Ruey Hsieh Research Fellow, Institute of Economics, Academia Sinica, Taipei, Taiwan.

Andrew M. Jones Professor, Department of Economics and Related Studies, University of York, Heslington, York, UK.

Theodore Joyce Professor, Department of Economics and Finance, Baruch College, New York, USA, and Research Associate, National Bureau of Economic Research, New York, USA.

Robert Kaestner Professor, School of Public Affairs, Baruch College, New York, USA, and Research Associate, National Bureau of Economic Research, New York, USA.

Kamhon Kan Associate Research Fellow, Institute of Economics, Academia Sinica, Taipei, Taiwan.

Don Kenkel Associate Professor, Department of Policy Analysis and Management, Cornell University, Ithaca, NY, USA.

Chien-Fu Jeff Lin Professor, Department of Economics, National Taiwan University, Taipei, Taiwan.

Jin-tan Liu Professor, Department of Economics, National Taiwan University, Taipei, Taiwan.

Sara Markowitz Assistant Professor, Department of Economics, Rutgers University, Newark, USA and Faculty Research Fellow, National Bureau of Economic Research, New York, USA.

Kerry Anne McGeary Assistant Professor, Department of Economics, University of Miami, FL, USA.

Rima Nair PhD Candidate, Department of Economics, University of Illinois at Chicago, Chicago, IL, USA.

John A. Rizzo Professor, Graduate Program in Health Services Management and Policy, College of Medicine and Public Health and Senior Research Scholar in the Center for Health Outcomes, Policy and Evaluation Studies at the Ohio State University, Columbus, Ohio, USA.

Henry Saffer Professor of Economics, Kean University, New York, USA, and Research Associate, National Bureau of Economic Research, New York, USA.

Mau-Shan Shi Associate Research Fellow, Institute of Economics, Academia Sinica, Taipei, Taiwan.

Frank A. Sloan J. Alexander McMahon Professor of Health Policy and Management and Professor of Economics, Duke University, Durham, NC, USA.

V. Kerry Smith University Distinguished Professor, Department of Agriculture and Resources Economics, North Carolina State University, Raleigh, NC, USA.

John A. Tauras Assistant Professor, Department of Economics, University of Illinois at Chicago, Chicago, IL, USA.

Donald H. Taylor, Jr. Assistant Research Professor, Center for Health Policy, Law and Management, Terry Sanford Institute of Public Policy, Duke University, Durham, NC, USA.

Wei-Der Tsai Assistant Professor, Graduate Institute of Industrial Economics, National Central University, Chungli, Taiwan.

Ping Wang Professor, Department of Economics, Vanderbilt University, Nashville, TN, USA.

Gary A. Zarkin Senior Program Director, Center for Economics Research, Research Triangle Institute, NC, USA.

Acknowledgements

Academia Studies in Asian Economies serve to assimilate the findings of research conducted by the faculty of the Institute of Economics, Academia Sinica and studies presented at conferences sponsored by the Institute.

The Institute of Economics is one of the 24 research units of Academia Sinica, the leading academic institution in Taiwan. Its goals are to conduct and promote academic research in economics. Its faculty conducts research in all areas of economics, with emphasis on issues related to Asian economies. To promote economic research, each year the Institute organizes a number of international conferences on several areas in economics, especially those relevant for Asian economies. The papers included in this volume were selected from those presented at the Taipei International Conference on Health Economics held at the Institute on March 25–26, 1999. Over 200 conference participants from seven countries contributed papers and discussed issues concerning health behavior and health insurance.

Many individuals and institutions contributed to the success of the conference and this volume. We owe a special debt of gratitude to Dr Yuan-Tseh Lee, President of Academia Sinica and Dr Sheng-Cheng Hu, Director of the Institute of Economics, for their encouragement and support. We are grateful to the Health Economics Program of the National Bureau of Economic Research, the National Science Council, the Ministry of Health, and the Bureau of National Health Insurance in Taiwan for generous financial support. We are grateful to Min-Hui Hsu for her excellent assistance and to the staff of the Institute of Economics for their efficient logistic support.

1. The economics of substance use and abuse: the role of price

Michael Grossman*

1 INTRODUCTION

The economics of substance use and abuse deals with the consumption of goods that share two properties. First, they are addictive in the sense that an increase in past consumption of the good leads to an increase in current consumption. Second, their consumption harms the consumer and others. This second property makes them of interest from policy, legal, and public health perspectives. Clearly, not every addictive good harms the user and others. A person can be addicted to jogging, classical music, detective novels, attending church, and other activities that do not harm others and may yield future benefits to the individual in addition to increases in current utility. But the consumption of such substances as cigarettes, alcohol, cocaine, marijuana, and heroin can harm the consumer and others. For example, cigarette smoking has been labeled as the largest preventable cause of death by the last three annual US Surgeon General's Report on Smoking and Health. Motor vehicle accident mortality is the leading cause of death of persons between the ages of one and 35 in the US, and alcohol is involved in almost 50 percent of these fatal accidents. The consumption of cocaine and other illicit substances results in deaths due to drug overdoses and the violence that accompanies the purchase and sale of illegal drugs. The existence of external costs (harm to others) and ignored internal costs (harm to self) suggests a possible justification for government intervention. This policy may not, however, be justified if it generates substantial external costs, or if the costs of eliminating the harms are greater than the costs arising from the harms.

Currently, developed countries pay much more attention to harmfully addictive substances than do developing countries. This is not surprising since these substances account for much larger percentages of premature mortality and morbidity in the developed regions of the world. Table 1.1

*Table 1.1 Percentages of total years of life lost due to premature mortality from tobacco, alcohol, and illicit drug use, by regions of the world, 1990**

Region	Tobacco use (%)	Alcohol use (%)	Illicit drug use (%)
1. Established Market Economies	16.0	5.1	1.4
2. Formerly Socialist Economies of Europe	16.3	5.7	0.6
3. India	0.7	1.4	0.1
4. China	4.9	1.8	0.4
5. Other Asian Islands	1.7	1.6	0.2
6. Sub-Saharan Africa	0.4	2.0	0.1
7. Latin America and Caribbean	1.7	5.9	0.8
8. Middle Eastern Crescent	1.3	0.2	0.1
Developed Regions (1–2)	16.2	5.4	1.1
Developing Regions (3–8)	1.5	1.8	0.2

Note: * Percentages of total pertain to years of life lost due to tobacco use, for example, as a percentage of total years of life lost due to ten risk factors (the three in the table and malnutrition, poor water supply, unsafe sex, occupation, hypertension, physical inactivity, and air pollution) by region.

Source: Murray and Lopez (1996, pp. 313–14).

shows that tobacco, alcohol, and illicit drug use accounted for 23 percent of total years of life lost due to premature mortality in developed regions but only 4 percent of total years of life lost in developing regions in 1990. That situation, however, is extremely likely to change within the next two decades. At the present time, diarrhoeal diseases cause 3 million annual deaths worldwide. Practically all of these deaths occur in developing countries. Murray and Lopez (1996) predict that this number will fall to 1.2 million by the year 2020. At the same time, they forecast that tobacco deaths will increase from 3 million to 8.4 million, with almost 90 percent of this increase occurring in the developing world. This increase can be traced to relatively high smoking rates in the developing world and to potential growths in these rates in the future. Most of what I have to say deals with research on the demand for harmful substances in the US and a few other developed countries and public policies pursued by these countries. But this body of literature is very relevant to the developing world since substance abuse is likely to impose a continually increasing burden of disease in the region in the near future.

The US government and those of many other countries have chosen to regulate some addictive substances (for example, cigarettes and alcohol) via taxation; minimum purchase age laws; restrictions on consumption in schools, the workplace, and public places; and stiff fines for driving under the influence of alcohol. They have chosen to outlaw other substances (for example, cocaine, heroin, opium, and marijuana). Taxation, other forms of regulation, and bans raise the prices of these substances. In addition, bans create black markets and encourage criminal activities that may harm innocent victims.

The full price of addictive goods can be defined broadly to include not only the money price but such indirect cost elements as the monetary value of the travel and waiting time required to obtain the good, the monetary value of the expected penalties for possession of illegal drugs or conviction of drunk driving, and the monetary value of the adverse health effects. The responsiveness of these substances to full price is an important parameter in determining the optimal level of taxation and the impacts of legalization. The economics of substance use and abuse is very relevant to these issues because recent theoretical advances predict that addictive goods should be more sensitive to price than previously believed. A growing body of empirical studies confirms this prediction.

2 PRICE TRENDS IN THE UNITED STATES

Much of the research that I shall be discussing deals with the effects of money price on consumption and abuse and on interactions between money price and other components of full price. It is natural to focus on money price given the pre-eminence of the law of the downward-sloping demand function. Moreover, money price is a convenient variable for governments to manipulate via excise taxation. Taxes are ‘blunt instruments’ because they impose welfare cost on non-abusers. But the enforcement and administrative costs of such policies as minimum purchasing ages are likely to be much higher than those associated with taxation (Grossman et al. 1994).

Given my emphasis on money price and on US data and policy, it is instructive to examine trends in the real prices of cigarettes, alcohol, cocaine, and marijuana (the money price of each substance divided by the consumer price index for all goods). Figure 1.1 shows trends in real cigarette, beer, wine, and distilled spirits prices from 1975 through 1999. This period encompasses most of the US anti-smoking campaign which dates to the issuance of the first Surgeon General’s Report on Smoking

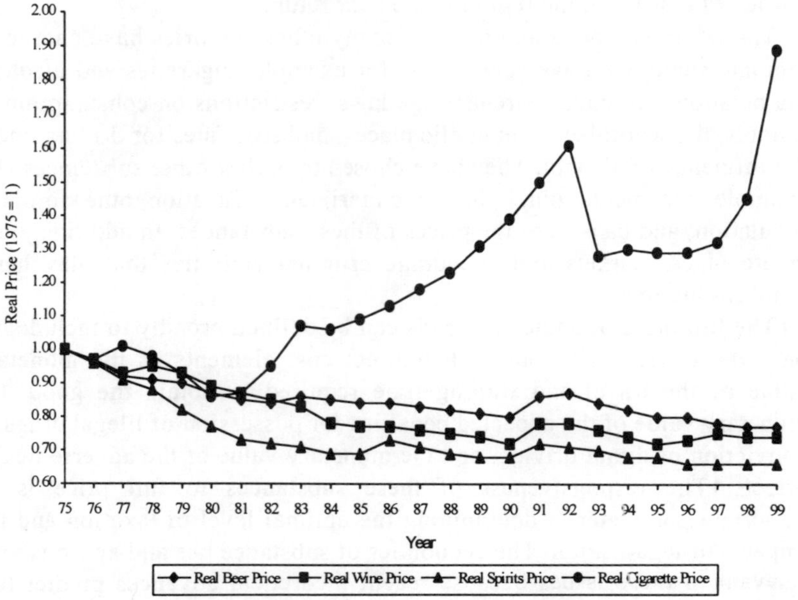

Sources: Consumer price index and alcoholic beverage prices from Bureau of Labor Statistics (various years). Cigarette prices from Orzechowski and Walker (2000).

Figure 1.1 Real alcohol and cigarette prices, 1975–99

and Health in 1964. It includes the entire campaign to reduce deaths from motor vehicle accidents by discouraging alcohol abuse. This campaign began in the mid-1970s and has been expanded to include other outcomes of alcohol abuse.

The figure shows that the real prices of alcohol and cigarettes have declined significantly for long periods during which the anti-smoking and anti-drinking campaigns have been in effect. These declines can be traced in part to the stability in nominal terms of the federal excise tax rates on cigarettes and alcohol (see Table 1.2). In the case of cigarettes, the real price fell by 15 percent between 1975 and 1980 (and by 20 percent between 1965 and 1980) before rising by 88 percent between 1980 and 1992. This large increase resulted in part from the three federal tax hikes. The 18 percent decline in price between 1992 and 1997 was generated by a cut of 40 cents in the nominal price of a pack of Marlboro cigarettes by the Philip Morris Companies in April 1993, which was matched by competitors soon after. Since 1997, the real price has risen by 43 percent in response to the settlement of the state lawsuits filed against cigarette

Table 1.2 Federal excise tax rates on alcoholic beverages and cigarettes, 1951–present

	Distilled Spirits
1951–Sept. 1985	$10.50 per proof gallon
Oct. 1985–1990	$12.50 per proof gallon
1991–present	$13.50 per proof gallon
	Beer
1951–1990	16 cents per six pack
1991–present	32 cents per six pack
	Wine
1951–1990	3 cents per bottle
1991–present	21 cents per bottle
	Cigarettes
1951–1982	8 cents per pack
1983–1990	16 cents per pack
1991–1992	20 cents per pack
1992–1999	24 cents per pack
2000–2001	34 cents per pack
2002	39 cents per pack

makers to recover Medicaid funds spent treating diseases related to smoking.

The downward trends in real price for beer, wine, and distilled spirits are much more dramatic. These reductions between 1975 and 1990 were 20, 28, and 32 percent, respectively. Since the tax rates on all three beverages were raised in 1991, real price declines amounted to 11 percent for beer, 5 percent for wine, and 8 percent for spirits.

Trends in the real prices of cocaine and marijuana for the period from 1981 through 1997 are shown in Figure 1.2. These prices are based on purchases made by drug enforcement agents to apprehend drug dealers. Despite large allocations of resources to interdiction and criminal justice as part of the Federal War on Drugs, the real price of one pure gram of

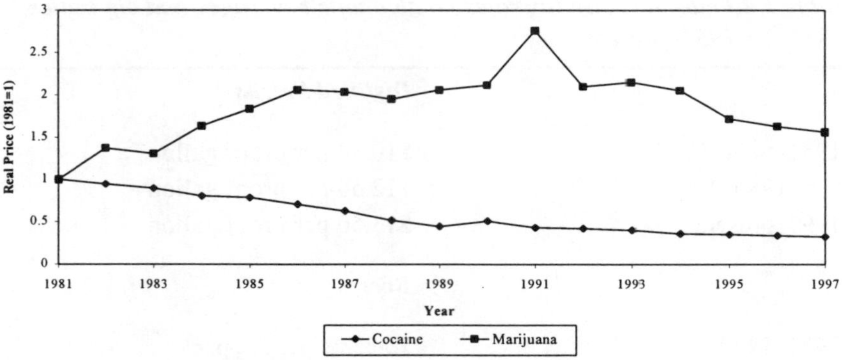

Source: Johnston et al. (1999).

Figure 1.2 Real prices of one gram of pure cocaine and one gram of marijuana, 1981–97

cocaine fell by 67 percent between 1981 and 1997. Most of this decline took place in the 1980s. One factor causing it was the development of the production sector and the results of learning-by-doing that followed the reintroduction of cocaine into the US market in the early 1970s after a long period of absence. A second was vertical integration, which reduced the number of levels in the chain of distribution and the cost of wholesaling and retailing. Finally, there was a shift to low-cost labor as the professionals who dealt cocaine in the 1970s were replaced by unemployed residents of urban ghettos in the 1980s. By contrast, the real price of marijuana rose until 1991 but has since declined by 43 percent.[1]

Declines in real prices of cigarettes, alcohol, and illicit drugs are inconsistent with campaigns to discourage their use. Clearly, for cigarettes and alcohol, one can question a policy that allows real tax rates to fall unless there is a consensus that the current tax exceeds the one that fully offsets external and ignored internal costs. I return to this issue at the end of this chapter. Here I note that consumption of the goods in question has declined since the early 1970s for all age groups. But for high school seniors the following indicators have risen since 1992 or 1993: the percentage using marijuana in the past month, the percentage using marijuana daily, the percentage who engaged in binge drinking in the past two weeks (consumption of five or more drinks of alcohol in a row), the percentage who smoked cigarettes in the past month, and the percentage who smoked cigarettes daily in the past month (Johnston et al. 1998).[2] As we shall see, both theory and empirical evidence suggest that youths are more sensitive to changes in the money price of addictive goods than adults. Since most addictions begin early in life (for example, 90 percent of smokers begin the habit as teenagers), policies to prevent the onset of these behaviors in adolescents might be the most effective method to curb them in all segments of the population.

3 BASIC CONCEPTS

One can approach the demand for a harmful addiction from three perspectives: a conventional model of consumer behavior which ignores addiction, a myopic model of addictive behavior which ignores the future consequences of current consumption, and a rational model of addictive behavior which incorporates future consequences. The latter approach is developed by Becker and Murphy (1988) in their seminal treatment of the economics of addiction. Since the first two approaches are nested within the Becker–Murphy framework, I emphasize this perspective. Given its somewhat controversial nature, I indicate at the outset that in my view, Becker and Murphy's main contribution is to suggest that it is a mistake to assume that addictive goods are not sensitive to price. Even if one does not accept all the aspects of their model, one can examine this proposition in the context of the standard theory of consumer behavior.[3]

An increase in past consumption of an addictive good raises current consumption because it increases the marginal utility of current consumption of that good (the increase in satisfaction or utility caused by an increase in consumption of the good). This is the reinforcement property of an addictive good stressed by psychologists. A harmful addiction, the focus of my discussion, is one in which past consumption has detrimental effects on current utility, such as reductions in health and therefore in utility caused by cigarette smoking, excessive alcohol use, and the use of cocaine. Harmful addictions exhibit the physiological property of tolerance in the sense that the utility from a given amount of current consumption is lower when past consumption is higher. Note that I follow most of the literature in using the terms addiction and habit as synonyms. Consumers are myopic if they ignore the effects of current consumption on future utility when they determine the optimal or utility-maximizing quantity of an addictive good in the present period. On the other hand, they are rational or farsighted if they take account of future effects of current consumption when they determine the optimal quantity of an addictive good in the present period.

Interest in addictive behavior by economists dates to Alfred Marshall. Writing in 1920, he noted:

> Whether a commodity conforms to the law of diminishing or increasing return, the increase in consumption arising from a fall in price is gradual; and, further, habits which have once grown up around the use of a commodity while its price is low are not quickly abandoned when its price rises again. (Marshall 1920: 807)

In this quote Marshall anticipates the differences between long-run and short-run price responses that play an important role in rational models of addiction. Most economists who have studied this behavior since Marshall have assumed myopia or imperfectly rational behavior. I classify two types of models under the general rubric of myopia. In one, consumers ignore the effects of current consumption on future utility when they determine the optimal quantity of an addictive good in the present period. In this class of models, past consumption affects current consumption through an accumulated stock of past consumption (for example, Houthakker and Taylor 1970; Pollak 1970). In the second class of models, consumers have inconsistent short-run and long-run preferences (for example, Schelling 1978; Thaler and Shefrin 1981). At any one point in time the individual is both a 'far-sighted planner and a myopic doer' (Thaler and Shefrin 1981: 392), with the planner and the doer in conflict.

Empirical applications of myopic addiction focus on the first class of models and are based on the pioneering work by Houthakker and Taylor (1970). They argue that the stock of a commodity should have a positive impact on its current consumption in the presence of habit formation if the commodity is non-durable. If it is durable, a negative stock effect is possible due to inventory adjustment. Houthakker and Taylor fit demand functions for a variety of goods for the US and several countries in Western Europe using annual time-series data. They find a considerable amount of evidence in support of habit formation.

More recent examples of myopic demand functions are contained in studies by Grabowski (1976), Johnson and Oksanen (1977), Baltagi and Levin (1986), and Baltagi and Griffin (1995). The first, second, and fourth studies report positive and significant impacts of past consumption of alcohol on current consumption of alcohol. The third study contains the same finding for cigarette consumption.

In sharp contrast to the myopic addiction studies, Becker and Murphy (1988) assume that consumers take account of future effects of current consumption when they determine the optimal amount of an addictive good in the current period. They use this notion to construct a model of rational addiction that among other things contains the first explicit derivation of long- and short-run demand functions for addictive goods in the case of farsighted consumers. The conventional wisdom is that addictive goods are not sensitive to price, possibly because small changes in the consumption of these goods cause large changes in the marginal benefit of consumption. Contrary to this conventional wisdom, Becker and Murphy stress that the demand for addictive goods may be responsive to price in the long run. They also stress that the quantity demanded of an addictive good is negatively related not only to the current price of the good but also to its past and future price. Economists define a set of goods to be complements if a reduction in the price of one good causes consumption of all of them to rise. In the Becker–Murphy model of rational addiction, the quantities of an addictive good consumed in different periods are complements.

Becker et al. (1994) show that the Becker–Murphy model generates a demand function for consumption of an addictive good in period t (C_t) of the form

$$C_t = \alpha C_{t-1} + \beta\alpha C_{t+1} + \theta P_t. \tag{1.1}$$

Here, P_t is the price of C_t. Other determinants of current period consumption are suppressed. Since α and β are positive and θ is negative, current consumption is positively related to past and future consumption (C_{t-1} and C_{t+1}, respectively) and negatively related to current price. In particular, α measures the effect of an increase in past consumption on the marginal benefit of current consumption. This parameter also measures the effect of an increase in future consumption on the marginal benefit of current consumption. The larger the value of α the greater is the degree of reinforcement or addiction. Equation (1.1) highlights the source of intertemporal complementarity in the rational addiction model. It arises because increases in past or future consumption (caused by reductions in past or future prices) cause current consumption to rise.

Equation (1.1) also implies that the short-run price elasticity, which holds past consumption constant, must be smaller than the long-run price elasticity, which allows past consumption to vary. This property does not hold in general for a non-addictive good. Hence, comparisons between the price elasticities of the two types of goods may be misleading if they are not based on long-run price elasticities. Put differently, since past consumption reinforces current consumption, the price response grows over time in the case of an addictive good. For example, a price increase in 1999 would reduce consumption in 1999 which in turn would cause consumption in 2000 and in all future years to fall *ceteris paribus*. Indeed, the long-run price response is greater the higher the degree of addiction or reinforcement.

The parameter β in equation (1.1) is the time discount factor and is equal to $1/(1 + r)$, where r is the rate of time preference for the present.

Typically, economists and psychologists assume that this discount factor is smaller than one because people are impatient. They prefer to consume 100 units of a good today instead of consuming 100 units of the same good tomorrow. The smaller the time discount factor (the greater the rate of time preference for the present) the smaller is the effect of future consumption or future price on current consumption. In the case of perfectly myopic behavior, β equals zero (*r* equals infinity), and future variables have no impact on current decisions. This is the sense in which a myopic model of addiction is nested within a rational model of this behavior.

Time preference for the present enters this and other models of optimal consumption over the life cycle because consumers are assumed to maximize a lifetime utility function defined as the discounted sum or present value of utility in each period or at each age, where β is the discount factor. While the discount factor is usually taken to be exogenous or given, Becker and Mulligan (1997) point out that consumers have incentives to make investments that *lower* the rate of time preference for the present. This is because the present value of utility is *higher* the smaller is the rate of time preference for the present. Becker and Mulligan provide examples of such investments. They write (1997: 735):

> Purchases of particular goods, such as newspapers, can distract one's attention away from current pleasures and toward future ones. A person ... may spend additional time with his aging parents in order to better appreciate the need for providing for his own old age. People may also purchase disciplinary devices, such as a piggy bank or membership in a Christmas Club which help a person sacrifice current consumption.

There are important interactions between time preference and addiction. On the one hand, people who discount the future more heavily are more likely to become addicted (Becker and Murphy 1988). On the other hand: 'Since a decline in future utility reduces the benefits from a lower discount on future utilities, greater consumption of harmful substances would lead to higher rates of time preference by discouraging investments in lowering these rates' (Becker and Mulligan 1997: 744). Thus, 'harmful addictions induce even rational persons to discount the future more heavily, which in turn may lead them to become more addicted' (Becker and Mulligan 1997: 744).

Extensions of the above framework imply differential price responses by age, income, and education in the case of addictive goods (Becker et al. 1991b). The total cost of addictive goods to consumers equals the sum of the good's price and the money value of the future adverse effects, such as the negative effects on earnings and health from smoking, heavy drinking, or heavy dependence on cocaine.[4] Future costs tend to be less important to poorer, less-educated, and younger consumers because they generally place a smaller monetary value on health and other harmful future effects than richer, more-educated, and older consumers who have higher wage rates. Moreover, the poor, youths, and the less educated are likely to have lower time discount factors (higher rates of time preference for the present) than the rich, adults, and the more educated (Becker and Mulligan 1997). It follows that the poor, youths, and the less educated are more sensitive to changes in money prices of addictive goods, whereas the middle- or upper-income classes, adults, and the more educated respond more to changes in the perceived or actual harmful consequences that take place in the future. Becker (1992) also shows that interactions between peer pressure, which is much more important for youths than for adults, and addiction predict greater price sensitivity by youths.

If the parameter α in equation (1.1) is zero or if consumers ignore the addictive properties of the substances under discussion, a conventional model of the demand for these substances emerges.[5] Yet all the factors just mentioned except for interactions between peer pressure and addiction still operate to produce differential price responses. In particular, youths are expected to be more sensitive to changes in money prices of addictive goods than adults because they value the future health consequences less, discount the future more heavily, and are more sensitive to peer pressure. In addition, the fraction of disposable income that a youth allocates to harmful substances is likely to exceed the corresponding fraction that an adult allocates to these substances. An increase in the fraction of income spent on a good raises the absolute value of the uncompensated (money income-constant) price elasticity of demand.

One common criticism of the Becker–Murphy formulation is that it assumes perfect foresight or ignores uncertainty. Orphanides and Zervos (1995) modify the model to allow for uncertainty about the probability of becoming addicted but do not provide a framework for empirical research. Therefore, it is worth noting that Becker et al. (1994) do not ignore uncertainty about future prices and other future variables. Instead, they incorporate this phenomenon into their empirical framework by distinguishing between, for example, anticipated and unanticipated future price effects.

Consider the effect on consumption in period t of a price change in period $t + 1$. The effect is fully anticipated if the price change is known as of the planning date (period 0). On the other hand, it is unanticipated if it does not become known until period t. In the latter case, past consumption

(consumption in period $t - 1$) remains constant, while in the former case past consumption varies. Put differently, the future consumption variable in equation (1.1) is expected future consumption. The one-sided forward solution of this second-order difference equation results in an equation in which C_t depends on C_{t-1}, P_t, and all future prices. Unanticipated future price effects and future life-cycle events (for example, marriage) are obtained from this equation. The two-sided forward and backward solution of equation (1.1) yields C_t as a function of P_t, all past prices, and all future prices. Anticipated future price effects and future life-cycle events are obtained from this equation. Since past consumption varies when future effects are anticipated, unanticipated effects are smaller in absolute value than anticipated effects.[6]

More generally Becker et al. (1991a) point out that uncertainty about the addictive properties of a certain substance can be introduced into their model. That is, the consumer assumes that the substance will affect utility and the marginal utility of consumption next period with probability π and will not affect these variables next period with probability $1 - \pi$. In that case, the coefficient of future consumption in equation (1) becomes $\pi\beta\alpha$. Not surprisingly, the introduction of this type of uncertainty reduces the size of future effects.[7]

4 EMPIRICAL EVIDENCE

In this section I summarize empirical evidence that highlights the importance of price, particularly money price, as a determinant of the demand for harmful substances. I begin with studies that obtain price effects in the context of the Becker–Murphy (1988) rational addiction model and then consider evidence that emerges from research using myopic or conventional approaches. The rational model has been applied successfully to the demand for cigarettes by Chaloupka (1991); Keeler et al. (1993); Becker et al. (1994); and Tauras (1998). It also has been applied successfully to the demand for alcohol by Grossman (1993) and by Grossman et al. (1998) and to the demand for cocaine by Grossman and Chaloupka (1998). All these studies report negative and significant price effects, positive and significant past and future consumption effects, and larger long-run than short-run price elasticities.

The cigarette and alcohol studies capitalize on the substantial variation in prices across the United States that exists due primarily to the very different state excise tax rates on these goods. The cocaine study draws on cocaine prices based on local purchases made by drug enforcement agents to apprehend drug dealers. These prices are higher in cities and states that both impose relatively stiff fines and prison terms on persons convicted of selling cocaine and allocate more resources to apprehending and convicting dealers. Typical short-run and long-run price elasticities of demand in these studies are –0.40 and –0.75 for cigarettes; –0.41 and –0.65 for alcohol measured by the number of drinks in the past year; –0.79 and –1.00 for alcohol measured by cirrhosis mortality (a standard index of excessive alcohol consumption); and –0.70 and –1.35 for cocaine consumption.[8]

The studies just mentioned and others contain additional support in favor of the economic approach to addictive behaviour. Chaloupka (1991) finds that smoking by the less educated is considerably more responsive to changes in cigarette prices than is smoking by the more educated; a similar result has been obtained by Townsend (1987) with British data. Lewit et al. (1981), Lewit and Coate (1982), Chaloupka and Grossman (1996), Chaloupka and Wechsler (1997), Lewit et al. (1997), Evans and Huang (1998), Evans and Farrelly (1998), and Harris and Chan (1999) report that youths respond more to cigarette prices than adults. By contrast, the information that began to emerge in the early 1960s about the harmful long-run effects of smoking has had a much greater effect on smoking by the rich and more educated than by the poor and less educated (Farrell and Fuchs, 1982 for the US; Townsend 1987 for Britain).

The negative relationship between age and the price elasticity of demand for cigarettes is worth highlighting because it is very robust across a number of studies, and it suggests that price hikes are an extremely effective instrument to discourage youths from beginning to smoke. Table 1.3 contains cigarette price elasticities by age from nine studies – two completed in the early 1980s and seven completed since 1996. Both the price elasticity of participation and the unconditional price elasticity (the sum of the price elasticity of participation and the price elasticity of the number of cigarettes smoked conditional on positive smoking) are shown. While estimates for a given age group vary from study to study, the negative correlation between the absolute value of the elasticity and age is striking.[9]

I have stressed the importance of the negative effect of price on youth participation in the consumption of harmful substances because changes in participation by youths primarily reflect start behavior. At older ages, changes in participation are due mainly to decisions to cease consumption. Quits are key outcomes because most of the health effects at issue are reversible.

As predicted by myopic and rational addiction models, Yen and Jones (1996) find that an increase in peak past cigarette consumption lowers the quit probability in a large representative survey of British adults. They are

Table 1.3 Cigarette price elasticities, by age

Study	Age group	Participation elasticity	Unconditional elasticity*
Lewit, Coate, and Grossman (1981)	12–17	−1.20	−1.45
Lewit and Coate (1982)	20–25	−0.74	−0.94
	26–35	−0.44	−0.48
	over 35	−0.15	−0.30
Chaloupka and Grossman (1996)	12–17	−0.68	−1.31
Chaloupka and Wechsler (1997)	College students	−0.53	−1.12
Lewit et al. (1997)	14–15	−0.88	Not computed
Evans and Huang (1998)	High school seniors	−0.50	Not computed
Evans and Farrelly (1998)	18–24	−0.36	−0.63
	25–39	−0.21	−0.42
	40+	+0.01	−0.01
	18+	−0.11	−0.22
Harris and Chan (1999)	15–17	−0.83	−1.00
	18–20	−0.52	−0.78
	21–23	−0.37	−0.64
	24–26	−0.20	−0.66
	27–29	−0.10	−0.32
Gruber and Zinman (2000)	High school seniors	−0.66	−0.85

Note: * Unconditional elasticity is sum of participation elasticity and quantity smoked conditional on participation elasticity.

not able to estimate direct price effects because there is no variation in price in their data. Their results suggest, however, that an increase in past price causes quits to rise.

Douglas (1998) provides somewhat more definitive evidence on the role of price in the decision to stop smoking in a US survey. The rational addiction model predicts that the quit probability should be positively related to current, past, and future price. The latter effect occurs because an increase in future price lowers future consumption. In turn, current consumption falls perhaps to zero. Despite high correlations among the current price, the price next year (future price), and the price last year (past price), Douglas finds positive and significant future price coefficients in his quit equations. This indicates that smokers in his sample are forward looking. The current and past price coefficients are not significant, but Douglas includes the number of cigarettes smoked per day at a peak period in his hazard equations. Clearly, past price may operate through this variable, suggesting that it should be omitted from the equations.

As in the case of cigarettes, cocaine consumption by teenagers and young adults appears to be more price sensitive than consumption by adults (Grossman and Chaloupka 1998; Chaloupka et al. 1999; Saffer and Chaloupka 1999). These three studies do not consider consumption by the homeless and by prison inmates, who may behave very differently from the population at large. Caulkins (1996), however, reports an even larger price elasticity of demand for cocaine of –2.50 using data on the percentage of persons arrested and brought to booking facilities in different cities within the United States who tested positive for cocaine based on urine specimens. Bretteville-Jensen and Sutton (1996) obtain a price elasticity of demand for heroin of –1.23 in a sample of non-dealing heroin users who participated in a needle exchange program in Oslo, Norway.

Historical data indicate that opium users responded to price during periods when its consumption was legal. Van Ours (1995) estimates a short-run price elasticity of demand of –0.70 and a long-run price elasticity of –1.00 in the Dutch East Indies (now Indonesia) during Dutch colonial rule, for the years 1922–38. Liu et al. (1999) report similar findings in a study of the demand for opium in the Japanese Colony of Taiwan during the period from 1914 through 1942.

Excessive alcohol consumption is perhaps the most common example of a legally addictive good next to cigarette smoking. The two goods are not, however, linked to adverse health outcomes and to addiction in the same way. There is overwhelming evidence that smoking has detrimental health effects. One can usually focus on whether and how much an individual smokes since these measures are highly correlated with the smoking-related costs of interest.[10] With alcohol, the situation is more complex. Unlike cigarettes, many persons regularly consume small quantities of alcohol. Most individuals who consume alcohol do not harm themselves or others; indeed, moderate alcohol consumption has been shown to lower the risk of coronary heart disease in men. Instead, the adverse effects of alcohol spring from the overuse or misuse of this substance. Examples include cirrhosis of the liver, drunk-driving crashes, workplace accidents, various forms of violent behavior, and failure to complete college or high school.

Given the above, the following findings are particularly notable. The short-run and long-run price elasticities of the number of drinks of alcohol in a panel sample of young adults are substantial, yet are smaller than the corresponding elasticities of cirrhosis mortality in a time series of state cross-sections (Grossman et al. 1998; Grossman 1993). Cook and Tauchen (1982) report that a one dollar increase in the state excise tax on distilled spirits lowers the age-adjusted cirrhosis mortality rate by approximately the same percentage as it lowers per capita consumption of distilled spirits. Using a similar methodology and a time series of countries, Saffer (1991) finds that the price elasticity of cirrhosis mortality is three times larger than the price elasticity of per capita ethanol consumption.

Kenkel (1993) reports large price elasticities for the number of days with five or more drinks in the past year, which is another standard measure of the incidence of heavy consumption: –0.92 for persons of all ages and –2.24 for youth between the ages of 18 and 21. This suggests that young drinkers, like young smokers and young consumers of cocaine, are quite sensitive to price. Similar findings using measures of frequent and heavy drinking by youths are summarized by Grossman et al. (1994). Kenkel also reports a strong positive association between the measure of heavy drinking and the reported number of occasions of drunk driving in the past year. This provides a plausible mechanism for the negative relationship between fatal motor vehicle crashes (many of which are alcohol related) and the price of alcohol, which is found in many studies (see Grossman et al. 1994 for a summary).

Additional consequences of alcohol overuse or misuse fall as the cost of alcohol rises. These include workplace accidents (Ohsfeldt and Morrisey 1997); violent crime (Chaloupka and Saffer 1992; Cook and Moore 1993b); child abuse (Markowitz and Grossman 1998); suicide (Sloan et al. 1994); failure to complete college (Cook and Moore 1993a); and failure to complete high school (Yamada et al. 1996).

Evidence on the effects of other components of the total price of a harmful substance on consumption and consequences are more limited.[11] State and local bans on cigarette smoking in the workplace and in other public places curtail smoking in the United States (Wasserman et al. 1991; Evans et al. 1999). Increases in state minimum legal ages for the purchase and consumption of alcohol in the late 1970s and 1980s lowered the frequency and quantity of heavy drinking and the motor vehicle accident mortality rate of 18 to 20 year olds (Kenkel 1993; Grossman et al. 1994). Minimum age effects tend to be smaller than the price effects, possibly because drinking-age laws are difficult (costly) to enforce. Some state laws that increase the certainty that a drunk driver will be apprehended and convicted, and the penalty paid if convicted, lower the incidence of both drunk driving and the motor vehicle accident mortality rate (Chaloupka et al. 1993; Kenkel 1993; Ruhm 1996). The evidence is mixed, however, and the effects are modest, possibly because the perceived probabilities of apprehension and conviction are small.

Eleven US states decriminalized the possession of small amounts of marijuana between 1973 and 1978. Some studies find that this increased the use of marijuana, while others do not (see Chaloupka et al. 1999 for a summary and new estimates). These mixed results may arise because nearly every state liberalized its treatment of marijuana possession in the 1970s. Chaloupka et al. (1999) report that marijuana use and cocaine use by US high school seniors are inversely related to state fines for conviction of possession. These effects are weak most likely because the probability of apprehension and conviction is low.

5 POLICY IMPLICATIONS

Since harmful addictions are sensitive to price, the government can discourage these behaviors by taxation or by bans. In the United States, federal and state excise taxes account for approximately 30 percent of the price of cigarettes and approximately 20 percent of the price of alcohol. Cocaine may sell for as much as 20 times its free market price (Miron and Zwiebel 1995). My discussion implies that cigarette smoking, alcohol abuse, and the consumption of illicit substances would rise substantially if tax rates were lowered or cocaine, marijuana, and heroin were legalized. But this observation does not justify the current policies. Revenue considerations aside, taxation of harmful addictions is justified only if there are external costs or ignored internal costs associated with these behaviors. Bans can be viewed in a similar manner. I illustrate these issues with respect to cigarette and cocaine consumption because alcohol control is discussed in detail by Grossman et al. (1994).

Consider the optimal tax on cigarettes. There is widespread agreement that smoking has the potential to generate external costs because the premiums paid by smokers for health and life insurance do not fully reflect their excess use of medical care services and their higher probability of death (Manning et al. 1991; Viscusi 1995). The lower Social Security and pension payments to smokers who die earlier offset some of these costs.

Some parents behave in ways that harm their children's health, and the health of spouses or unrelated persons can be worsened by the actions of smokers. The best example of these external costs is the harm done to their fetuses by pregnant women who smoke. Numerous studies show that these women are more likely to miscarry and to give birth to low-weight infants. Some of these infants die within the first month of life. Many more require extensive neonatal intensive care and suffer long-term impairments to physical and intellectual development. According to some, maternal smoking during pregnancy should not be treated as a cost imposed on one person by another and ignored by the smoker, because pregnant women may already have taken into account the impacts of their behavior on their infants. Since they still choose to smoke, the benefits to them outweigh the potential costs. Others argue that at least some pregnant women who smoke do so because they lack information about the effects of their behavior or heavily discount the future consequences of their current actions.

Similar issues arise in considering the detrimental health effects suffered by non-smokers from secondhand smoke. The US Environmental Protection Agency estimates that these effects include annually roughly 3000 additional lung cancer deaths, between 9000 and 17,000 additional deaths due to heart disease as well as a host of other respiratory illnesses. When these effects are attributed to the smoking behavior of a spouse, the costs are internal because most economists consider the family as the relevant economic decision-making unit. While children are members of this unit 'they are relatively powerless to affect consumption decisions that may influence their health, especially when they are very young' (Warner et al. 1995: 382). Increases in morbidity and mortality suffered by non-smokers in the workplace and other public places clearly are external costs of smoking.

As I indicated above, smoking generates ignored internal costs if consumers have imperfect information about the risks of smoking or behave in a myopic fashion. In response to the first US Surgeon General's Report on Smoking and Health in 1964, smoking participation rates of more-educated consumers declined rapidly in the late 1960s and early 1970s. In this period educated consumers were more likely to quit smoking and less likely to begin than less-educated consumers. These data imply differential ability to process new information as a function of education and possibly some government action. It is still true today, after more-than 30 years of providing information, that the more educated are less likely to smoke than the less educated despite the massive anti-smoking campaign that has been mounted by federal and state governments.

It is tempting to attribute the recent data to more future-oriented behavior by the more educated rather than to differences in information. Indeed, a survey taken by Viscusi (1995) shows that both smokers and non-smokers overestimate, not underestimate, the probability of death and illness from lung cancer due to tobacco. Teenagers, who have less information and are less future oriented than adults, actually attach much higher risks to smoking than the rest of the population. Schoenbaum (1997), however, finds that, among current heavy smokers in the Health and Retirement History Survey, expectations of reaching age 75 were nearly twice as high as actuarial predictions. Moreover, other risks of cigarette smoking, including the risk of becoming addicted, may be underestimated.

The addiction studies previously summarized suggest that smokers and consumers of other addictive goods are farsighted in the sense that they anticipate the expected future consequences of their current actions. Consumers who behave in this manner reduce their current consumption in response to an increase in future price. This is exactly what these studies find. Yet some persons, particularly the young and the poor, may discount the future much more heavily than other segments of the population.

The story with regard to cocaine consumption is somewhat similar. Consumption by pregnant women harms their fetuses. Cocaine use, like excessive alcohol use, may cause motor vehicle fatalities and violent behavior and crime. On the other hand, Miron and Zwiebel (1995) argue convincingly that drug prohibition, rather than drug consumption, promotes violence. I disagree, however, with their prediction of modest increases in consumption if drugs were legalized, based on the US experience with alcohol prohibition from 1920 to 1933. More recent research suggests sharper increases. For example, Grossman and Chaloupka (1998) predict that a 10 percent reduction in the price of cocaine would increase consumption by young adults by almost 14 percent in the long run.

The endogenous nature of time preference and interactions among time preference, addiction, and peer pressure are the strongest justifications for government concern with the cigarette and cocaine decisions of its citizens. Some persons may lack information about the process and outcomes of investments in time preference. The existing distribution of income and imperfections in the capital market may limit the ability of certain individuals to make these investments. Given society's concern with the welfare of its children, these issues are particularly troublesome if some parents ignore or are unaware of the benefits of making their children future oriented. Similar issues arise if poor pregnant women or young children smoke or use cocaine because they have high rates of time preference for the present.

These concerns justify government information and education programs, taxation, and other policies to curtail consumption, especially by youths. Such policies are often second-best solutions because they impose welfare costs on others. For example, taxing cigarettes to curtail consumption by children or pregnant women imposes costs on other smokers in the form of higher prices. Perhaps the first-best solution is to encourage investments designed to make persons more future oriented since such investments will simultaneously curtail the use of a variety of addictive substances. But much more research dealing with the determinants of time preference is required before this policy can be offered as a substitute for taxation and other forms of regulation.

I have not provided enough information in this chapter to compute the optimal tax on cigarettes or to evaluate whether the use of cocaine, marijuana, or heroin should be legalized. With cigarette taxes, a primary unresolved issue relates to what harmful consequences should be treated as external. For legalization, a cost–benefit analysis of many effects is needed to decide between a regime in which cocaine and other drugs are legal and a regime in which they are not. What I can conclude is that permanent increases in price caused by excise tax increases or permanent reductions in price caused by legalization will have substantial effects on the use of addictive goods. These strong price effects have been proven over and over in the literature and should not be ignored in the policy debate.

While this debate currently receives much more attention in the developed world than in the developing world, that situation is very likely to change in the future for reasons indicated at the beginning of this chapter. Thus developing countries have much to learn from the research that I have summarized. Similar studies using data for these countries deserve a very high priority on an agenda for future research.

Studies of the role of US cigarette companies in developing country markets also deserve a high priority on this agenda. Given the increasing hostile legal environment that these companies face in the domestic market, they are very likely to try to expand exports in the future. Chaloupka and Laixuthai (1996) report that per capita consumption of cigarettes in Japan, Taiwan, South Korea, and Thailand increased by almost 10 percent after the markets in these countries were opened to US cigarettes in the 1980s and early 1990s. Hsieh et al. (1999) present additional evidence that opening the Taiwan market to imported cigarettes has increased overall consumption.

6 CONTRIBUTIONS OF THIS VOLUME

The following sixteen chapters in this volume extend the frontiers of research on the economics of substance use and abuse in a variety of extremely significant ways. They are organized around five topics: rational addiction, risk perception and time preference, the costs of substance use, criminal violence and substance use, and demand analysis. Part I contains chapters on theoretical and empirical aspects of rational addiction. Don Kenkel and Ping Wang integrate economic research on the effects of alcohol on worker productivity with models of rational addiction as a form of consumer behavior. This allows them to examine theoretically and empirically the relationship between alcohol abuse and post-schooling human capital investment in the context of a framework in which the rates of time preference and human capital depreciation are positively related to alcohol abuse. Paul Contoyannis and Andrew M. Jones incorporate adjustment costs and future health costs into a model of the decision to quit smoking by British consumers. Their main finding is that there is a non-monotonic relationship between the probability of quitting and previous consumption, with the highest probabilities found among light and heavy smokers. Kamhon Kan and Wei-Der Tsai address the same issue in a Taiwan sample and report similar results.

Part II contains chapters dealing with risk perception and time preference. Frank A. Sloan, Donald H. Taylor Jr. and V. Kerry Smith address the question of whether US smokers adequately assess the health risks of this behavior. They find that heavy elderly smokers are too optimistic about their life expectancies. Tsu-tan Fu, Kamhon Kan, and Jin-tan Liu find that Taiwanese betel quid chewers underestimate the health risks of this behavior. Consumption by chewers is quite sensitive to price, with a short-run price elasticity of approximately –0.60 and a long-run elasticity of at least –1.00. David M. Bishai develops a methodology to estimate rates of time preference from data on wages and job risks and to include these rates in rational addiction estimates of demand functions for alcohol. In a US panel of alcohol consumers, persons who have higher rates of time preference for the present have more days in the past month on which they consumed six or more drinks.

Part III is concerned with the costs of substance use. All three chapters present results with US data. John A. Rizzo deals with the labor productivity costs of cigarette smoking as reflected by increased unemployment and work disability. These costs are concentrated among males 40 years of age and over and amount annually to approximately $4000 per smoker in 1998 dollars. Robert Kaestner and Theodore Joyce examine whether substance use causes unintended pregnancies. They uncover a causal effect in the case of alcohol consumption among white non-Hispanic women. Michael T. French, Alphonse G. Holtmann, Kerry Anne McGeary, and Gary A. Zarkin study the relationship between substance use and workplace attendance. They show that the use of cigarettes, alcohol, and illicit drugs is negatively related to attendance, measured by full days absent from work, leaving work early, or arriving at work late.

Part IV focuses on a specific negative consequence of substance abuse: criminal violence. Michael Grossman and Sara Markowitz consider the effects of variations in alcoholic beverage prices among states of the US on violence on college campuses. Their principal finding is that the incidence of each of four types of violent behavior is inversely related to the price of beer in the state in which the student attends college. Henry Saffer examines the effects of illicit drug control expenditures by US state and local governments and the state excise tax rate on beer on arrests, property crime, property damage, and the use of force. Both increased drug control spending and increased beer taxes reduce crime, with larger effects observed for youths than for adults. Sara Markowitz studies the impacts of alcohol beverage control policies on criminal violence in cross-sectional surveys conducted in each of 18 developed countries in 1989 and 1992. Her results suggest that higher alcoholic beverage prices lead to lower incidence of robbery, assault, and sexual assault.

Part V deals with demand analysis. The first three studies employ US data, while the last employs Taiwanese data. John A. Tauras and Frank J. Chaloupka examine the impact of cigarette prices on the decision to quit smoking by young adult males and females. Price has a positive and significant effect on quit probabilities for both genders, with somewhat larger elasticities reported for males than for females. Likwang Chen and Matthew Farrelly consider whether the presence of children is associated with men's cigarette consumption and whether this relationship has changed since the early 1980s. They find the negative association between the presence of young children and smoking by highly educated fathers was much stronger in the 1990s than in the 1980s. Rima Nair, Frank J. Chaloupka, Michael Grossman, and Henry Saffer study the differential responses of alcohol consumption by high school seniors cross-classified by race and gender to alcohol taxes and minimum legal drinking ages. They find significant differences in the impact of alcohol control policies on drinking among these subgroups, suggesting that a blanket approach to curtail this behaviour by all youths is not appropriate. Chee-Ruey Hsieh, Mau-Shan Shi, and Chien-Fu Jeff Lin examine the impact of trade liberalization on per capita alcohol consumption in Taiwan. Their results suggest that consumption rose after the market was opened to US producers in 1987 and that this occurred because the price of alcohol declined and non-price competition increased.

NOTES

* I wish to thank Gary S. Becker, Sara Markowitz, and Kevin M. Murphy for helpful comments and William Rhodes and Patrick Johnston for providing data on the prices of cocaine and marijuana.

1 Since drug enforcement officials focus on apprehending cocaine dealers, marijuana prices are based on many fewer observations than cocaine prices. Marijuana prices are not adjusted for purity, and an increase in purity may account for some of the increase in price prior to 1991. While these prices should be interpreted with caution, the downward trend in the 1990s has been reported by Rhodes et al. (1994), Rhodes and Pittayathikhun (1996), and Office of National Drug Control Policy (1998).

2 Very recent data from Monitoring the Future (2000) – a national survey of youths between the ages of 12 and 17 – reveal a decline in teenage smoking of approximately 12 percent between 1997 and 1999. As pointed out above, the real price of cigarettes rose by 43 percent in that period.

3 For critiques of the Becker–Murphy model, see Akerlof (1991) and Kleiman (1999).

4 I abstract from indirect costs associated with time required to make purchases and with expected penalties for conviction of use.

5 The rational addiction model generates a reduced-form demand function in which current consumption depends on current price and on past and future prices. Conventional demand studies of harmful substances fit reduced-form demand functions with past and future prices omitted. In the context of the addictive model, the price coefficients that they obtain may be viewed as biased estimates of long-run price effects. To those who do not accept the assumptions of the rational addictive model or the empirical evidence in support of it (perhaps because they think that the econometric tests of it are too taxing on the data), the price coefficients in the conventional studies are unbiased.

6 Technically, the formulas for unanticipated price changes in Appendix A of Becker et al. (1994) should be modified to allow the marginal utility of wealth to vary. But since the share of consumption in period $t + 1$ in wealth is likely to be small, this modification would not change the basic results.

7 Orphanides and Zervos (1995) address the issue of updating of probabilities due to information received from experimentation with consumption of addictive goods. Becker et al. (1991a) do not cover this topic.

8 Rational addiction studies of the demand for cigarettes by Labeaga (1993) and Conniffe (1995) are less supportive than those mentioned above but use data that

contain limited price variation. Waters and Sloan (1995) obtain positive but very small past and future consumption coefficients in their study of the demand for alcohol. The survey that they employ contains measures of current and past consumption of alcohol but lacks a measure of future consumption. They use an ingenious procedure to obtain an estimate of future consumption, but their study is hampered by the absence of a direct measure of this key variable.

9 DeCicca et al. (1998) fail to find negative price effects in a study of smoking initiation by teenagers. This result emerges, however, only after they include dichotomous variables for each state of the US in a panel that spans a very short four-year time period. It is extremely plausible that there is not enough price variation in the data to estimate a demand function once state dummies are included as regressors in a sample that spans only four years.

10 Some debate exists with regard to this proposition. Evans and Farrelly (1998) report that cigarette excise tax hikes lead smokers to shift to higher tar and nicotine cigarettes. Their estimated effects are so large that many of the health benefits generated by reduced smoking participation are eliminated. On the other hand, Moore (1996) finds that state cigarette excise tax increases lead to decreases in mortality due to heart disease, cancer, and asthma and that a 10 percent tax hike would save over 5000 lives per year.

11 For a much more detailed treatment of this topic, see Chaloupka and Pacula (2000). They also consider the issue of whether cigarettes, alcohol, and illicit drugs are substitutes or complements – a subject that I do not address due to space constraints. They summarize a number of studies that contain the tentative conclusion that these substances are complements. Thus, an increase in the price of one harmful substance is reinforcing in the sense that it causes consumption of that substance and others to fall.

REFERENCES

Akerlof, G.A. (1991), 'Procrastination and obedience', *American Economic Review*, **81**(2): 1–19.

Baltagi, B. and J.M. Griffin (1995), 'A dynamic model for liquor: the case for pooling', *Review of Economics and Statistics*, **75**(3): 545–54.

Baltagi, B. and D. Levin (1986), 'Estimating dynamic demand for cigarettes using panel data: the effects of bootlegging, taxation and advertising reconsidered', *Review of Economics and Statistics*, **68**(1): 148–55.

Becker, G.S. (1992), 'Habits, addictions and traditions', *Kyklos*, **45**(3): 327–46.

Becker, G.S., M. Grossman and K.M. Murphy (1991a), 'An empirical analysis of cigarette addiction', Cambridge, MA: National Bureau of

Economic Research Working Paper 3322, Revised.

Becker, G.S., M. Grossman and K.M. Murphy (1991b), 'Rational addiction and the effect of price on consumption', *American Economic Review*, **81**(2): 237–41.

Becker, G.S., M. Grossman and K.M. Murphy (1994), 'An empirical analysis of cigarette addiction', *American Economic Review*, **84**(3): 396–418.

Becker, G.S. and C.B. Mulligan (1997), 'The endogenous determination of time preference', *Quarterly Journal of Economics*, **112**(3): 729–58.

Becker, G.S. and K.M. Murphy (1988), 'A theory of rational addiction', *Journal of Political Economy*, **96**(4): 675–700.

Bretteville-Jensen, A.L. and M. Sutton (1996), 'Under the influence of the market: an applied study of illicitly selling and consuming heroin', York, England: Discussion Paper 147, University of York, Centre for Health Economics.

Bureau of Labor Statistics, US Department of Labor (various years), *Monthly Labor Review, Consumer Price Index – Detailed Report*, and Bureau of Labor Statistics Home Page, www.bls.gov.

Caulkins, J.P. (1996), 'Estimating elasticities of demand for cocaine and heroin with DUF data', Pittsburgh: Working Paper, Heinz School of Public Policy, Carnegie Mellon University.

Chaloupka, F.J. (1991), 'Rational addictive behavior and cigarette smoking', *Journal of Political Economy*, **99**(4): 722–42.

Chaloupka, F.J and M. Grossman (1996), 'Price, tobacco control policies and youth smoking', Cambridge, MA: National Bureau of Economic Research Working Paper 5740.

Chaloupka, F. J., M. Grossman and J.A. Tauras (1999), 'The demand for cocaine and marijuana by youth', in F.J. Chaloupka, M. Grossman, W.K. Bickel and H. Saffer (eds), *The Economic Analysis of Substance Use and Abuse: An Integration of Econometric and Behavioral Economic Research*, Chicago: University of Chicago Press, pp. 133–55.

Chaloupka, F.J. and A. Laixuthai (1996), 'U.S. trade policy and cigarette smoking in Asia', Cambridge, MA: National Bureau of Economic Research Working Paper 5543.

Chaloupka, F.J. and R.L. Pacula (2000), 'Economics and anti-health behavior: the economic analysis of substance use and abuse', in W. K. Bickel and R. Vuchinich (eds), *Reframing Health Behavior Change with Behavioral Economics*, Mahwah, NJ: Lawrence Erlbaum Associates, pp. 89–111.

Chaloupka, F.J. and H. Saffer (1992), 'Alcohol, illegal drugs, public policy, and crime', presented at the annual meeting of the Western

Economic Association International, San Francisco, CA, July.

Chaloupka, F.J., H. Saffer and M. Grossman (1993), 'Alcohol-control policies and motor-vehicle fatalities', *Journal of Legal Studies*, **22**(1): 161–86.

Chaloupka, F.J. and H. Wechsler (1997), 'Price, tobacco control policies and smoking among young adults', *Journal of Health Economics*, **16**(3): 359–73.

Conniffe, D. (1995), 'Models of Irish tobacco consumption', *Economic and Social Review*, **26**(4): 331–47.

Cook, P.J. and M.J. Moore (1993a), 'Drinking and schooling', *Journal of Health Economics*, **12**(4): 411–30.

Cook, P.J. and M.J. Moore (1993b), 'Economic perspectives on reducing alcohol-related violence', in S.E. Martin (ed.), *Alcohol and Interpersonal Violence: Fostering Multidisciplinary Perspectives*, National Institute on Alcohol Abuse and Alcoholism Research Monograph No. 24. Washington, DC: US Government Printing Office, pp. 193–211.

Cook, P.J. and G. Tauchen (1982), 'The effect of liquor taxes on heavy drinking', *Bell Journal of Economics*, **13**(2): 379–90.

DeCicca, P., D. Kenkel and A. Mathios (1998), 'Putting out the fires: will higher taxes reduce youth smoking?', Ithaca, NY: Working Paper, Department of Policy Analysis and Management, Cornell University.

Douglas S. (1998), 'The duration of the smoking habit', *Economic Inquiry*, **36**(1): 49–64.

Evans, W.N and M.C. Farrelly (1998), 'The compensating behavior of smokers: taxes, tar and nicotine', *Rand Journal*, **29**(3): 578–95.

Evans, W.N., M.C. Farrelly and E. Montgomery (1999), 'Do workplace smoking bans reduce smoking?', *American Economic Review*, **89**(4): 728–47.

Evans, W.N. and L.X. Huang (1998), 'Cigarette taxes and teen smoking: new evidence from panels of repeated cross-sections', College Park, MD: Working Paper, Department of Economics, University of Maryland.

Farrell, P. and V.R. Fuchs (1982), 'Schooling and health: the cigarette connection', *Journal of Health Economics*, **1**(3): 217–30.

Grabowski, H.G. (1976), 'The effects of advertising on the interindustry distribution of demand', *Explorations in Economic Research*, **3**(1): 21–75.

Grossman, M. (1993), 'The economic analysis of addictive behavior', in M.E. Hilton and G. Bloss (eds), *Economics and the Prevention of Alcohol-Related Problems*, National Institute on Alcohol Abuse and Alcoholism Research Monograph No. 25, Washington, DC: US

Government Printing Office, pp. 91–123.

Grossman, M. and F.J. Chaloupka (1998), 'The demand for cocaine by young adults: a rational addiction approach', *Journal of Health Economics*, **17**(4): 427–74.

Grossman, M., F.J. Chaloupka, H. Saffer and A. Laixuthai (1994), 'Effects of alcohol price policy on youth: a summary of economic research', *Journal of Research on Adolescence*, **4**(2): 347–64.

Grossman, M., F.J. Chaloupka and I. Sirtalan (1998), 'An empirical analysis of alcohol addiction: results from the Monitoring the Future panels', *Economic Inquiry*, **36**(1): 39–48.

Gruber, J. and J. Zinman (2000), 'Youth smoking in the U.S.: evidence and implications', Cambridge, MA: National Bureau of Economic Research Working Paper 7780.

Harris, J.E. and S.W. Chan (1999), 'The continuum-of-addiction: cigarette smoking in relation to price among Americans 15–29', *Health Economics*, **8**(1), 81–6.

Houthakker, H.S. and L. Taylor (1970), *Consumer Demand in the United States: Analysis and Projections*, 2nd and enlarged edition, Cambridge, MA: Harvard University Press.

Hsieh, C.R., T.W. Hu and C.F.J. Lin (1999), 'The demand for cigarettes in Taiwan: domestic versus imported cigarettes', *Contemporary Economic Policy*, **17**(2): 223–34.

Johnson, J.A. and E.H. Oksanen (1977), 'Estimation of demand for alcoholic beverages in Canada from pooled time series and cross sections', *Review of Economics and Statistics*, **59**(1): 113–18.

Johnston, L.D., P.M. O'Malley and J.G. Bachman (1998), *National Survey Results on Drug Use from the Monitoring the Future Study, 1975–1997. Volume I: Secondary School Students*, Washington, DC: US Government Printing Office.

Johnston, P., W. Rhodes, K. Carrigan and E. Moe (1999), 'The price of illicit drugs: 1981 through second quarter of 1998', Cambridge, MA: Abt Associates Working Paper.

Keeler, T.E., T. Hu, P.G. Barnett and W.G. Manning (1993), 'Taxation, regulation, and addiction: a demand function for cigarettes based on time-series evidence', *Journal of Health Economics*, **12**(1): 1–18.

Kenkel, D.S. (1993), 'Drinking, driving, and deterrence: the effectiveness and social costs of alternative policies', *Journal of Law and Economics*, **36**(2): 877–913.

Kleiman, M.A.R. (1999), 'Comment', in F.J. Chaloupka, M. Grossman, W.K. Bickel and H. Saffer (eds), *The Economic Analysis of Substance Use and Abuse: An Integration of Econometric and Behavioral Economic Research*, Chicago: University of Chicago Press, pp. 242–

47.
Labeaga, J.M. (1993), 'Individual behavior and tobacco consumption: a panel data approach', *Health Economics*, **2**(2): 103–12.
Lewit, E.M. and D. Coate (1982), 'The potential for using excise taxes to reduce smoking', *Journal of Health Economics*, **1**(2): 121–45.
Lewit, E.M., D. Coate and M. Grossman (1981), 'The effects of government regulation on teenage smoking', *Journal of Law and Economics*, **24**(3): 545–69.
Lewit, E.M., A. Hyland, N. Kerrebrock and K.M. Cummings (1997), 'Price, public policy, and smoking in young people', *Tobacco Control*, **6** (supplement 2): S25–S30.
Liu, J.T, J.L. Liu, J.K. Hammitt and S.Y. Chou (1999), 'The price elasticity of opium in Taiwan, 1914–1942', *Journal of Health Economics*, **18**(6): 795–810.
Manning, W.G., E.B. Keeler, J.P. Newhouse, E.M. Sloss and J. Wasserman (1991), *The Costs of Poor Health Habits*, Cambridge, MA: Harvard University Press.
Markowitz, S. and M. Grossman (1998), 'Alcohol regulation and domestic violence towards children', *Contemporary Economic Policy*, **16**(3): 309–20.
Marshall, A. (1920), *Principles of Economics*, 8th edn, London: The Macmillan Company.
Miron, J.A. and J. Zwiebel (1995), 'The economic case against drug prohibition', *Journal of Economic Perspectives*, **9**(4): 175–92.
Monitoring the Future (2000), 1999 overview of key findings. Monitoring the Future Home Page, www.isr.umich.edu/src/mtf.
Moore, M.J. (1996), 'Death and tobacco taxes', *Rand Journal*, **27**(2): 415–28.
Murray, C.J.L. and A.D. Lopez (1996), 'Quantifying the burden of disease and injury attributable to ten major risk factors', in C.J.L. Murray and A.D. Lopez (eds), *The Global Burden of Disease*, Cambridge, MA: Harvard University Press, pp. 295–324.
Ohsfeldt, R.L. and M.A. Morrisey (1997), 'Beer taxes, workers' compensation, and industrial injury', *Review of Economics and Statistics*, **79**(1): 155–60.
Office of National Drug Control Policy (1998), *What America's Users Spend on Illegal Drugs, 1988–1998*, Washington, DC.: Office of National Drug Control Policy.
Orphanides, A. and D. Zervos (1995), 'Rational addiction with learning and regret', *Journal of Political Economy*, **103**(4): 739–58.
Orzechowski, W. and R. Walker (2000), *The Tax Burden on Tobacco*, Vol. 34, Arlington, VA: Orzechowski & Walker.

Pollak R.A. (1970), 'Habit formation and dynamic demand functions', *Journal of Political Economy*, **78**(4), part 1: 745–63.

Rhodes, W., R. Hyatt and P. Scheiman (1994), 'The price of cocaine, heroin, and marijuana, 1981–1993', *Journal of Drug Issues*, **24**(3): 383–402.

Rhodes, W. and T. Pittayathikhun (1996), 'Prices of illicit drugs', Cambridge, MA: Abt Associates Working Paper.

Ruhm, C.J. (1996), 'Alcohol control policies and highway vehicle fatalities', *Journal of Health Economics*, **15**(4): 435–54.

Saffer, H. (1991), 'Alcohol advertising bans and alcohol abuse: an international perspective', *Journal of Health Economics*, **10**(1): 65–80.

Saffer, H. and F.J. Chaloupka (1999), 'The demand for illicit drugs', *Economic Inquiry*, **37**(3): 401–11.

Schelling, T.C. (1978), 'Egonomics or the Art of Self-management', *American Economic Review*, **68**(2): 291–4.

Schoenbaum, M. (1997), 'Do smokers understand the mortality effects of smoking? Evidence from the Health and Retirement Survey', *American Journal of Public Health*, **87**(5): 755–9.

Sloan, F.A., B.A. Reilly and C. Schenzler (1994), 'Effects of prices, civil and criminal sanctions, and law enforcement on alcohol-related mortality', *Journal of Studies on Alcohol*, **55**(4): 454–65.

Tauras, J.A. (1998), 'Price, clean indoor air laws, addiction, and cigarette smoking', PhD dissertation, University of Illinois at Chicago.

Thaler, R.H. and H.M. Shefrin (1981), 'An economic theory of self-control', *Journal of Political Economy*, **89**(2): 392–406.

Townsend, J.L. (1987), 'Cigarette tax, economic welfare and social class patterns of smoking', *Applied Economics*, **19**(2): 355–65.

Van Ours, J.C. (1995), 'The price elasticity of hard drugs: the case of opium in the Dutch East Indies, 1923–1938', *Journal of Political Economy*, **103**(2): 261–79.

Viscusi, W.K. (1995), 'Cigarette taxation and the social consequences of smoking', in J.M. Poterba (ed.), *Tax Policy and the Economy*, Vol. 9, Cambridge, MA: MIT Press, pp. 51–101.

Warner, K.E., F.J. Chaloupka, P.J. Cook, W.G. Manning, J.P. Newhouse, T.E. Novotny, T.C. Schelling and J. Townsend (1995), 'Criteria for determining an optimal cigarette tax: the economist's perspective', *Tobacco Control*, **4**(4): 380–86.

Wasserman, J., W.G. Manning, J.P. Newhouse and J.D. Winkler (1991), 'The effects of excise taxes and regulations on cigarette smoking', *Journal of Health Economics*, **10**(1): 43–64.

Waters, T.M and F.A. Sloan (1995), 'Why do people drink? Tests of the rational addiction model', *Applied Economics*, **27**: 727–36.

Yamada, T., M. Kendix and T. Yamada (1996), 'The impact of alcohol consumption and marijuana use on high school graduation', *Health Economics,* **5**(1): 77–92.

Yen, Y.S. and A.M. Jones (1996), 'Individual cigarette consumption and addiction: a flexible limited dependent variable approach', *Health Economics*, **5**(2): 105–17.

PART I

Rational Addiction

2. Rational addiction, occupational choice and human capital accumulation

Don Kenkel and Ping Wang*

1 INTRODUCTION

Addiction to a substance like alcohol can be viewed from many perspectives: as a psychiatric medical condition; as a public health and safety problem; as a problem threatening worker productivity; and as an extreme form of consumer behavior. Most economic research on addictions takes one of the last two perspectives. The most recent comprehensive study suggests that alcohol problems in the US in 1995 led to productivity losses of $77.1 billion (see Harwood et al. 1998). Moreover, there is good evidence that drinking reduces individuals' investment in schooling, limiting their lifetime earnings potential (see, for example, Cook and Moore 1993). Kenkel and Wang (1999) establish some benchmark empirical patterns describing relationships between alcoholism, job choice, and post-schooling human capital investment. Another line of economic research extends the rational model of the consumer to explain addictive behavior (Becker and Murphy 1988; Orphanides and Zervos 1995). The primary objective of the chapter is to explore theoretically the relationships between alcohol abuse and post-schooling human capital investment to integrate research on rational addiction with research on alcohol and worker productivity.

This chapter makes a first step toward establishing a theory by developing a generalized rational addiction model in which occupation and post-schooling human capital accumulation are endogenously determined. The framework is also general enough to allow for time discounting and human capital depreciation to depend on individual addictive behavior. The forward-looking behavior of the rational addict implies that the labor market consequences of alcohol abuse will be anticipated. This allows us to examine the dynamic effect of rational addiction on labor market decisions, including occupational choice and on-the-job accumulation of human capital. In addition, we can explore the short- and long-run consequences of some relevant public policies, such as an alcohol tax, a wage income tax, and an education subsidy.

Our model builds on the rational addiction model of Becker and Murphy (1988). Although not the only economic model of addiction, the rational addiction model has been very influential because it both explains well-known features of addictions (such as abrupt or cold-turkey quitting behavior) and generates testable predictions about addictive behavior (for more discussion see Grossman 1993). In particular, Becker and Murphy show that by holding the marginal utility of wealth (λ) constant, the λ-constant demand for the addictive good depends on not only the current price but also the past and future prices. By reducing past consumption, higher past prices lead to a lower consumption stock and thus lower marginal utility of current consumption, reducing current demand (which can be called the conventional addiction effect). By decreasing future consumption, higher future prices result in a higher shadow price of current consumption, also reducing current demand (the rational addiction effect). The long-run price elasticity of addictive demand consequently exceeds the short-run elasticity in absolute value. The main hypotheses on addictive consumption demand can be tested empirically when the utility function is quadratic (for example, see Chaloupka 1991; Keeler et al. 1993; Becker et al. 1994; Moore and Cook 1994; Waters and Sloan 1995; and Grossman et al. 1998). All these studies find evidence supporting the rational addiction approach to cigarette and/or alcohol consumption. However, it is notable that these empirical tests of the rational addiction model focus almost exclusively on the impact of future prices on current demand and on the relationship between short-run and long-run price elasticities.

A major shortcoming is that in the previous rational addiction studies, the rational addict is not allowed to take into account future consequences of current consumption through productivity effects.[1] Beyond our focus on the productivity effects, we also try to fully incorporate the implications of multiple equilibria as well as many features of addiction, including cold-turkey quitting, vintage-distribution of new addictions, and regret. One approach to explaining addiction is to move away from the concept of rationality (Schelling 1984; Akerlof 1991). Alternatively, Orphanides and Zervos (1995) build a rational addiction model that incorporates learning and regret. However, introducing departures from rationality or perfect foresight also tends to remove empirical content. While this chapter retains the assumptions of rational, forward-looking addicts, it will try to shed new light on interesting and important phenomena in the labor market by undertaking further study of the dynamic productivity effects of alcohol abuse.

The main contributions of our chapter to the existing literature are fivefold. First, rational addicts' consumption behavior interacts with occupational choice and post-school human capital accumulation. Second, the shape of the dynamic wage profile depends on the alcohol status: alcohol dependents have a flatter profile compared to the non-dependents. Third, addictive stock-dependent time preference and human capital depreciation together cause the job package of fringe benefits to be less generous for alcoholics. As a consequence, the wage loss from alcoholism may significantly understate the true productivity loss. Fourth, due to the interplays between consumption and labor market decisions, an education subsidy may be as effective as an alcohol tax for discouraging excessive drinking. Finally, information may play a crucial role when self-fulfilling expectations-driven multiplicity is present. Minimizing informational frictions can enhance the effectiveness of public policy.

The organization of the remainder of the chapter is as follows. Section 2 reviews research on alcohol and the labor market, including some simple but we hope convincing empirical evidence documenting the relationship between alcohol consumption and post-school human capital accumulation. These benchmark empirical patterns motivate our construction of a dynamic general equilibrium model of rational addiction in Section 3, where the labor market is an integrated part of the basic environment. Section 4 presents the optimization of the model, which leads to a dynamical system of 7×7 with two contemporaneous price variables solved recursively after deriving the quantity and intertemporal price variables. Section 5 characterizes the asymptotically balanced growth equilibrium and illustrates the underlying dynamic properties. In particular, we examine how workers' consumption choices interact with their labor market decisions, including occupational choice, on-the-job human capital accumulation, and the resulting wage dynamics. We illustrate the possibility of multiple equilibria in the sense that a continuum of transition paths converges to a finite number of asymptotically balanced growth paths (that is, both local and global indeterminacy). Finally, we conclude the chapter in Section 6 by offering some interesting avenues for future research.

2 ADDICTION AND LABOR MARKET OUTCOMES: EVIDENCE FROM THE NLSY DATA

Most studies of the effect of alcohol abuse in the labor market have been conducted within the static human capital framework using cross-sectional data. Since critical reviews of these studies exist elsewhere (for example, see Cook 1991 and Mullahy 1993), it is only necessary to highlight here some of the main results and shortcomings. These studies estimate models in which current earnings or income are specified to be a function of exogenous current drinking. They generally conclude that problem drinking causes earnings losses in the range from 10 to over 20 percent (compare Harwood et al. 1984 and Rice et al. 1990). In contrast, moderate drinking appears to be associated with higher earnings. For example, French and Zarkin (1995) find an inverse U-shaped relationship where wages peak at 1.5 to 2.5 drinks per day while Zarkin et al. (1998) find that male drinkers earn 7 percent more than non-drinkers (but somewhat surprisingly do not find evidence that this earnings differential disappears or becomes negative for heavier drinkers). A series of studies by Mullahy and Sindelar (1991, 1993, 1995) go beyond the conventional research line by addressing more subtle effects of alcohol abuse on productivity through indirect channels such as labor market participation, schooling, and marital status. Kenkel and Ribar (1994) argue that methodological shortcomings of many of these studies tend to yield estimates that are biased away from finding any negative effect of drinking on earnings. Kenkel and Ribar use a variety of approaches to address these shortcomings, including instrumental variables (IV) analysis. Their IV results provide the strongest indication that alcohol problems reduce earnings, yielding point estimates that alcohol problems cause about a 30 percent drop in earnings. A remaining shortcoming is that existing work fails to carefully address labor market dynamics related to the productivity effects of alcohol abuse despite some good evidence that supports for the detrimental effect of alcohol abuse on schooling (for example, see Benham and Benham 1982; Mullahy and Sindelar 1989; and Cook and Moore 1993).

To address this last shortcoming, we now present some simple empirical exercises to establish a plausible relationship between alcohol addiction and labor market outcomes. The primary data used herein comes from the panels of the National Longitudinal Survey of Youth (NLSY), which contains detailed economic and demographic information for 12,686 individuals who were between 14 and 21 years old in 1979. Annual data on work behavior and incomes are available for each individual in the survey; retention is roughly 90 percent. The NLSY has become a standard data source for empirical labor economics. Questions allowing measurements of alcohol consumption and problem drinking were added to various waves of the NLSY. The exact wording and types of questions vary, but the set of questions asked in 1989 can be used to construct measures of alcohol abuse and alcohol dependence that correspond to the American Psychiatric Association's *Diagnostic and Statistical Manual of Mental Disorders*, third edition, revised (DSM-IIIR) definitions. Another advantage of the NLSY is that it allows us to focus on young adults. The NLSY sample provides a look at individuals at the age when they simultaneously are at high risk of alcohol problems and are making key decisions about their occupation and future career.

We restrict our attention to the examination of the NLSY data of the 1989 wave for male workers. Non-working individuals are excluded because they do not face directly a choice between alcohol consumption and labor market decisions (although they do enjoy some fringe benefits through spouse coverages and/or government subsidies). In Table 2.1, we provide a partial listing of sample means for relevant labor market outcomes and alcohol measures available in the 1989 wave. The 'alcohol-dependency' status is defined by the DSM-IIIR criteria. Tables 2.1–2.6 summarize some relevant empirical findings concerning alcohol addiction and post-school labor market outcomes.

In Table 2.2, we provide a descriptive analysis of 1989 NLSY data for men, which indicates some of the questions to be explored. The results suggest that statistically significant group differences between alcohol-dependent and non-dependent workers (at the 1 percent confidence level). Relatively speaking, alcohol-dependent workers have on average received lower pensions, health/life/dental insurance, paid sick leave/vacation, and training opportunities. Such reduction in non-wage fringe benefits ranges from 6 to 13 percentage points. On the other hand, alcohol-dependent workers have suffered more (by 4 percentage points) on-the-job injury. Thus, we may conclude that alcoholics seem to be in 'bad jobs'.

To further explore this issue, we perform an econometric analysis, based on a companion paper, Kenkel and Wang (1999, see especially Tables 2, 3 and 9 therein). The estimates in Table 2.3 are from 14 probit models, where the dependent variable in each model indicates that the respondent reported receiving the fringe benefit in question. In addition to alcohol-dependency status the models also include as explanatory variables measures of individual and family background, including year of birth, ethnicity, the individual's standardized score on the Armed Forces Qualifying Test (AFQT), and whether at age 14 the individual lived in a non-intact family, attended religious services regularly, read magazines, or had a library card. In this way, the models attempt to control for many background variables that are potentially correlated with alcohol abuse. The models do not include current human capital variables such as schooling, job tenure, and marital status. Even though these are also potentially correlated with alcohol abuse, they are also potentially

Table 2.1 NLSY variable means–full sample, 1989

Variable	Men		Women	
	Mean	Standard deviation	Mean	Standard deviation
1989 Outcomes				
Log(earnings)	9.48	(0.88)	8.99	(1.07)
Log(hours/100)	7.57	(0.55)	7.25	(0.79)
Marriage	0.46	(0.50)	0.54	(0.50)
Alcohol dependence	0.20	(0.40)	0.08	(0.28)
Alcohol abuse	0.15	(0.36)	0.05	(0.23)
Heavy drinking	2.01	(3.09)	0.63	(1.75)
Days drinking per month	6.44	(7.92)	2.81	(4.99)
Personal characteristics				
African origin	0.27	(0.44)	0.26	(0.44)
Latino origin	0.16	(0.37)	0.16	(0.37)
Year of birth	60.65	(2.22)	60.51	(2.22)
Religious	0.41	(0.49)	0.49	(0.50)
Interview status	0.12	(0.32)	0.06	(0.24)
Health status	0.04	(0.19)	0.05	(0.21)
Completed high school	0.80	(0.40)	0.84	(0.37)
Completed college	0.16	(0.37)	0.17	(0.37)
AFQT score	183.45	(39.87)	184.44	(36.38)
Children	1.04	(1.18)	1.47	(1.29)
Family background				
Mother's education	9.99	(4.17)	10.17	(3.84)
Mother's education missing	0.07	(0.26)	0.05	(0.22)
Father's education	9.25	(5.29)	9.19	(5.23)
Father's education missing	0.15	(0.35)	0.15	(0.35)
Non-intact family at age 14	0.32	(0.47)	0.33	(0.47)
Siblings	3.88	(2.65)	3.96	(2.68)
Magazines at age 14	0.55	(0.50)	0.54	(0.50)
Alcoholic mother/stepmother	0.04	(0.19)	0.05	(0.23)
Alcoholic father/stepfather	0.18	(0.38)	0.23	(0.42)
Other alcoholic relative	0.23	(0.42)	0.25	(0.44)

Table 2.2 Job characteristics by problem-drinking status, 1989 NLSY data

Job characteristic	Alcohol-dependent workers	Alcohol non-dependent workers	*T*-test for hypothesis of no group differences
Pensions	0.46	0.55	4.85***
Training opportunities	0.38	0.44	2.90***
Health insurance	0.71	0.77	3.93***
Life insurance	0.58	0.65	3.86***
Paid sick leave	0.47	0.60	6.59***
Dental insurance	0.47	0.52	2.80***
Paid vacation	0.71	0.78	4.06***
Attended on-the-job training	0.16	0.16	0.19
On-the-job injury	0.12	0.08	3.45***

Note: The definition of alcohol dependence is based on DSM-IIIR criteria. Statistical significance is denoted by *, ** and *** at 0.10, 0.05 and 0.01 percent levels, respectively.

Table 2.3 Alcohol-dependency status and fringe benefits, 1989 NLSY data for men

	Sample proportion	Effect of alcohol dependency on probability	
Health insurance	0.764	–0.064***	(0.018)
Life insurance	0.643	–0.055***	(0.021)
Paid sick leave	0.575	–0.105***	(0.022)
Dental insurance	0.509	–0.046**	(0.022)
Paid vacation	0.774	–0.059***	(0.018)
M(p)aternity leave	0.485	–0.047**	(0.023)
Retirement plan	0.534	–0.090***	(0.022)
Employee discounts	0.453	0.006	(0.022)
Flexible work schedule	0.437	0.018	(0.022)
Profit-sharing	0.288	–0.012	(0.020)
Training opportunities	0.423	–0.037*	(0.022)
Child care	0.042	0.001	(0.008)
Paid/subsidized meals	0.160	0.001	(0.016)
Parking	0.540	–0.007	(0.021)

Notes: Probit coefficient has been transformed to show the effect on the probability of a discrete change of the alcohol-dependency dummy variable from zero to one. Standard errors in parenthesis. Models also include measures for year of birth, ethnicity, non-intact family/religious attendance/magazines/library card at age 14, mother's and father's education, siblings, and AFQT score.

endogenous. With these variables excluded from the models, we estimate the total impact of alcohol abuse on the receipt of fringe benefits, noting that part of the total impact may be through the channels of reduced schooling and marital status.

The probit coefficients have been transformed to show the effect on the probability of a discrete change of the alcohol-dependency dummy variable from zero to one; the proportion of the sample receiving each fringe benefit is also reported for a point of reference. Alcohol dependency is associated with a 5 to 10 percentage point reduction in the probability of receiving most major fringe benefits including health insurance, paid sick leave, paid vacations, and retirement plans. The estimates in Table 2.4 suggest that relative to their non-dependent peers, alcohol-dependent workers were almost 40 percent (or 3.3 percentage points) more likely to suffer an on-the-job injury. This together with results in Table 2.3 reinforces previous findings in Table 2.2, indicating that alcohol-dependent workers are indeed in jobs with worse non-wage attributes.

We next turn to examining the distribution of earnings by occupation and by alcohol-dependency status, seeking to address whether alcoholics are also facing a disadvantage in wages. We obtain simple ordinary least squares (OLS) regression results in Table 2.5, reporting the effect of alcohol dependency on earnings, after controlling for schooling, tenure, marriage and other job characteristics. The total earnings loss associated with alcohol dependency is of 9.8 percent, or about \$2100 at the average earnings in the sample. Only 4.6 percent (\$1000) is the direct effect of alcohol dependency while the remaining 5.2 percent (\$1100) is the indirect effect of alcoholism through the measured human capital variables.

Finally, we can use these data to begin to explore the relationships between alcohol dependency and occupation and earnings. Since occupational requirements concerning workers' drinking habits are not directly observable, we can only study general occupational differences, comparing the proportions of alcohol non-dependents and dependents in different occupational categories. Table 2.6a indicates that about 37.5 percent of non-dependents are in white-collar occupations, compared to only 30.9 percent of dependents. In contrast, only 48.1 percent of non-dependents are in blue-collar occupations, compared to 57.9 percent of dependents. There is also a smaller difference showing that alcohol dependents are less likely to be in service occupations. Table 2.6b presents mean and median earnings by occupation and alcohol-dependency status. Among those workers in white-collar occupations, alcohol dependents appear to earn nearly as much as non-dependents.

Table 2.4 Alcohol-dependency status and job characteristics, 1989 NLSY data for men

	Sample proportion (or mean of continuous variable)	Effect of alcohol dependency on probability (or OLS coefficient for continuous variable)	
Occupation	0.159	–0.025*	(0.013)
Like job very much	0.328	0.029	(0.018)
Injury/illness occurred at job	0.088	0.033***	(0.011)
ln (number of employees)		–0.235***	(0.090)

Note: See notes to Table 2.3.

Table 2.5 Alcohol-dependency and earnings, 1989 NLSY data for men

	(1)	(2)	
Alcohol dependent	–0.098** (0.035)	–0.046*	(0.030)
Schooling		0.054***	(0.007)
Tenure		0.003***	(0.0003)
Married		0.244***	(0.025)
White-collar occupation		0.317	(7.994)
Blue-collar occupation		0.225	(0.036)
Log (number of employees at job)		0.055	(0.005)
Attended training		0.151***	(0.033)

Note: In the OLS regressions, the dependent variable is ln(earnings). See also notes to Table 2.3.

Table 2.6a Occupation by alcohol-dependency status, 1989 NLSY data for men

Occupational status	Alcohol non-dependent	Alcohol-dependent
White collar	**37.5**	**30.9**
Professional and technical	13.9	10.1
Managers and administrators	11.4	10.5
Sales workers	4.3	3.2
Clerical workers	7.9	7.1
Blue collar	**48.1**	**57.9**
Craftspeople	19.2	25.0
Operatives	19.1	20.1
Non-farm laborers	9.9	12.8
Service workers	**12.0**	**9.6**
Farmers/farm workers	**2.2**	**1.5**

Table 2.6b Earnings, by occupation and alcohol-dependency status, 1989 NLSY data for men

Occupational status	Median earnings ($)		Mean earnings ($)	
	Non-dependent	Dependent	Non-dependent	Dependent
White collar ($n=1619$)	**25,000**	**25,000**	**28,398**	**27,252**
Professional and technical ($n=584$)	29,000	29,300	31,186	31,325
Managers and administrators ($n=505$)	26,000	25,000	30,087	29,505
Sales workers ($n=181$)	25,750	27,000	30,412	25,467
Clerical workers ($n=349$)	18,950	18,500	20,056	18,994
Blue collar ($n=2202$)	**18,000**	**15,000**	**18,941**	**16,807**
Craftspeople ($n=898$)	20,400	16,500	21,224	18,378
Operatives ($n=853$)	18,000	15,000	18,758	16,718
Non-farm laborers ($n=451$)	12,000	14,000	14,763	13,805
Service workers ($n=513$)	**15,000**	**13,000**	**16,032**	**15,433**
Farmers/farm workers ($n=94$)	**10,000**	**5000**	**13,012**	**6257**

There are virtually no differences in median earnings between the two groups, while mean earnings are somewhat higher for non-dependent workers. In contrast, in terms of either median or mean earnings, alcohol-dependent workers in blue-collar occupations earn less than non-dependent workers. Alcohol-dependent service workers earn somewhat less than non-dependents. There appears to be a large difference in the earnings of non-dependent and alcohol-dependent farm workers, but this should be interpreted cautiously due to the small cell sizes.

Of course, these findings are preliminary as they are based only on the 1989 wave of the NLSY data for men only. Nevertheless, they in general suggest that there are interrelationships between alcohol abuse and labor market outcomes: while alcoholics are likely in bad jobs in both wage and non-wage compensations, alcohol dependents are likely to be sorted into blue-collar jobs rather than white-collar or service occupations. Such empirical links between alcohol consumption, occupational choice and human capital reflected by wage and non-wage attributes remain open to be explored in a dynamic general-equilibrium framework.

3 THE MODEL

By developing a generalized general-equilibrium framework for additive behavior, we extend the existing rational addiction literature in two significant ways. First, it integrates the labor market into the intertemporal choice environment to study the dynamic interactions between alcohol addiction, occupation choice, labor supply and human capital investment. Second, it considers two additional channels of the detrimental effects of alcohol consumption – by raising the time discount rate and by reducing human capital accumulation. In general equilibrium, this structure allow us to characterize the dynamic paths of alcohol consumption and price as well as the lifetime wage-earning profile. The model builds on an infinite-horizon, perfect-foresight framework in continuous time with inelastic leisure and constant population normalized to unity. The adoption of the continuous-time framework is not only for technical convenience but also provides a sharp distinction between stocks and flows, which is particularly relevant to the considerations of addictive behavior.

Before proposing the theoretical framework formally, it would be useful to summarize the importance of these considerations in comparing potential productivity loss and wage loss due to alcohol abuse. In the empirical literature on alcohol abuse, estimating the impact of alcoholism on earnings has proven to be a difficult methodological challenge. Kenkel and Wang (1999) point out a methodological shortcoming that has received little attention to date: wage differences are unreliable estimates of the productivity losses from alcoholism if there are important differences in the non-wage attributes of the jobs of problem drinkers. To see the possible biases, consider a simple model of job choice depicted graphically in Figure 2.1(A). The indifference curves drawn are based on the assumption that the worker has homothetic preferences over after-tax wage earnings (W) and the level of a fringe benefit (F) (or other non-wage job attribute). The worker's opportunity set is described by the negatively sloped schedule $W(F)$ showing possible combinations of wages and fringes employers can offer, given the worker's level of productivity. For simplicity, it will be assumed that $W(F)$ is linear. The worker's optimizing job choice is thus given by the tangency of an indifference curve and the $W(F)$ schedule. In the absence of endogenous human capital depreciation, alcohol abuse causes a parallel shift of the opportunity line $W(F)$ downward to $W'(F)$, thus resulting in proportional changes in productivity and wage losses. In principle, the absolute value of productivity loss may be greater or less than that of wage loss, depending on the slope of the opportunity line.

However, it may be more natural to consider non-homothetic preferences as a direct consequence of endogenous time discounting. As one can see from Figure 2.1(B), changes in productivity and wage losses due to alcohol abuse are no longer proportional. The left panel of Figure 2.1(B) shows the possibility that the observed wage loss overestimates the productivity loss in the case when the alcoholic has stronger preferences for the fringe benefit than does a non-alcoholic. For example, the alcoholic might be more willing to accept lower wages in return for more generous health insurance, flexible hours and sick leave. This is in part due to the possibility that the benefits of a health insurance fringe may accrue more time-proximately for addicts than non-addicts. In this case, part of the observed difference in the wages earned by alcoholics and non-alcoholics is actually the compensating differential for the higher level of fringe benefits. Put differently, even if there were no productivity loss from alcoholism, alcoholics would choose to earn less but receive more generous fringes.

More plausibly and interestingly, the alcoholic has weaker preferences for the non-wage job attribute than does a non-alcoholic, as shown in the right panel of Figure 2.1(B). In this case the observed earnings losses underestimate the true productivity loss. The preference effect reinforces the income effect shown in Figure 2.1(A). This particular case can be motivated several ways. First, Becker et al. (1991) argue that people with relatively high rates of time preference are more likely to become addicts.

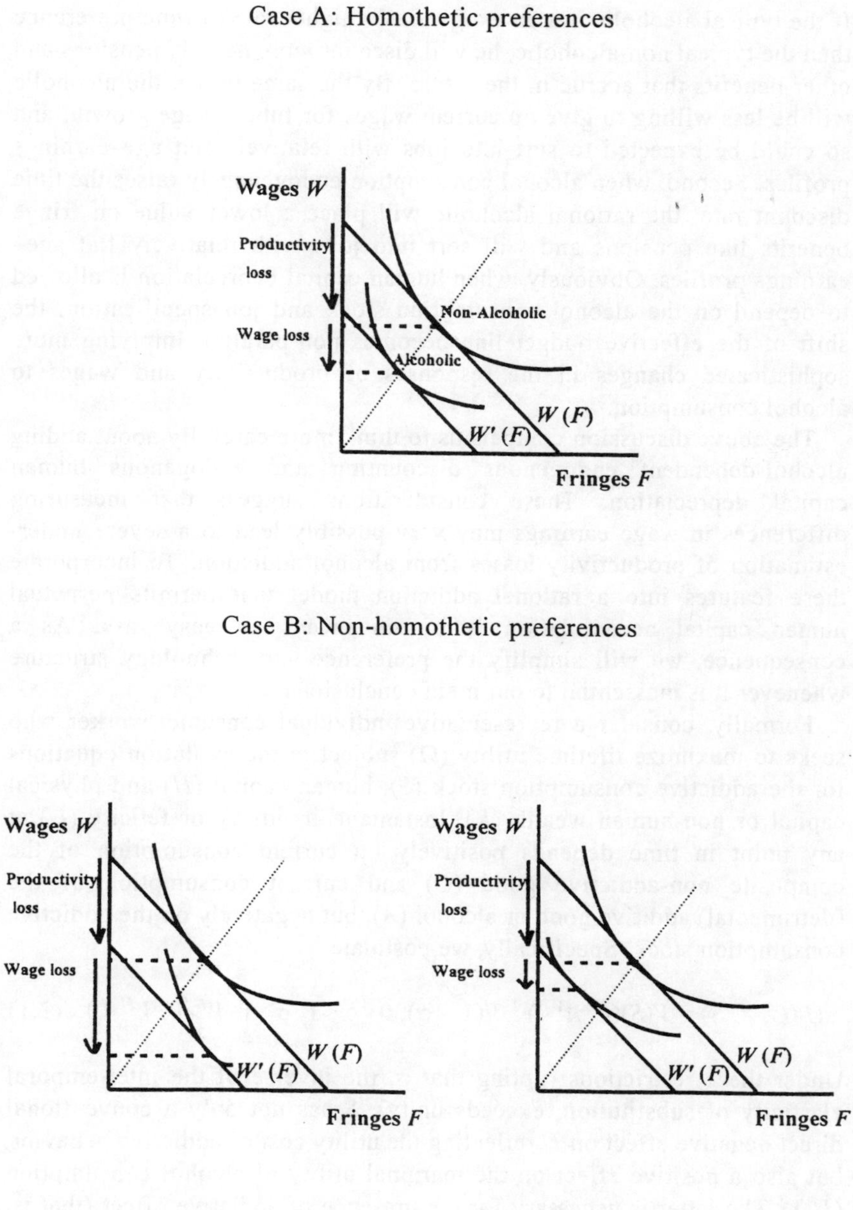

Figure 2.1 Productivity versus wage losses

If the typical alcoholic has an exogenously higher rate of time preference than the typical non-alcoholic, he will discount more heavily pensions and other benefits that accrue in the future. By the same token, the alcoholic will be less willing to give up current wages for future wage growth, and so could be expected to sort into jobs with relatively flat age–earnings profiles. Second, when alcohol consumption endogenously raises the time discount rate, the rational alcoholic will place a lower value on fringe benefits like pensions and will sort into jobs with relatively flat age–earnings profiles. Obviously, when human capital depreciation is allowed to depend on the alcohol consumption stock and job specification, the shift of the effective budget line becomes non-parallel, implying more sophisticated changes in the responses of productivity and wages to alcohol consumption.

The above discussion compels us to think more carefully about adding alcohol-dependent endogenous discounting and endogenous human capital depreciation. These considerations suggest that measuring differences in wage earnings may very possibly lead to a severe under-estimation of productivity losses from alcohol addiction. To incorporate these features into a rational addiction model that permits perpetual human capital accumulation is by no means an easy task. As a consequence, we will simplify the preference and technology structure whenever it is inessential to our main conclusions.

Formally, consider a representative individual consumer/worker who seeks to maximize lifetime utility (Ω) subject to the evolution equations for the addictive consumption stock (S), human capital (H) and physical capital or non-human wealth (K). Instantaneous utility or felicity (U) at any point in time depends positively on current consumption of the composite non-addictive good (C) and current consumption of the (detrimental) additive good or alcohol (A), but negatively on the addictive consumption stock. Specifically, we postulate:

$$U(C, A, S) = V(S)(C^{\alpha}A^{1-\alpha})^{1-\sigma}/(1-\sigma),\ 0<\alpha<1,\ \sigma>1,\ V'>0,\ V''<0. \quad (2.1)$$

Under these restrictions (noting that σ, the inverse of the intertemporal elasticity of substitution, exceeds unity), S has not only a conventional direct negative effect on U reflecting the utility cost of addictive behavior, but also a positive effect on the marginal utility of alcohol consumption (U_A). The latter is necessary for the presence of addictive effect (that is, Pareto complementarity between current and future consumption) and is a natural force for dynamic instability due to the non-convergence of the accumulation process.

Let the evolution process of alcohol consumption stock be:

$$\dot{S} = A - \pi S,\ 0<\pi<1; \tag{2.2}$$

that is, the current alcohol consumption flow net of depreciation of the past consumption stock adds to the accumulation of the current stock. As in Grossman (1972) and Ehrlich and Chuma (1990), consumption decisions have health and longevity implications. Due to its effects on human health, the stock of alcohol consumption is allowed to affect the length of lifetime (which has been ignored in the existing literature). Rather than using an uncertain lifetime model, this effect is simply captured in the present research by an increase in the cumulated subjective discount rate (Δ):

$$\dot{\Delta} = \delta(A - \pi S),\ \delta' > 0,\ \delta'' < 0,\ \Delta(0) = 0,\ -\frac{(A-\pi S)\,\delta''}{\delta'} \le D \in R_+. \tag{2.3}$$

That is, an increase in current and past alcohol consumption is allowed to result in a higher subjective discount rate, implying that the individual may become more impatient given an increased probability of alcohol-related death. Since the discount rate depends on the consumer's choice variable, our model follows in the spirit of the existing endogenous preference literature (compare Ryder and Heal 1973; Epstein 1987; Becker et al. 1989; and Becker and Mulligan 1997).

The lifetime utility can thus be written as:

$$\Omega = \int_0^\infty V(S)(C^\alpha A^{1-\alpha})^{1-\sigma}/(1-\sigma)\exp\{-\int_0^t \delta[A(i) - \pi S(i)]di\}dt. \tag{2.4}$$

Due to path-dependent discounting, it is necessary to define the marginal utility of alcohol consumption in the Volterra derivative sense as the increment in Ω caused by a small increase in A along the addictive consumption path at a time near a particular date T:

$$\partial_V \Omega_T(\{A\}) = \partial U(\cdot(T))/\partial A -$$
$$\delta'(A(T))\{\int_0^\infty U(\cdot)\exp[-\int_T^t \delta(A(i) - \pi S(i)di]dt\}\exp[-\int_0^T (A(t) - \pi S(t))dt].$$

Should the discounting rate be constant over time, the Volterra defined above is equivalent to the standard concept of marginal utility $\partial U(\cdot)/2A$. To ensure the marginal utility of alcohol be positive, we assume the direct marginal utility of alcohol consumption exceeds its adverse effect via increased impatience (that is, the second term in the Volterra derivative).

Moreover, we also need to modify the concept of the rate of time preference. Specifically, we define it as:

$$\rho_T = -\frac{d}{dT}\log \partial_V \Omega_T(\{A\})\big|_{A=0} =$$
$$\delta \frac{\partial U(\cdot(\mathrm{T}))/\partial A - \delta' U(\cdot(\mathrm{T}))/\delta}{\partial U(\cdot(\mathrm{T}))/\partial A - \delta' \{\int_T^{\infty} U(\cdot)\exp[-\int_T^{t} \delta(A(i) - \pi S(i))di]dt\}},$$

which measures the rate at which the marginal utility of alcohol consumption falls along a locally constant path. This time preference rate measure reduces to the conventional one when discounting is constant over time (under which the fraction on the right-hand side becomes unity). Under the assumption of positive marginal utility, the denominator of that fraction is positive. Thus, as long as the numerator is positive, we ensure the positiveness of the time preference rate. To guarantee the strict concavity of the Hamiltonian we assume: $U_{AA} - U_A \delta'' / \delta' < 0 \; \forall A > 0$. In order for the optimization to be sensible, we need to ensure the boundedness of the lifetime utility: $U/\delta \le \Omega_0 e^{\delta_0 \Delta}$ for $\Omega_0 > 0$ and $\delta_0 \in (0, 1)$. Under this condition, the lifetime utility is bounded above by a positive constant $\Omega_0/(1-\delta_0)$. These regularity conditions will be imposed throughout the whole chapter.

The non-addictive consumption good is produced with the use of physical capital $Z = \mu K$ $(0 < \mu < 1)$ and human capital-augmented effective labor $L = vH$ $(0 < v < 1)$ via a constant-returns-to-scale technology $F(\mu K, vH) = vHf(z)$, where μ and v represent the fraction of physical capital and time, respectively, devoted to the non-addictive good production and z denotes factor proportion $(\mu K/vH)$. The production of alcohol is simply assumed to depend on physical capital alone via a linear technology (with a constant scaling factor $M > 0$). This assumption together with the human capital evolution equation specified below allows us to restrict our factor allocation choice to two dimensional (μ and v only). Denote w as the (before-tax) real wage rate in effective units (thus, $W = wH$ is the standard wage rate measure). The evolution of non-human wealth is governed by:

$$\dot{K} = \Lambda(n)F(\mu K, vH) + pM(1-\mu)K - \tau_W wvH - C - (1+\tau_A)pA, \quad (2.5)$$

where p denotes the (before-tax) mill price of alcohol in units of the non-addictive consumption goods; τ_W and τ_A are the wage income tax and the alcohol consumption tax rates; and Λ is a productivity measure, depending on the occupation specification n ($\Lambda' > 0$ and $\Lambda'' < 0$). In contrast to the existing literature, job selection is endogenous and consumption and labor decisions are interactive. Let $n \in [0,1]$, where $n = 0$ indicates a job most suitable for problem drinkers and $n = 1$ is for non-drinkers. In reality, a higher n is associated with a job requiring better human capital/health maintenance or more intensive on-the-job training. Equation (2.5) specifies that the net-of-tax output, $Y = \Lambda F + PM(1 - \mu)K$, can be allocated to consumption of both non-addictive and addictive goods and savings which enhance non-human wealth.

The increment of human capital, on the other hand, relies on the current production of human capital net of depreciation:

$$\dot{H} = B(1-v)H - \eta(n)G(S/K)H,\ G' > 0,\ G'' > 0, \tag{2.6}$$

where ηG measures the endogenous rate of human capital depreciation ($\eta' > 0$ and $\eta'' > 0$). Due to its detrimental effect on health, the alcohol consumption stock increases the rate of depreciation of human capital. By improving nutrition and medical care, an increase in non-human wealth retards human capital depreciation. Notably, the size of the former effect is assumed to be job specific: for a job most suitable for problem drinkers ($n = 0$), human capital depreciation is insensitive to alcohol additions (that is, the correspondent value of η is low). For simplicity, assume G to exhibit constant elasticity: $G = (S/K)^{\zeta}/\zeta$, $\zeta > 1$. Comparing (2.5) and (2.6), selecting a higher n increases productivity (and hence the rate of return on human capital), but at the expense of higher human capital maintenance cost (as reflected by the endogenous human capital depreciation). This tension will provide an endogenous determination of occupation choice.

To close the model, we consider a government that balances its budget at any point in time. It collects wage income and alcohol consumption tax to finance an infrastructural or environmental spending required to maintain the non-economic status of the society (which is assumed to be a fixed proportion to output:

$$\beta Y = \tau_W wvH + \tau_A pA,\ 0 < \beta < 1. \tag{2.7}$$

Denote the co-state variables associated with the evolution equations of S, K and H as λ_S, λ_K and λ_H, respectively. Thus the ratio $q = \lambda_H/\lambda_K$ measures the relative price of human capital investment. In equilibrium, perfect competition in the factor market implies that factor returns must equal marginal products:

$$w(z,n) = \Lambda(n)(f - zf_z) \text{ and } r(z,n) = \Lambda(n) f_z. \tag{2.8}$$

By full employment in the factor market, we have:

$$vz + (1-\mu)(K/H) = (K/H). \tag{2.9}$$

Finally, material balances in the goods market require that the supply of and the demand for each consumption good be equal:

$$C = \Lambda F \text{ and } A = M(1-\mu)K. \tag{2.10}$$

4 DYNAMIC OPTIMIZATION

This environment can be thought of as a dynamic two-sector (goods and human capital investment), general-equilibrium model with two types of consumption goods (non-addictive and addictive) and with a general recursive utility in the sense that both past and current consumption (of the addictive good) can affect the instantaneous utility and the cumulated subjective discount rate.

The first step toward solving this model is to conduct the Uzawa transformation by converting the calendar time (t) into the psychological time (Δ) using the identity: $dt = d\Delta/\delta(A-\pi S)$. The transformed optimization problem can then be solved using standard optimal control techniques. It contains five control variables concerning consumption, factor allocation and occupation choice (C, A, μ, v and n) and three state variables consisting of the reproducible stocks (S, K and H). After deriving the necessary and sufficient conditions for optimization, one can then transform the whole system back to conventional calendar time.

Applying Palivos et al. (1997), we can show that this class of constant-returns, recursive utility model can yield non-degenerate asymptotically balanced growth equilibrium at which the common rate of growth of C, A, S, K and H is positive and asymptotically constant. This growth rate is strictly positive provided that the scaling factor B dominates the sum of the maximum rates of time discounting and human capital depreciation. Recalling from the previous section that the elasticity of marginal discounting $[(A - \pi S)\delta''/\pi']$ is bounded above, our model will accept an asymptotically balanced growth path as long as the elasticity of marginal felicity with respect to the alcohol consumption stock (SV''/V) and the subjective discount rate (δ) are asymptotically constant.

Define $\gamma = \lambda_S/\lambda_K$. To characterize the dynamical system, we apply the technique developed by Bond et al. (1996) by transforming the non-stationary variables into ratios to human capital: $c = C/H$, $a = A/H$, $s = S/H$ and $k = K/H$. We then use eight first-order conditions, three evolution equations, one full-employment condition, two material balance conditions, and the government budget constraint (where one is redundant by Walras's law) to obtain the following relationships.

First, optimal occupation choice implies

$$\Lambda'(n)/\eta'(n) = q\,, \tag{2.11}$$

implying that n can be written as a decreasing function of q alone. Intuitively, when the relative price of human capital investment is higher, it discourages labor sorting toward that requiring higher skills and human capital maintenance. This general-equilibrium relationship between job selection and intertemporal pricing has been completely ignored in the existing literature.

Second, cross-sector (after-tax) factor return equalization yields:

$$r(z, n) = Mp \text{ and } (1-\tau_W)w(z, n) = q\,. \tag{2.12}$$

Combining these relationships with the factor market equilibrium condition, we have:

$$z = z(q),\ n = n(q),\ p = p(q) \text{ and } w = w(q)\,. \tag{2.13}$$

When human capital accumulation is labor intensive, one obtains: $z' > 0$, $p' < 0$ and $w' > 0$.

Third, the intertemporal no-arbitrage condition, by equating the capital gain of human capital from changes in q with the difference in the rates of returns on K and H, gives:

$$\dot{q}/q = Mp(q) + q\eta(n)G(s/k)(1+\xi\ /k) - B. \tag{2.14}$$

Note that there is another no-arbitrage condition pinning down the evolution of γ. However, due to the complexity of the model, we ignore any possible general-equilibrium effects through changes in γ and thus proceed to solve for the equilibrium consistent with any given path of γ. By utilizing (2.13) and (2.14), the alcohol price and the (effective) wage dynamics can be derived as:

$$\dot{p}/p = (qp'/p)[Mp(q) + q\eta(n)G(s/k)(1+\xi\ /k) - B] \tag{2.15}$$

$$\dot{w}/w = (qw'w)[Mp(q) + q\eta(n)(G(s/k)(1+\xi\ /k) - B], \tag{2.16}$$

which indicate that the dynamics of the alcohol price and the effective wage rate must depend on q, s and k. Equations (2.14)–(2.16) together with the optimal job selection schedules from (2.11), $n(q)$, clearly illustrate the dynamic interactions between alcohol pricing, occupation choice and wage earnings.

Fourth, full employment (for K) and material balance (for A) provide the validity of expressing μ and v as functions of (q, k, a):

$$\mu(a,k) = 1 - \frac{a}{Mk} \text{ and } v(q,a,k) = \frac{k}{z(q)}\left(1 - \frac{a}{Mk}\right) \tag{2.17}$$

Thus, as the capital–labor ratio is higher, more physical and human capital inputs will be devoted to goods production, whereas the effects of alcohol consumption are opposite. While the relative price of human capital investment has no direct influence on the allocation of physical capital, it encourages human capital to be devoted to the education sector.

Fifth, the Keynes–Ramsey equations, governing intertemporal consumption efficiency, generate:

$$\begin{aligned}&[1+\alpha(\sigma-1)]\frac{\dot{c}}{c} + (1-\alpha)(\sigma-1)\frac{\dot{a}}{a} - \frac{SV'}{V}\frac{\dot{s}}{s} = Mp + \\ &\eta G[\frac{\xi}{k} + \sigma - \frac{SV'}{V}] - B(1-v)[\sigma - \frac{SV'}{V}] - \delta,\end{aligned} \tag{2.18}$$

$$\begin{aligned}&\frac{s\gamma}{p}\frac{\dot{s}}{s} + \frac{k}{p}\frac{\dot{k}}{k} = (1 + \frac{s\gamma + k}{p})[\eta G - B(1-v)] + (a - \pi s) \\ &[\frac{\gamma}{p} + \frac{1-\alpha}{\alpha}\frac{c}{ap} - (1+\tau_A)][\frac{\delta}{(A-\pi S)\delta'}].\end{aligned} \tag{2.19}$$

Finally, manipulation of (2.2), (2.5), (2.6) and (2.17) yields two transformed equations for the dynamics of (s, k):

$$\dot{s}/s = a/s + \eta(n)G(s/k) - B(1-v) - \pi \tag{2.20}$$

$$\begin{aligned}&\dot{k}/k = \Lambda(n)vf(z)/k + pa/k + \eta(n)G(s/k) - \\ &\tau_W wv/k - c/k - (1+\tau_A)ap/k - B(1-v).\end{aligned} \tag{2.21}$$

The dynamic system is captured by five differential equations, (2.14), (2.18)–(2.21), governing the rates of change of q, c, a, s and k, respectively. Two additional conditions are required to ensure the existence of the relative price path and non-degenerate growth: sup_q

$[r(q) - w(q)/p(q)] > \delta - \eta > inf_q[r(q) - w(q)/p(q)]$ and $\beta[1 - v(q,k,a)] > \eta[n(q)]G(s/k)$, where the first equation permits a well-defined price path governed by (2.14) and the second guarantees positive rate of growth of the underlying economy. Once these above transformed quantity and intertemporal price variables are solved, the dynamics of p and w can then be determined recursively with the use of (2.15) and (2.16).

5 CHARACTERIZATION OF THE ASYMPTOTICALLY BALANCED GROWTH AND THE DYNAMICS

Under the specifications of the preference structure and production technologies and the regularity conditions presented in Sections 2 and 3, there exists a non-degenerate *asymptotically balanced growth path* (ABGP) on which all the transformed variables $\{q, c, a, s, k, p, w\}$ are asymptotically constant with an asymptotic growth rate $\theta > 0$ (see Proposition 4 of Palivos et al. 1997).

Utilizing Propositions 2, 3, 5 and 6 of Bond et al. (1996), we can examine the stability properties of the model and provide the necessary theoretical structure toward understanding the dynamics of both price variables, the wage rate as well as quantity variables (especially in our interest, addictive consumption, labor effort and human capital investment). In particular, one can combine (2.6) and (2.16) to obtain the dynamic wage profile $W=wH$:

$$\begin{aligned} \dot{W}/W = {} & (qw^{\prime}/w)Mp(q) + B[1 - v - (qw^{\prime}w)] \\ & - \eta(n)G(s/k)[1 - q(1+\xi/k)]. \end{aligned} \tag{2.22}$$

Though we are able to study analytically the asymptotically balanced growth rates and stability properties, it is clear that the dynamics cannot be fully characterized, since the individual decision rule and the dynamic system are highly non-linear.[2] This is due to the joint considerations of habit formation/endogenous time preferences and labor market decisions (v, H and n). Nevertheless, we may still draw some useful conclusions by imposing further simplifying assumptions (which will be employed in the discussion below).

What are the model implications for rational addiction behavior? Conventional rational addiction models focus on the effects of future and past prices on current alcohol consumption. Our framework further suggests that a forward-looking individual's alcohol consumption *and* labor decisions depend on the current state variables as well as the entire (past and future) path of exogenous variables. In particular, when deciding about current alcohol consumption, work effort and occupation, the rational addict will anticipate the effects of alcohol abuse on human capital accumulation and the induced wage effects. Labor decisions can thus offer additional tests for rational versus myopic addiction.

Equation (2.22) illustrates the wage dynamics. Due to the consideration of endogenous time preferences and occupation choice, the corresponding wage profile for a drinker is expected to be flatter than for a non-drinker – a rational drinker will accumulate less human capital and work more at earlier ages and face a slow increase in wage earnings onwards. Specifically, a drinker in our model is associated with a lower n, which by reducing the productivity results in a lower rate of wage growth (direct productivity effect).

Even by omitting the relative price effect (which is valid if $\eta \ll B$), there are still two additional channels for n to influence the wage-earning profile. First, a lower n leads to a lower rate of return (r) in the non-addictive good sector and, by factor price equalization, results in a lower rate of return in the alcohol sector. The latter requires the alcohol price to fall, which through intertemporal no-arbitrage decreases the rate of wage growth (alcohol price effect). Second, given the same rate of return, a lower n creates a downward pressure on the rate of return in the non-addictive good sector and hence demands an offset force from a reduction in the factor proportion (z). As a consequence, the s/k ratio decreases, resulting in a lower rate of wage growth (alcohol stock effect).

All these effects imply that a rational drinker faces a flatter wage profile, which is again empirically testable. Mullahy and Sindelar (1993) find differences in the labor market consequences of alcoholism over the life cycle that are suggestive of the predicted pattern. Young adults with alcohol problems appear to earn slightly more than their non-alcoholic peers, but large negative impacts of alcohol abuse appear in the prime working ages (approximately 30–59 years old). Of course, this cross-sectional evidence, which compares different individuals of different ages at a point in time, may be misleading on the pattern of wages over the life cycle for a given individual.

An immediate problem is a possible observational equivalence between rational addictions and the ability of the employers to screen for alcohol abuse – both result in similar work and occupational choice outcomes. We do not explicitly model the demand side of the labor market, but a natural assumption would be that employers try to sort alcoholic workers into low n jobs. As a result, observing alcoholic workers in jobs with flat wage profiles could be due to rational addicts or due to effective employer screening. Additional tests are required to disentangle these two alternative hypotheses. Suppose job selection is a consequence of employment screening. Then future policy such as an alcohol tax or an education subsidy (that is, a negative wage tax) would not affect current occupation choice and work effort. In contrast, a rational addict will react to these policy changes. For example, our model indicates that an anticipated future alcohol tax raises the alcohol price. Thus, it discourages alcohol consumption and encourages human capital accumulation, which by increasing real wage earnings makes job selection of a higher n more attractive.

On the other hand, an anticipated education subsidy will enhance human capital accumulation and by encouraging a choice of a higher n, reduce the demand for alcohol. A large number of empirical studies document that people with more schooling human capital make healthier lifestyle choices, such as avoiding cigarette and alcohol addiction. Previous studies explore whether schooling causes the healthier behaviors by improving people's knowledge of the health consequences of the addictions (Kenkel 1991). Our model suggests a more subtle way schooling can 'cause' healthier lifestyles: more schooling places the individual on optimal trajectories of choice variables that are inconsistent with alcohol addictions. Moreover, a rational addict will also take into account the job package of fringe benefits related to future health, including pensions and insurance. In particular, these benefits are expected to be less generous for an alcohol-dependent. This is mainly due to endogenous time preference (so an alcohol-dependent cares less about pensions) and endogenous human capital depreciation (so an alcohol-dependent picks a package with less human capital maintenance required). Thus alcohol policy can affect labor market outcomes whereas education policy can influence addictive behavior. Any policy evaluation without a full account for such interplays may be biased.

Finally, we note that this class of model may lead to multiple balanced growth equilibrium paths. Differently from the threshold multiplicity as in Becker and Murphy (1988), our model may have a continuum of equilibrium paths leading to a unique asymptotically balanced growth path. As a consequence, the selection of a specific equilibrium path does not depend on history (initial conditions) but relies solely on expectations (self-fulfilling prophecies). An individual who believes in a strong future labor market is more likely to avoid being addicted to alcohol and thus to choose an occupation that has a relatively higher elasticity of human capital depreciation in response to alcoholism. Therefore, he or she accumulates more capital and receives a higher wage, fulfilling the original expectations. In the presence of self-fulfilling expectations-driven multiplicity, dynamic indeterminacy emerges. An immediate consequence is that it is difficult to evaluate the effect of any public policy in transition to the asymptotically balanced growth path. Thus, to enhance the effectiveness of public policy, one must minimize informational frictions, hoping to reduce expectations-caused volatility.

6 CONCLUDING REMARKS

This chapter only begins to explore alcohol addiction and the labor market, leaving many interesting avenues for future research. First, it would be interesting to study the effect of alcoholism on job duration and unemployment spells. This can be done by introducing the addictive behavior into the dynamic search model. Intuitively, heavy drinkers would face limited choice of occupations in order to prevent severe human capital depreciation and possible job loss. On the one hand, this increases search duration and unemployment spells. On the other hand, this makes drinking workers more willing to stay at a given job, until a critical point when job loss occurs.

Second, the employment effects of alcoholism cannot be completely analysed without separating the intensity of work effort from labor hours. In particular, work effort depends crucially on the worker's health. The rational addiction model described above can be readily modified (at expenses of simplifying the basic structure) to disentangle work effort from hours. While alcoholism may reduce employment measured by hours, it also reduces labor productivity due to lower work effort intensity. Since in certain types of jobs, wages are not sensitive to work effort, it is expected that more frequent drinkers would be likely to select such occupations. Both of these extensions have empirical implications. Specifically, in addition to the alcohol consumption and labor market data described above, we can construct measures of job duration and occupation classifications in the NLSY data. Thus it is possible to investigate the possible relationships between alcohol abuse and job duration, as well as between the degree of alcoholism and the productivity elasticity of wage earnings. These will have positive value-added to the empirical labor search literature summarized in Devine and Kiefer (1991).

NOTES

* We would like to thank Mike Grossman, Chee-Ruey Hsieh, an anonymous referee and participants of the Taipei International Conference on Health Economics (Institute of Economics, Academia Sinica) for helpful comments.

Needless to say, the usual disclaimer applies.

1 In the original model Becker and Murphy (1988) include productivity effects by assuming earnings are a concave function of the stock of addictive consumption capital. To derive an empirical rational addiction demand function, Becker et al. (1994) make several simplifying assumptions, including the assumption that earnings are independent of addictive consumption. Other empirical studies using the rational addiction framework maintain that assumption.

2 This is true even when V exhibits constant-relative-risk-aversion, δ is an inverse exponential function and F takes the Cobb–Douglas form.

REFERENCES

Akerlof, George (1991), 'Procrastination and obedience', *American Economic Review Papers and Proceedings*, **81**: 1–19.

Becker, Gary, Michael Grossman and Kevin Murphy (1991), 'Rational addiction and the effect of price on consumption', *American Economic Review, Papers and Proceedings*, **81**: 237–41.

Becker, Gary, Michael Grossman and Kevin Murphy (1994), 'An empirical analysis of cigarette addiction', *American Economic Review*, **84**(3): 396–418.

Becker, Gary and Casey Mulligan (1997), 'The endogenous determination of time preference', *Quarterly Journal of Economics*, **112**(3): 729–58.

Becker, Gary and Kevin Murphy (1988), 'A theory of rational addiction', *Journal of Political Economy*, **96**(4): 675–700.

Becker, Robert A., John H. Boyd III and B.Y. Sung (1989), 'Recursive utility and optimal capital accumulation. I. Existence', *Journal of Economic Theory*, **47**: 76–100.

Benham, Lee and A. Benham (1982), 'Employment, earnings, and psychiatric diagnosis', in Victor Fuchs (ed.), *Economic Aspects of Health*, Chicago: University of Chicago Press, pp. 203–20.

Bond, Eric, Ping Wang and Chong K. Yip (1996), 'A general two-sector model of endogenous growth with physical and human capital: balanced growth and transitional dynamics', *Journal of Economic Theory*, **68**(2): 149–73.

Chaloupka, Frank (1991), 'Rational addictive behavior and cigarette smoking', *Journal of Political Economy*, **99**(4): 722–42.

Cook, Philip (1991), 'The social costs of drinking', in *Expert Meeting on Negative Social Consequences of Alcohol Use*, Oslo: Norwegian Ministry of Health and Social Affairs, pp. 49–74.

Cook, Philip and Michael J. Moore (1993), 'Drinking and schooling', *Journal of Health Economics*, **12**: 411–29.

Devine, Theresa and N.M. Kiefer (1991), *Empirical Labor Economics: The Search Approach*, New York, NY: Oxford University Press.

Ehrlich, Isaac and Hiroyuki Chuma (1990), 'A model of the demand for longevity and the value of life extension', *Journal of Political Economy*, **98**(4): 761–82.

Epstein, Lawrence (1987), 'A simple dynamic general equilibrium model', *Journal of Economic Theory*, **41**: 68–95.

French, Michael and Gary Zarkin (1995), 'Is moderate alcohol use related to wages? Evidence from Four Worksites', *Journal of Health Economics*, **14**(3): 319–44.

Grossman, Michael (1972), *The Demand for Health: A Theoretical and Empirical Investigation*, National Bureau of Economic Research Occasional Paper 119, New York: Columbia University Press, pp. 1–38.

Grossman, Michael (1993), 'The economic analysis of addictive behavior', in Gregory Bloss and Michael Hilton (eds), *Economic and Socioeconomic Issues in the Prevention of Alcohol Related Problems*. Rockville, MD: National Institute on Alcohol Abuse and Alcoholism, pp. 91–123.

Grossman, Michael, Frank Chaloupka and Ismail Sirtalan (1998), 'An empirical analysis of alcohol addiction: results from the Monitoring the Future panels', *Economic Inquiry*, **36**(1): 39–48.

Harwood, H.J., A.M. Cruze, P.L. Kristiansen, J.J. Collins and D.C. Jones (1984), *Economics Costs to Society of Alcohol and Drug Abuse and Mental Illness: 1980*, Research Triangle Park, NC: Research Triangle Institute.

Harwood, Henrick J., Douglas Fountain and Gina Livermore (1998), *The Economic Costs of Alcohol and Drug Abuse in the United States, 1992*, Rockville, MD: US Department of Health and Human Services, National Institutes of Health, National Institute on Drug Abuse, Office of Science Policy and Communications; National Institute on Alcohol Abuse and Alcoholism, Office of Policy Analysis.

Keeler, Theodore E., Teh-wei Hu, Paul Barnett and Willard Manning (1993), 'Taxation, regulation, and addiction: a demand function for cigarettes based on time-series evidence', *Journal of Health Economics*, **12**(1): 1–18.

Kenkel, Donald S. (1991), 'Health behavior, health knowledge, and schooling', *Journal of Political Economy*, **99**(2): 287–305.

Kenkel, Donald S. and David Ribar (1994), 'Alcohol consumption and young adults' socioeconomic status', *Brookings Papers on Economic Activity-Micro* (June): 119–61.

Kenkel, Donald S. and Ping Wang (1999), 'Are alcoholics in bad jobs?', in Frank J. Chaloupka, Michael Grossman, Warren K. Bickel and Henry Saffer (eds), *The Economic Analysis of Substance Use and Abuse: An Integration of Econometric and Behavioral Research*, National Bureau of Economic Education, Chicago, IL: University of Chicago Press, pp. 251–78.

Moore, Michael J. and Philip J. Cook (1994), 'The demand for alcohol by youths: empirical models of habit formation and addiction with unobserved heterogeneity', mimeo, Fuqua School of Business, Duke University.

Mullahy, John (1993), 'Alcohol and the labor market', in Gregory Bloss and Michael Hilton (eds), *Economics and the Prevention of Alcohol Related Problems*, Rockville, MD: National Institute on Alcohol Abuse and Alcoholism, pp. 141–74.

Mullahy, John and Jody Sindelar (1989), 'Life-cycle effects of alcoholism on education, earnings, and occupation', *Economic Inquiry*, **26**(2): 272–82.

Mullahy, John and Jody Sindelar (1991), 'Gender differences in labor market effects of alcoholism', *American Economic Review Papers and Proceedings*, **81**(2): 161–5.

Mullahy, John and Jody Sindelar (1993), 'Alcoholism, work and income', *Journal of Labor Economics*, **11**(3): 494–520.

Mullahy, John and Jody Sindelar (1995), 'Employment, unemployment, and problem drinking', National Bureau of Economic Research Working Paper No. 5123, May.

Orphanides, Athanasios and David Zervos (1995), 'Rational addiction with learning and regret', *Journal of Political Economy*, **103**(4): 739–58.

Palivos, Theodore, Ping Wang and Jianbo Zhang (1997), 'On the existence of balanced growth equilibrium', *International Economic Review*, **38**(1): 205–24.

Rice, Dorothy P. (1993), 'The economic cost of alcohol abuse and dependence, 1990', *Alcohol Health and Research World*, **17**(1): 10–12.

Rice, Dorothy P., Sander Kelman, Leonard S. Miller and Sarah Dunmeyer (1990), *The Economic Costs of Alcohol and Drug Abuse and Mental Illness: 1985*, Report submitted to the Office of Financing and Coverage Policy of the Alcohol, Drug Abuse, and Mental Health Administration, U.S. Department of Health and Human Services, San Francisco, CA: Institute for Health & Aging, University of California.

Ryder, Harl E., Jr. and Geoffrey M. Heal (1973), 'Optimal growth with intertemporally dependent preferences', *Review of Economic Studies*, **40**: 1–31.

Schelling, Thomas (1984), 'Self-command in practice, in policy, and in a theory of rational choice', *American Economic Review Papers and Proceedings*, **74**: 1–11.

Waters, Teresa M and Frank Sloan (1995), 'Why do people drink? Tests of the rational addiction model', *Applied Economics*, **27**: 727–36.

Zarkin, Gary A., Michael T. French, Thomas Mroz and Jeremy W. Bray (1998), 'Alcohol use and wages: new results from the National Household Survey on Drug Abuse', *Journal of Health Economics*, **17**(1): 53–68.

3. Addiction and adjustment costs: an empirical implementation

Paul Contoyannis and Andrew M. Jones*

1 INTRODUCTION

Recent papers by Yen and Jones (1996) and Suranovic et al. (1999) have argued that the impact of addiction on the decision to quit smoking should be modeled using the concept of adjustment costs. We illustrate the implications of incorporating adjustment costs and future health costs into a model of the decision to quit smoking and apply the model to panel data from the British Health and Lifestyle Survey (HALS). We then present estimates for the prevalence of quitting prior to the first wave of the survey (1984) and the incidence of quitting between the first and second waves (1991), finding robust evidence of a non-monotonic relationship between the probability of quitting and previous consumption, with the highest probabilities found among light and heavy smokers. We use data on actual survival rates to proxy the perceived improvement in life expectancy associated with quitting, but we do not find clear evidence of the effect predicted by Suranovic et al. But measures of current health do have a significant impact on quitting and our results reinforce those in Jones (1996) and Hsieh (1998). These findings are consistent with self-reported data from the HALS survey which show that 34 percent of men and 26 percent of women cite experience of illness as a reason for quitting, while 30 percent of men and 23 percent of women cite fear of future ill-health.

We find the probability of quitting to be increasing in age, a result consistent with the evidence of increasing duration dependence of the hazard of quitting in Forster and Jones (2000) and Douglas (1998), and with the theoretical predictions of Suranovic et al. (1999) and others, but contradictory to the predictions of Becker and Murphy (1988). This suggests that the benefits of quitting will increase relative to the costs as an individual gets closer to the point where the length and quality of life become affected by the chronic effects of smoking.

2 ADDICTION ASYMMETRY AND ADJUSTMENT COSTS

It is generally accepted that withdrawal effects, and the associated craving, are important features of nicotine dependence. One interpretation of this phenomenon is that a cost of adjustment is incurred if an individual reduces their consumption of tobacco. Atkinson (1974) argues that the concept of adjustment costs offers an improvement on the conventional approach towards habit formation. The important feature of this model is that adjustment costs are asymmetric and only apply to reductions in consumption.

More recently, Jones (1987, 1999) argues that, for economists concerned with modeling addiction, two stylized features of withdrawal effects stand out. First, the effects are asymmetric and only occur when consumption falls below its previous level. Second, once a threshold has been passed the role of consumption is not simply to provide satisfaction, but also to ward off the unpleasant consequences of withdrawal. In this respect withdrawal can be thought of as increasing the efficiency of current consumption. From this perspective it seems appropriate to write the direct utility function in terms of an intermediate production function $\phi(C)$, and allow for an asymmetry in the 'marginal productivity' of current consumption around the individual's reference level of consumption, C^R. The reference level of consumption could simply be consumption in the previous period. But an intuitive alternative would be to use the level of consumption that 'maintains the habit' by keeping the habit stock constant,

$$C^R = \delta S. \tag{3.1}$$

One possible specification of $\phi(.)$ is the linear form,

$$\phi^-(.) = C - a(Z) + b(Z).(C - C^R), \text{ if } C < C^R, \tag{3.2}$$

and

$$\phi^+(.) = C \text{ if } C \geq C^R. \tag{3.3}$$

In this case a can be interpreted as the fixed effect of withdrawal, while b can be interpreted as a constant marginal effect of withdrawal, with the levels of a and b determined by the vector of exogenous variables Z. For example, withdrawal effects could be an increasing function of past consumption.

The gist of the model is that, as a result of withdrawal effects, the marginal productivity of current consumption is asymmetric, implying a discontinuity in the slope of the indifference curves. With withdrawal effects defined by (3.2) and (3.3), the utility function will be non-differentiable at the reference level of consumption, and it is possible to establish the conditions under which the consumer's indifference curves are either kinked or non-convex. If $a = 0$, with a single addictive good and the linear specification (2, 3), the condition for kinked rather than non-convex indifference curves is simply $b > 0$.[1]

The existence of non-convex indifference curves due to $a \neq 0$, or $b < 0$, can lead to discontinuous responses to changes in exogenous variables such as prices or income. In particular they can lead to cold-turkey quitting from an interior solution at C^R to a corner solution at $C = 0$. Non-convexities are central to the prediction of cold-turkey quitting in the models of Barthold and Hochman (1988), Becker and Murphy (1988), Michaels (1988), Yen and Jones (1996), and Suranovic et al. (1999).

Yen and Jones (1996) develop an empirical model of the simultaneous decisions of how many cigarettes to smoke and whether to quit smoking. This is based on the tradeoff between the expected benefits of quitting for the smoker's health, wealth and self-esteem and the fixed costs of quitting associated with nicotine dependence and withdrawal. The influence of nicotine dependence is modeled as a fixed cost of quitting. Yen and Jones assume that expected fixed costs (A) depend on a vector of variables, including past consumption, and a random error reflecting unobservable individual heterogeneity. The expected benefits of quitting (B), in terms of health, wealth and self-esteem, will depend on how much the individual would have smoked otherwise. These benefits are likely to increase with the individual's level of cigarette consumption. The decision to quit smoking depends on the expected net benefit of quitting, ($B - A$). By assuming that the fixed costs of adjustment (A) and the individual's desired level of cigarette consumption are both functions of a set of explanatory variables and random error terms, Yen and Jones derive an econometric specification taking the form of a 'double-hurdle' model. A feature of their model is that variables that have no (or small) influence on the fixed costs of quitting are expected to have equal and opposite effects on quitting and on the level of smoking. This reflects the intuition that, conditional on overcoming the fixed costs of quitting, heavier smokers have the greatest incentive to quit. By the same reasoning, the econometric specification suggests that it would not be appropriate to assume independence of the error terms in the double-hurdle model, and that there will tend to be a negative correlation between the error terms.

A recent theoretical contribution by Suranovic et al. (1999) recognizes the withdrawal effects of quitting and the importance of the delayed health effects of smoking. Their approach views addiction as repetitive, compulsive, and damaging, as defined by Kuhn et al. (1998). For example, Suranovic et al. (p. 4) state that 'repetitive usage of a good is not sufficient to call consumption of that good an addiction .... Instead, addiction requires that someone would like to either cease or reduce habitual consumption but is unable to do so'. This idea is incorporated into their model as asymmetric adjustment costs. Their model predicts that individuals will get 'hooked' and can be regarded as 'unhappy addicts'.[2] The model shows how different forms of adjustment costs will lead to gradual or cold-turkey quitting, while providing a rationale for smoking cessation programmes and nicotine replacement therapies, and showing how aging can induce quitting.

Suranovic et al. use a specification of the utility function that is additively separable in smoking and other consumption. The utility associated with current smoking (C) at age α is assumed to consist of three components,

$$U_\alpha(C) = B_\alpha(C) - L_\alpha(C) - A_\alpha(C), \tag{3.4}$$

where $B_\alpha(.)$ represents the direct benefits of consumption and is assumed to be increasing and concave, $L_\alpha(.)$ represents future losses which are modeled as the impact of continued smoking on the present value of expected utility streams, and $A_\alpha(.)$ represents the costs of adjustment associated with withdrawal. Rather than allowing for full intertemporal rationality, Suranovic et al. assume a form of bounded rationality in which the individual takes account of the impact of current consumption on future health but does not plan the optimal path of future consumption. In particular, W_t, the level of instantaneous utility at time t, is implicitly assumed independent of the decision to continue or quit smoking. The loss $L_\alpha(.)$ is related to the reduction in life expectancy from smoking, given the individual's history of smoking and is equal to

$$L_\alpha(.) = V(S_\alpha, 0) - V(S_\alpha, C) = \int_{T_\alpha + \alpha - \beta(S_\alpha + C)}^{T_\alpha + \alpha - \beta S_\alpha} e^{-\sigma(t-\alpha)} W_t \, dt \tag{3.5}$$

where W_t is instantaneous utility at time t, σ is the rate of time preference, and T_α is the life expectancy of a non-smoker at age α which is reduced by the stock of addiction, S_α and by current smoking C. For simplicity, Suranovic et al. assume that the impact of smoking on life expectancy is linear and is indicated by the parameter β.

Under their assumptions, L is increasing and convex in current consumption and increases with age; as death is brought forward a higher discount rate is applied to the final years of life. This further implies that the incentive to quit also increases with age. Smoking can become a net 'bad' with aging, with the utility of consumption becoming negative as the impact on future health outweighs the direct benefits of consumption. Hence Suranovic et al. predict that consumption will decline with age. This contradicts the conclusion of Becker and Murphy (1988). In their model the impacts of addictive consumption are immediate and continual, leading to an increase in consumption as individuals age.

Individuals start smoking at an age when the anticipated health effects are heavily discounted. Also, although the model relies on bounded rationality and does not allow for forward planning of future consumption, Suranovic et al. speculate that the anticipated costs of quitting would also be heavily discounted. Once consumption ensues, the addictive stock accumulates and costs of adjustment set in. Costs of adjustment are assumed to be asymmetric around the habitual level of consumption and to depend on the level of consumption and the addictive stock. Suranovic et al. show that different assumptions about the shape of the cost of adjustment function lead to different styles of quitting. Convex adjustment costs (giving kinked indifference curves) are associated with gradual quitting. Concave adjustment costs (giving non-convex indifference curves) are associated with cold-turkey quitting. A mixture of concave and convex portions leads to predictions that are consistent with the 'stages of change' view of addiction, where repetitive consumption is followed by gradual reduction and then cold-turkey quitting.[3]

As mentioned earlier, 'cold-turkey' quitting is predicted by other models; the role of non-convexities in inducing the decision to quit an addictive behavior abruptly appears ubiquitous. Whether in the fully rational, intertemporal framework of Becker and Murphy (1988), the myopic models of Michaels (1988), and Barthold and Hochman (1988), or the pragmatic, imperfect foresight models of Yen and Jones (1996), and Suranovic et al. (1999), non-convexities are often necessary and sometimes sufficient to induce cold-turkey quitting. Although we may be offered hints by previous work, Jones (1999) suggests that until a theoretical model is developed which is able to combine the possibilities of non-convexities and multiple optima with unbounded rationality, the theoretical and empirical implications of the simplification of imperfect foresight are difficult to judge. This requires a model which is able to tackle the mathematical complexities created by incorporating adjustment costs into a model assuming full intertemporal rationality.

3 SOME PREVIOUS EMPIRICAL EVIDENCE ON QUITTING

Jones (1994) argues that an approach that treats withdrawal effects as fixed costs, which must be overcome to quit smoking, offers a theoretical foundation for the double-hurdle specification employed by Jones (1989a). This relies on addiction being a major determinant of the individual's ability to quit, a claim that was explored using a cross-sectional sample of 3801 ex- and current smokers from the HALS. The paper finds that a range of variables significantly influence quitting. In particular, those whose health is fair or poor are less likely to have quit, as are those with poor respiratory performance, and those who are not disabled. However, conclusions drawn from these results must remain tentative, given the retrospective nature of the data. It is problematic to use current health when predicting the stock of quitters and current smokers. However, being an ex-smoker consists of a sequence of decisions to remain an ex-smoker, and as such current health should influence whether we observe an ex- or current smoker.

The results suggest that past consumption does not influence the desire to quit, as measured by the individual reporting a serious attempt to quit smoking, but does influence their success in actually quitting. This gives empirical support to the idea that, due to addiction, many smokers are ‘locked-in’ to a pattern of behavior they would prefer to abandon – the ‘unhappy addicts’ described by Suranovic et al. However, whether past health impacts positively or negatively on the decision to quit cannot be observed using these data, and so the causes of flows, or new quits, remain largely obscured; we cannot tell whether an individual decided to quit for curative or preventive reasons. This is further examined by Shmueli (1996) and Jones (1996).

Shmueli argues that unobserved heterogeneity in time since quitting masks the true relationship between health and smoking cessation. He constructs synthetic cohorts of smokers using Israeli survey data, and finds that the endogeneity status and the sign of the coefficient of present health varies considerably according to the time passed since quitting, finding that the cohorts composed of those who smoked recently quit for curative reasons, unlike the result found by Jones (1994) for the stock of quitters. In response, Jones (1996) uses the second wave of the HALS to allow analysis of the influence of health at the time of the original survey, health at the time of the follow-up survey, and experience of ill-health during the intervening period on the flow of new quits over the 1984–91 period. Exogeneity is not rejected and the results suggest that the relationship between health and smoking cessation cannot be summarized by a definitive curative or preventive relation. In particular, those who reported excellent or good health at the time of the original survey were more likely to have quit (preventive), while those who reported a serious illness or injury during the period or had poor or ill health at the end of the period were more likely to have quit (curative).

Motivated by a Bayesian learning framework, Hsieh (1998) interprets changes in health as a measure of the influence of new information on the perception of the health risks of smoking. The model is applied to new quits between the 1989 and 1993 waves of the Taiwan Survey of Health and Living Status of the Elderly. Health status is measured by self-assessed health, chronic illness, and the number of limiting conditions. The paper finds that worsening health status increases the probability of quitting. It also finds that the probability of quitting increases with age and with the level of past cigarette consumption which is measured by dummy variables for light (1–9), moderate (10–20), and heavy (21+) consumption.

Sander (1995) focuses on the influence of schooling, rather than of health, for the decision to quit. He uses data from the US National Opinion Research Center's General Social Survey for the years 1986–91 to estimate probit equations for quitting. These are estimated for samples of men and women aged 25 and over. The paper pays particular attention to the possibility of unobservable heterogeneity bias arising from the correlation between schooling, quitting, and a 'third factor' such as the individual's rate of time preference. However, tests do not reject the exogeneity of the schooling variables. Sander finds that schooling increases the probability of quitting. It is notable, however, that the estimated models only control for a limited range of other covariates (age, ethnic group, and region).

Yen and Jones (1996) estimate Box–Cox double-hurdle models and various nested forms using the subsample of 'smokers' from the HALS. The Box–Cox formulation differs from previous hurdle models (Cragg 1971; Jones 1989a), by allowing the conditional distribution of observed consumption to be non-normal. Previous peak consumption is found to increase the level of current consumption and the probability of participation. The variables reflecting health have the same effects as in Jones (1994) on quitting, while having the opposite effects on the level of consumption. Those in higher socioeconomic groups are more likely to have quit, but those that have not quit are likely to smoke more than those in lower socioeconomic groups. Interestingly, these results are not robust to alternative specifications, indicating the importance of controlling for error dependence and sample-selection. These empirical findings provide some support for the adjustment cost specification and the intuition that, once the fixed costs associated with addiction are overcome, it is the heavier smokers who have the greatest incentive to quit.

An alternative to estimating probit or double-hurdle type models to deal with binary measures of quitting is to use duration analysis. Then the number of years of smoking prior to the decision to quit can be used to estimate the hazard of quitting. This approach can also be used to estimate the hazard of starting, based on the age at which an individual starts smoking (Douglas and Hariharan 1994; Douglas 1998).

Jones (1995) estimates a simple parametric model for the hazard of quitting using a Weibull specification. This is estimated using retrospective data on years of smoking prior to the 1984 Health and Lifestyle Survey. The results show that the hazard of quitting is reduced by past smoking and by the presence of other smokers in the household, and that the hazard is influenced by gender, marital status, employment status, education, and health. The hazard function shows increasing duration dependence. Forster (1997) develops this analysis of the HALS data and estimates Cox proportional and stratified hazard models, applying tests for mis-specification from the biostatistics literature.

Douglas (1998) deals with the hazards of both starting and quitting in a combined model. This is estimated using the 1987 US National Health Interview Survey. The empirical specification uses a split-population model based on an ordered probit which is used to distinguish between those who never start, those who start and will eventually quit and those who start and never quit. The hazard function for quitting shows increasing duration dependence and is influenced by ethnic group, marital status, income, education, future prices, past consumption, anti-smoking regulations, and health information.

4 AN EMPIRICAL FRAMEWORK

Here we propose a simple empirical model based on the adjustment cost models proposed by Yen and Jones (1996) and Suranovic et al. (1999), and similar to the specification proposed in Jones (1999). The model implies that the perceived benefits of quitting smoking are an (increasing) function of the impact of cigarette consumption on expected health. It is assumed that these expectations are formed on the basis of the individual's current information, including their current level of cigarette consumption.

The individual's decision to quit during the period $[t, t+1]$, given that they are a smoker at t, is modeled by comparing their level of utility as a smoker and as a non-smoker. The individual will quit if the benefit in terms of future utility exceeds the cost of quitting. Following Yen and Jones and Suranovic et al., we assume that the net benefits of quitting depend on the impact of smoking on expected future health. These are offset by adjustment costs which depend on the individual's history of smoking.

The participation equation can be expressed to reflect Suranovic et al.'s utility function, equation (3.4). So, a smoker will continue to smoke if

$$\mu_t = B_t(.) - L_t(.) - A_t(.) > 0. \tag{3.6}$$

$B(.)$ is the net direct benefit of continuing to smoke. Suranovic et al. suggest that current benefits will include the pleasurable effects of nicotine and peer group approval, offset by the effects of social disapprobation. In our application $B(.)$ is assumed to include measures of social, educational, marital and employment status, and the presence of other smokers in the individual's household.[4]

$A(.)$ includes the cost of adjustment which is assumed to be a function of the reference level of consumption and the addictive stock. In our application these are measured by the initial number of cigarettes smoked. We use a quadratic function of consumption to allow for convexity or concavity in the shape of the adjustment cost function. As noted by Suranovic et al., this allows alternative quitting styles to be represented, including the possibility of cold turkey.[5]

$L(.)$ is the net effect of quitting on discounted future utility. In our empirical application we equate this with the reduction in lifespan associated with smoking, weighted by the delay before the reduction occurs. This is measured by estimating a Weibull duration model. The Weibull specification has proved to be an adequate empirical model for lifespan in previous analysis of our dataset (Forster 1997), and it has the convenient property that it gives a closed-form expression for the predicted lifespan. Predicted lifespan takes the form $(xb - 0.5772/p)$ where p is the duration-dependence parameter.

Our approach to computing the difference in lifespan due to continued cigarette smoking estimates survival models as a function of the stock of consumption, measured by previous peak consumption multiplied by years of smoking. Predicted lifespan with quitting, T_0, is then computed on the basis of the current value of the stock, assuming that the individual's lifespan is conditional on their current stock and that no further additions are made. Lifespan with continued smoking, T_C, is computed by taking the number of additional years the individual would smoke, $(T_0 - Age)$, and adding the implied additional stock to their current stock. T_C is then predicted using this augmented stock value. The measure of benefits is then approximated as being proportional to $(T_0 - T_C)$.[6] T_C will be a lower bound for lifespan under continued smoking (and hence lead to an upper bound for the benefits of quitting), as it employs previous peak consumption and the assumption that the individual will live to T_0. However, it is likely that under continued smoking the individual will live to a value less than T_0, leading to overestimation of the implied additional stock.

We have experimented with different approaches to account for the impact of discounting due to the delay before the individual experiences the reduction in life expectancy. The first follows Suranovic et al. and multiplies $(T_0 - T_C)$ by $\exp(-\sigma (T_C - \alpha))$.[7] The second approach uses the implicit discount factor $1/(T_C - \alpha)$.[8] These predictions depend on the full set of regressors in the Weibull model and therefore reflect the socioeconomic characteristics, allowing individuals to have different expected benefits for given values of age and addictive stock. We present results using the implicit discount factor approach, as this avoids an arbitrary assumption concerning the choice of the rate of time preference. Although the use of the implicit discount factor approach may lead to inconsistent intertemporal decisions, this does not contradict substantively the model of Suranovic et al., given their assumption of imperfect foresight. Once the measure of L has been constructed, equation (3.6) can be augmented with a random error term and estimated. This can be performed using a probit model for the binary variable indicating whether the individual quits, or as a survival model for the hazard of quitting, using information on the number of years of smoking prior to quitting. Here we present estimates derived using probit models for quitting.

Before moving to a discussion of the data and results, it is important to consider the identification of the model that we are estimating. First, if we had the true measure of L for each individual we may be concerned with the potential for unobserved heterogeneity bias, as unobservables which induce quitting may also increase the benefits from doing so. However, given that the variables included in the lifespan equation are exogenous in the quit equation, our prediction of L is independent of whether an individual actually quit and the unobservables which drive quitting. In this sense our estimator can be viewed as an instrumental variable estimator. Second, it should be noted that we rely heavily on the non-linear functional form of the Weibull model to ensure identification of the quitting equations. However, we do not rely wholly on non-linearity; we restrict the quitting equation to exclude the stock variable as the value of this variable is dependent on whether an individual quit, and if included would induce issues of reverse causality to become pertinent.

5 DATA

HALS is a national representative sample of adults living in private households in Great Britain (Cox et al. 1987, 1993). Carried out by Social and Community Planning Research, the first wave of data (HALS1) were collected between Autumn 1984 and Summer 1985 during two home visits; first an hour-long interview, followed by a nurse visit to collect physiological measurements and data on cognitive function. Individuals were also asked to fill in a self-completion questionnaire. The available sample has information on 9003 individuals, although some gave incomplete responses. This is exemplified by the response rate falling to 53.7 percent for the nurse visit and self-completion questionnaire, relative to 73.5 percent when considering the interview alone. The sample has been compared to the 1981 Census of Population in order to gauge its representativeness. Among respondents who completed all three stages of the survey, there is a slight excess of women, particularly elderly women, and some under-representation of those households with lower incomes and education levels. However, the overall conclusion of the authors is that 'the study appears to offer a good and representative sample of the population' (Cox et al. 1987, p.1). The second wave of the data (HALS2) was collected in 1991 and includes 5352 interviewees.

As we are concerned with the cessation rather than the initiation of smoking we concentrate on two subsamples of respondents. The first allows us to estimate the prevalence of quitting and consists of those individuals who defined themselves as current regular or ex-regular cigarette smokers at HALS1. The second restricts the sample to those who were current regular smokers at HALS1 and allows us to analyse the incidence of new quits over the seven years between HALS1 and HALS2.[9] After excluding missing values on the relevant variables, the sample size for the first sample is 4381, of whom 1870 had quit prior to HALS1. For the second it is 1469, of whom 298 quit between the two surveys.

The expected health benefit of quitting, L_a (.), is computed using data on the actual age of death of a subset of the respondents. Respondents to the original survey were notified to the Office of Population Censuses and Surveys (OPCS) and flagged on the National Health Service (NHS) central register. Information from the death certificate of those who died is forwarded to the survey team at the University of Cambridge. Data on the date and cause of death is available up to November 1995. We use age at death as the dependent variable for our survival analysis. Individuals who were still alive in November 1995 are treated as right censored and their actual age is used. In our sample, 19 percent of males and 10 percent of females were known to have died at this point. As the data come from a cross-section of those alive at the time of HALS1, we allow for left truncation of the data (see Forster 1997). It is also important to note that while a small proportion of individuals were known to have died, $L_\alpha(.)$ is computed for all individuals in our sample, whether censored or otherwise. However, given these proportions we may expect imprecise, although consistent, estimates of the expected benefits of quitting, and potentially poor estimates of the impact of $L_\alpha(.)$ in the quitting equations. However, against this must be weighed the benefit of reducing the potential for unobserved heterogeneity bias if we used the actual value of $L_\alpha(.)$, as noted in the previous section. The survival models are intended to capture the incremental effect of current cigarette consumption on expected lifespan, given the individual's previous history of smoking and given their current state of health. Cigarette consumption is measured by a stock variable constructed as the product of previous peak consumption and the number of smoke years (stock). Health status is measured by a dummy variable for the presence of a longstanding illness or disability (disability) and by self-assessed health, with dummy variables for excellent, good and poor health (health-ex, health-gd, health-pr) relative to an average person of the same age, with fair as the reference category. To allow for different impacts of exogenous variables on the hazard functions for males and females, we split the sample by gender and estimate separate Weibull models for men and women.[10]

Equation (3.6) can be estimated as a binary choice model. In the case of the probit models, smoking cessation is measured as a binary variable equal to one if the respondent is a current regular smoker and zero if they have quit. For the prevalence sample consisting of ex- and regular smokers at HALS1, cigarette consumption is measured by the previous peak consumption of each individual. For the probit models using the incidence sample consisting of regular smokers at HALS1, cigarette consumption is measured by the typical number of cigarettes per day.

Other independent variables in the models are dummy variables for occupational socioeconomic group (regsc1–regsc5), with higher values indicating lower occupational status; the reference category is between groups two and three. A set of educational dummies indicates the highest formal qualification level achieved (noqual, alevels, Higher National

Diploma (hnd), degree); the reference category is 'O' levels, between no qualifications and 'A' levels. We also include a set of marital status indicators (widow, divorced, separated, single) with married as the reference category and a set of work-status dummies (part-time, retired, sick-leave, keep-house, unemployed) where full-time is the reference category. Also included are a set of ethnic status dummies (Indian/ Pakistani, black African/West Indian, other non-white) where the reference category is white/European. Other variables are age and powers of age (age, age2, age3), and a dummy for whether an individual is a house owner (house-owner). Although our measure of the future health benefits is confined to the impact of smoking on expected lifespan we condition on self-assessed health and an indicator of disability in order to pick up the influence of morbidity as well as the influence of a shortened lifespan. Finally, we include dummy variables relating to environmental smoking including the presence of other smokers in the household (other smokers) and parental smoking history (mother smoked, father smoked, both smoked). Further details on the variables used in our analysis are provided in Cox et al. (1987).

6 RESULTS

6.1 Predicted Lifespan

Table 3.1 presents results from the Weibull models for lifespan. The coefficents, β, are presented in the log-relative hazard form where coefficients greater than one indicate an increase in the hazard and those less than one indicate an increase. For males, an educational gradient can be tentatively observed in the direction expected, with those with no qualifications and with other or professional/vocational qualifications expecting to lead a shorter life. In line with expectations, self-assessed health appears to be a good predictor of the probability of mortality; there is a discernible gradient in expected lifespan. The stock variable is a significant predictor of lifespan in the direction expected. The duration dependence parameter p is significantly greater than one, indicating positive duration dependence; the hazard of dying increases rapidly with age. For females, the educational gradient observed tentatively for males is not discernible. The effect of self-assessed health on the probability of mortality is also diminished, although the gradient is clearer. The stock variable is again significant and in the expected direction, with the duration dependence parameter again significantly greater than one.

Table 3.2 presents summary statistics for the Weibull estimates of predicted lifespan for the prevalence sample. As expected, mean predicted lifespan is lower for males than for females. Two features are particularly noteworthy. First, the mean expected benefit of quitting is about twice as large for females relative to males. Second, there is much more variability

Table 3.1 Weibull models for lifespan

	Males (*N* = 2195)		Females (*N* = 2186)	
	Coef.	Std. error	Coef.	Std. error
regsc1	1.154	0.400	0.655	0.273
regsc2	1.219	0.225	0.482***	0.128
regsc3	0.933	0.155	0.928	0.196
regsc4	1.107	0.201	0.815	0.195
regsc5	1.022	0.236	1.146	0.302
noqual	1.643*	0.424	0.911	0.252
alevels	1.265	0.477	0.977	0.451
hnd	1.055	0.377	0.854	0.377
degree	0.934	0.310	0.640	0.302
other/prof	1.771*	0.532	1.568	0.565
mother smoked	1.043	0.422	1.138	0.497
father smoked	0.908	0.130	0.766	0.152
both smoked	0.835	0.164	0.795	0.188
disability	1.110	0.115	1.226	0.189
health-ex	0.753*	0.111	0.610**	0.143
health-gd	0.736**	0.089	0.777	0.129
health-pr	1.360*	0.236	1.289	0.291
stock	1.0002***	0.00006	1.0004***	0.0001
p	6.976		7.653	
Log *L*	96.12		–51.23	
χ^2 (18)	56.71		50.22	
Prob > χ^2	0.000		0.000	
RESET (p)	0.496		0.909	

Note: All estimation was performed using *STATA* version 6. In all cases we used robust standard errors to compensate for potential mis-specification of the error distribution. In all tables asterisks above coefficient estimates represent significance of the estimated parameters at the 10 (one asterisk), 5 (two asterisks) and 1 (three asterisks) percent levels, respectively.

Table 3.2 Predicted lifespans computed for the prevalence sample

Male ($N = 2195$)		Mean	Min	Max
	T_C	74.36	60.83	83.72
	T_0	75.67	61.08	84.89
	T_0–T_C	1.31	0.00	9.01
Female ($N = 2186$)				
	T_C	77.38	59.88	95.63
	T_0	80.13	64.21	96.56
	T_0–T_C	2.75	0.00	16.82

Note: See note to Table 3.1.

Table 3.3 Predicted lifespans computed for the incidence sample

Male ($N = 645$)		Mean	Min	Max
	T_C	74.16	60.83	82.91
	T_0	75.77	61.08	84.89
	T_0–T_C	1.61	0.00	6.79
Female ($N = 824$)				
	T_C	76.34	60.20	91.72
	T_0	79.49	66.60	95.66
	T_0–T_C	3.15	0.00	16.82

Note: See note to Table 3.1.

in the estimates of the benefits of quitting for females than for males. Hence, if individuals do respond to the future benefits of quitting, we are more likely to observe this result for females than males.

Table 3.3 presents summary statistics for the Weibull estimates of predicted lifespan for the incidence sample. The results are comparable to the prevalence sample, albeit with an increased mean expected benefit of quitting for both males and females. However, the relative mean benefit from quitting is comparable to the results for the prevalence sample.

6.2 Quitting

Table 3.4 presents results from the Probit model for the prevalence sample; those who were current or ex-regular smokers at HALS1. All models pass a RESET based on including squared, cubed, and quartic values of the linear index. The results are presented as marginal effects

Table 3.4 Probit models for continuation-prevalence sample

	Males (N = 2195)		Females (N = 2186)	
	dF/dx	Std. error	dF/dx	Std. error
regsc1	–0.091	0.072	–0.135**	0.065
regsc2	–0.015	0.044	0.016	0.040
regsc3	0.039	0.040	0.069*	0.036
regsc4	0.075*	0.045	0.023	0.040
regsc5	0.083	0.059	0.117**	0.047
noqual	0.055	0.038	0.034	0.034
alevels	0.037	0.070	0.005	0.063
hnd	–0.023	0.046	–0.032	0.047
degree	–0.087*	0.052	–0.090*	0.048
other/prof	0.142**	0.052	–0.015	0.069
widow	0.070	0.060	0.134***	0.037
divorced	0.288***	0.054	0.149***	0.042
separated	0.172**	0.077	0.179***	0.054
single	0.223***	0.041	0.091*	0.044
part-time	0.122	0.079	–0.049	0.035
retired	0.071	0.052	–0.007	0.052
sick leave	0.084	0.069	0.040	0.091
keephouse	–0.078	0.231	–0.057*	0.033
unemployed	0.149***	0.042	–0.008	0.073
Indian/Pakistani	0.337***	0.076	0.106	0.203
black African/West Indian	–0.125	0.116	0.035	0.178
other non-white	0.192	0.133	0.177	0.097
age	–0.029	0.021	–0.042**	0.019
age2	0.439	0.424	0.900**	0.414
age3	–0.293	0.279	–0.652**	0.278
house owner	0.149***	0.051	–0.034	0.051
other smokers	0.280***	0.024	0.239***	0.023
mother smoked	0.014	0.071	0.001	0.057
father smoked	–0.072*	0.042	0.003	0.039
both smoked	–0.040	0.046	–0.006	0.040
disability	–0.078***	0.028	–0.089***	0.028
health-ex	–0.160***	0.035	–0.091**	0.038
health-gd	–0.114***	0.030	–0.054*	0.028
health-pr	–0.024	0.057	0.084*	0.047
$L(.)$	0.278	1.06	0.952	0.757
cigmax	0.016***	0.003	0.025***	0.004
cigmax2	–0.002***	0.0004	–0.004***	0.0005
Min-P(Quit)-Cigmax	38		33	
Log L	–1218.30	–	–1193.63	–
χ^2 (37)	463.34	–	433.15	–
Prob > χ^2	0.000	–	0.000	–
Pseudo R-sq	0.1983	–	0.1741	–
RESET Prob > χ^2	0.1096	–	0.762	–

Note: See note to Table 3.1.

for the continuous regressors and as average effects on the probabilities of continued smoking for the binary indicators.

For males, marital status is a strong predictor of quitting; the divorced, separated, and single are significantly more likely to have continued smoking regularly than the married. The presence of other smokers in the household has a similar effect. Disability increases the probability of quitting, while excellent self-assessed health increases the probability of quitting by approximately twice that of disability. In this sense, the 'curative' element in quitting is half as important as the 'preventive' or preservative element, at least for males (Shmueli 1996). Further there is some appearance of a gradient in the effect of self-assessed health. These conclusions should, however, be tempered by concerns about reverse causality, as it may be that those who have quit report better self-assessed health for precisely that reason. The 'preventive' element should also be captured by the impact of discounted reduction in lifespan. However, this coefficient is *positive* for both males and females. However, in neither case is the estimate significantly different from zero.

The effect of previous peak consumption is quadratic, displaying a *U*-shaped relationship between past consumption and the probability of quitting. Moderate smokers have a lower probability of quitting than both light and heavy smokers, with the minimum around 38 cigarettes per day. In our prevalence sample, about 20 percent of male smokers consume more than this amount. This result sheds new light on previous studies which had suggested that the impact of past consumption on the probability of quitting was monotonically decreasing. These include Jones (1994) who used a linear relationship and Hsieh (1998) who used dummy variables. However, Hsieh defined heavy smoking as 21 or more cigarettes per day. The result obtained here is comparable to Kan and Tsai (1999) who found a *U*-shaped relationship with a minimum at about 50 cigarettes per day using a sample of elderly Taiwanese.

For females, marital status is again a significant predictor of quitting; however, unlike for males, widowhood significantly reduces the probability of quitting while the effect of having never married is reduced. The presence of other smokers in the household again significantly increases the likelihood of continuation. Although the impact of disability is similar to that for males, the impact of excellent health is approximately halved; for females the preventive and curative effects are of a similar magnitude. Furthermore, for women the gradient with respect to self-assessed health is more pronounced. Again the parameter estimate for the benefits of quitting variable is *positive*, but insignificant. As for males, we observe a quadratic relationship between the probability of quitting and previous peak consumption, with the minimum around 33

Table 3.5 Probit models for continuation-incidence sample

	Males ($N = 623$)		Females ($N = 819$)	
	dF/dx	Std. error	*dF/dx*	Std. error
regsc1	0.020	0.119	0.079	0.044
regsc2	0.043	0.064	–0.004	0.047
regsc3	–0.029	0.060	0.025	0.041
regsc4	0.016	0.066	0.072*	0.038
regsc5	0.013	0.088	0.003	0.063
noqual	–0.002	0.053	0.037	0.037
alevels	–0.087	0.113	–0.117	0.084
hnd	–0.100	0.074	0.017	0.051
degree	–0.085	0.098	–0.025	0.056
other/prof	–0.038	0.078	0.025	0.077
widow	–0.076	0.144	0.107**	0.031
divorced	0.096	0.069	0.029	0.047
separated	0.007	0.115	0.075	0.053
single	0.105	0.059	0.055	0.047
part-time	–	–	0.014	0.038
retired	–0.125	0.108	0.078	0.044
sick leave	–0.098	0.125	0.103	0.050
keephouse	–	–	0.014	0.036
unemployed	0.016	0.052	0.051	0.064
Indian/Pakistani	0.168	0.061	0.003	0.202
black African/West Indian	–	–	–	–
other non-white	–	–	–0.109	0.172
age	0.030	0.033	0.024	0.024
age2	–1.023	0.740	–0.507	0.538
age3	0.937*	0.536	0.260	0.386
house owner	0.166*	0.097	0.026	0.065
other smokers	0.086**	0.038	0.058**	0.030
mother smoked	–0.039	0.103	0.088	0.045
father smoked	–0.079	0.077	–0.001	0.048
both smoked	–0.024	0.079	0.028	0.049
disability	–0.062	0.043	0.036	0.031
health-ex	0.031	0.055	–0.126***	0.054
health-gd	–0.060	0.041	–0.059*	0.032
health-pr	0.066	0.074	–0.167**	0.085
$L(.)$	–0.118	0.832	–0.308	0.375
cigday	0.016***	0.005	0.025***	0.005
cigday2	–0.002*	0.001	–0.004***	0.001
Min-P(Quit)-Cigday	44		29	
Log L	–307.34	–	–341.64	–
χ^2 (33/36)	65.09	–	100.84	–
Prob > χ^2	0.0007	–	0.000	–
Pseudo R-sq	0.0971	–	0.1272	–
RESET Prob > χ^2	0.3467	–	0.3282	–

Note: See note to Table 3.1.

cigarettes per day, slightly lower than for males but the proportion of females smoking more than this amount is also lower than for males at about 10 percent.

Table 3.5 presents results from the probit models for the incidence sample; those who were current smokers at HALS1. As for the prevalence sample, all models pass a RESET including squared, cubed, and quartic powers of the linear index. However, the models show much less explanatory power than exhibited using the prevalence sample, as indicated by the relative values of the pseudo-R^2 measures. This is particularly true for males.

For males, very few individual variables remain significant. However, this is not only due to an inflation of standard errors; the absolute values of the majority of coefficients are also reduced. The estimated effect of a discounted reduction in expected lifespan is now negative, but again insignificant. However, the impact of past consumption remains stable. Again there is a *U*-shaped relationship with a minimum at about 44 cigarettes per day.

Similar findings are evident for females. However, although the impact of disability is now insignificant (and positive), the effect of self-assessed health remains. Interestingly, the effect of excellent self-assessed health is increased, while poor self-assessed health also significantly increases the probability of quitting. It may be that curative and preventive effects are now both working through self-assessed health, while the disabled that remain in the sample are the more addicted. This is in line with the results for the prevalence sample. The effect of a discounted reduction in expected lifespan is negative, but it is again insignificant. The impact of consumption is again *U*-shaped with a minimum at 29 cigarettes per day. The proportion of individuals smoking more than the minima in the incidence sample is about 2 percent for both males and females. This suggests that, in line with the results obtained using the prevalence sample, a substantial proportion of heavy smokers had already quit by HALS1, or that they had reduced consumption between the two surveys.

7 CONCLUSION

In the empirical part of this chapter we have attempted to specify models of the prevalence and incidence of quitting that build on previous empirical work by Jones (1994) and Yen and Jones (1996) and that reflect the recent theoretical contribution by Suranovic et al. (1999). We have used data on actual survival rates to proxy the perceived improvement in life expectancy associated with quitting, but we do not find clear evidence of the effect predicted by Suranovic et al. But measures of current health do have a significant impact on quitting and our results reinforce those in Jones (1996) and Hsieh (1998). These findings are consistent with self-reported data from the *HALS* survey which show that 34 percent of men and 26 percent of women cite experience of illness as a reason for quitting, while 30 percent of men and 23 percent of women cite fear of future ill-health.

We find the probability of quitting to be increasing in age, a result consistent with the evidence of increasing duration dependence of the hazard of quitting in Forster and Jones (2000) and Douglas (1998), and with the theoretical predictions of Suranovic et al. and others. This suggests that the benefits of quitting will increase relative to the costs as an individual gets closer to the point where the length and quality of life become affected by the chronic effects of smoking.

We find evidence of non-linearity in the relationship between the probability of quitting and the level of past cigarette consumption. This result is robust for males and females for both the prevalence and incidence samples. The relationship is non-monotonic with plots showing that the probability of quitting is highest for those with low and high levels of past consumption, while the probability of quitting is lowest for those in the mid-range (about 20–40 cigarettes per day). Kan and Tsai (1999) find the same pattern in their analysis of Taiwanese data. This evidence is consistent with the hypothesis of different styles of quitting depending on the initial consumption level. Light smokers may be those who are less addicted and are more likely to quit gradually by continuous adjustment in the number of cigarettes smoked. Heavy smokers may be more addicted and more likely to quit by 'cold turkey'. An alternative interpretation of this result is that it is due to a correlation between unobserved health and cigarette consumption. However, excluding the *observed* health variables leaves the estimates of the marginal effects unchanged to three decimal places. We therefore consider this explanation improbable.

NOTES

* Data from the Health and Lifestyle Survey (HALS) were supplied by the ESRC Data Archive. However, neither the original collectors of the data nor the archive bear any responsibility for the analyses or interpretations presented here. We are grateful for research funding from the ESRC award no. R000222492, and for comments from Tadashi Yamada, Peter Zweifel and an anonymous referee. We also thank participants at the Taipei International Conference on Health

Economics, the International Workshop on Nicotine Dependence, Lausanne, the Arne Ryde symposium, Lund, the Institute for Fiscal Studies (IFS) Health Economics seminar, and the York Seminars in Health Econometrics (YSHE).

1 Jones (1989b) uses a similar framework in incorporating the tolerance effects of addiction in the cost function, while maintaining constant preferences.

2 The potential for unhappy addiction appears to be borne out by the self-reported responses of current smokers in the longitudinal follow-up of the Health and Lifestyle Survey (HALS2), which we use in our empirical analysis. In particular 72 percent of current smokers report that they want to quit. Of these 65 percent claim that they would definitely quit if they could do so easily; a further 19 percent say they would probably quit, while only 16 percent say that they would not.

3 The stages of change perspective also applies to the predicted price responsiveness in the model. Those who are just starting and those who are about to quit are expected to be price responsive, while those who are addicted will be unresponsive (Harris and Chan 1999). An implication is that the analysis of aggregate price effects may be misleading if the tobacco consumer distribution changes as prices vary, and will also mask these different responses.

4 The utility function in Suranovic et al. (1999) is contingent on age. In our empirical analysis we condition on a cubic function of age.

5 Kan and Tsai (1999) adopt the same approach in their study of quitting and re-initiation of smoking among a sample of the elderly in Taiwan. They interpret the quadratic term as a way of allowing for Becker and Murphy's (1988) prediction of cold-turkey quitting in the context of strong adjacent complementarity.

6 The difference in discounted utility will be proportional to $T_0 - T_C$ if undiscounted utility is assumed constant over this period.

7 We experimented with $\sigma = 0.05$ in our empirical application. The results for this approach are not presented in this chapter.

8 For both approaches we set the loss $L(.)$ equal to $T_0 - T_C$ for those individuals whose predicted lifespan is less than or equal to one year greater than their current age. This affects a total of 34 out of 4381 individuals.

9 In the incidence sample the probability of quitting is conditioned on the individual's characteristics, including their health status at the time of HALS1. This should reduce the possibility of the results being affected by reverse causality.

10 It would have been possible to estimate the survival models including never-smokers, rather than our sample which consists of ever-smokers only. However, while bringing efficiency gains, this approach may confound the impact of starting and quitting if the coefficients in the model differ for ever- and never-smokers. Forster (1997) finds using Cox proportional hazard models that it is appropriate to split the sample into ever-smokers and never-smokers when

estimating models of lifespan.

REFERENCES

Atkinson, A. (1974), 'Smoking and the economics of government intervention', in M Perlman (ed.), *The Economics of Health and Medical Care*, London: Macmillan, pp. 428–41.

Barthold, T. and H. Hochman, (1988), 'Addiction as extreme seeking', *Economic Inquiry*, **26**: 89–106.

Becker, G. and K. Murphy (1988), 'A theory of rational addiction', *Journal of Political Economy*, **96**: 675–700.

Cox, B., F. Huppert and M. Whichelow (1993), *The Heath and Lifestyle Survey: Seven Years On*, Aldershot: Dartmouth, 1st edn.

Cox, D., M. Blaxter, J. Fenner, J. Golding and M. Gore (1987), *The Health and Lifestyle Survey*, London: Health Promotion Research Trust, 1st edn.

Cragg, J. (1971), 'Some statistical models for limited dependent variables with applications to the demand for durable goods', *Econometrica*, **39**: 829–44.

Douglas, S. (1998), 'The duration of the smoking habit', *Economic Inquiry*, **36**: 49–64.

Douglas, S. and G. Hariharan (1994), 'The hazard of starting smoking: estimates from a split population duration model', *Journal of Health Economics*, **13**: 213–30.

Forster, M. (1997), 'Economics, inequalities in health, and health-related behaviour', PhD thesis, University of York.

Forster, M. and A. Jones (2000), 'The role of tobacco taxes in starting and quitting smoking: duration analysis of British data', Centre for Health Economics Discussion Paper 176, University of York.

Harris, J. and S. Chan (1999), 'The continuum of addiction: cigarette smoking in relation to price among Americans aged 15–29', *Health Economics*, **8**: 81–6.

Hsieh, C.-R. (1998), 'Health risk and the decision to quit smoking', *Applied Economics*, **30**: 798–804.

Jones, A. (1987), 'A theoretical and empirical investigation of the demand for addictive goods', PhD thesis, University of York.

Jones, A. (1989a), 'A double-hurdle model of cigarette consumption', *Journal of Applied Econometrics*, **4**: 23–39.

Jones, A. (1989b), 'A systems approach to the demand for alcohol and tobacco', *Bulletin of Economic Research*, **41**: 85–105.

Jones, A. (1994), 'Health, addiction, social interaction and the decision to quit smoking', *Journal of Health Economics*, **13**: 93–110.

Jones, A. (1995), 'A microeconometric analysis of smoking in the UK. Health and lifestyle survey', Centre for Health Economics Discussion Paper 139, University of York.

Jones, A. (1996), 'Smoking cessation and health: a response', *Journal of Health Economics*, **15**: 755–9.

Jones, A. (1999), 'Adjustment costs, withdrawal effects, and cigarette addiction', *Journal of Health Economics*, **18**: 125–37.

Kan, K. and W.-D. Tsai (1999), 'Rational cessation and re-initiation of cigarette smoking: evidence from Taiwan', Presented at Taipei International Conference on Health Economics, 25–7 March.

Kuhn, C., S. Swartzwelder and W. Wilson (1998), *Buzzed*, New York: W.W. Norton & Co., 1st edn.

Michaels, R. (1988), 'Addiction, compulsion, and the technology of consumption', *Economic Inquiry*, **26**: 74–88.

Sander, W. (1995), 'Schooling and quitting smoking', *Review of Economics and Statistics*, **129**: 191–8.

Shmueli, A. (1996), 'Smoking cessation and health: a comment', *Journal of Health Economics*, **15**: 751–4.

Suranovic, S., R. Goldfarb and T. Leonard (1999), 'An economic theory of cigarette addiction', *Journal of Health Economics*, **18**: 1–29.

Yen, S. and A. Jones (1996), 'Individual cigarette consumption and addiction: a flexible limited dependent variable approach', *Health Economics*, **5**: 105–17.

4. Rational cessation and re-initiation of cigarette smoking: evidence from Taiwan

Kamhon Kan and Wei-Der Tsai*

1 INTRODUCTION

Due to their inability to explain the inconsistence of smokers' behavior using the neoclassical framework, early researchers largely regarded cigarette smoking as irrational (for example, Strotz 1956; Pollak 1968; Elster 1979; McKenzie 1979; Winston 1980; and Schelling 1978, 1984a, 1984b) or myopic (for example, Houthakker and Taylor 1966; and Pollak 1975), and claimed that cigarette smoking behavior could not be studied using standard economic theory. By definition, in making a decision a rational consumer maximizes utility subject to the available information and opportunity sets. Hence rational consumers will consider all possible consequences of their choices such that, if they have perfect information on the consequences, they will not regret a decision that they have made. Because of its addictive nature, cigarette smoking behavior seems inconsistent with the rationality postulate. For example, to earlier researchers it seemed puzzling that some individuals would pick up the harmful habit and regret it later (reflected by their quiting behavior); smokers' lifetime cigarette consumption path looks time inconsistent (see Strotz 1956); and cigarette smokers are ambivalent over the decision to quit (see Schelling 1978; Winston 1980; and Thaler and Shefrin 1981). Because of the difficulty of modeling addiction, the addictive characteristics of cigarette smoking are seldom accounted for in early empirical studies of cigarette smoking behavior (for example, Lewit and Coate 1982; Baltagi and Levin 1986).

Recently, by incorporating the dependence of current consumption level on past consumption, some researchers are able to reconcile cigarette smoking with rationality.[1] A notable example is Becker and Murphy (1988). Several hypotheses are developed in Becker and Murphy

(1988) and Becker et al. (1991). The most important one is 'adjacent complementarity', that is, current consumption positively depends on past consumption. This implies that current consumption is inversely related to all prices (past, current and future). The study by Becker and Murphy (1988) has stimulated a sequence of studies that empirically test the rationality of cigarette smoking and other addictive substances. For example, Chaloupka (1990, 1991) uses micro data and Perkurinen (1991), Keeler et al. (1993), Becker et al. (1994) and Bardsley and Olekalns (1998) use time-series data to study cigarette smoking behavior in the context of the Becker–Murphy (1988) model. They all support the rationality of cigarette smoking.[2]

Another important prediction of the Becker–Murphy (1988) rational addiction model is 'strong adjacent complementarity' (that is, the case of strong addiction) which will lead to unstable steady states. Nevertheless, the popularity of empirical testing of the implications related to adjacent complementarity has not extended to those arising from strong adjacent complementarity. Perhaps this is because most researchers regard the consistency of the implications of strong adjacent complementarity with actual behavior as too apparent to warrant empirical testing. It is true that quitting behavior is frequently observed for smokers. However, strong adjacent complementarity actually implies a specific consumption trajectory leading to cessation. On the other hand, a careful search of the literature reveals that there does not exist any empirical evidence on the 'binge' phenomenon of cigarette consumption.

The purpose of this chapter is to investigate the implications of strong adjacent complementarity of Becker and Murphy's (1988) rational addiction model. More specifically, we investigate the implication that an increase in past consumption of cigarettes will increase current consumption at a decreasing rate, and that the effect of past consumption will eventually become negative leading to cessation of cigarette smoking, that is, cold turkey. While substantial empirical evidence substantiates the positive dependence of current cigarette consumption on past, not much is known about whether further increases in cigarette consumption will lead to cessation.

Another implication of rational addiction is the existence of cycles of addiction, that is, binges. In the case of smoking, cigarette consumption over time will exhibit cycles with excess consumption leading to cessation, followed by re-initiation of the habit.

The empirical work in this study is based on panel data of elderly individuals in Taiwan. The advantage of focusing on elderly individuals is that the adverse effects of smoking usually crop up increasingly when a smoker reaches an advanced age. Thus, for elderly smokers aging exerts a positive impact on the decision to quit; this may represent shocks to the stock of addiction in the sense of Becker and Murphy (1988). This helps us identify the effects of addiction on the decision to quit. The empirical results support Becker and Murphy's strong adjacent complementarity implication in the context of cigarette smoking. We find that past cigarette consumption has a negative effect on the decision to quit. However, its effect becomes positive when past consumption reaches a certain level, implying that the strongly addicted tend to quit abruptly. Nevertheless, it is not likely that ex-smokers will start smoking again when their health becomes better. Thus, the existence of binges in cigarette consumption is not identified.

The organization of the rest of the chapter is as follows. The empirical models are illustrated in Section 2. The data source and variables used in the empirical investigation are described in Section 3. The estimation results are reported and discussed in Section 4. A conclusion is given in Section 5.

2 EMPIRICAL MODEL

The rational addiction model is developed by Becker and Murphy (1988). This model has attracted and revived much interest in the economics of addiction and motivated many empirical analyses on the issue. Most of these empirical analyses focus on the relationship between future prices or consumption level, and current consumption implied by adjacent complementarity. The current study examines other implications arising from the rational addiction hypothesis, namely, 'cold turkey' and 'binge'.

2.1 Cold Turkey

Becker and Murphy's (1988) theory of addiction predicts that because of adjacent complementarity, the time $t-1$ cigarette consumption level will have a negative effect on the likelihood of quit at time t because consumption at $t-1$ will increase the stock of addiction for time t. However, when the level of time $t-1$ consumption is sufficiently high, strong complementarity creeps in, that is, future adjustment cost will become very high so that past consumption will hasten quitting. In other words, there exists a (second-order) non-linear relationship between past cigarette consumption and likelihood of quit.

The test of the above hypothesis is based on a sample of elderly individuals.[3] The test is based on the following model:

$$Q_{it} = x_{it}\beta + \alpha_1 q_{it-1} + \alpha_2 q_{it-1}^2 + \varepsilon_{it}, \tag{4.1}$$

where q_{it-1} is the number of cigarettes consumed by smoker i in period $t - 1$, x_{it} is a vector of socioeconomic variables (for example, age, changes in health status and so on), ε_{it} is a mean-zero, unit-variance, independent and normally distributed error term, β, α_1 and α_2 are parameters to be estimated, and Q_{it} is a latent variable so that

$$I_{qit} = \begin{cases} 1 \text{ (that is, quit), if } Q_{it} > 0; \\ 0 \text{ (that is, continue smoking), if } Q_{it} \leq 0. \end{cases} \tag{4.2}$$

In (4.2), I_{qit} is an indicator variable, with $I_{qit} = 1$ if i quit by time t and $I_{qit} = 0$ if i continues smoking. This specification of the quit decision constitutes a probit model. The rational addiction theory predicts that $\alpha_1 < 0$ and $\alpha_2 > 0$, and the critical consumption level which triggers quitting cold turkey is $-\alpha_1/2\alpha_2$.

It is noted that the variable q_{it-1} is likely to be an endogenous variable, that is, Q_{it} and q_{it-1} to some extent are jointly determined so that the error term ε_{it} is correlated with q_{it-1}. If this kind of endogeneity is not controlled, biased estimates will be obtained from the estimation of (4.1). To account for the endogeneity of q_{it-1}, the estimation of (4.1) is performed jointly with an auxiliary regression of q_{it-1} with the method of maximum likelihood, that is, a recursive simultaneous equation system is estimated.[4] The auxiliary regression equation of q_{it-1} is specified as

$$q_{it-1} = z_{it-1}\gamma + u_{it-1}, \tag{4.3}$$

where z_{it-1} is a vector of respondent characteristics pertaining to $t-1$, γ is a vector of coefficients to be estimated and u_{it-1} is a normally distributed error term with mean zero and standard deviation σ. ε_{it} and u_{it-1} are correlated with the correlation coefficient denoted by ρ. Below is the likelihood function:

$$\mathcal{L} = \prod_{\forall i} \left[\Phi\left(\frac{x_{it}\beta + \alpha_1 q_{it-1} + \alpha_2 q_{it-1}^2 + \rho(q_{it-1} - z_{it-1}\gamma)}{\sqrt{1-\rho^2}}\right) \right]^{I_{qit}}$$

$$\times \left[1 - \Phi\left(\frac{x_{it}\beta + \alpha_1 q_{it-1} + \alpha_2 q_{it-1}^2 + \rho(q_{it-1} - z_{it-1}\gamma)}{\sqrt{1-\rho^2}}\right) \right]^{(1-I_{qit})} \quad (4.4)$$

$$\times \phi\left(\frac{q_{it-1} - z_{it-1}\gamma}{\sigma}\right).$$

The parameter estimates are obtained by maximizing the log likelihood, that is, ($\mathcal{L}$), with respect to all parameters.

It is noted that model (4.1) is not a structural model of rational addiction. It is because we only have past (that is, $t-1$) and current (that is, t) information but do not have future (that is, $t+1$) information in our two-period panel data. Thus, the above model constitutes a habit formation model.

2.2 Binge

In the literature, there are few studies looking at the phenomenon of binging, that is, a temporary increase in consumption above the normal or long-run level. If the swing in consumption is large enough, we may observe a period of abstinence followed by another of indulgence.[5] According to Becker and Murphy (1988), two stocks of consumption capital are needed to create oscillations between abstinence and addiction. In the case of smoking behavior, the two consumption stocks could be interpreted as the stock of health and the stock of addiction. When an individual starts smoking, the stock of addiction capital may rise faster than deterioration in health stock. However, when the health stock is sufficiently low (that is, health problems start to appear) the individual may reduce smoking or quit. However, when health stock is replenished after a bout of abstinence, the individual may start smoking again.

To test this binge behavior, the following model is specified:

$$R_{it} = x_{it}\gamma + D_{it}\delta + u_{it}, \quad (4.5)$$

where D_{it} is a dummy variable indicating ex-smoker i's health has improved between periods $t-1$ and t, u_{it} is a mean-zero, unit-variance, independent and normally distributed error term, and γ and δ are parameters to be estimated, and R_{it} is a latent variable indicating the propensity to re-initiate smoking with

$$I_{rit} = \begin{cases} 1 \text{ (that is, re initiate), if } R_{it} > 0; \\ 0 \text{ (that is, stay abstinent), if } R_{it} \leq 0. \end{cases} \tag{4.6}$$

In the above equation, I_{rit} is an indicator variable, denoting re-initiation if it equals one and not re-initiating if it equals zero. The parameters in equation (4.5) are estimated by a probit model. The rational addiction hypothesis predicts that $\delta > 0$. The estimation of the above model is based on two different samples: a subsample of individuals who were not smokers in 1989 and a subsample of ex-smokers before the survey year 1989. These individuals' decision to start smoking in 1993 is explained by their change in health status and some other socioeconomic characteristics.

There is an admonition to our analysis of binge. In our analysis we examine binging behavior by looking at the alternation between abstinence and restarting. Nevertheless, binging may take a much less extreme manifestation, for example, in the form of oscillations between high consumption level and low consumption. Thus, while we can conclude the existence of binge in cigarette smoking if we find supportive results, that is, $\delta > 0$; we cannot negate the existence of binge if we find the contrary.

3 DATA AND VARIABLES

The data used in this study are based on the Survey of Health and Living Status of the Elderly, which is a nationally representative sample of the elderly in Taiwan. This survey was conducted by the Taiwan Provincial Institute of Family Planning, and the Population Studies Center and Institute of Gerontology at the University of Michigan in 1989 to collect information on the social, economic and demographic status of 4049 individuals aged 60 and over. A follow-up survey was conducted in 1993. The sample size reduced sharply to 3155 in 1993. The attrition of respondents between the two surveys is largely due to death.[6]

Three different subsamples are extracted from the 1989–93 panel of respondents for the empirical work. The first is a subsample of individuals who were smokers in 1989. This subsample is used in the investigation of smoking cessation behavior. The definition of variables used and their sample statistics are reported in Table 4.1. The statistical

Table 4.1 Descriptive statistics – decision to quit

Variable	Mean (Std dev.)	Definition
QUIT93	0.1816 (0.3857)	Dependent variable: = 1 if quit smoking in 1993; = 0 otherwise
NCIGAR89	14.8823 (9.3251)	Number of cigarettes consumed per day in 1989
$NCIGAR89^2$	308.3769 (596.1146)	NCIGAR89 squared
AGE89	67.0940 (5.7866)	Age of respondent in 1989
EDUC	4.9063 (4.1512)	Years of schooling received by respondent
HG2P	0.2857 (0.4519)	= 1 if (self-evaluated) health of respondent deteriorated between 1989 and 1993; = 0 otherwise
HP2G	0.4228 (0.4942)	= 1 if (self-evaluated) health of respondent improved between 1989 and 1993; = 0 otherwise
DINCOME	–0.0460 (1.5448)	Change in average monthly income between 1989 and 1993 (in 10 thousands)
INCOME89	1.4655 (1.4044)	Average total monthly income in 1989 (in 10 thousands)
MALE	0.9081 (0.2890)	= 1 if respondent is male; = 0 otherwise
NOSPOUSE	0.1012 (0.3017)	= 1 if respondent lost spouse between 1989 and 1993; = 0 otherwise
MARR89	0.7514 (0.4323)	= 1 if respondent is married in 1989; = 0 otherwise
HEALTH89	2.5403 (1.0633)	Self-evaluated health status of respondent: = 1 if excellent, = 2 if good, = 3 if fair, = 4 if poor, = 5 if poor
Observations		919

Table 4.2 Descriptive Statistics – decision to start smoking

Variable	Subsample	
	NON-SMOKER=1	EX-SMOKER=1
START93	0.0245 (0.1548)	0.0666 (0.2495)
AGE89	68.7459 (6.7033)	68.6602 (6.6556)
EDUC	3.6513 (4.5131)	5.8844 (4.6535)
HG2P	0.2837 (0.4509)	0.2581 (0.4380)
HP2G	0.4150 (0.4928)	0.4448 (0.4973)
DINCOME	–0.0379 (1.4147)	0.0326 (1.4685)
INCOME89	1.3629 (1.4934)	1.6588 (1.6202)
MALE	0.3990 (0.4898)	0.9075 (0.2900)
NOSPOUSE	0.0907 (0.2873)	0.0860 (0.2806)
HP2G × EX-SMOKER	0.1019 (0.3026)	– –
Observations	1800	387

Notes
NON-SMOKER denotes whether a respondent was a non-smoker in 1989 (who may or may not have smoked before 1989); equals 1 if yes, equals 0 otherwise.
EX-SMOKER denotes whether a respondent was a smoker before 1989 and has quit by 1989; equals 1 if yes, equals 0 otherwise.
START represents whether a respondent started smoking in 1993; equals 1 if yes and equals 0 otherwise.

characteristics of the other two subsamples for the 'start smoking' decision are presented in Table 4.2. The two subsamples consist of, respectively, respondents who did not smoke in 1989 (but may or may not have smoked before 1989), and respondents who were smokers before 1989 and have quit by 1989.

Being critical explanatory variables, the variables HG2P and HP2G deserve further elaboration. Their construction is based on the variables HEALTH89 and its counterpart for 1993, that is, HEALTH93. An improvement in health (that is, HP2G = 1) is defined as HEALTH93 <

HEALTH89, and likewise, a deterioration in health (that is, HG2P = 1) is defined as HEALTH93 > HEALTH89.

4 RESULTS DISCUSSION

The estimation results are displayed in Tables 4.3 and 4.4.[7] In Table 4.3 the results pertaining to the decision to quit suggest that the number of cigarettes consumed in 1989 has a negative impact on the decision to quit. This demonstrates adjacent complementarity. However, as the number of cigarettes consumed grows the impact will become positive as suggested by the positive coefficient of the variable $NCIGAR89^2$. The turning point is when the number of cigarettes consumed reaches 48.03.[8] This result gives support to strong adjacent complementarity of Becker and Murphy (1988). However, in the sample there are only ten respondents (that is, about 1 percent of the sample) whose daily average cigarette consumption exceeded this level. This suggests that 'cold turkey' is not a very common phenomenon in cigarette smoking.

The rest of the results in Table 4.3 are very much in accordance with intuition as well as results obtained by previous studies. The parameter estimate associated with AGE indicates that age exerts a positive impact on the decision to quit. As suggested, for example, by Suranovic et al. (1999), since the health problems, whether associated with smoking or not, usually start or get serious as a person reaches an advanced age, then aging itself is a strong enough reason for some smokers to quit smoking.

The result pertaining to HG2P (that is, health deteriorates) indicates that when a smoker's health deteriorates he/she is prone to quit smoking. However, when a smoker's health improves (that is, HP2G = 1) his/her propensity to quit smoking is not significantly affected.

As implied by the positive coefficient of DINCOME (denoting change in income between 1989 and 1993), an increase in income will prompt a smoker to quit. This positive coefficient is contradictory to intuition which suggests that an improvement in economic situation should discourage quitting. However, an improvement in economic status may lead to higher value of life, that is, being more health conscious. That is, the results are consistent with the fact that health is a normal good, and the positive income effect of health is stronger than that of demand for cigarettes.[9] The same explanation may explain why the variable INCOME89 (income level in 1989) also has a (marginally significant) positive effect on the decision to quit. However, when a smoker lost his/her spouse (when NOSPOUSE = 1), the quit decision is not affected.

Eduction level (denoted by EDUC) does not have any explanatory

Table 4.3 The quit decision

	QUIT93	NCIGAR89
CONSTANT	–2.8586	32.3471
	(–4.225)	(7.253)
NCIGAR89	–2.1026e–2	–
	(–2.097)	–
$NCIGAR89^2$	2.1887e–4	
	(1.658)	–
AGE89	0.0289	–0.1182
	(3.258)	(–1.876)
EDUC	6.7517e–3	–0.2233
	(0.605)	(–2.754)
HG2P	0.2416	–
	(2.196)	–
HP2G	–0.1790	–
	(–1.438)	–
DINCOME	0.0671	–
	(1.999)	–
INCOME89	0.0722	0.3563
	(1.717)	(1.485)
MALE	0.2053	–6.2472
	(1.150)	(–5.159)
NOSPOUSE	0.1156	–
	(0.833)	–
MARR89	–	–0.7301
	–	(–1.009)
HEALTH89	–	–0.1997
	–	(–0.623)
σ	–9.2526	
	3640.5240	
ρ	–0.0983	
	(–3.3630)	
Log likelihood	–3818.445	
Observations	919	

Note: Numbers in parentheses are *t*-statistics.

Table 4.4 Decision to start smoking

	Non-smoker	Ex-smoker
CONSTANT	–0.5756	–0.4749
	(–0.683)	(–0.392)
AGE89	–0.0131	–0.0246
	(–1.162)	(–1.453)
EDUC	–0.0016	–0.0123
	(–0.092)	(–0.473)
HG2P	0.0461	–0.1779
	(0.319)	(–0.787)
HP2G	–0.2060	0.0767
	(–1.062)	(0.339)
DINCOME	0.0642	0.0175
	(1.439)	(0.250)
INCOME89	–0.0023	0.0015
	(–0.042)	(0.019)
MALE	–0.3032	0.76141
	(–2.043)	(2.768)
NOSPOUSE	0.0461	0.3334
	(0.243)	(1.231)
HP2G × EX-SMOKER	0.7679	–
	(3.173)	–
Log likelihood	–231.9897	–111.2987
Observations	1800	387

Note: Numbers in parentheses are *t*-statistics.

power on the decision to quit even though education level is related to more efficient learning of health risk of smoking (see Viscusi 1989, for a discussion). Furthermore, the gender of the respondent (denoted by SEX) is statistically insignificant in the quit equation. However, in Hsieh (1998) all these variables are statisitically significant in affecting the decision to quit. The major difference in the econometric specification between the current study and Hsieh's (1998) is the inclusion of previous consumption level (that is, NCIGAR89 and NCIGAR89^2) in the current study. This demonstrates that previous consumption level is sufficient for summarizing most of the influence of socioeconomic characteristics on the quit decision.

The results pertaining to the cigarette consumption equation, displayed in the second column of Table 4.3, are quite consistent with intuition: year of schooling (EDU), and a smoker's gender and age have statistically significant negative impacts on the level of consumption, while income level (denoted by INCOME89), marital status (MARR89) and health status (HEALTH89) do not exert any significant impact on the consumption decision.

In Table 4.4, the estimation results corresponding to the 'start' decision are presented. In the first column (heading: Non-smokers), the estimation employs all individuals who were not smokers in 1989. Most of the variables are not statistically significant except MALE (gender of the individual) and HP2G × EX-SMOKER which denotes an interaction term of HP2G (improvement in health status between 1989 and 1993) and EX-SMOKER (the individual had a smoking habit before 1989). This seems to indicate binging. However, when only ex-smokers are used in the estimation, no variable is statistically significant in affecting the decision to start smoking even though an improvement in the situation (for example, health, income, and so on) should have a positive impact, according to the rational addiction theory.

Our empirical results do not provide supportive evidence of the existence of binge in cigarette smoking. However, there are caveats which call for caution in the interpretation of the results pertaining to binge. The interval between the two observations (4 years, between 1989 and 1993) may be too large. There may be cycles of higher frequencies in between the two points in time, and looking at behavior at only the two points in time (that is, 1989 and 1993) may not reveal these cycles. Also, binge may appear as variations in the quantities of cigarette consumption, which are not captured by our empirical work where binge is defined as alternating between abstinence and re-initiating.

5 CONCLUSION

In this chapter, the behavior of smoking cessation and re-initiation is studied from the perspective of the rational addiction model of Murphy and Becker (1988). The rational addiction model predicts that, when there is a shock requiring a reduction in cigarette consumption for moderate cigarette addicts, the degree of addiction will have a negative effect on quitting the smoking habit; however, due to strong complementarity, heavy addicts will be more likely to quit. In other words, the relationship between the degree of addiction and cigarette consumption is non-linear. Another phenomenon that is predicted by the rational addiction theory is 'binging'. In the case of cigarette smoking, binging could be in the form of oscillation between a bout of addiction and a period of abstinence.

Becker and Murphy (1988) assert that quitting cold turkey does happen to strong addicts and the consumption pattern of addicts does exhibit binging and therefore that their theory explains these two phenomena. However, there is not much empirical evidence to support their claim. The present study treats them as hypotheses derived from the theory and examines their empirical validity.

Based on a panel of elderly individuals in Taiwan, the above predictions are examined. The empirical results indicate that strong addicts are more likely to stop smoking abruptly. However, the estimation results are not supportive of the binging hypothesis. When health or income improves, the likelihood for an ex-smoker to start smoking again is not significantly affected.

NOTES

* We would like to thank two anonymous reviewers, Michael Grossman and, especially, Chee-Ruey Hsieh for thorough and insightful comments and suggestions. We are solely responsible for any remaining errors.

1. The dependence of current consumption on past consumption, that is, habit formation, was recognized long before the Becker–Murphy paper. However, the Becker–Murphy paper is among the first to incorporate habit formation in a rational choice model.
2. Despite this, some more recent studies still model the decision to smoke as irrational (see Chesney and Hazari 1998) and smokers choose cigarette consumption with bounded rationality (see Suranovic et al. 1999).
3. The data will be described in Section 3.
4. The system is recursive in the sense that an endogenous variable appears on the right-hand side of one of the two equations.
5. In the Becker–Murphy (1988) paper, binge is defined as bouncing between overconsumption and underconsumption, for example, cycles of overeating and dieting.
6. There are 671 of the respondents in the 1989 survey who had passed away by 1993. Among them, 33.68 percent were smokers.
7. It is noted that in our empirical study, we do not have price as a regressor. Unlike, for example, in the US where regional variation in cigarette price (which is quality independent and is mainly due to local sales taxes) is great enough to produce meaningful results; in Taiwan there is not much regional cigarette price variation. In Taiwan, all contemporal price variations solely reflect quality/brand differences. Nevertheless, the omission of price in our regressions does not

create any problems for us. On the one hand, the effect of price on cigarette consumption is not a focus of our study. On the other hand, the omission of price in the regressions is unlikely to create bias in the results. This is so because (quality-independent) price is supposed to be exogenous to all individual socioeconomic variables.

8 That is, $\frac{-\alpha_1}{2\alpha_2} = 48.03$. With a *t*-value of 2.1886, it is statistically significant. The calculation of the standard error of $\frac{-\alpha_1}{2\alpha_2}$ is based on the *delta* method. In short, if a variable μ is a function of a vector of variables *v*, such that $\mu = f(v)$, the variance of μ equals $\frac{\partial f(v)}{\partial v'} var(v) \frac{\partial f(v)}{\partial v}$, where *var*(*v*) denotes the variance-covariance matris of *v*.

9 We thank a referee for pointing out this explanation.

REFERENCES

Baltagi, B.H. and D. Levin (1986), 'Estimation dynamic demand for cigarette using panel data: the effects of bootlegging, taxation, and advertising reconsidered', *Review of Economics and Statistics*, **68**(1): 148–55.

Bardsley, P. and N. Olekalns (1998), 'Cigarette and tobacco consumption: have anti-smoking policies made a difference?', Working Paper, Department of Economics, University of Melbourne.

Becker, G.S., M. Grossman and K.M. Murphy (1991), 'Rational addiction and the effect of price on consumption', *American Economic Review*, **81**: 237–41.

Becker, G.S., M. Grossman and K.M. Murphy (1994), 'An empirical analysis of cigarette addiction', *American Economic Review*, **84**(3): 396–418.

Becker, G.S. and K.M. Murphy (1988), 'A theory of rational addiction', *Journal of Political Economy*, **96**(4): 675–700.

Chaloupka, F.J. (1990), 'Men, women, and addiction: the case of cigarette smoking', Working Paper No. 3267, National Bureau of Economic Research.

Chaloupka, F.J. (1991), 'Rational addiction behavior and cigarette smoking', *Journal of Political Economy*, **99**(4): 722–42.

Chesney, M. and B. Hazari (1998), 'Irrational entry, rational exit', *Journal of Mathematical Economics*, **29**(1): 1–13.

Elster, J. (1979), *Ulysses and the Sirens: Studies in Rationality and Irrationality*, Cambridge: Cambridge University Press.

Houthakker, H.S. and L.D. Taylor (1966), *Consumer Demand in the United States, 1929-1970: Analyses and Projections*, Cambridge, MA: Harvard University Press.

Hsieh, C.-R. (1998), 'Health risk and the decision to quit smoking', *Applied Economics*, **30**: 795–804.

Keeler, T.E., T.-W. Hu, P.G. Barnett and W.G. Manning (1993), 'Taxation, regulation and addiction: a demand function for cigarettes based on time-series evidence', *Journal of Health Economics*, **12**(1): 1–18.

Lewit, E.M. and D. Coate (1982), 'The potential for using excise taxes to reduce smoking', *Journal of Health Economics*, **3**(2): 121–45.

McKenzie, R.B. (1979), 'The non-rational domain and the limits of economic analysis', *Southern Economic Journal*, **46**(1): 145–57.

Perkurinen, M. (1991), *Economic Aspects of Smoking: Is There a Case for Government Intervention in Finland*?, Helsinki: Vapk-Publishing.

Pollak, R. (1968), 'Consistent planning', *Review of Economic Studies*, **35**: 201–8.

Pollak, R. (1975), 'The intertemporal cost of living index', *Annals of Economic and Social Measurement*, **4**: 179–95.

Schelling, T.C. (1978), 'Economics, or the art of self-management', *American Economic Review*, **68**: 290–94.

Schelling, T.C. (1984a), 'The intimate contest for self-command', *The Public Interest*, **60**: 94–113.

Schelling, T.C. (1984b), *Choice and Consequence*, Cambridge, MA: Harvard University Press.

Strotz, R.H. (1956), 'Myopia and inconsistency in dynamic utility maximization', *Review of Economic Studies*, **23**: 165–80.

Suranovic, S.M., R.S. Goldfarb and T.C. Leonard (1999), 'An economic theory of cigarette addiction', *Journal of Health Economics*, **18**: 1–30.

Thaler, R. and H.M. Shefrin (1981), 'An economic theory of self control', *Journal of Political Economy*, **89**: 392–406.

Viscusi, K. (1989), 'Prospective reference theory: toward an explanation of the paradoxes', *Journal of Risk and Uncertainty*, **2**: 235–63.

Winston, G.C. (1980), 'Addiction and backsliding: a theory of compulsive consumption', *Journal of Economic Behavior and Organization*, **1**(4): 295–324.

PART II

Risk Perception and Time Preference

5. Are smokers too optimistic?

Frank A. Sloan, Donald H. Taylor, Jr. and V. Kerry Smith*

1 INTRODUCTION

Smoking is a major source of mortality and morbidity in countries throughout the world (for example, Peto et al. 1992). In contrast to many involuntary sources of risk that people face, smoking is a private choice. Nonetheless, it has received special attention from policy makers for at least three decades. To most public health experts, smokers seem irrational. The US Surgeon General and others have warned about adverse health effects of smoking; yet seemingly intelligent people continue to smoke. Moreover, a large fraction of teenagers and young adults start smoking in the face of targeted warnings and other efforts to limit their access to cigarettes and ability to smoke in public and private places (Jacobson and Wasserman 1997). To some policy makers, these choices imply that people do not understand how to make choices in the presence of risk.

The conclusion is at odds with a substantial set of alternative evidence. People make decisions everyday that involve risk. Driving to work, flying to a distant city, or engaging in dangerous recreational activities (for example, scuba diving, rock climbing) are all choices that imply people recognize that they must accept risks to realize other outcomes contributing to their well-being.[1] The economist's perspective generally begins from the premise that people know what is best for themselves. This presumption relies on each individual knowing the consequences of their actions so that an *informed choice* is made.[2] The debate over smoking policies in the United States is fundamentally about what constitutes an informed choice. That is, it questions whether those starting to smoke or those continuing, in the presence of what appears to many as an overwhelming set of evidence documenting serious health consequences, are actually making informed decisions.

An economic model of behavior in the presence of risk generally assumes that each individual knows or can form subjective beliefs about the risks (that is, the probabilities) of all the events that can affect his or her well-being. In this framework, the causal line of reasoning in the model flows from information to risk perception and then ultimately to behavior. This logic leads to a focus on the information to risk perception stage of model in evaluations of what constitutes an informed choice.

At practical levels, however, we know that the process is not so simple. When a person takes action to acquire information, this is a behavioral choice related to the decision to change behavior. For example, changing one's diet based on new information about fiber and the risk of cancer is connected to the choice to pay attention to that information in the first place. Because of these connections, a person's efforts to enhance knowledge about risk should depend on the events at risk. The consequences of faulty brakes are likely to be more important for a long driving trip than determining the odds it will rain on that same trip.

Any effort to understand people's risk perceptions must acknowledge the multiple reasons for unobserved heterogeneity that can prevent an analyst from knowing all aspects of how people judge the risks they face. As a result, efforts to evaluate whether smoking is an informed choice can, and do, lead to different judgments. These differences can be partially explained by assumptions analysts made in trying to uncover the full dimensions of the information–perception–behavior nexus with incomplete data.

This chapter summarizes our evaluation of how information and behavior affect risk perceptions over time. We exploited unique characteristics of a survey of the near elderly, the Health and Retirement Study (HRS). This national panel study includes birth cohorts 1931–41 and their spouses. Each respondent in the panel was interviewed every two years beginning in 1992. Three waves of interviews were available for our analysis. We focused on respondents' reported longevity expectations, elicited using a question originally suggested by Hamermesh (1985).

Our analysis considered three aspects of these longevity expectations. The first involved consistency between these subjective perceptions and actual outcomes. This consistency was evaluated based on a comparison of mean values and micro analysis of deaths among HRS respondents. In the analysis of mean values, we assessed the relationship between mean subjective perceptions and life tables for selected demographic groups. The HRS also permitted a micro-level analysis of longevity expectations of respondents who died between Waves 1 and 2 (1992 to 1994) and those dying between Waves 2 and 3 (1994 to 1996).

Second, we considered how current behavior (that is, smoking versus not) and changes in that behavior affected these expectations. Third, we investigated how longevity perceptions were updated in response to what is arguably the most direct health information an individual can receive – serious health shocks. The HRS's panel structure allowed a test of the influence of general and smoking-related health shocks between Waves 1 and 2 on longevity expectations reported in Wave 2.

In Section 2, we describe the Bayesian-updating model used in past research and empirical evidence on risk perceptions and smoker status. A major limitation of this research reflects reliance on a single cross-section. Our new empirical evidence, based on the first three waves of HRS, is presented in Section 3. These findings suggest that smokers experience relatively more adverse health-related outcomes. These events are then translated into reduced subjective probabilities of living to age 75. Finally, contrary to much of the earlier evidence, we find that heavy smokers are too optimistic about their life expectancies.

2 BACKGROUND

In the United States, various efforts aimed at achieving major decreases in smoking and compensating for injuries attributed to smoking are being considered. The possible actions include increased taxation of tobacco products, broad-based information programs, and greater reliance on tort claims. Non-smokers can be adversely affected as neighbors of smokers, as stockholders, taxpayers, and as insurance premium payers (Manning et al. 1991). Smokers can experience effects through pecuniary losses they incur, time losses by self and family members, and various types of non-pecuniary losses, including pain and suffering, associated with smoking-related disease. The newest development in the US that is likely to affect tobacco firms in the future is the increasing role of tort as a means for compensating smoking 'victims'. Recent decisions have confirmed that 'victims' can extend beyond the individual smoker and his or her family.

A major issue in this tort litigation involves the extent to which individuals correctly perceive risks inherent in their smoking decisions (Hanson and Logue 1998). This is a special concern when it has been argued that tobacco companies withheld pertinent health information from the public and/or engaged in misleading advertising. Claims and counterclaims raise important empirical issues. To what extent have individuals been able to make informed decisions about smoking? This depends on how individuals use information to form expectations about their risks from smoking. Answers to these questions are offered based on evaluations of the information available to smokers – from both the public sources conveyed through the media as well as from more personal signals, such as their own and the health of other people they know. If smokers do perceive their risks accurately, then they should be expected to bear the cost of smoking-related diseases that arise due to smoking. Conversely, if, as a result of misleading claims by tobacco companies, smokers systematically underestimate the risks from smoking, including the probabilities of acquiring smoking-related diseases, then the companies may be found to be culpable. Of course, misperception may occur for several reasons. Thus, finding underestimation of risks is probably a necessary but not a sufficient condition for establishing liability of tobacco companies.

A second question concerns the extent to which addiction to tobacco compromises the economic model that maintains that people make rational choices. Becker and Murphy's (1988) rational addiction model suggests that people make a rational choice based on available information about whether to start consuming an addictive product. Nonetheless, even if that initial choice is rational, smokers may experience regret 'after the fact', as new information from smoking research becomes public, or as people learn about their own susceptibility to more specific health effects. People are likely to be heterogeneous with regard to the harmful effects of an addictive good (Orphanides and Zervos 1995). Subjective beliefs about the effect of such a good on one's own health are plausibly updated via a Bayesian learning process. This activity can take place as a smoker consumes the good (or observes others who smoke, such as close relatives, who may have common genes). According to this perspective, those who receive bad news over time use the information to update their perceptions and may, as a result, regret having become addicted.

2.1 Early Results

Viscusi's (1990) well-cited study for the United States considered two issues. First, to what extent do smokers have a correct perception of the probability of harm from smoking? Second, does risk perception affect actual smoking behavior? That is, are persons who perceive that the probability of harm is relatively high less likely to smoke? One reason for addressing the latter question was to gauge the validity of his measure of smoking risk. In a companion study, Viscusi (1991) evaluated the extent to which risk perceptions vary by age.

Conceptually, Viscusi's model is identical to the Bayesian updating model widely used in insurance (Lemaire 1985). In that framework, the individual is assumed to have a prior estimate of the probability, P_{t-1}, that a particular event will occur. The current probability, P_t, is hypothesized to be a weighted function of a respondent's initial assessment, P_{t-1}, along with the risk equivalent, r_t, implied by any new information that motivated the revision. Respondents are assumed to assign a precision, θ, to the prior (or baseline) assessment, P_{t-1}. They also form a gauge of the precision, γ, of the beliefs implied by the new information, r_t. The posterior or current assessment of his or her odds of a particular event occurring, for example, living to 75 or more, P_t, is then a weighted average of prior beliefs, scaled by the relative 'information' associated with that prior (θ / (θ + γ)) and the new information, expressed as a risk equivalent, r_t, weighted by the relative precision (γ /(θ +γ)) as in equation (5.1):

$$P_t = \frac{\theta P_{t-1} + \gamma r_t}{\theta + \gamma}. \tag{5.1}$$

To answer the first question, Viscusi (1990) studied responses from a 1995 national survey asking people to evaluate: 'Among 100 cigarette smokers, how many of them do you think will get lung cancer because they smoke?'. In telephone surveys conducted in Durham, North Carolina in 1990 and 1991, Viscusi varied the questions to explore the sensitivity of the risk responses to changes in question formulation, particularly to changes in the base number of smokers (Viscusi 1992, p. 76).

Responses were compared to actual life tables. When his estimates were compared to the actual probabilities, both smokers and non-smokers tended to overestimate risks of smoking. That is, they were too pessimistic. He also found that respondents who attached a greater risk to smoking were less likely to engage in such behavior. Consistent with the Bayesian updating framework, reported risk perceptions were greater for the younger age cohorts among whom overall lung cancer risks were appreciably overestimated. This group presumably based judgments on public information from a variety of sources, including public anti-smoking campaigns. Older persons, by contrast, may have relied to a greater extent on personal experiences and those of their relatives and close acquaintances.[3]

Using regression analysis with a number of other covariates, Viscusi (1992) found that current and former smokers, *ceteris paribus*, had lower assessments of the lung cancer probability from smoking. This tendency was more apparent for current than former smokers (pp. 125–8). Also, people who had heard messages that smoking 'shortens life' were less likely to smoke, but other messages had no impact on the propensity to smoke ('dangerous to health', 'bad, not dangerous', 'not bad for health').

Some of the explanatory variables representing responses to attitude probes from the national survey also had negative and statistically significant impacts on the probability of smoking (smoking 'causes lung cancer', 'causes any cancer', 'affects health'; 'know people who died'; 'general health effects'). Interestingly, people who believed that smoking is 'habit forming' were more likely to smoke (pp. 97–8).

Before they were required to do so by government mandate, advertising by tobacco companies did not publicize the health risks from smoking. Some people, now older, were exposed to such campaigns at the time they decided to start smoking.[4] Examples of misleading claims are posted on several websites resulting from tobacco litigation (for example, www.tobacco.org).

Some empirical evidence suggests that, whatever the content of cigarette advertisements, consumers were not seriously misled when making the decision of whether or not to smoke. The consensus from several econometric studies that studied the effect of aggregate cigarette advertising expenditures on cigarette consumption is that no statistically significant effect has been found.[5] Nor have studies of bans on cigarette advertising shown a consistent effect on smoking (Chaloupka and Warner 2000). By contrast, many of the econometric studies of 'counter-advertising' campaigns have suggested that such programs have deterrent effects (Chaloupka and Warner 2000). Public information dissemination about risks of particular activities and diseases from other sources may be inaccurate because some risks are rarely publicized (for example, diabetes, certain forms of cancer) and others are stressed in the media (for example, homicides, drownings, motor vehicle accidents) (Fischhoff et al. 1988).

Data from Taiwan confirm the association between risk perceptions and smoking status that Viscusi found for the US. In a two-equation analysis, one for smoking and the other for risk perception, Liu and Hsieh (1995) found that risk perceptions exerted a significantly negative effect on the probability of smoking. They also found that the Taiwanese overestimated the probability of contracting lung cancer from smoking, although the subjective probabilities were lower than in Viscusi's sample. Younger persons had higher risk perceptions than older persons, again presumably because they have less personal experience with consequences of smoking than persons in older age cohorts.

Hsieh et al. (1996) assessed the impact of anti-smoking campaigns in Taiwan using the above framework. They found that such campaigns had a statistically significant effect on health knowledge which in turn reduced the probability of smoking. An anomalous finding, seemingly not consistent with Bayesian updating, was that persons with smoking-related illnesses had significantly lower health knowledge (related to smoking risks).[6] However, this may be an artifact of the authors' having only one cross-section.

Hsieh et al.'s findings are also consistent with a result obtained by Jones (1994), using a single cross-section from the United Kingdom, namely that smokers having (self-assessed) fair or poor health at the survey date were less likely to succeed in quitting smoking, holding the degree of addiction to the habit and other factors constant. Again, this may be an artifact reflecting the role that health variables may reflect in a single cross-section. In these situations, health measures may be proxy variables for other types of individual heterogeneity that is not accounted for by the models' other explanatory variables.

In earlier research, Kenkel (1991a) studied whether health knowledge affected cigarette smoking, heavy drinking, and exercise. His results were similar to those from the studies, cited above, in that more knowledgeable persons were less likely to smoke, even when knowledge was treated as an endogenous variable jointly determined with the decision to smoke. Respondents to the national US survey used by Kenkel (1991b) were quite knowledgeable about the adverse effects of smoking. His results also suggested that 'healthy behaviors' tend to occur together in 'healthy' people (that is, those who do not smoke or drink excessively are more likely to exercise). Such a finding is consistent with other work demonstrating that the use of certain preventive health services (for example, mammography) is higher among women with healthier overall lifestyles. These findings were obtained after controlling for perceived risk of breast cancer (Cole et al. 1997).

Viscusi's risk perception questions have been criticized from several different perspectives (see Hanson and Logue 1998; Schoenbaum 1997; Chaloupka and Warner 2000). Hanson and Logue, who presented the most extensive critique, identified three general issues that have also been expressed by the other critics of Viscusi's conclusions. First, the risk perception question was phrased in a way that could be interpreted as a request for 'factual' information about smokers rather than as a personalized assessment of risk. In this context, respondents to the survey used by Viscusi (and Liu and Hsieh) were free to overestimate the health risks of smoking, but at the same time, they may not have felt these overinflated risk perceptions applied to themselves. Personalized risk, rather than general risk, should affect individual behavior (Fishbein and Aizen 1975).[7]

The second issue concerns the extent of brand-specific smoking risk information that is available to consumers. That is, even if people did know the generic health risks from smoking, they would also need to know the risks of smoking particular brands and types of cigarettes. This issue is reinforced by the recent results from Evans and Farrelly (1998) indicating that smokers faced with higher cigarette taxes purchased longer cigarettes and cigarettes higher in tar and nicotine.

Finally, even if individuals overstate the absolute health risks of smoking, they may overestimate the risks of other hazards to which they are exposed. To the extent that people's decisions are based on the relative risks of actions leading to comparably serious outcomes, then it is the extent of overstatement across these alternatives that is important to their behavior.[8]

2.2 Research Stimulated by Viscusi's Findings

Viscusi's findings together with the settlement of the states' tort case against US tobacco firms have focused renewed attention on smokers' risk perceptions. To reconsider Viscusi's conclusions, Schoenbaum (1997) compared subjective probabilities of living to age 75 or more. Using data from Wave 1 of HRS, he compared subjective longevity expectations with life-table values for the probabilities of living to age 75 or more for never, former, current light, and current heavy smokers. This analysis was completed separately for men and women who were aged 50–62. Because of limitations in the life tables, the comparison was limited to whites, using data from Wave 1 of HRS. Schoenbaum found that people underestimated the risk of death by age 75 given their smoking status in 1992 (current smoker, former smoker or never smoked).

Table 5.1 summarizes the framing of the risk perception questions used by Viscusi and HRS. The risk perception questions used by Viscusi and Liu and Hsieh were identical and differed substantially from the HRS longevity questions used by Schoenbaum. The former investigators asked about one disease, lung cancer (representing 55 deaths per 100,000 among smokers in the US) and people's perceptions of the risk that smokers would contract this disease because of smoking. The HRS elicited estimates of each respondent's personal assessment of living to 75 years or older. The question was not linked to smoking. As a result, the questions did not 'lead' respondents by asking, given you are a smoker, what is the chance you will live to 75?

2.3 Relationship of Past Research to Our Empirical Analysis

The question posed by the chapter's title, 'Are smokers too optimistic?' has not been conclusively answered by past research. In our empirical analysis described below, we extended Schoenbaum's (1997) analysis of of Wave 1 HRS data by tracking changes in risk perceptions in the HRS

Table 5.1 Alternative framings of risk/longevity perception questions

A. Viscusi's Risk Perception Questions[a]

- **Basic**

  Among 100 cigarette smokers, how many of them do you think will get lung cancer because they smoke?
- **Sample Testing**[b]

  Among 100 cigarette smokers, how many of them do you think will die from lung cancer because they smoke?

B. HRS Longevity Expectation Questions

- **Wave 1**

  Set-up

  Next I would like to ask you about the chances that various events will happen in the future. Using any number from zero to ten where 0 equals absolutely no chance and 10 equals absolutely certain …

  What do you think are the chances that you will live to be 75 or more?
- **Wave 2**

  Set-up

  Now I am going to ask about the chances of various events happening to you. Please answer the questions in terms of percent chance. Percent chance must be a number from 0 to 100, where '0' means there is absolutely no chance, and '100' means that it is absolutely certain …

  What is the percent chance you will live to be 75 or more?

Notes

[a] Liu and Hsieh (1995) repeated the same question in their survey in Taiwan.

[b] Viscusi (1992) used this question to evaluate the effects of identifying specifically death due to lung cancer in a small telephone survey in Durham, NC.

through three waves of HRS – a four-year follow-up period. In addition, we measured health outcomes, including mortality, of current, former, and never smokers at Wave 1 for up to four years after the Wave 1 interview. We found that smokers tend to be overly optimistic, not only in a cross-section, but also about the health implications of quitting the habit. In addition, our analysis of HRS data included investigation of health trajectories of smokers, gauged in terms of both mortality and morbidity.

3 METHODS

3.1 Sample

The HRS is a national panel study of birth cohorts 1931–41 and their spouses, if married. Respondents to Wave 1 HRS, conducted in 1992, ranged from 51–61 years of age (with some spouses being younger or older than this). Some 12,652 persons (7600 households) were included in the baseline survey, with oversamples of minorities and Floridians (Juster and Suzman 1995). The HRS contains extensive information on health behaviors, health and functional status, and each respondent's subjective longevity perceptions. Respondents are resurveyed every two years. From the HRS, we analysed three samples composed from the HRS panel to consider three issues: (a) the relationship between subjective longevity assessments and life tables; (b) the effects of changes in smoking behavior for longevity assessments; and finally (c) the impact of health shocks between Waves 1 and 2, as new information, on respondents' subjective beliefs about longevity.

The first analysis focused on a subset of Wave 1 of the HRS sample, confined to whites, because this is the group estimated in the Rogers and Powell-Griner (1991) life tables, which were also used by Schoenbaum (1997). The last sample was composed of all individuals responding to the HRS Wave 2 interviews (including spouses) who also responded to Wave 1 (N = 11,492). The second was limited to all persons responding to the longevity to age 75 question in Waves 1–3 or persons dying by Waves 2 or 3.

3.2 Risk Perception, Health and Smoking Status Variables Used in the Analysis

Our measure of risk perception was the same as that used by Schoenbaum, each respondent's self-reported subjective probability of living to 75 or more years of age (see Table 5.1). Each individual in a household was asked this question in each wave. Responses were re-scaled to the zero to one interval. The health-shock variables measured unexpected events that we hypothesized would cause respondents to re-evaluate their personal longevity expectations. All health shocks were events that occurred between the waves and represented the onset of new, serious health conditions. For example, if a respondent reported a heart attack at Wave 2 that had occurred since Wave 1, and reported no history of heart attacks, this represented a health shock. We classified health shocks as smoking related and general (Table 5.2). Smoking-related health shocks were those

Table 5.2 Health and disability variables

Variable	Description
Risk perceptions	See Table 5.1
Smoking-related health shock	All persons with newly occurring congestive heart attack, heart failure, or stroke in Wave 2 who spent at least 3 days in hospital between Waves 1 and 2. All newly occurring chronic lung disease which resulted in some disability. All persons with newly occurring cancers identified by US Surgeon General as being smoking related
General health shock	All persons with newly diagnosed diabetes in Wave 2 and accidents leading to 3-day hospitalization between Waves 1 and 2. All persons with surgery to replace a joint after fracture between Waves 1 and 2, those with non-smoking-related cancers (cancers other than those identified by US Surgeon General as smoking related), and all other persons who said they had a new, serious medical condition in Wave 2 and had a 3-day hospital stay between Waves 1 and 2
Positive information	For each variable, we identified whether or not the condition existed in Wave 1. For those with each condition, we identified persons for whom the condition did not worsen in ways described by the variable's heading by Wave 2
High blood pressure and no cardiovascular shock	
Smoking-related cancer and no spread to other organs	
Heart disease history and no shock	
Upper body limitations	Difficulty in running or jogging, walking one block, walking across room, sitting for 2 hours, getting up after sitting for long periods, stooping, kneeling, or crouching, climbing one flight of stairs after resting
Lower body limitations	Difficulty in lifting or carrying 10 lbs (for example, bag of groceries), bathing or showering without help, pulling or pushing large objects like living room chair
Fine motor limitations	Difficulty in picking up a dime from a table, eating without help, dressing without help For each limitation variable, we determined whether the count of limitations increased, or decreased/stayed the same between Waves 1 and 2

health events found to have an elevated relative risk for death among smokers by the US Surgeon General (US Department of Health and Human Services 1990). These were cardiovascular and cerebrovascular diseases, cancers that are related to smoking, and severe chronic lung disease such as emphysema, as reported by HRS respondents.

To ensure that health shocks were serious health events, and hence powerful 'shocks', we applied a screen to all reports of heart attack, congestive heart failure, and stroke requiring that the person had reported at least three days in the hospital between Waves 1 and 2 (although the data did not indicate that the reported shock was responsible for a particular hospital stay).[9] For newly occurring cases of severe chronic lung disease (for example, bronchitis and emphysema), the respondent had to state that this illness limited his or her ability to work or do household chores. For cancers that were smoking related, no hospital stay screen was used because diagnosis is more clear-cut, and the treatment for some types of cancer has been shifted to outpatient facilities.

For general health shocks, we used the onset of serious medical conditions that were elicited from HRS respondents and that have not been linked conclusively to smoking. General medical shocks were: onset of diabetes that resulted in a hospitalization (suggesting newly diagnosed, uncontrolled, or severe diabetes); an accident in which a person was knocked unconscious and spent at least three days in a hospital between Waves 1 and 2; surgery to replace a joint after a fracture; and the report of any other serious medical condition with a three-day hospital stay. Finally, the new occurrence of a cancer in an organ not identified as smoking related (for example, prostate cancer) was also considered a general medical shock.[10]

Even in this near elderly age group, pre-existing chronic conditions are fairly common. To the extent that the condition did not worsen, this may have been considered to be 'good news' by those affected individuals and may have caused them to raise their subjective probabilities of living to age 75. The pre-existing health states included two measures of heart disease, one for smoking-related cancers, and one for other cancers. The heart conditions were binary variables identifying cases for which a condition existed previously but did not get worse between the waves. Such worsening was measured by whether or not the person was hospitalized for a cardiovascular event between Waves 1 and 2. Such conditions were separated into: (a) cases with pre-existing high blood pressure in Wave 1 (but no history of heart attacks, strokes, or congestive heart failure) who did not experience a heart attack, congestive heart failure, or stroke between Waves 1 and 2; and (b) cases for which the respondent reported having a history of heart disease in Wave 1 but did not have a new occurrence or report worsening of heart disease. The cancer measures were also binary variables identifying respondents who reported a smoking-related cancer at Wave 1, but did not have it spread to another organ between Waves 1 and 2. Only cancers reported as occurring in 1982 or later were included.

The last set of health indicators used the two waves to identify changes in reported lower body and upper body limitations. These measures were based on reports of specific activity limitations. We used the count of reported limitations to evaluate whether the limitations increased, stayed the same, or improved between the two waves. Smoking status was elicited for all respondents to both Waves 1 and 2. The information allowed people to be classified as current smokers, former smokers, and never smoked.

4 RESULTS

4.1 Smoking Status at Wave 1 and Subsequent Mortality

Consistent with past research, smoking hastened death among HRS respondents. To assess the impact of smoking status on mortality, we used the full sample Wave 1 HRS (N =12,652) and followed everyone to Wave 2. Between Waves 1 and 2, a total of 227 persons (1.8 percent) died, and 1336 were lost to follow-up.[11] Judging on the basis of the probability of survival from Wave 1 to Wave 2 (two years) and from Wave 1 to Wave 3 (four years), the never smokers fared much better than did current and former smokers as of the Wave 1 interview (Table 5.3). By Wave 2 (1994), the probability of current smokers dying was 0.018 higher for current Wave 1 smokers than for persons who had never smoked as of that date. Between current and former smokers, the differential was 0.0077. We assessed mortality by Wave 3 for persons answering both Waves 1 and 2 (N =11,316). By Wave 3, the overall death rate was slightly higher than that observed between Waves 1 and 2, and the survival gap between current smokers, former smokers, and persons never smoking widened.

4.2 Comparison of Subjective Probabilities to Life-table Estimates of the Probability of Living to Age 75 at Wave 1

The comparative mortality data in our sample provide a frame of reference. The HRS data are too small in terms of numbers of respondents and follow-up period. Thus, to compare subjective and objective probabilities of surviving to age 75, we used a life table that projects

Table 5.3 Smoking status at wave 1 and subsequent mortality through wave 3

	Wave 1 smoking status			
	Current 3438	Former 4588	Never 4626	χ^2
Dead at Wave 2	94 (2.73%)	90 (1.96%)	43 (0.93%)	37.6*
Dead at Wave 3	113 (3.72%)	91 (2.18%)	43 (1.02%)	59.1*

Note: * Dead at Wave 2 are those persons who responded to Wave 1, but died before the Wave 3 interview. Dead at Wave 3 are those persons who died between Waves 2 and 3 contingent upon responding to both Waves 1 and 2.

survival probabilities based on smoking status.

We compared subjective probabilities, measured at Wave 1, to objective, life-table estimates of the probability of living to age 75 at an aggregate level. The life table and hence our sample were limited to whites; further, the life table stratified current smokers into two groups—those smoking 25+ and less than this per day. We also constructed groups corresponding to former smokers and those who never smoked.

White males who never smoked were remarkably accurate in forecasting their own probabilities for living to age 75 as defined by life tables. For all but one of the age categories, the perceived probability was within 0.01 or less of the actual probability (Table 5.4). Only for the 65–69 age group were those who never smoked unduly pessimistic about their chances of living to 75 – 0.67 for the perceived probability versus 0.75 for the actual probability. Overall for white males (subjective less life table over ages), the estimated differential was –0.018 and was significantly different from zero, suggesting slight pessimism. Nonetheless, this is a very close correspondence that is generally consistent for overall averages like this one with the findings reported by Hamermesh (1985).

Former white male smokers were somewhat less accurate in predicting their life expectancies, those in their 50s being somewhat overly optimistic and those in older age groups being somewhat pessimistic. Respondents in the age group 65–69 assessed accurately their probability of living to 75. A similar but somewhat more erratic pattern characterized the responses of smokers who consumed fewer than 25 cigarettes per day in Wave 1. Current smokers who consumed more than this amount daily were much too optimistic about their life expectancy. The differentials were particularly great for heavy smokers who were in their 50s.

Table 5.4 Comparison of subjective and life-table probability of living to age 75 by smoking status at Wave 1

Age range	Current				Former		Never	
	25 + cigs		< 25 + cigs					
	Subjective probability	Life-table probability	Subjective probability	Life-table probability	Subjective probability	Life-table probability	Subjective probability	Life-table probability
White males								
50–54	0.51	0.25[a]	0.58	0.56	0.64	0.60[c]	0.65	0.66
55–59	0.50	0.26[a]	0.57	0.59	0.63	0.62	0.68	0.67
60–64	0.58	0.30[a]	0.60	0.63	0.61	0.66[c]	0.69	0.70
65–69	0.60	0.36[b]	0.54	0.69[c]	0.72	0.72	0.67	0.75
70–74	0.65	0.50	0.76	0.80	0.79	0.82	0.82	0.82
White females								
50–54	0.63	0.29[a]	0.63	0.73[a]	0.69	0.67	0.72	0.82[a]
55–59	0.55	0.32[a]	0.62	0.74[a]	0.69	0.69	0.70	0.83[a]
60–64	0.57	0.34[b]	0.66	0.77[b]	0.66	0.72[b]	0.66	0.84[a]
65–69	–	0.39	0.81	0.80	0.68	0.78	0.70	0.87[b]
70–74	–	0.50	1.00	0.87	0.88	0.86	0.70	0.92

Notes

The comparisons are for whites only. Subjective probabilities came from HRS. Life-table estimates from Rogers and Powell–Griner (1991). Standard error calculated using the following formula, square root of pq where p is the probability of living to 75 for a given comparison, and q is $1 - p$.

[a] $p < 0.001$.
[b] $p < 0.05$.
[c] $p < 0.10$.

Using the life table as the 'gold standard', white females who never smoked were too pessimistic about their chances of living to age 75. Female former smokers were more accurate, while those who were light smokers under age 65 tended to be pessimistic. In this case, as with the white males, females who smoked 25+ cigarettes daily were much too optimistic about their longevity expectations.

4.3 Determinants of Difference between Subjective and Objective Probabilities of Living to Age 75

Life tables represent population averages. Individuals may differ from population averages because of systematic biases in cognition (see Kahneman and Tversky 1981, 1982). They may also differ because of characteristics that are obvious to them but which are 'smoothed' in average life tables. To investigate whether smokers differ from former and never smokers in terms of their Wave 1 assessments of living to 75, we estimated an equation for the difference between an individual's subjective assessment and the life-table average assigned to them based on their age and gender using HRS data from Wave 1. We specified the difference as the dependent variable in a regression with smoking status among the covariates. Other explanatory variables were gender, cognition (number of words correctly recalled), and educational attainment.

Holding several other factors constant, current smokers overestimated the probability of living to 75 by 0.13 (Table 5.5). Former smokers, *ceteris paribus*, overestimated this probability by about half this much on average, that is, by 0.066. Males tended to be overly optimistic, overestimating the probability by 0.068. Persons in higher-income households, those with a college degree and who scored relatively well on the HRS test of cognitive status also tended to overestimate the probability of living to 75. Rather than reflect relative optimism, the latter results may be due to objective increases in life expectancy associated with higher income, cognition, and education. The life tables did not disaggregate on the basis of these variables. The same cannot be said for the discrepancy by gender and smoking status since the life tables accounted for these factors.

A final gauge of the subjective longevity assessments is given in Figure 5.1. This bar graph displays the longevity assessments of those HRS respondents who died between waves in the year before they died. These responses were grouped into five classes and reported separately for those dying between Waves 1 (1992) and 2 (1994) (with the longevity assessment in Wave 1) and between Waves 2 and 3 (1996) (with the longevity expectation in Wave 2). The vertical axis plots the percent

Table 5.5 Differences in subjective and life-table probabilities of living to age 75 at Wave 1

	Coef.	Std. error	*P*-value	Mean
Male	0.0680	0.0071	< 0.000	0.50
Household income, Wave 1 ('0000)	0.0047	0.0007	< 0.000	4.74
College degree or more	0.2960	0.0093	0.002	0.18
Cognition (# words recalled)	0.0067	0.0013	< 0.000	6.23
Former smoker, Wave 1	0.0660	0.0081	< 0.000	0.38
Current smoker, Wave 1	0.1330	0.0089	< 0.000	0.27
Intercept	–0.1800	0.0110	< 0.000	

Notes

$N = 7364$.

A t-test for the null hypothesis that the difference between the longevity perceptions and the probablitity from the life table indicates a significant difference. The mean difference was − 0.018.

of respondents that reported longevity expectations in each class (for either Wave 1, the first bar, or Wave 2, the second bar) who died. Thus, a little over 5 percent of HRS respondents stating probabilities of living to 75 or more between 0.0 and 0.2 in Wave 1 died by Wave 2. About 5.5 percent of those who gave probabilities in this range in Wave 2 died by Wave 3. Even at this simple level, there is a consistent pattern – people who died appear to have anticipated it with a lower subjective probability of living to 75 or more.

To further investigate determinants of survival, we estimated two probit models to describe the factors associated with deaths between Waves 1 and 2 and Waves 2 and 3. The estimated parameters for all demographic variables were all consistent with our prior expectations. People who died in Wave 2 were older, more likely to be male, more likely to have smoked in Wave 1, and less likely to be married. The same relationships held for deaths in Wave 3, given that the person responded to Waves 1 and 2. In addition, health shocks (both smoking and general) that occurred between Waves 1 and 2 were significant predictors of death by Wave 3. Increased limitations in activities between Waves 1 and 2 (upper body, lower body, and fine motor) were also predictive of death by Wave 3. Of particular interest, the self-assessed probability of living to age 75 in the wave before death was negative and a statistically

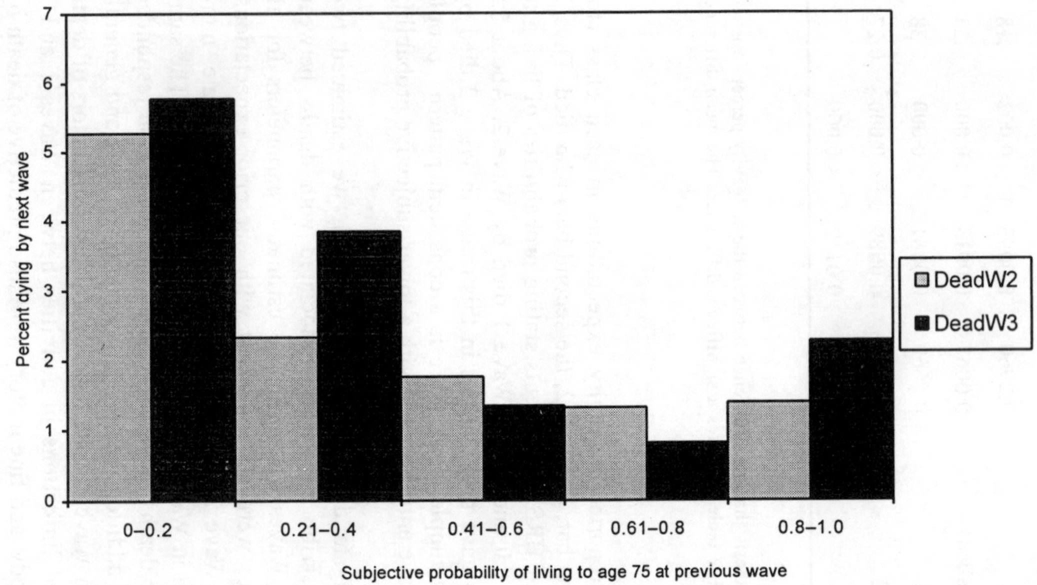

Note: Solid bars show the probability of dying by Wave 2, given the person's subjective probability of surviving to age 75 at Wave 1. Shaded bars show the probability of dying by Wave 3, given survival to Wave 2 and the person's subjective probability of living to age 75 at Wave 2.

Figure 5.1 Subjective probability of living to age 75 and subsequent mortality

significant predictor of mortality at the next wave. This result would suggest that people are consistently anticipating their own mortality. This held true for Wave 1 expectations and between Waves 1 and 2 as well as Wave 2 expectations and between Waves 2 and 3.

4.4 Smoking Status Transitions, Waves 1–3, and Perceived Probabilities of Surviving to Age 75

Given that smokers tended to be overly optimistic about the probability of surviving to age 75 at the baseline interview, we next inquired how subjective probabilities changed with intertemporal changes in smoking status. Some persons interviewed in Wave 1 did not survive to Wave 3 (see Table 5.3 above). We also compared how well people predicted their own death by smoking status in Wave 1. This comparison provides another indication of the validity of the probability questions in HRS.

To analyse how changes in smoking status (smoking transitions) influence expressed risk perceptions, we followed 11,543 Wave 1 respondents to Waves 2 and 3 (Table 5.6). Only persons surviving (and responding to) all three waves of HRS, or those dying between Waves 1 and 2 or 2 and 3 conditional upon responding to Waves 1 and 2 were included in Table 5.6.

One stylized fact that clearly emerges from the Table 5.6 transition matrix is a point also evident from Figure 5.1. Persons who subsequently died were much less optimistic about their chances of living to 75 years of age than were survivors. Persons who were current or former smokers at Wave 1 and who died by Wave 2 had a mean expectation of living to 75 of 0.46 and 0.47, respectively. This compares to the overall sample mean of 0.65 at Wave 1.

A second pattern from Table 5.6 is that smokers who died were more pessimistic about their chances of living to 75 than were others who died. Among current smokers who died by Wave 2, the perceived probability of living to 75 was 0.46 compared to 0.56 for those who never smoked. By contrast, former smokers who died were about as optimistic about living to 75 as were then current smokers (0.47 for former versus 0.46 for current). Non-smoking respondents who died must have incorporated other health signals in making their assessment.

Persons who died by Wave 3 revised their assessments downward over time, implying that expectations do not simply drop just before an imminent death, but seem to follow a downward trajectory in anticipation of death. Even among persons who subsequently died, smokers were more pessimistic than former smokers or those who never smoked.

Table 5.6 Smoking transition matrix: updating of subjective probability of living to age 75 with time and behavior, Waves 1–3

1992: Wave 1	Current smoker	Former smoker	Never smoker
N	3145	4185	4213
Live 75 Wave 1	0.60	0.66	0.67

1994: Wave 2	Smoke	Dead	Not Smoke	Smoke	Dead	Not Smoke	Smoke	Dead	Not Smoke
N	2555	94	496	158	90	3937	25	43	4145
Live 75 Wave 1	0.60	0.46	0.60	0.64	0.47	0.66	0.56	0.56	0.67
Live 75 Wave 2	0.58		0.61	0.62		0.65	0.53		0.65

1996: Wave 3	Smoke	Dead	Not smoke	Smoke	Dead	Not smoke	Smoke	Dead	Not smoke	Smoke	Dead	Not smoke	Smoke	Dead	Not smoke	Smoke	Dead	Not smoke
N	1906	90	384	125	23	318	84	7	55	70	84	3527	12	1	8	1	42	3827
Live 75 Wave 1	0.59	0.51	0.64	0.63	0.50	0.60	0.63		0.67	0.61	0.52	0.67	0.44	–	–	–	0.61	0.67
Live 75 Wave 2	0.59	0.46	0.60	0.64	0.45	0.61	0.63		0.60	0.64	0.40	0.66	0.42	–	–	–	0.52	0.65
Live 75 Wave 3	0.58	–	0.60	0.60	–	0.62	0.59		0.69	0.66		0.67	0.50	–	–			0.68

Notes

N = 11,543 respondents who are followed up completely; either answered all three waves, or who were identified as dead between Waves 1 and 2, or between Waves 2 and 3.

Live 75, Wave 1 is mean longevity expectation stated in Wave 1, Live 75, Wave 2 is mean longevity expectation stated in Wave 2, and Live 75, Wave 3 is mean longevity expectation stated in Wave 3. Mean expectation is suppressed.

The effect of smoking cessation on risk perceptions is less clear. Among Wave 1 current smokers, there was no difference in the perceived probability of living to age 75 among those who quit and those who kept smoking by the Wave 2 interview date (0.60 for both groups). However, for those persons who said they were former smokers at Wave 1 but were smoking again at Wave 2 (3.4 percent of 1992 former smokers), the perceived probability of living to 75 at Wave 1 was slightly higher for those who remained non-smokers than for those who started to smoke again (0.66 versus 0.64). Only 25 out of the 4213 persons who reported never smoking at Wave 1 had begun smoking by 1994. These 25 persons were most pessimistic about living to 75 at Wave 1 among those who survived to the Wave 2 interview, rating the probability of surviving to 75 at only 0.56. Persons who survived to Wave 2 but were lost to the sample by Wave 2 tended to be more optimistic about living to 75 than either those who survived and responded or died by the 1994 interview date.

In most cases, patterns in the perceived probabilities accord with common sense. This consistency was maintained both cross-sectionally and over time. Comparing the perceived probability of surviving to 75 among Wave 1 and 2 (1994) smokers, there was a 0.02 drop in the probability of living to 75 as assessed at Wave 1 versus Wave 2. By contrast, for persons who smoked in 1992 but stopped by Wave 2, there was a 0.01 increase in this probability. For former smokers in Wave 1 who started again by Wave 2, there was a 0.02 drop in the probability of living to 75. For those who continued to abstain from smoking, the probability fell by a smaller amount – by 0.01. For the small group of never smokers at Wave 1 who smoked in Wave 2, the perceived probability of living to 75 dropped by 0.03. However, the probability for Wave 1 never smokers who continued to abstain from smoking fell from 0.67 to 0.65. As for the former smokers who continued to abstain, one would generally have expected the perceived probability to rise as they approached age 75.[12]

4.5 Changes in Longevity Expectations After Cessation Related to Life Tables

Given that most changes in perceived probabilities of surviving to age 75 were plausible, how well do the changes in subjective probabilities compare with changes in actual survival probabilities conditional on quitting? We next examined how subjective probabilities changed with changes in smoking behavior and how realistic these changes were.

Based on a life table, changing from a former to a current smoker consuming fewer than 25 cigarettes daily reduced the probability of living to 75 from between 0.02 to 0.04 for males and from 0.01 to 0.06 for females, depending on the age cohort (Table 5.4). Comparing these objective changes with the changes in subjective probabilities of living to 75 (Table 5.6), the changes in subjective probabilities appear consistent with the objective changes (for example, persons who stop smoking generally increase their expectation, those who start or resume decrease theirs). By contrast, life tables are based on large numbers of individuals, and, on average, the former smokers quit far more than one year ago.

Research from the Cancer Prevention Survey–II (CPS–II) suggests that cessation produces tangible health benefits almost immediately. However, both the duration since quitting and former smoking consumption were important in determining the change in probability of death within a given interval. Further, the story was different according to the health state of the person at the time they quit smoking. Persons who quit when they are already seriously ill had an even higher mortality rate in the short term compared to continuing smokers (US Department of Health and Human Services 1990, p. 78). However, persons who quit before having such an illness have an immediate (within one to two years) reduction in death rate compared to never smokers. On balance, a smoker needs to be a former smoker for six to seven years to obtain the maximum survival improvement (see US Department of Health and Human Services 1990 for a comprehensive assessment of the health benefits of smoking cessation, especially p. 78). This suggests that smokers who quit smoking may 'claim credit too quickly'. This is another sign of smoker optimism.

4.6 Health Transitions and Smoking Status – Wave 1 Current, Former, and Never Smokers

Mortality is only one measure of health, albeit the most accurately measured one. Before death, individuals may endure years of poor health and disability. We used the HRS to track changes in health between Waves 1 and 2, according to the person's smoking status at Wave 1.

Changes in health between Waves 1 and 2 (1992–94) can be considered the most personalized type of health information possible, and therefore might be important in influencing subsequent risk perception measures.[13] Persons who smoked at Wave 1 were much more likely to have experienced a smoking-related health shock by the Wave 2 interview than were former smokers or never smokers (Table 5.7. See Table 5.2 for definitions of smoking-related and general health shocks.). Although smoking-related shocks are more likely to occur among smokers, they also occur among non-smokers. Smokers were also more likely to have experienced a health shock between Waves 1 and 2 that was not directly attributable to smoking ($p < 0.01$). Such shocks included injuries, cancers not identified by the US Surgeon General as being smoking related, and other self-described serious conditions that newly occurred between waves. For such shocks, there was a 0.005 difference in the probabilities between current smokers and former smokers. Between current smokers and never smokers, the difference in probabilities was 0.016.

We also assessed changes in self-reported activity limitations between Waves 1 and 2. Increases in such limitations were relatively common (50.1 percent of the sample reported increased limitations in at least one of these variables) but such changes were not related to smoking status as reported at Wave 1.

Health shocks represent negative information to persons and should make persons more pessimistic, on average, regarding their chances of living to be 75 years of age or older. It is possible that persons might receive positive information that might, alternatively, make people more optimistic about their chances of living to 75. We defined a series of variables to represent such positive health shocks (see Table 5.2).

Smokers at Wave 1 were more likely to have a smoking-related cancer before that date and have experienced no spread in the cancer to other organs between Waves 1 and 2 than were former smokers and never smokers. This difference was related to the higher rate of smoking-related cancer at baseline. By contrast, former smokers were more likely to have had heart disease, but no adverse events signifying worsening of heart disease between Waves 1 and 2. This may have been related to the decision of smokers to quit smoking prior to Wave 1 because of their heart disease. Combining the three items – high blood pressure and no cardiovascular shock, no spread of smoking-related cancer, and no adverse events following heart disease at baseline into a single category – the probabilities of 'good news' from at least one of these sources were 0.10 for smokers, 0.13 for former smokers, and 0.085 for never smokers. In other analysis using HRS data, Smith et al. (2000) found that, in fact, these variables were not viewed by respondents as 'good news' in the sense that they did not positively update their expectation of living to 75 when they experienced these health signals. Apparently, the negative nature of the condition at baseline overwhelmed any positive information conveyed by a lack of worsening in that condition over the two-year period. It may take 'more time' for respondents to feel confident that there is, in fact, some positive signal.

4.7 Health Transitions among Wave 1 Smokers by Level of Daily Cigarette Consumption

Disaggregating the Wave 1 current smoking group into three subcategories, heavy (41+ cigarettes daily), moderate (20–40), and light smokers (1–19), perceived probabilities of living to 75 fell as the amount of baseline smoking increased (Table 5.8), also consistent with life tables and epidemiological literature (for example, US Department of Health and Human Services 1990). The difference between heavy and moderate was 0.03 and between moderate and light smokers was 0.08, both appreciable differences and statistically significant ($p < 0.01$).

Heavy smokers were more likely than persons in the other smoking categories to have experienced a smoking-related shock between Waves 1 and 2: 0.070 for heavy versus 0.065 for moderate and 0.048 for light smokers. Heavy smokers were more likely than other Wave 1 smokers to have experienced positive news of no spread of a smoking-related cancer

Table 5.7 Health transitions between Waves 1 and 2 by smoking status at Wave 1

	Current	Former	Never	Significance
Wave 1 Smoking status				
Live to 75, Wave 1	0.60	0.66	0.67	a
Changes between Waves 1 and 2				
Smoking related health shock	0.059	0.033	0.019	a
General health shock	0.062	0.057	0.046	a
Upper body limitations (worse)	0.220	0.210	0.220	
Lower body limitations (worse)	0.320	0.330	0.320	
Fine motor limitations (worse)	0.190	0.170	0.180	
Positive information				
High blood pressure and no cardiovascular shock	0.0032	0.0051	0.0034	
Smoking cancer and no spread	0.0110	0.0066	0.0041	a
Heart disease history and no shock	0.0870	0.1200	0.0780	a
At least 1 signal from above 3	0.1000	0.1300	0.0850	a
N	3051	4095	4170	

Notes

Table includes only those persons answering both Waves 1 and 2 of HRS. A total of 227 died between Waves 1 and 2.

a < 0.01.

One way ANOVA, testing the means between groups.

Table 5.8 Health transitions between Waves 1 and 2 by level of cigarette consumption at Wave 1

	Cigarette consumption			
Wave 1 Smoking consumption	Light	Moderate	Heavy	Significance
Live to 75, Wave 1	0.63	0.58	0.55	a
Changes between Waves 1 and 2				
Smoking shock	0.048	0.065	0.070	a
General shock	0.064	0.062	0.047	
Upper body (worse)	0.23	0.21	0.21	
Lower body (worse)	0.33	0.32	0.41	
Fine motor (worse)	0.20	0.18	0.24	c
Positive information				
High blood pressure and no cardiovascular shock	0.0054	0.0022	0	
Smoking cancer and no spread	0.014	0.0092	0.023	a
Heart disease history and no shock	0.086	0.087	0.093	
At least 1 positive signal (from 3 immediately above)	0.11	0.10	0.10	
N	1139	1897	90	

Notes

Light smoker = 1–19 cigarettes perday; moderate 20–40; heavy 41+.

a < 0.01 c < 0.10 one way ANOVA testing variance between groups.

to other organs within the two-year time span. No dose-response relationship was detected for general health shocks. The only other difference detected was slight evidence that heavy smokers were more likely to have experienced increased limitations in fine motor activity skills such as using a calculator ($p = 0.08$).

5 DISCUSSION AND CONCLUSION

This analysis has three primary findings. First, in answer to the question posed by this chapter's title, current smokers in general and, among such persons, those who consumed more cigarettes per day in particular, were overly optimistic about their chances of survival. This conclusion comes from an assessment of the subjective longevity as an estimate of the *level* of a survival probability. When we considered the updating process in response to new personalized information for smokers, former smokers, and those who never smoked, smokers responded more pessimistically to new information.

By contrast, women who never smoked appear to be too pessimistic about their life expectancies. The latter may have nothing to do with their smoking status *per se*, but may reflect unmeasured personal factors. The conclusion about smokers being overly optimistic even held after we accounted for other plausible determinants of the probability of living to age 75. These findings may well be of special interest because our measure of risk perceptions was a personalized risk rather than one applicable to an entire population.

Second, with data from a panel of near elderly, we were able to link changes in smoking status to changes in the subjective probability of living to age 75. We found directions of change in the probabilities in the right directions. Persons who quit smoking revised the probabilities upward, but they were probably too optimistic about the short-run effects on longevity of quitting. In fact, there is some evidence that survival is actually worse in the short run for quitters, probably because adverse health events led to the decision to quit (US Department of Health and Human Services, 1990, p. 78). In this sense, smokers who quit were overly optimistic as well. Being able to track persons over time makes an important addition to previous research. Schoenbaum (1997), who used the same data source as we, could reach the first but not this second conclusion because his analysis relied on only Wave 1 of the HRS. Our results differ from Viscusi's for plausible reasons. Our measure of risk was personalized. Further, we could cross-check our cross-sectional findings with panel data.

This aspect of our findings responds in part to Ayanian and Cleary's (1999) call for greater research on smokers' relative and absolute risk perceptions. The HRS panel structure allowed these risks to be compared across groups (smokers or not) and by level of smoking, as well as over time for each group. These authors' recommendation for greater attention to older, less-educated smokers is confirmed by our findings with the HRS's nearly elderly sample.

Third, evidence presented in this study is consistent with a large body of epidemiological literature that indicates that smoking is bad for your health. Smokers are more likely to die, and, if they survive, to experience additional adverse health effects. Adverse health effects begin to appear with greater frequency after age 50. The Health and Retirement Study is a rich source of information on health changes.

Our research has implications both for public policy and for future research. The finding that smokers are overly optimistic provides a clear contrast to the tobacco companies' defense that persons who smoke are making a fully informed choice, one that they should have a right to make. Nonetheless, our findings do not offer the equivalent of a 'smoking gun'. We still do not know how judgments about risk and underlying preferences are formed. For one, many smokers may have been duped, in spite of a general cultural acknowledgment and understanding that smoking is harmful to your health. It may be that many smokers simply did not know *how* bad their choices would turn out to be at the time they made them. To study this matter in depth, it will be necessary to ask parallel questions of younger persons, including those at the age at which smoking tends to be initiated.

NOTES

* This chapter was supported in part by a grant from the Robert Wood Johnson Foundation through its Substance Abuse Policy Research Program, located at Wake Forest University, Winston-Salem, NC, to investigate 'Risk perception, information, and smoking decisions'.

1. Jakus and Shaw (1996) found that experienced rock climbers do adjust in response to hazard warnings. Technical ability increases their willingness to accept hazards, but as the severity of the events at risk increases (for example, broken bones versus death) climbers do adjust their route selections to mitigate the risks involved.
2. See Johnson et al. (1998) for a discussion of what constitutes informed choices in the context of risk communication experiments.
3. Viscusi's updating model was estimated with a single cross-section. As a result, the roles he discussed for these demographic characteristics in the models for risk perceptions are conjectures that rely on accepting the updating framework as a maintained hypothesis. Moreover, they require fairly specific roles for the independent variables in influencing unobserved elements in that framework.
4. According to Viscusi (1992, p. 41), very few health claims by tobacco companies directly implied that smoking was good for a person's health. 'Positive health claims, including testimonials by doctors and athletes were usually more specific. In some cases the ads claim that cigarettes aided digestion, provided relaxation, improved one's concentration, or improved one's disposition'. However, he presented no empirical evidence to support his assertion. Thus, the contrary assertion that material presented in tobacco litigation is representative of advertising practices seems at least as plausible.
5. These studies have been based on aggregate data. Some critics have suggested that studies using micro data would be conclusive. Lewit et al. (1981) used direct measures of the number of pro- and anti-smoking ads that youths saw on

television. They found empirical evidence that televised pro-smoking ads increased consumption of cigarettes by youths.

6 Ippolito (1981) suggested that after some point in the life cycle concerns about the health risks would be dominated by the consumption benefits from smoking. That is, the gains in the life extension are dominated by the increased satisfaction.

7 Analysis of individuals' responses to information about radon's health risks, developed as part of a study of the effectiveness of risk communication in promoting mitigation, also confirmed this conclusion. See Smith et al. (1989).

8 This same point also applies in criticizing 'conservatism' (for example, over statement of risks) in public risk assessments. Rather than providing greater safety, this strategy misallocates resources and could well lead to higher, not lower, risks imposed on consumers. The same conclusion could be reached for private decisions with differences in the 'conservatism' in risk perceptions.

9 This screen was imposed because preliminary analysis showed some implausible reports of health shocks with no corresponding hospital stays. The primary goal of all screens was to verify that the newly reported condition, whether or not it was smoking related, was indeed serious.

10 Cancers not identified as smoking related included breast and prostate cancers, two of the leading causes of cancer mortality among females and males, respectively. There have been published reports showing smokers at elevated risk of these cancers, but they were not officially designated as smoking related by the US Surgeon General in 1989 (before our study period). It appears likely that more cancer sites will be considered to be smoking related in the future.

11 Some 233 persons are contained in the HRS Wave 2 'tracker file' with a notation of being dead. Six of these persons were initially screened for HRS but never completed a Wave 1 interview, and so have been discarded. Of the 227 persons who died between Waves 1 and 2, 176 had proxy interviews completed on their behalf in Wave 2. The other 51 were identified as dead by the National Death Index. The large number of lost to follow-ups was likely due to the lengthy nature of the HRS. We investigated persons lost to follow-up and found that their live to 75 expectations in Wave 1 were similar, on average, to those of never smokers.

12 There were a substantial number of missing values to the live to 75 question. In Wave 1 (N = 12,652), 7.7 percent of current smokers, 6.7 percent of former, and 7.0 percent of never smokers had missing values for the live to 75 expectation question. Smith et al. (2000) found that poor cognition was an important determinant of having a missing value on the live to 75 variable, holding other variables including educational attainment and other demographic variables constant. Cognition was measured by the number of words from a list of 20 that could be correctly recalled, and the number of relationships/analogies out of seven that were correctly assessed as measured in Wave 1 HRS. Schoenbaum

(1997) reported only on white respondents and reported that 'less than 1 percent' of these cases had a missing value on the live to 75 variable. Our calculations showed 6 percent missing for white respondents. We matched the responses in our data set to the code book of the public release HRS and perfectly replicated the code book. This discrepancy results because Schoenbaum used an earlier release of the data and some observations that were listed as an answer of 0 on the live to 75 question were most likely determined to be missing after HRS staff cleaned the data.

13 We did not analyse Wave 2 to 3 transitions because HRS had not yet produced the detailed data needed for the health-shock variables.

REFERENCES

Ayanian, John Z. and Paul D. Cleary (1999), 'Perceived risks of heart disease and cancer among cigarette smokers', *Journal of the American Medical Association*, **281**(11): 1019–21.

Becker, G.S. and K.M. Murphy (1988), 'A theory of rational addiction', *Journal of Political Economy*, **96**(4): 675–700.

Chaloupka, F. and K. Warner (2000), 'The economics of smoking', in Joseph P. Newhouse and Anthony Culyer (eds), *The Handbook of Health Economics*, Amsterdam: Elsevier Science, pp. 1539–627.

Cole, S.R., R.J. McDermott, C.A. Bryant, C. Sorrell and M. Flynn (1997), 'Beliefs and mammography screening', *American Journal of Preventative Medicine*, **13**(6): 439–43.

Evans, William and Matthew Farrelly (1998), 'The compensating behavior of smokers: taxes, tar, and nicotine', *Rand Journal of Economics*, **29**(3): 578–95.

Fischhoff, Baruch, Paul Slovic and Sarah Lichtenstein (1988), 'Knowing what you want: measuring labile values', in David E. Bell, Howard Raiffa and Amos Tversky (eds), *Decision Making: Descriptive, Normative, and Prescriptive Interactions*, Cambridge: Cambridge University Press, pp. 398–421.

Fishbein, M. and I. Aizen (1975), *Belief, Attitude, Intention, and Behavior: An Introduction to Theory and Research*, Reading, MA: Addison-Wesley.

Hamermesh, Daniel S. (1985), 'Expectations, life expectancy, and economic behavior', *Quarterly Journal of Economics*, C (May): 389–408.

Hanson, Jon D. and Kyle D. Logue (1998), 'The costs of cigarettes: the economic case for ex post incentive-based regulation', *Yale Journal of Law*, **107**: 1163–361.

Hsieh, Chee-Ruey, L.-Y. Yen, J.-T. Liu and C.J. Lin (1996), 'Smoking, health knowledge, and anti-smoking campaigns: an empirical study in Taiwan', *Journal of Health Economics*, **15**(1): 87–104.

Ippolito, Pauline M. (1981), 'Information and the life cycle consumption of hazardous goods', *Economic Inquiry*, **19**: 529–58.

Jacobson, Peter D. and Jeffrey Wasserman (1997), *Tobacco Control Laws: Implementation and Enforcement*, Santa Monica, CA: Rand Corporation.

Jakus, P.M. and D. Shaw (1996), 'An empirical analysis of rock climbers' responses to hazard warnings', *Risk Analysis*, **16**(4): 581–6.

Johnson, F. Reed, Ann Fisher, V. Kerry Smith and William H. Desvouges (1998), 'Informed choice of regulated risk? Lessons from a study in radon risk communication', *Environment*, **30**(4): 12–5, 30–5.

Jones, A.M. (1994), 'Health, addiction, social interaction and the decision to quit smoking', *Journal of Health Economics*, **13**(1): 93–110.

Juster, F. Thomas and R. Suzman (1995), 'An overview of the health and retirement study', *The Journal of Human Resources*, **30**, S7–S56.

Kahneman, Daniel and Amos Tversky (1981), 'The framing of decisions and the psychology of choice', *Science*, **211**: 453–8.

Kahneman, Daniel and Amos Tversky (1982), *Judgement under Uncertainty: Heuristics and Biases*, Cambridge: Cambridge University Press.

Kenkel, Donald S. (1991a), 'Health behavior, health knowledge, and schooling', *Journal of Political Economy*, **99**(2): 287–305.

Kenkel, Donald S. (1991b), 'What you don't know really won't hurt you', *Journal of Political Analysis and Management*, **10**(2): 304–9.

Lemaire, Jean (1985), *Automobile Insurance: Actuarial Models*, Boston, MA: Kluwer-Nijhoff.

Lewit, E.M., D. Coate and M. Grossman (1981), 'The effects of government regulation on teenage smoking', *Journal of Law and Economics*, **24**(3): 545–69.

Liu, Jin-Tan and Chee-Ruey Hsieh (1995), 'Risk perception and smoking behavior: empirical evidence from Taiwan', *Journal of Risk and Uncertainty*, **11**(2): 139–57.

Manning, W.G., E.B. Keeler, J.P. Newhouse, E.M. Sloss and J. Wasserman (1991), *The Costs of Poor Health Habits*, London UK: Harvard University Press.

Orphanides, A. and D. Zervos (1995), 'Rational addiction with learning and regret', *Journal of Political Economy*, **103**: 739–58.

Peto, R., A.D. Lopez, J. Boreham, M. Thun and C. Heath, Jr. (1992), 'Mortality from tobacco in developed countries: indirect estimation from national vital statistics', *Lancet*, **339**: 1268–78.

Rogers R.G. and E. Powell-Griner (1991), 'Life expectancies of cigarette smokers and nonsmokers in the United States', *Social Science and Medicine*, **32**: 1151–9.

Schoenbaum, Michael (1997), 'Do smokers understand the mortality effects of smoking? Evidence from the Health and Retirement Survey', *American Journal of Public Health*, **87**(5): 755–64.

Smith, V. Kerry, William H. Desvousges, Ann Fisher and F. Reed Johnson (1989), *Communicating Radon Risk Effectively: A Mid-Course Evaluation*, Report of the Surgeon General, Washington, DC: US Department of Health and Human Services.

Smith, V. Kerry, Donald H. Taylor, Frank A. Sloan, F.R. Johnson and W.H. Desvousges (2000), 'Do smokers respond to health shocks?', Duke University, Center for Health Policy, Law and Management, unpublished manuscript.

US Department of Health and Human Services (1990), *The Health Benefits of Smoking Cessation: A Report of the Surgeon General 1990*, Rockville, MD: Centers for Disease Control.

Viscusi, W. Kip (1990), 'Do smokers underestimate risks?', *Journal of Political Economy*, **98**(6): 1253–68.

Viscusi, W. Kip (1991), 'Age variations in risk perceptions and smoking decisions', *The Review of Economics and Statistics*, **73**(4): 577–88.

Viscusi, W. Kip (1992), *Smoking: Making the Risky Decision*, New York: Oxford University Press.

6. Health risk perception and betel quid consumption in Taiwan

Tsu-tan Fu, Kamhon Kan and Jin-tan Liu

1 INTRODUCTION

Betel quid chewing has been prevalent in Asia for many centuries, especially in countries such as India, Pakistan, Sri Lanka, Thailand, Malaysia, China, Papua New Guinea and the Pacific islands. It is estimated that the betel chewing population is at least 200 million (Ko et al. 1992). In Taiwan, betel quid chewing is a tradition among aborigines and is common among farmers and laborers in the southern regions. Betel quid chewing has become very popular in Taiwan in recent decades, despite warnings on the health risks associated with it. In 1996, the population of chewers was estimated at 2.5 million, about one-tenth of Taiwan's population. The percentage of youths in the betel chewing population is increasing.[1]

Betel quids are prepared differently in different countries. In Taiwan, they are prepared in two different ways: a fresh areca nut together with white and red lime simply wrapped in a betel leaf is mainly used by aborigines; whereas a lengthwise piece of unripe piper betel fruit and lime paste sandwiched between two halves of an areca nut is popular among Taiwanese. Betel quids, similar to cigarettes, are possibly addictive, with adverse health effects if consumed habitually (Murti et al. 1990; Sinor et al. 1990). Previous studies on health hazard from betel chewing have been mostly clinical as well as epidemiological. Clinical and experimental medicine research has provided adequate evidence that the betel nut itself is a possible carcinogenic agent for the induction of buccal and gingival malignancies. Habitual betel chewing could cause serious damage to tissues or organs such as oral submucosal, dentine and peridonotis, oral pharynx and the esophagus. Medical doctors also warn that pregnant women who chew betel habitually have a higher probability of fetal death, spontaneous abortion, or terogenic fetus. Swallowing betel quid juice may also cause hypercalcemia and may induce symptoms such as headache, anorexia, nausea, muscle pain or conscious disturbances (Han 1998).

Epidemiologic studies also show betel chewing to be related to oral leukoplakia and submucosal fibrosis. Research on betel chewing behavior in different countries has universally indicated that a higher incidence of oral cancer is found in areas with higher populations of betel chewers (Ko et al. 1992). Similar observations have been made in Taiwanese studies by Kwan (1976), Ko et al. (1992) and Yang et al. (1996), even though Taiwanese chewers usually do not chew betel quid together with tobacco leaves as taken by people in India or in other countries. It is also observed that the rapid increase in oral cancer in recent years is concomitant with an increase in betel chewers in Taiwan. In 1996, government statistics on the incidence of cancer ranked oral cancer to be the cancer with the seventh-highest death rate in Taiwan, whereas it was rated fifth for males.[2]

In addition to investigating the relationship between the incidence of buccal mucosa cancer and betel chewing, previous research also identified risk factors or sociodemographic variables that explain the Taiwanese betel quid chewing habit (Ko et al. 1992, 1995; Yang et al. 1996). However, these studies all failed to explain why the betel chewing population has experienced a rapid increase in recent years, even though betel quid chewing has been recognized to be carcinogenic.

Research on cigarette smoking behavior has found that perception of health risks associated with cigarette smoking plays a crucial and significant role in consumers' decision to smoke (Viscusi 1989; Kenkel 1991; Hsieh et al. 1996). It found that individuals having a higher health risk perception would have a lower probability of smoking. A similar pattern is expected for betel chewing, since both betel chewing and cigarette smoking are associated with health risks. But, until now there has been no attempt to investigate betel chewing behavior empirically.

In this chapter, we shall first measure Taiwanese males' perception of the health risks associated with betel quid chewing. Information on risk perception is then used to examine its impact on the betel chewing decision as well as its consumption. Other factors that may affect the betel chewing decision and its consumption will also be identified. We then test whether betel quid chewing is addictive. The relationship between price elasticity of demand and level of addiction is also examined.

2 DATA

2.1 The Survey

A randomly stratified telephone survey was conducted in Taiwan in October 1997 to provide data for this study. Because of the low prevalence rate of betel chewing among females,[3] the low financial ability of children to buy betel quids and the difficulty for the elderly to answer correctly some of the health risk-related questions, only adult males aged between 18 and 65 were interviewed.

The survey consisted of two parts. In the first part, a total of 728 individuals were interviewed. Of these, 652 finished the interview, and 66 were current betel quid chewers.[4] To investigate betel chewers' consumption and buying behavior more thoroughly, we needed a large sample of chewers. Therefore we conducted a second survey based on a choice-base sampling procedure, where we increased the number of random draws in the same stratification as in the first survey.[5] However, only those who were current chewers were selected for interview. As a result, an additional 158 current chewers completed the interview in the second survey. Therefore, in total we have 224 current chewers out of 810 respondents in the full sample.

In addition to information on individuals' betel quid purchase and consumption, information concerning their socioeconomic background, social interaction, risk preferences, and health risk knowledge was also collected in the survey.

2.2 Prevalence of Betel Quid Chewing

In 1991, Ko et al. (1992) conducted a survey of local residents in Kaohsiung county, southern Taiwan. They found the prevalence rate of betel chewing was 9.8 percent for all age groups. They also found a 46.5 percent prevalence rate for local people in their house-to-house survey. In another survey of adolescent students in southern Taiwan by Yang et al. (1996), students in a junior high school and in a vocational senior high school were interviewed in 1992. Yang et al. found that the prevalence rate was 1.9 percent for junior highs and 10.2 percent for vocational senior highs. They also showed a higher prevalence rate for males than for females. The prevalence rate of betel chewing in our random sample is about 16 percent; that is, 108 betel chewers out of 652 respondents. This is higher than that found by Ko et al. in 1991. However, under our definition of current chewers, those respondents whose daily consumption of betel quid is at least one betel quid will be regarded as current or habitual chewers. Thus, the prevalence rate of current chewers on betel chewing is about 10 percent, that is 66 chewers out of 652 respondents in the random sample, whereas we have a total of 224 current chewers in the full sample.

3 HEALTH RISK PERCEPTION IN BETEL QUID CHEWING

3.1 Risk Perception Indicators

Health risks associated with betel quid chewing are evidenced in medical research. During the last decades, information on human health risks has been widely disseminated to the inhabitants of Taiwan by government health authorities and private health protection groups through formal education in schools and the public media. However, until now no research has ever been conducted to investigate or report on the degree of betel quid health risk perception in Taiwan.

In measuring the health risk of betel quid chewing, three kinds of indicators are used in this study. The first adopts Viscusi's (1985a, 1985b) subjective risk perception measure where individuals were asked their perception of the probability that habitual betel chewers would suffer from oral cancer. The second is widely used in the public health literature: respondents were asked to access their subjective odds ratios of developing oral cancer from betel chewing. The third follows Kenkel (1991), by asking a set of questions related to symptoms or diseases associated with betel chewing and constructing an index based on respondents' knowledge of them.

In this chpater, only results pertaining to the last indicator are reported, because there are significant gaps in the data obtained for the first two. However, results on the comparisons of all three indicators can be found in Fu et al. (1998), where all three risk perception indicators are shown to have a negative and significant impact on Taiwanese betel quid chewing participation.

3.2 Health Knowledge Index

A list of diagnostic disease categories associated with betel quid chewing was provided by physicians and dentists for our evaluation of respondents' health risk knowledge: oral ulcer, oral submucosal fibrosis, leukoplakia, asthma, peptic ulcer and oral cancer. Respondents in the survey were asked if they were aware that they could contract these diseases through habitual betel quid chewing. The question is based on a check list design. Respondents choose one of the following answers: 'possible', 'depends', 'impossible' and 'don't know'.

Table 6.1 shows the distribution of respondents' knowledge of these six diseases. While results indicate that more than half of the respondents know that habitual betel quid chewers can develop oral ulcer, oral submucosal fibrosis, peptic ulcer and oral cancer, the health risk of

Table 6.1 Distribution of respondents' awareness of the possibility of contracting diseases caused by betel quid chewing (%)

Disease	Sample	Respondent	Possible	Depends	Impossible	Don't know
Oral ulcer						
	Random	Non-chewers	84.1	3.2	3.6	9.0
		Chewers	71.2	6.1	18.2	4.5
	Full	Chewers	69.2	7.6	16.1	7.1
Oral submucosal Fibrosis						
	Random	Non-chewers	60.9	6.0	13.3	19.8
		Chewers	53.0	4.5	39.4	3.0
	Full	Chewers	58.0	3.1	34.4	4.5
Leukoplakia						
	Random	Non-chewers	48.5	4.9	10.8	35.8
		Chewers	28.8	6.1	43.9	21.2
	Full	Chewers	35.7	5.4	34.8	24.1
Asthma						
	Random	Non-chewers	19.1	5.5	36.3	39.1
		Chewers	13.6	0.0	71.2	15.2
	Full	Chewers	9.8	1.8	67.9	20.5
Peptic ulcer						
	Random	Non-chewers	72.0	3.2	10.2	14.5
		Chewers	62.1	1.5	25.8	10.6
	Full	Chewers	64.3	2.7	25.4	7.6
Oral cancer						
	Random	Non-chewers	87.9	3.1	3.4	5.6
		Chewers	69.7	6.1	15.2	9.1
	Full	Chewers	73.2	5.8	13.8	7.1

Note: In the random sample, there are 652 individuals in total, of which 66 are betel quid chewers and 586 non-chewers. In the full sample, there are 810 individuals in total, of which 224 are betel quid chewers.

Source: Telephone survey conducted by the authors.

leukoplakia and, especially, asthma are less well known to respondents. By comparing responses by chewers and non-chewers in the random sample, we find that there is a lower percentage of chewers choosing 'possible' for most diseases except oral submucosal fibrosis. This implies that, in general, chewers have a relatively lower health risk perception than non-chewers.

Following Kenkel (1991), for each health knowledge question, we assign a score of '+1' if choosing 'possible', and '0' if choosing 'impossible', 'don't know', or 'depends'. The health knowledge index (HKI) for each respondent is defined as the summation of the scores for all health knowledge questions. The average HKI for non-chewers is 3.73 and it is 2.98 for current chewers in the random sample, whereas it is 3.10 for current chewers in the full sample. The frequency distributions of respondents' HKI are shown in Table 6.2. Results showed that 36.9 percent of non-chewers have HKI scores of less than 4, compared to 57.6 percent of current chewers with less than 4. These distributions seem to

Table 6.2 Frequency distribution of respondents' health knowledge index (%)

Health knowledge index	Random sample (652)				Full sample[1] (810)	
	Non-chewers (586)		Chewers (66)		Chewers (224)	
	%	Cumulative %	%	Cumulative %	%	Cumulative %
HKI = 0	4.3	4.3	9.1	9.1	8.5	8.5
HKI = 1	6.0	10.2	21.2	30.3	14.3	22.8
HKI = 2	10.8	21.0	4.5	34.8	12.5	35.3
HKI = 3	15.9	36.9	22.7	57.6	17.4	52.7
HKI = 4	26.8	63.7	21.2	78.8	22.8	75.4
HKI = 5	27.8	91.5	12.1	90.9	19.6	95.1
HKI = 6	8.5	100.0	9.1	100.0	4.9	100.0
Total[2]	100		100		100	

Notes

1. Full sample is the choice-based sample in our survey with a total of 810 sample respondents, among which random sample has 652 sample respondents.
2. Totals rounded.

indicate that those who do not chew betel quids (non-chewers) have better health knowledge than current chewers.

4 ECONOMETRIC MODELS

In this section we introduce the econometric models that are employed in this study to investigate betel quid consumption behavior and its interaction with the HKI. The empirical work employs two different samples of individuals.

The first is the random sample which contains 652 individuals. Using this sample, the discrete decision of whether to consume betel quids or not is studied. The second is a choice-based sample or full sample which oversamples betel quid consumers. We use this sample to study the continuous decision of betel quid consumption.

4.1 Discrete Decision

Based on the first sample, the main focus of the empirical investigation is on individuals' discrete decision of whether to consume betel quids and its interaction with the HKI. Since the betel quid consumption decision is binary, we employ a probit model for the estimation, that is,

$$C_i = \beta_0 + \beta_1^{'} x_i^c + \beta HKI_i + u_i \qquad (6.1)$$

where x_i^c is a vector of socioeconomic variables pertaining to i, HKI_i is individual i's HKI score, u_i is a mean-zero, normally distributed error term, and C_i is an (unobservable) latent variable that can be interpreted as individual i's propensity to consume betel quids. While C_i is latent, the discrete decision I_i of whether i is a betel quid consumer is observed. The variable C_i is related to whether individual i consumes betel quids in the following way:

$$I_i = \begin{cases} 1, & \text{that is, consumes betel quid, if } C_i > 0; \\ 0, & \text{that is, non-consumer, otherwise.} \end{cases} \qquad (6.2)$$

In the above equation, the variable HKI_i may be an endogenous variable, that is, HKI_i may be correlated with u_i. To take account of the endogeneity between I_i and HKI_i, the variable HKI_i is modeled explicitly:

$$HKI_i = \alpha_0 + \alpha_1 x_i^h + e_i, \tag{6.3}$$

where x_i^h is a vector of socioeconomic variables and u_i is a mean-zero, normally distributed error term.[6]

The estimation of models (6.2) and (6.3) is through a two-stage method. In the first stage, a reduced form of model (6.3) (that is, using all distinct variables in x_i^c and x_i^h as regressors) is estimated using ordinary least square (OLS). In the second stage, based on the first-stage estimation, the predicted value of HKI_i (denoted by $H\hat{K}I_i$) is derived and $H\hat{K}I_i$ is used as a surrogate of HKI_i in the estimation of model (6.2).

4.2 Continuous Decision

The sample used in the estimation consists of all betel quid habitual consumers. The continuous decision is modeled as in the following:

$$Q_i = \gamma_0 + \gamma_1' x_i^q + \gamma_2 HKI_i + \varepsilon_i \tag{6.4}$$

where Q_i is the amount of betel quid consumed by the i'th consumer, x_i^q is a vector of socioeconomic variables and ε_i is a mean-zero normally distributed error term. As in the discrete model above, the potential endogeneity of HKI_i is handled using a two-stage method where $H\hat{K}I_i$ is used to replace HKI_i in the estimation.

5 EMPIRICAL RESULTS

5.1 Definition of Variables and Descriptive Statistics

Variables used in the empirical work are defined in Table 6.3. There are four groups of variables: sociodemographic, social interaction, risk preferences and health risk perception. Descriptive statistics are also shown in Table 6.3. The average age of the respondents is about 37, the average number of years of education is 9.6, and the average monthly household income is about 50 thousand NT dollars (equivalent to US$1700). In general, the non-chewers have relatively more education and higher risk preference as well as health risk knowledge. Also, this group contains a lower proportion of individuals working outdoors, having other family members who are betel quid chewers and having friends who are chewers in Taiwan.

Table 6.3 Variable definitions and statistics

Variable	Definition	Random sample		Full sample
		Non-chewers	Chewers	Chewers
Sociodemographic				
AGE	Years of age	37.7509 (11.1712)	35.9697 (10.2702)	37.0938 (10.3843)
EDUYEAR	Years of education received	11.6962 (3.3507)	10.0606 (2.9450)	9.6116 (2.8905)
PRICE	Price per portion (NT$)		2.8161 (1.0937)	2.9085 (1.0272)
Q	Weekly consumption amount in October (portion)		196.3529 (204.6427)	177.5045 (186.0965)
Q_{-1}	Weekly consumption in June (portion)		65.2745 (116.6156)	56.0893 (101.2772)
INCOME	Total household income per month (NT$10,000)	5.0119 (5.9679)	5.3939 (5.4832)	5.0558 (6.5544)
$INCOME^2$	Income squared (NT$10,000)	60.6741 (251.8848)	58.7045 (201.1765)	68.3292 (284.3619)
OUTDOOR	= 1 if work outdoor, = 0 otherwise	0.1962 (0.3975)	0.5303 (0.5029)	0.4330 (0.4966)
TAIWANESE	= 1 if Taiwanese, = 0 otherwise	0.7901 (0.4076)	0.8636 (0.3458)	0.7902 (0.4081)
MARRIED	= 1 if married, = 0 otherwise	0.7287 (0.4450)	0.6667 (0.4750)	0.7545 (0.4314)
REGION	= 1 if lives in regions producing betel quid, =0 otherwise	0.0734 (0.2610)	0.1364 (0.3458)	0.1429 (0.3507)
VULGAR	= 1 if feels that betel chewing is vulgar, =0 otherwise	0.8532 (0.3542)	0.7273 (0.4488)	0.6205 (0.4863)
Social interaction				
FAMILY	= 1 if betel chewing family members, = 0 otherwise	0.0102 (0.1008)	0.1970 (0.4008)	0.2277 (0.4203)
FRIEND	= 1 if betel chewing friend, = 0 otherwise	0.8242 (0.3809)	0.9545 (0.2099)	0.9643 (0.1860)
Risk belief / information				
HARMFUL	= 1 if agrees that chewing 5 or more betel quid per day is harmful to health, = 0 otherwise	0.4590 (0.4987)	0.2879 (0.4562)	0.1563 (0.3639)
NOTHARMFUL	= 1 if agrees that chewing 5 or more betel quid per day does not affect health at all, = 0 otherwise	0.0768 (0.2665)	0.3636 (0.4847)	0.5089 (0.5010)
HEARD	= 1 if heard that piper betel fruit and lime paste is carcinogenic, = 0 otherwise	0.8259 (0.3795)	0.8182 (0.3887)	0.8125 (0.3912)
Health risk perception				
HKI		3.7253 (1.5352)	2.9848 (1.8102)	3.1027 (1.7081)
Observations		586	66	224

Note: Standard deviations in parentheses.

Table 6.4 Betel quid chewing decision (random sample)

Variable	HKI	Chewing
Constant	2.3975	0.4341
	(6.422)**	(0.574)
Sociodemographic		
AGE	–0.0123	–0.0245
	(–2.234)**	(–2.308)**
EDUYEAR	0.0573	–0.1179
	(2.898)**	(–3.416)**
INCOME	0.0364	0.1394
	(1.516)	(3.402)**
INCOME^2	–0.0007	–0.0031
	(–1.297)	(–2.727)**
OUTDOOR		0.6607
		(3.908)**
TAIWANESE		0.2914
		(1.205)
MARRIED		–0.2058
		(–0.963)
REGION		0.5916
		(2.325)**
VULGAR		–0.0133
		(–0.061)
Social interaction		
FAMILY		1.7223
		(4.927)**
FRIEND		0.3470
		(1.115)
Risk belief / information		
HARMFUL	0.8906	
	(7.824)**	
NOTHARMFUL	–0.8098	
	(–4.389)**	
HEARD	0.7347	
	(5.047)**	
Health risk perception		
HKI		–0.2460
		(–2.025)**
$\overline{R^2}/F$	0.2603/33.73	
Log-likelihood		–158.3717

Notes
t-statistics in parentheses.
** significant at 5 percent.

5.2 Estimation of Health Risk Perception Equation

Results of the health risk perception equation for betel chewing are shown in Table 6.4. It is found that sociodemographic variables such as *AGE* and *EDUYEAR* are significant in explaining respondents' health risk perception. The negative sign of *AGE* indicates that younger respondents have higher risk perception. This result is expected because those who are younger are likely to be better at absorbing information. An alternative explanation for this negative effects of age may be a result of the more widely known adverse health effects of betel chewing as well as a dramatic increase in social pressure against betel chewing in recent years. If older people acquired their information and beliefs about betel before information was widely available, that could also explain the negative coefficient. The positive sign of *EDUYEAR* implies that respondents with a higher education level have higher risk perception. This result is consistent with that of Kenkel (1991), which indicates that schooling may improve allocative efficiency in the choice of health inputs by improving individuals' health knowledge. However, as pointed out by Kenkel (1991) and Farrell and Fuchs (1986), the education effect on the risk perception could be picking up omitted unobservable differences across individuals such as rates of time preference. Nevertheless, such effects may be weak since an income variable is included in the equation as a control variable. The results also show that respondents' income levels have a positive impact on their risk perception, although the effect is not very significant statistically.

In addition, individual risk beliefs and new risk information of betel chewing could contribute to the formation of health risk perception. Results pertaining to risk beliefs and information variables, that is, *HEARD*, *HARMFUL* and *NOTHARMFUL*, in Table 6.4 show that their impacts on individuals' risk perceptions are significant. Those who agree that chewing five or more betel quids a day is harmful to health (*HARMFUL*) have higher perceived risk, whereas those who do not agree (*NOTHARMFUL*) have lower perceived risk. The significance of information received (*HEARD*) also indicated that those who have ever heard about any anti-betelnut-chewing information from the mass media or private sources would have a better knowledge of the risk of betel chewing.

5.3 Estimation of Betel Quid Chewing Decision

A two-stage probit model is used for the estimation of the betel quid chewing participation equation. Results in Table 6.4 show that the betel chewing decision is significantly explained by sociodemographic, social interaction and risk perception variables. The negative sign of *AGE* implies that those who are younger have a higher propensity to chew betel quids. Since the younger chewers are also shown to have higher risk perception, it is plausible to imply that those younger chewers are eager to explore betel quid chewing primarily to satisfy their curiosity or to submit to peer pressure. Similar attitudes have also been found in Yang et al.'s (1996) study on adolescents' betel nut chewing behavior. The coefficient of *EDUYEAR* has a negative sign, indicating that education reduces the likelihood of betel chewing, which also confirms the results of studies by Ko et al. (1992) and Yang et al.

Income is assumed to influence betel chewing in two ways: higher income may represent higher ability to consume betel nuts, whereas it may also reveal higher appreciation of health. The impact of household income on the likelihood of betel chewing is shown to be quadratic, which implies that the impact of income on chewing decisions will be dominated first by the income effect, and then by the health deterrent effect. That is, the tendency to chew betel is higher as household income increases. But such a tendency decreases once household income reaches a certain level. The probability of chewing is maximized when income reaches NT$224,838, which is the income level for the top 0.3 percent in Taiwan. As indicated by Ko et al. (1992), betel quid chewing may induce a feeling of well-being, overcome sensations of hunger, exhaustion or irritability, and offer an image of toughness and strength, thus it became a habit mainly of blue-collar workers. We use the variable *OUTDOOR*, those who work mainly outdoors, as the proxy for blue-collar workers. The statistically significant and positive sign of the coefficient of *OUTDOOR* indicates that those who work outdoors have a higher likelihood of chewing betel quids. Other sociodemographic variables representing racial difference (*TAIWANESS*), marital status (*MARRIED*), and chewer's image (*VULGAR*) are not significant. However, the positive sign of the coefficient of *REGION* regional difference seems to indicate that respondents in those betel nut production regions have a higher tendency to be a chewer.

Since betel chewing in Taiwan is very common and has become a way of socializing, betel quids are often served at social occasions in rural areas, and in the southern regions of Taiwan. The economic literature introduces social interaction as a form of externality. Individual utility functions are assumed to be interdependent with other individuals' consumption (Becker 1974; Pollak 1976; Jones 1994). We have utilized this externality concept to analyse whether the preference of other smokers may affect an individual's decision to quit. In this chapter, we design two dummy variables as proxies for the externality effect. The *FAMILY*, defined as betel chewers in the family, captures the social influence of family members in the individual's household. Similarly, *FRIEND*, defined as whether a respondent has friends or workmates who are betel quid chewers, captures social influence outside the household.

A respondent will feel comfortable or regard betel chewing as a way of communication if some of his/her family members or his/her friends or workmates are betel chewers. Our results show that social interaction or peer pressure affects betel quid chewing behavior significantly. The positive sign of *FAMILY* indicates that having family members who are chewers increases the likelihood of chewing. A similar positive effect is also found for *FRIEND*, but it is not statistically significant.

The impact of health risk perception on cigarette smoking participation in previous studies such as Viscusi (1985b, 1991) and Liu and Hsieh (1995) has been shown to be negative and significant. The risk perception variable is proxied by direct or indirect measures of health knowledge. Kenkel (1991) used a direct measure of health knowledge based on the number of illnesses that individuals correctly associate with smoking, whereas Jones (1994) adopted an indirect indicator of health knowledge to indicate whether an individual has received advice from his or her doctor, spouse, relative or friend to quit smoking. Both studies have shown a significant impact of health knowledge on an individual's smoking or quit smoking decision. In this chapter, we adopted Kenkel's (1991) method and constructed the HKI for betel quid chewing. The empirical results in Table 6.4 showed that HKI, representing individual risk perception, has a significant and negative impact on the tendency to be a betel quid chewer. Thus, there is evidence that health risk perception plays an important role in betel quid chewing behavior.

5.4 Estimation of Betel Quid Consumption Decisions

Consumption of betel quids is estimated by a two-stage least squares method, where the risk perception equation and betel quid consumption equation are estimated jointly. Variables used in this estimation are similar to the preceeding estimation for chewing decisions except that the price variable is included in the former model only. The inclusion of the price variable is to measure the responsiveness of betel consumption to price changes. The estimation is based on the subsample of betel quid consumers. This is equivalent to the second part of a two-part model. A total of 224 habitual chewers, those who regularly chew at least one portion of betel quid daily, were selected from the full sample for the estimation.

The estimation results show that *INCOME*, *PRICE* and *REGION* are significant in explaining betel quid consumption behavior. The coefficient of *PRICE* is negative. That is, the substitution effect is negative. This is consistent with consumption theory. Also, the *INCOME* coefficient is positive so that the betel quid is a normal good. The effects of PRICE and *INCOME* together imply that the demand curve of betel quids is downward sloping. The statistically significant and positive coefficient of *REGION* can be explained by easier access to betel quids for residents in betel production regions. Other sociodemographic variables in Table 6.5, although exhibiting the expected signs, are statistically insignificant.

Social interaction variables show insignificant effects on betel quid consumption. This is contrary to the results in Table 6.4 pertaining to the betel quid chewing decision. Meanwhile, Table 6.5 shows that risk perception (HKI) plays an insignificant role in betel quid consumption. This is also contrary to the results on the chewing decision.

5.5 Addiction Analysis of Betel Quid Consumption

Addiction is shown to be a common characteristic of some products with health risks. Previous research on addictive behavior is mostly related to cigarette smoking (see Becker et al. 1994, for a detailed discussion). There is also some research on alcohol drinking (Grossman et al. 1998) and gambling (Elster 1999). In this section, we analyse empirically the addictive nature of betel quid consumption.

Having consumption data for two consecutive periods, our data allow us to test only whether betel quid is habitual; we cannot test the rational addiction hypothesis as proposed by Becker and Murphy (1988). Following models testing addiction in previous research, we add the log of past consumption level ($\text{Log}Q_{-1}$) to the consumption equation. If the coefficient of $\text{Log}Q_{-1}$ is positive and significantly different from zero, implying that an increase in past consumption level leads to an increase in current consumption, then we can claim that betel quid consumption is addictive. The estimate in EQ(2) of Table 6.5 confirms that betel quid is addictive.[7] The positive sign of past consumption level ($\text{Log}Q_{-1}$) has a significantly positive impact on current consumption level. Therefore, similar to alcohol drinking, cigarette smoking and gambling, betel chewing can be regarded as addictive behavior, although as yet it has not been proven to be rational addiction.

Price elasticity is often used to measure the responsiveness of consumption to a price change. Price elasticity for betel consumption is –0.5663 (in EQ(1) of Table 6.5) or –0.6415 (in EQ(2) of Table 6.5). The long-run elasticity for model 2 is 1.12.[8] These are quite close to the

Table 6.5 Betel quid consumption decision and addiction analysis (full sample)

Variable	HKI	Consumption: Log(Q)		
		EQ(1)	EQ(2)	EQ(3)
Constant	1.4759	5.2810	4.3018	4.9532
	(2.109)**	(5.381)**	(5.071)**	(5.235)**
Sociodemographic				
AGE	−0.0110	−0.0155	−0.0144	−0.0156
	(−1.046)	(−1.302)	(−1.414)	(−1.533)
EDUYEAR	0.1236	0.0315	0.0157	0.0148
	(3.068)**	(0.668)	(0.389)	(0.368)
INCOME	0.0483	0.0860	0.0501	0.0502
	(1.060)	(1.818)*	(1.229)	(1.238)
$INCOME^2$	−0.0012	−0.0015	−0.0010	−0.0011
	(−1.184)	(−1.435)	(−1.102)	(−1.152)
Log*PRICE*		−0.5633	−0.6415	−1.2167
		(−1.994)**	(−2.650)**	(−2.791)**
LogQ_{-1}			0.4231	0.2142
			(8.931)**	(1.511)
Log*PRICE** LogQ_{-1}				0.2116
				(1.570)
OUTDOOR		−0.2163	−0.0457	−0.0003
		(−1.050)	(−0.258)	(−0.002)
TAIWANESE		0.2792	0.2994	0.3058
		(1.093)	(1.370)	(1.405)
MARRIED		−0.1929	0.0524	0.0711
		(−0.732)	(0.231)	(0.314)
REGION		0.6833	0.3857	0.3864
		(2.237)**	(1.466)	(1.475)
VULGAR		0.0206	−0.1067	−0.0882
		(0.092)	(−0.552)	(−0.457)
Social interaction				
FAMILY		−0.2194	−0.3323	−0.3466
		(−0.881)	(−1.555)	(−1.629)
FRIEND		0.0805	−0.2508	−0.3112
		(0.144)	(−0.522)	(−0.649)
Risk belief / information				
HARMFUL	0.9370			
	(3.045)**			
NOTHARMFUL	−0.5480			
	(−2.395)**			
HEARD	1.0074			
	(3.800)**			
Health risk perception				
HKI		−0.1413	−0.0144	−0.0204
		(−0.942)	(−0.111)	(−0.157)
$\overline{R^2}$	0.2447	0.0402	0.3053	0.3105
F	11.319	1.719	8.002	7.696

Notes

t-statistics in parentheses.

* significant at 10 percent.

** significant at 5 percent.

price elasticity of cigarette smoking found by previous research. Research on cigarette smoking has also found that price elasticity may vary with the length of study period, income level, education and age (Becker et al. 1994). In the current study, interestingly we find that the price elasticity of betel quid consumption varies with the individual's addiction level. In the estimation of EQ(3) of Table 6.5, we include the cross-product of *PRICE* and past consumption, $\text{LogP*Log}Q_{-1}$. By such specification, price elasticity (η) can be derived as a function of past consumption.

According to the estimated results in EQ(3), the price, past consumption level and their cross-product term variables are shown to be significant. The price elasticity of betel quid consumption is calculated as $\eta = -1.2167 + 0.2116\text{*Log}Q_{-1}$. These estimates indicate that the responsiveness to price of betel quid consumption becomes smaller once past consumption increases. The relative irresponsiveness to price of those heavy consumers seems to imply that taxation-like policy instruments will be less effective for betel quid consumers with a higher level of addiction. However, since the long-run price elasticity is –3.06 (according to model 3), all betel quid chewers will be responsive to a price change in the long run.[9]

6 CONCLUDING REMARKS

In this chapter, we investigate the relationship between individuals' health risk perception and their chewing and consumption decisions of betel quids. The data come from a survey conducted in 1997 in Taiwan.

In general, respondents have good knowledge of some diagnostic diseases associated with betel chewing. We also find that betel chewers had a lower health risk perception than non-chewers. To model betel chewing decisions and consumption behavior, two-stage methods are used. Empirical results show that risk perception plays a significant role in the betel quid chewing decision, whereas risk perception is insignificant in affecting betel consumption. The price of betel quids and household income level are significant factors in betel quid consumption behavior.

The short-run price elasticity of demand for betel quid is estimated to be –0.64, which implies that a 10 percent increase in price would result in a 6.4 percent decrease in the amount of betel quid consumed. It is interesting to find that the price responsiveness of betel quid consumption is negatively correlated with the level of addiction. Price elasticity becomes smaller in absolute value as an individual is more addicted to betel chewing.

Several policy implications can be derived from the findings of this study. First, recent anti-betel-quid-chewing campaigns strongly promoted by health authorities and private health protection groups will help to increase the health risk perception of individuals in Taiwan by distributing more information on health knowledge associated with betel chewing. It is expected that such efforts could have significant effects on the tendency to chew betel quid, without reducing the amount of betel quid consumed by chewers. Second, consumption taxes will reduce betel quid consumption, since the price elasticity of demand for betel quid is negative, about –0.65. Third, the effect of taxation on betel quid consumption would be less effective for heavy betel chewers in the short run. However, with a long-run price elasticity of –3.06, a tax hike will be effective even for heavy users. In this regard, information on health risk specifically associated with heavy consumption of betel quid needs to be investigated and emphasized in the anti-betel-quid-chewing campaigns. Such promotion may increase the health perception of heavy chewers or induce more social pressure and advice from their family members, which would provide a conducive atmosphere in which their betel chewing behavior could be modified.

NOTES

1. A survey in 1991 by Ko et al. (1992) estimated that there are approximately 2 million betel chewers in Taiwan. The estimate by Fu and Huang (1998) was 2.5 million betel chewers in 1997.
2. The oral cavity cancer death rate in Taiwan was 4.86 per 100,000 population in 1996. The highest death rate caused by cancer in 1996 was 130.41 per 100,000 population by malignant neoplasms. However, the oral cavity cancer death rate was 8.53 per 100,000 population for males, as compared to 163.29 per 100,000 male population for malignant neoplasms in 1996.
3. Ko et al. (1992) showed that the prevalence rate for women in Taiwan was 1.6 percent in their survey, which is about one-sixth of that of men.
4. A current betel quid chewer is defined as one who has chewed at least one portion of betel quid daily on average during the last 12 months. In our first-round survey, we have 66 current chewers by this definition. Some 42 chewers, who reported having betel chewing behavior but consumed less than one portion daily on average in the last 12 months, are defined as irregular chewers. These irregular chewers were not regarded as current chewers in the betel chewing participation and consumption analysis of this chapter. However, in calculating the prevalence rate of betel chewing in Taiwan, we added these 42 irregular chewers to the 66 current chewers as the numerator.
5. Increasing the sample size of chewers is important because current betel quid

chewers comprise about 10 percent of the Taiwanese male population. If the choice-based sampling scheme were not adopted, out of 652 respondents (the total number of respondents that we currently have in the random survey), we would get only about 66 betel quid chewers, which would not allow us to study the consumption behavior of betel quid chewers comprehensively. For example, a small betel chewer sample would not allow us to study the effect of the dummy variable *REGION*, which has a low mean value, because of insufficient variation for *REGION*.

6 The price of betel quids is not used as a regressor. This is because the price of betel quids is unobservable for non-consumers. This is a common problem for consumption studies with non-consumers in the data. Theoretically, one can impute the prices for non-consumers based on the prices collected for the consumers. Computationally it is not difficult. However, we may encounter the problem of heteroskedasticity arising from using generated variables (where there are measurement errors and these measurement errors will become part of the disturbance term). Here, to avoid this complication, we sacrifice additional interesting results by not imputing the prices for non-consumers.

7 It is noted that the variable $\text{Log}Q_{-1}$ is based on the respondent's recall of the previous betel quid consumption level. There may be measurement errors in Q_{-1} and these errors are likely to be positively correlated with the current consumption level. Since memory is not perfect, recalling, to some extent, involves estimation and this estimation is likely to be conditional on a respondent's current consumption level. The relationship between the recalled past consumption level and the current one should be positive. This implies that the higher the respondent's current consumption is, the higher will be his/her recall (estimate) of the past consumption level. As a result, the coefficient of $\text{Log}Q_{-1}$ may be overestimated.

8 The long-run elasticity is calculated by keeping the consumption level constant, that is, $Q_t = Q_{t-1}$, $\eta = \beta/(1-\alpha)$.

9 The long-run price elasticity in model 3 is $\varepsilon_\ell = \beta(1-\alpha)/(1-\alpha\,\gamma\,\text{Log}P)^2$, where β is the coefficient for $\text{Log}P_t$, α is the coefficient for $\text{Log}Q_{t-1}$ and γ is the coefficient for $\text{Log}P_t * Q_{t-1}$. The short-run price elasticity is $\varepsilon_s = \beta + \gamma * \text{Log}Q_{t-1}$.

REFERENCES

Becker, Gary S. (1974), 'A theory of social interactions', *Journal of Political Economy*, **82**(6): 1063–93.

Becker, G.S. and K.M. Murphy (1988), 'A theory of rational addiction', *Journal of Political Economy*, **96**: 675–700.

Becker, G.S., M. Grossman and K.M. Murphy (1994), 'An empirical analysis of cigarette addiction', *The American Economic Review*, **84**(3):

396–418.

Elster, Jon (1999), 'Gambling and addiction', in Jon Elster and Ole-Jorgen Skog (eds), *Getting Hooked: Rationality and Addiction*, Cambridge, MA: Cambridge University Press, pp. 208–34.

Farrell, P. and V.R. Fuchs (1986), 'Schooling and health: the cigarette connection', in Victor R. Fuchs (ed.), *The Health Economy*, Cambridge, MA and London: Harvard University Press, pp. 243–54.

Fu, T.T. and W.T. Huang (1998), 'The production, marketing and consumption of betel nut in Taiwan', Paper presented at the conference on Problems Associated with Betel Quid Chewing in Taiwan, Academia Sinica, Taipei, Taiwan (in Chinese).

Fu, T.T., K. Kan, J.T. Liu and S. Chen (1998), 'Consumer behavior of betel quid chewing in Taiwan: a survey', Institute of Economics, Academia Sinica, Research Report, Taiwan (in Chinese).

Grossman, M., F.J. Chaloupka and I. Sirtalan (1998), 'An empirical analysis of alcohol addiction: results from the Monitoring the Future panels', *Economic Inquiry*, **36**(1): 39–48.

Han, L.C. (1998), 'Health damage of betel chewing', Paper presented at the conference on Problems Associated with Betel Chewing in Taiwan, Academia Sinica, Taipei, Taiwan (in Chinese).

Hsieh, Chee-Ruey, Lee-Lan Yen, Jin-Tan Liu and Chyongchiou-Jeng Lin (1996), 'Smoking, health knowledge, and anti-smoking campaigns: an empirical study in Taiwan', *Journal of Health Economics*, **15**: 87–104.

Jones, A.M. (1994), 'Health, addiction, social interaction and the decision to quit smoking', *Journal of Health Economics*, **13**: 93–110.

Kenkel, D.S. (1991), 'Health behavior, health knowledge, and schooling', *Journal of Political Economy*, **99**: 287–305.

Ko, Ying-Chin, Tai-An Chiang, Shun-Jen Chang and Shu-Feng Hsieh (1992), 'Prevalence of betel quid chewing habit in Taiwan and related sociodemographic factors', *Journal of Oral Pathology and Medicine*, **21**: 261–4.

Ko, Y.C., Y.L. Wang, C.H. Lee, M.J. Chen, L.M. Lin and C.C. Tsai (1995), 'Betel quid chewing, cigarette smoking and alcohol consumption related to the oral cancer in Taiwan', *Journal of Oral Pathology and Medicine*, **24**: 450–53.

Kwan, Hsueh-Wan (1976), 'A statistical study on oral carcinomas in Taiwan with emphasis on relationship with betel nut chewing: a preliminary report', *Journal of Formosa Medical Association*, **75**: 497–505.

Liu, Jin-Tan and Chee-Ruey Hsieh (1995), 'Risk perception and smoking behavior: empirical evidence from Taiwan', *Journal of Risk and Uncertainty*, **11**: 139–57.

Murti, P.R., P.C. Gupta, R.B. Bhonsle, D.K. Daftary, F.S. Mehta and J.J. Pindborg (1990), 'Effect on the incidence of oral submucous fibrosis of intervention in the areca nut chewing habit', *Journal of Oral Pathology and Medicine*, **19**: 99–100.

Pollak, Robert (1976), 'Interdependent preference', *American Economic Review*, **66**(3): 309–20.

Sinor, P.N., P.C. Gupta, P.R. Murti et al. (1990), 'A case-control study of oral submucous fibrosis with special reference to the etiologic role of areca nut', *Journal of Oral Pathology and Medicine*, **19**: 94–8.

Viscusi, W.K. (1985a), 'Are individuals Bayesian decision makers?', *American Economic Review*, **75**: 381–5.

Viscusi, W.K. (1985b), 'A Bayesian perspective on biases in risk perception', *Economic Letter*, **17**: 59–62.

Viscusi, W.K. (1989), 'Prospective reference theory: toward an explanation of the paradoxes', *Journal of Risk and Uncertainty*, **2**: 235–63.

Viscusi, W.K. (1991), 'Age variation in risk perception and smoking decisions', *American Economic Review*, **80**: 257–61.

Yang, Mei-Sang, I-Hung Su, Jung-Kwang Wen and Ying-Chin Ko (1996), 'Prevalence and related risk factor of betel quid chewing by adolescent students in Southern Taiwan', *Journal of Oral Pathology and Medicine*, **25**: 69–71.

7. Life-cycle changes in the rate of time preference: testing the theory of endogenous preferences and its relevance to adolescent substance use

David M. Bishai

1 INTRODUCTION

Empirical measurement of subjects' rates of time preference requires observations of subjects trading marginal future consumption against marginal present consumption. Although health behavior involves trades across time – pleasure increments now versus health decrements later – drawing inference on rates of time preference observed in this context is complicated by a lack of common currency. The work of Thaler and Rosen (1976) and later Moore and Viscusi (Viscusi and Moore 1989; Moore and Viscusi 1990) established that observing labor markets where subjects trade higher wages in exchange for higher occupational fatality risk could be a useful means of measuring rates of time preference.

This chapter extends the models of Moore and Viscusi by (i) relaxing the assumption that workers are perfectly informed about occupational fatality risk; and (ii) implementing a model of endogenous time preference. The extended model is applied to data from the National Longitudinal Survey of Youth (NLSY) to test Becker and Mulligan's (1997) suggestion that subjects adapt their rates of time preference as their future prospects and mental capacities develop. The extended model yields measures of time preference for each subject for each period. The validity of the time preference measures is explored by testing their relationship to alcohol use in the NLSY.

The term 'time preference' refers to a subject's capacity to value future events.[1] The formation of consistent plans for intertemporal consumption places restrictions on the relationship between future satisfaction and current satisfaction. In theory, there is little reason for an optimal plan to change when nothing has changed but calendar time. In 1956, Strotz described the alternative conditions that were necessary for time consistency: (i) the discount function is an exponential function of the time which would elapse between the present and future consumption; or (ii) the discount function is purely a function of calendar time; or (iii) the discount function is a function of other values whose evolution is completely determined by calendar time (Strotz 1956).

The presumption of dynamic consistency is a staple of models of intertemporal choice. The typical assumption is constant exponential discounting.[2] The presumption is defended by suggesting that agents can have perfect foresight into the future dynamic evolution of their discount rates and employ precommitment strategies to enforce adherence to an optimal plan. In reality the question of whether human subjects have discount functions that support dynamically consistent planning is an empirical one. There has been little evidence to support constant exponential discounting (Thaler 1981; Ainslie and Haslam 1992; Loewenstein and Prelec 1992; Cairns and van der Pol 1997). This has led to greater consideration of alternative discounting models and a concern that dynamic inconsistency, if true, would invalidate basic assumptions required to apply rational choice models to environmental, health, and safety regulations (Loewenstein 1996).

One important form of dynamic inconsistency is the possibility that the cognitive limitations of teenagers might render them incapable of foreseeing changes in their time preference rates that will render them more concerned with their future welfare when they are older. If human development during the life course imposes dynamic inconsistency, it would offer an alternative explanation for the wave of regret that accompanies retrospection on the indiscretions of youth. Accounts of 'regret' require an unforeseeable shift in the potential for harm from an activity. Orphanides (1994) explains the regret from addictive behavior as rooted in unforeseeable shifts in the potential of young people to become addicted. Unforeseeable shifts in time preference would account for regret of non-addictive youthful behaviors such as unsafe sex, petty crime, and delinquency. Even if one granted that teenagers are fully informed about the risks from smoking, drinking, and unsafe sex, one would hesitate to press the welfare properties of a *laissez-faire* approach to policies in this arena, if cognitive limitations made teenage risk choices dynamically inconsistent. A preliminary step to this line of inquiry is the estimation of valid measures of time preference during youth and across the life cycle.

2 METHODS: MEASURING TIME PREFERENCE IN INDIVIDUAL SUBJECTS IN THE NLSY

Past attempts to obtain measures of time preference in individuals have used direct survey methods to assess self-reported time preference (Fuchs 1982; Viscusi et al. 1987). But to study life-cycle variation in time preference one would require data on a sizable longitudinal cohort. Here, I identify individual measures of time preference in the context of panel data on individuals making repeated choices between money and danger.[3] Labor economists have devoted considerable attention to identifying the wage–risk tradeoff locus over the past four decades. See England (1992) for one review. This literature on compensating variations has recently been expanded to permit identification of the discount rate and the coefficient of risk aversion using readily available data on wages and occupational risk (Moore and Viscusi 1988; Viscusi and Moore 1989; Viscusi 1993). It can be shown (Viscusi and Moore 1989) that in weighing the local danger premium, a subject must consider the lifetime value of the extra wages discounted by survival probability and discounted because of time preference.

The initial problem is the maximization of lifetime utility which can be written as:

$$\underset{p_j}{\text{Max}} V = U[w(\pi_j)][1 - p_j(\pi_j) - p_x(\pi_x)] \sum_{t=1}^{\infty} \{\beta_j [1 - p_j(\pi_j) - p_x(\pi_x)]\}^{t-1} \quad (7.1)$$

where:

$U(\,)$ is the utility function.

$p_j(\pi_j)$ is the perceived occupational fatality risk as a function of *true* occupational risk π_j and $p_x(\pi_x)$ is the perceived life-table fatality risk as a function of *true* lifet-able risk, π_x.

$(1 - p_j - p_x)^t$ is the perceived probability of surviving at least t periods given exposure to the perceived job fatality risk p_j, and life-table-driven perceived fatality risk p_x.

$w(\pi_j)$ is the payoff of the *j*th agent as a function of the occupation (and risk) selected.

β_j is the discount rate of the *j*th agent.

The model in equation (7.1) modifies the Viscusi and Moore model by breaking the identification of perceived risk with actual risk. Imperfect knowledge of risk is modeled by incorporating the process whereby subjects perceive the fatality risks as 'prospects' (Kahneman and Tversky

1979) 'p' which have a functional association with the *true* risks now symbolized with Greek characters 'π_j' and 'π_x.'

In this stripped-down model, the subject selects once and for all their occupation which is parameterized only by its fatality risk. That choice determines the subject's wages according to $w(p_j)$ and the subject's survival $(1 - p_j)$ for the subsequent t periods.

Noting that $\sum_{t=1}^{\infty}[\beta(1-p)]^{t-1} = 1/[1 - \beta\,(1 - p)]$, equation (7.1) can be expressed as:

$$\underset{p_j}{\text{Max}}\, V = \frac{U[w(\pi_j)](1-p_j-p_x)}{[1-\beta(1-p_j-p_x)]}. \tag{7.2}$$

The first order condition is:

$$\frac{U'[w(\pi_j)](1-p_j-p_x)(\frac{\partial w}{\partial \pi_j})}{1-\beta(1-p_j-p_x)} - \frac{U[w(\pi_j)]\frac{\partial p_j}{\partial \pi_j}}{1-\beta(1-p_j-p_x)}$$
$$- \frac{\beta U[w(\pi_j)](1-p_j-p_x)\frac{\partial p_j}{\partial \pi_j}}{[1-\beta(1-p_j-p_x)]^2} = 0. \tag{7.3}$$

Solving for $\partial w/\partial \pi_j$ yields

$$\frac{\partial w}{\partial \pi_j} = \frac{U[w(p_j)]}{U'[w(p_j)]}\left(\frac{1}{1-p} + \frac{\beta}{1-\beta\,(1-p)}\right)\left(\frac{\partial p_j}{\partial \pi_j}\right). \tag{7.4}$$

To estimate the model I will need to apply functional forms to $U(\,)$ and $w(p_j)$.

Viscusi and Moore (1989) explore the constant relative risk aversion (CRRA) utility functional form which can be parameterized as $U = (w^c - 1)/c$. The limiting case of the CRRA utility function that turns out to be of interest for both exposition and estimation is $c \rightarrow 0$ in which case the CRRA utility function approaches the familiar logarithmic utility function. I thus assume:

$$U = [\log(w)]. \tag{7.5}$$

With this functional form

$$\frac{U}{U'} = w\log(w) \tag{7.6}$$

and (7.4) can be rewritten as:

$$\frac{\partial w}{\partial \pi_j} = w\log(w)\left(\frac{1}{1-p_j-p_x} + \frac{\beta}{1-\beta\,(1-p_j-p_x)}\right)\frac{\partial p_j}{\partial \pi_j}. \tag{7.7}$$

Noting that $d\log w/d\pi = (1/w)^*(dw/d\pi)$ and rearranging yields:

$$\left(\frac{1}{1-p_j-p_x} + \frac{\beta}{1-\beta\,(1-p_j-p\,)}\right)^{-1}\frac{\partial \log(w)}{\partial \pi_j} = \log(w)\frac{\partial p_j}{\partial \pi_j} \tag{7.8}$$

which can be simplified to yield

$$\left[(1-p_j-p_x)-\beta\,(1-p_j-p_x)^2\right]\frac{1}{\frac{\partial p_j}{\partial \pi_j}}\frac{\partial\, log(w)}{\partial \pi_j} = \log(w). \tag{7.9}$$

Viscusi and Moore note that in actual practice the mortality risk is so low that the approximation $1 - p = (1 - p)^2$ is warranted. With this approximation (7.9) becomes:

$$\log(w) = (1-\beta)\left[\frac{(1-p_j-p_x)}{\frac{\partial p_j}{\partial \pi_j}}\right]\frac{\partial \log(w)}{\partial \pi_j}. \tag{7.10}$$

Augmenting (7.10) with a vector of observed variables x_k and a vector of unobservable μ variables that may account for individual differences in tastes yields:

$$\log(w) = (1-\beta)\left[\frac{(1-p_j-p_x)}{\frac{\partial p_j}{\partial \pi_j}}\right]\frac{\partial \log(w)}{\partial \pi_j} + \sum_k \alpha_k x_k + \mu. \tag{7.11}$$

With an approximation that the perception of job fatality, $p_j(\pi_j)$ is a linear function of the true job fatality, for example, $p(\pi) = k^*\pi$ then the relationship between wages and the market can be expressed as:

$$\log w_j = C + (1 - \beta_j)\,[(1/k) - \pi_j - \pi_x](d\log w_j/d\pi_j) + \alpha_j{}^*X_j + \mu_{wj} \quad (7.12)$$

The intuition for equation (7.12) is straightforward. A positive coefficient on $d\log w/d\pi$ in equation (7.12) would indicate that higher subject wages are better explained by increases in 'attractive local wage offers for dangerous jobs' when the subject *perceives* a high probability of surviving his/her job risk and when the subject has a low discount rate (more immediate time preference).

To interpret $(1 - \beta_j)$ purely as a measure of time preference requires that statistical controls have been used for other mediators of the relationship between earnings and the danger premium. The foremost two confounders might be (i) economic desperation and (ii) intrinsic risk attitude. I shall control for desperation by using measures of family size, race, schooling, and gender as X_j variables. Parameterizing risk *attitude* within specialized functional forms like the constant relative risk aversion utility function offers one approach to making $(1 - \beta_i)$ a cleaner measure of 'time preference'.

Note that if subjects perceive their risk perfectly $k = 1$. With this assumption the coefficient of $(1 - \pi_j - \pi_x)\ d\log w/d\pi_j$ is an unbiased measure of $(1 - \beta_j)$. However, what if subjects do not perceive risk perfectly? If subjects underperceive risks it will make $1/k$ large, leading to data supporting a larger coefficient on the danger premium. The misspecification bias from assuming $k = 1$ will lead to estimates of $1 - \beta$ that are inordinately large. Because π_j and π_x are small, of the order of 10^{-5}, a good approximation for the magnitude of the misspecification bias is $1/k$.

Equation (7.12) imposes a restriction stating that other determinants of wages (X_j) such as schooling, age, gender, and so of will independently shift the relationship between wages and wage-risk offers up and down (changes in intercept) but they will not alter its slope. I shall loosen this restriction below.

In equation (7.12), the term $d\log w_j/d\pi_j$ represents the premium workers receive for danger in their local labor market and because it is not an official labor statistic, it must be computed. To compute it, I shall essentially use NLSY respondents as informants: they report to me their region, their wage, and their occupation. Using National Institute for Occupational Safety and Health (NIOSH)'s national traumatic occupational fatality data, I convert reported occupation into the fatality rate faced by that NLSY respondent in exchange for the wage he or she was given. The statistical model implemented is a regression of the form:

$$\log w_j = C + \sum_k [\beta_{1k}(D_k{*}\pi_j) + \beta_{2k}(D_k{*}\pi_j^2)] + \beta_x X + \varepsilon, \quad (7.13)$$

where D_k are dummy variables for region, and year.

Equation (7.13) is a representation of the hedonic market equilibrium for job safety (Kahn and Lang 1988). Controlling for other determinants of wages, the coefficient on occupational fatality will represent an equilibrium. Competition for workers between firms in a local labor market (determined by time and space) establishes the local balance between firms' willingness to invest in safer working conditions and their ability to simply raise wages to attract workers who are willing to jeopardize their survival for cash. Competition between workers for jobs establishes a similar balance between local workers' hedonic demand for better occupational survival poised against decrements in wages. As pointed out by Kahn and Lang (1988), were one simply to regress log wage on the X variables and on occupational risk *without the interactions*, the measures of the effect of $d\log w/d\pi$ would be endogenous in equation (7.12).

The empirical strategy is to conduct a first-stage regression of equation (7.13). The β_{1k} and β_{2k} coefficients are subsequently used to calculate a set of danger premiums using the derivative of (7.13) as follows:

$$\text{danger premium} = d\log w_j/d\pi_j = \sum_k (\beta_{1k})(D_k) + (\beta_{2k})(D_k)(\pi_j). \quad (7.14)$$

Viscusi and Moore (1989) treat $d\log w_j/d\pi_j$ as endogenous to an individual's wage equation and instrument it using age, education, gender, and race prior to inserting it in equation (7.12). In this analysis, $d\log w_j/d\pi_j$ is considered to be exogenous. Interacting $d\log w_j/d\pi_j$ with measures of $(1/k) - \pi_x - \pi_j$ in which I set $k = 1$ forms a new independent variable, $Z_j = (1 - \pi_x - \pi_j){*}\ d\log w_j/d\pi_j$.

To estimate $1 - \beta_j$ I note that it seems plausible that in (7.12) not just the intercept but the slope of the tradeoff between the danger premium and wages is a random coefficient that differs from individual to individual in general patterns suggested by Becker and Mulligan's (1997) theory of endogenous time preference. Becker and Mulligan's theory offers an account of the determination of time preference by suggesting that individuals may alter their time preference in part by spending time and effort in forming mental pictures of future pleasures. They cite as examples of such time and effort activities like acquiring information through schooling, access to print media, and time spent with older persons, particularly parents. Subjects endogenously invest effort in these activities in proportion to the agreeableness of their future life prospects.

For instance, Becker and Mulligan speculate that because church attendance offers repeated promise of future heavenly splendor it may lead attendants to endogenously develop ways to discount future splendor less.

I thus introduce a time preference determination equation inspired by Becker and Mulligan:

$$(1 - \beta_j) = A + \gamma_a * \text{age} + \gamma_s * \text{schooling} + \gamma_g * \text{gender} + \gamma_r * \text{race} + \gamma_f * \text{father} + \gamma_c * \text{church} + \mu_{\beta j} \quad (7.15)$$

which forms a multilevel system together with a shorthand version of equation (7.12)

$$\log w_{jt} = C + (1 - \beta_{jt}) * Z_{jt} + \gamma_j * X_{jt} + \mu_{wjt}. \quad (7.16)$$

In this system, person-rounds define the level 1 process and persons define the level 2 process. Multilevel estimation methods using Hierarchical Linear Modeling (HLM) software will be used to estimate all of the above parameters including the individual specific error term, $\mu_{\beta j}$. An alternative approach is to interact the observables from (7.15) with Z_{jt} in (7.16) and use the ordinary least squares (OLS) coefficients on the interaction terms to learn how the background variables affect time preference. These OLS coefficients could be used to estimate the average discount rate for a population based on population averages of the background variables. The goal of obtaining individual specific error terms cannot be realized using OLS.

3 DATA

The NLSY offers panel data on a cohort of 12,686 young persons aged 14 to 21 in 1979 followed up until when they are aged 29 to 37 in 1994 (see Table 7.1).

Table 7.2 describes the essential variables from NLSY to be included in the analysis of occupational choice. The national traumatic occupational fatality data from NIOSH contains occupation specific fatality rates for US workers. These data have been merged with the NLSY data in order to perform the occupational risk study.

From Table 7.2 one can get a sense of the magnitude of selection bias. Attrition shrinks the sample size from 12,686 to 8889, individuals who

Table 7.1 Cohort structure of NLSY

Year	Age																						
	14	**15**	**16**	**17**	**18**	**19**	**20**	**21**	**22**	**23**	**24**	**25**	**26**	**27**	**28**	**29**	**30**	**31**	**32**	**34**	**35**	**36**	**37**
79																							
80																							
81																							
82																							
83																							
84																							
85																							
86																							
87																							
88																							
99																							
90																							
91																							
92																							
93																							
94																							
obs	1	2	3	4	5	6	7	8	8	8	8	8	8	8	8	8	7	6	5	4	3	2	1

Note: Ages of subjects versus years of successive waves. The final row indicates the number of years in which the corresponding age group is observed.

Table 7.2 Variable definitions and means for wage-risk estimates

Variable	Years available	Number of obs in 1979	Number of obs in 1994	Mean conditional on no attrition and labor force participation	Source
Endogenous					
Annual real after tax wage	79–94	4657	7152	\$9163	NLSY
Danger premium ($d\log w/dp_j$)	79–94	4657	7152	0.0037	NTOF +
% Δ \$ per unit Δ in deaths/100K					NLSY
Calculated after regressing eqn (7.13)					
Exogenous included					
Job fatality rate (p_j) (deaths/100k)	90–91	4657	7152	4.6	NTOF
All cause mortality (deaths/100k)	1990	12,686	8889	134.6	NCHS
Years of schooling	79–94	12,686	8889	12.7	NLSY
Race (% African American)	79–94	12,686	8889	23.4%	NLSY
Gender (% female)	79–94	12,686	8889	48.5%	NLSY
Age	79–94	12,686	8889	25.5	NLSY
Number of dependents (incl. self)	79–94	12,686	8889	3.24	NLSY
Union status (% members)	79–94	4852	6881	16%	NLSY
Exogenous (Instruments for eqn (7.14))					
Period (4 quadrennial dummies)	79–94	12,686	8889	NA	NLSY
Pd1 (1979–1982)	79–82	12,686	NA	0.20	NLSY
Pd2 (1983–1986)	83–86	NA	NA	0.28	NLSY
Pd3 (1987–1990)	87–90	NA	NA	0.29	NLSY
Pd4 (1991–1994)	91–94	NA	8889	0.22	NLSY
Region (4 separate dummies)	79–94	12,686	8889	NA	NLSY
North East	79–94	12,686	8889	0.18	NLSY
South	79–94	12,686	8889	0.38	NLSY
North Central	79–94	12,686	8889	0.23	NLSY
West	79–94	12,686	8889	0.19	NLSY

Notes
NLSY = National Longitudinal Survey of Youth.
NTOF = National Traumatic Occupational Fatality data.
NCHS = National Center for Health Statistics.

can be followed over 16 years. Attrition means that observations on the effect of higher age and later period are conditional on sample non-attrition.

3.1 Multilevel Model Estimation

Equation system (7.15) and (7.16) is the multilevel system that will be estimated using the 15 waves of observations on however many of the 12,686 subjects in the NLSY report wages and occupations. Equation (7.15) describes phenomena at the level of the individual across successive rounds, while equation (7.16) describes phenomena at the level of the individual within each round. This approach is similar to that taken by Cairns and van der Pol (1997) whose analysis of two rounds of survey data on intertemporal preferences using multilevel models decisively favored the multilevel approach over OLS.

3.2 Computing Individual Time Preference Measures

In addition to examining the coefficients for equation (7.15) to assess the effects of age, education, and so on, on time preference, I shall compute individual measures of β_j that incorporate estimates of the individual specific fixed effects $\mu_{\beta j}$. Estimates of β_j can be derived which maximize the joint likelihood function for the system set up by (7.16).

3.3 Obtaining Unbiased Standard Errors

The assumption that successive observations of the behavior of the same subject are truly independent is likely to be false. The error terms generated by the same subject in different years are likely to be correlated and will result in heteroskedasticity. The multilevel model takes into account precisely this form of heteroskedasticity.

4 RESULTS

4.1 Determining the US Wage–Risk Locus for 1979–1994

Table 7.3 presents estimates of equation (7.13) which is a first-stage equation describing how the equilibrium wage–risk locus shifts across local markets defined by quadrennial periods and four regions composed of roughly 15 states each. Although this is hardly the proper specification to examine the effects of the productivity controls, it builds confidence

Table 7.3 Identification of the regional and period specific danger premia

Dependent variable (log of annualized after-tax earnings*)	Coefficient	*t*-statistic
N	116,405	
R^2	0.4282	
Job fatality * North East	0.0416	(16.24)
Job fatality² * North East	–0.0003	–(9.17)
Job fatality * North Central	0.0289	(11.41)
Job fatality² * North Central	–0.0002	–(6.23)
Job fatality * South	0.0306	(12.18)
Job fatality² * South	–0.0002	–(6.50)
Job fatality * West	0.0416	(16.36)
Job fatality² * West	–0.0003	–(9.27)
Job fatality * Period 1	–0.0311	–(12.24)
Job fatality² * Period 1	0.0002	(7.05)
Job fatality * Period 2	–0.0316	–(12.54)
Job fatality² * Period 2	0.0002	(7.12)
Job fatality * Period 3	–0.0275	–(10.87)
Job fatality² * Period 3	0.0002	(5.84)
Job fatality * Period 4	–0.0254	–(10.00)
Job fatality² * Period 4	0.0002	(5.36)
Highest grade completed	–0.0160	–(4.00)
Highest grade completed²	0.0025	(16.04)
Black	–0.0498	–(14.34)
Female	–0.1519	–(47.56)
Age	0.0725	(18.39)
Age²	–0.0010	–(13.69)
Job tenure	0.0010	(35.18)
Job tenure²	0.0000	–(19.86)
Experience in job market	0.0474	(25.41)
Experience²	–0.0005	–(3.85)
Union member	0.1725	(44.47)
Job satisfaction	–0.0318	–(16.64)
Family size	–0.0144	–(17.80)
Married	0.0490	(15.58)
Managerial**	0.2723	(51.58)
Technical sales	0.1831	(43.88)
Operators & fabricators	0.1258	(25.65)
Precision production	0.2327	(40.68)
Farm/Forestry/Fishing	–0.0513	–(6.39)
Constant	7.5184	(139.17)

Notes

* Hourly rate of pay * 2000 hours * (1-Tax rate).

** Excluded occupational dummy: service industries.

Period 1 = 79–82, Period 2 = 83–86, Period 3 = 87–90, Period 4 = 91–93.

to review the ways in which the long-established facts from labor economics are reaffirmed in Table 7.3.

- Marriage is associated with an increase in annualized wages of about 5 percent similar to previous findings (Daniel 1995).
- Each year of schooling is associated with an increase in annualized wages of about 5 percent similar to previous findings (Schultz 1988; Behrman et al. 1995).
- Workforce experience more than tenure in a given job is associated with increased wages similar to previous findings (Altonji 1987).
- Black race and female gender reduce annualized wages significantly (England et al. 1996).
- Union membership has a profound effect on wages (Leigh and Gill 1991).
- Occupational category controls appear to have reasonable effects, as does job satisfaction.

All of the interaction variables are significant, and their coefficients are used together with equation (7.14) to obtain individualized estimates of the local danger premia. Job fatality interactions with the occupational dummies were not used because of the theoretical requirement that the dummies should mark off separate markets for occupational safety. By the same token, substantial migration *on the basis of danger premia*, would invalidate the use of the regional dummies to identify the occupational risk versus wage market locus. There is no evidence to date for migration on the basis of geographical differences in compensating variations.

4.2 Determining the US Wage Determinants for 1979–1994

Table 7.4 presents parameters from the wage equation (7.16) which is estimated jointly with the time preference determination equation (7.15). The uninteracted covariates of wage have roughly the same coefficients in Table 7.4 as were noted in Table 7.3. The OLS estimates in Column I are derived by ignoring the existence of the time preference equation and simply including the uninteracted survival-adjusted danger premium, Z_j along with all of the X_{jt} variables (union membership, marital status, schooling and so on). The OLS estimates in Column II are derived by interacting each of the X_{jt} variables with survival-adjusted local danger premium. OLS standard errors are adjusted for heteroskedasticity using White's correction. The coefficients of these interacted variables (later shown in Column 1 of Table 7.5) confound both the effect of the X_t variable on $(1 - \beta)$ and the effect of $d\log w/dp$ on log wage. The interacted OLS estimates of the determinants of time preference lead to a distribution of different time preference rates which are shared by all

Table 7.4 *Estimating the wage equation in the NLSY*

Dependent variable (log of annualized after-tax earnings*)	Column I OLS		Column II OLS		Column III Unrestricted Maximum Likelihood	
	Coefficient	*t*-statistic	Coefficient	*t*-statistic	Coefficient	*t*-statistic
N	106,880		106,880		106,880	
Likelihood					-6.68E+04	
R^2	0.4383		0.4383			
Constant	7.5073	(87.82)	7.6120	(78.61)	7.7998	(130.7)
Survival adjusted local danger premium*	8.1250	(17.38)	*Distribution*		*Distribution Shown in Figure 7.1*	
Union member	0.1731	(29.38)	0.1721	(29.44)	0.1631	(40.56)
Married	0.0539	(10.5)	0.0625	(10.56)	0.0536	(16.15)
Family size	–0.0153	–(13.01)	–0.0164	–(12.6)	–0.0147	–(17.42)
Highest grade completed	–0.0226	–(2.48)	–0.0045	–(0.32)	–0.0267	–(5.43)
Highest grade²	0.0027	(7.52)	0.0020	(3.58)	0.0029	(15.32)
Experience in job market	0.0460	(18.48)	0.0356	(12.97)	0.0404	(19.46)
Experience²	–0.0003	–(1.98)	0.0000	(0.01)	–0.0002	–(1.53)
Age	0.0787	(14.53)	0.0747	(11.17)	0.0702	(16.22)
Age²	–0.0012	–(11.08)	–0.0013	–(9.62)	–0.0012	–(13.98)
Job tenure	0.0010	(25.65)	0.0010	(26.83)	0.0009	(33.21)
Job tenure²	–9.36E–07	–(14.84)	–9.6E–07	–(15.15)	–1.00E–06	–(17.61)
Job satisfaction	–0.0340	–(13.33)	–0.0339	–(13.37)	–0.0360	–(18.59)
Black	–0.0413	–(6.64)	–0.0306	–(4.46)	–0.0372	–(9.23)
Female	–0.1651	–(28.15)	–0.1731	–(25.1)	–0.1655	–(44.36)
North east			0.0223	(2.61)	–0.0098	–(1.24)
North central			–0.0929	–(6.45)	–0.1445	–(17.26)
South			–0.0928	–(7.32)	–0.1373	–(18.46)
Managerial**	0.2601	(29.51)	0.2584	(29.41)	0.2317	(42.71)
Operators & fabricators	0.1644	(23.01)	0.1556	(21.78)	0.1462	(29.7)
Technical sales	0.1753	(25.91)	0.1784	(26.48)	0.1593	(36.77)
Precision production	0.2711	(31.77)	0.2596	(30.31)	0.2322	(40.15)
Farm/forestry/fishing	0.0108	(0.77)	–0.0222	–(1.57)	–0.0157	–(1.98)
Period 2			0.0383	(6.48)	0.0347	(6.76)
Period 3			0.1457	(12.71)	0.1545	(21.08)
Period 4			0.2179	(12.63)	0.2163	(22.61)

Notes

* Computed value of dlog(wage)/d job fatality from Table 7.3, interacted with survival probability from lifetable.

** Excluded Occupational Dummy: Service Industries.

Period 1 = 79–82, Period 2 = 83–86, Period 3 = 87–90, Period 4 = 91–93.

persons having a given age/education/race/gender/ and so on.

The maximum likelihood (multilevel) estimates in Column III are random coefficients estimates produced by HLM which impose equation (7.15) as written, including the *person specific error term*. The $(1 - \beta)$ coefficients produced by the maximum likelihood technique were calculated for all subjects in the NLSY who ever participated in the labor market according to equation (7.15) which says $(1 - \beta_j) = A + \gamma_a * \text{age} + \gamma_s * \text{schooling} + \gamma_g * \text{gender} + \gamma_r * \text{race} + \gamma_f * \text{father} + \gamma_c * \text{church} + \mu_{\beta j}$. Output from the systems estimates includes the fixed effect term, $\mu_{\beta j}$, permitting one to impute a discount rate unique for each respondent. The distribution of values for $(1 - \beta)$ is displayed in Figure 7.1. The distribution is approximately normal and centered around a mean value of β of 5.3.

A Tau test (Bryk and Raudenbush 1992) rejected the null of non-random coefficient (for example, $1 - \beta$) on the danger premium, thus the multilevel maximum likelihood model offers the preferred set of estimates as well as the preferred specification.

4.3 Can We Infer the Proper Discount Rate for Society?

As can be seen from equation (7.12) the interpretation of the danger premium coefficients as indicators of the discount rate requires the assumption of perfect perception of occupational fatality rates (for

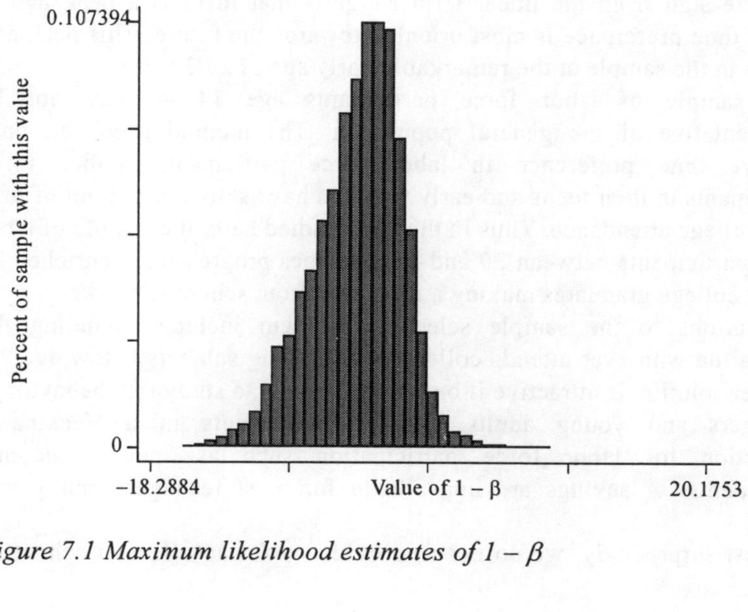

Figure 7.1 Maximum likelihood estimates of $1 - \beta$

example, $k = 1$). Although Viscusi and Moore (1989) implicitly make this assumption, on both theoretical and empirical grounds, its validity is questionable. An empirical rejection of perfect risk perception in the NLSY can be based on the finding that the average value of β at 5.3 is roughly tenfold higher than it would need to be to place the discount rate in its theoretical range of 0 – 1. If subjects underestimated the magnitude of their job fatality risk by at least a factor of 10 ($1/k = 0.1$), it would bring the mean estimate of β into the theoretical range. Unfortunately in the absence of information about the quality of risk perception, the empirical methods cannot deliver an absolute estimate of the population discount rate, or of the value of future life. For our purposes explaining relative variation in discount rates is fully sufficient and we now turn to this task.

4.4 The Determination of Time Preference

Table 7.5 indicates that controlling for covariates, young age, male sex, and white race are associated with an immediate time preference and/or a less acute perception of risk. There is no evidence to support the conjecture of Becker and Mulligan that religious participation would encourage a less immediate time preference. We find no evidence to support the hypothesis that the presence of a father early in life fosters the capacity to consider one's future persistence and a less immediate time preference. The significant coefficient on the age squared term with an opposite sign from the linear term suggests that there is a peak age at which time preference is most oriented towards the future. This peak age occurs in the sample at the remarkably early age of 23.3 years.

A sample of labor force participants age 14–34 may not be representative of the general population. The method used can only observe time preference in labor force participants. Labor force participants in their teens and early twenties have self-selected out of full-time college attendance. Thus in the data studied here, the sample of labor force participants between 20 and 25, becomes progressively enriched by recent college graduates making a transition from school to work.

Solutions to the sample selection problem include excluding the population who ever attends college or excluding subjects below age 25. Neither solution is attractive if one of the aims is to study risk behavior of teenagers and young adults. Typical instruments in a Heckman's correction for labor force participation such as spousal income, dependents, or savings are unavailable for most teenagers and young adults.

Most surprisingly, we do not find evidence for an effect of schooling

Table 7.5 Estimating time preference in the level 2 equation

Dependent variable is coefficient on (1 – π) *d*log*w*/*d*π	OLS* Coefficient	*t*-statistic**	Maximum likelihood Coefficient	*t*-statistic
Tau test for null of no random coefficients			618	
N	106,880		106,880	
Constant			–2.2082	–(1.81)
Lived with father in 1979	0.5276	(0.67)	1.2873	(1.53)
Religious attendance	0.1763	(0.77)	–0.3103	– (1.4)
Age	0.4323	(0.47)	–6.3707	–(3.93)
Age²	0.0032	(0.20)	0.1365	(3.45)
Highest grade completed	–2.6616	–(1.45)	0.0435	(0.03)
Highest grade²	0.1111	(1.67)	0.0482	(0.86)
Black	–1.9782	–(2.04)	–3.6676	–(3.69)
Female	2.7100	(3.1)	1.2739	(1.65)
Period 2	2.3159	(2.55)	3.8277	(2.73)
Period 3	2.6211	(1.62)	7.7066	(2.09)
Period 4	0.2505	(0.12)	–1.9350	–(0.22)
Married	–1.3113	–(1.68)	0.9411	(0.79)
Family size	–0.0304	–(0.16)	–0.4653	–(2.47)

Notes

Dependent variable is coefficient on local danger premium in Table 7.4.

* Model from Column II of Table 7.4.

** OLS standard errors adjusted for heteroskedasticity.

on time preference. According to the theory of endogenous preferences, schooling, by enhancing future earning potential would foster more attention to future great expectations. Part of the reason for finding no effect of schooling may have to do with the sample selection bias discussed above.

4.5 The Relationship of Time Preference to Risky Behavior

To assess the validity of time preference measures derived from studying compensating variations I test their performance in explaining differences in alcohol use. Measures of time preference have a prominent but infrequently tested association with health behavior in virtually all economic models of health behavior (Becker et al. 1990; Becker and Murphy 1988; Fuchs 1982; Grossman 1972; Grossman et al. 1994, 1996; Ribar 1994). Thus, empirical measures of time preference can also be used to assess the strength of this association. Health-promoting behaviors that pay off in the future are more enjoyable to individuals who have lower time preference. The theory of rational addiction (Becker et al. 1991; Becker and Murphy 1988) highlights the way in which past consumption of an addictive good increases the marginal utility of current consumption. The theory predicts that individuals who greatly discount the future are more likely to become addicted and will be more sensitive to shifts in the price of the commodity. The policy implication of the theory is to use price shifts to alter addictive consumption of those who discount the future (assumed to be youth) and use public information campaigns to alter addictive consumption of those who value the future (assumed to be educated, adults) (Becker et al. 1991). Indeed purely on the basis of the assumption that youth discount the future more than do adults, the occurrence of greater price responsivity among youth has been credited as evidence in favor of the theory of rational addiction (Becker et al. 1991; Grossman et al. 1994). The evidence that youth are more price sensitive than adults is actually inconsistent (Chaloupka and Wechsler 1995).

To apply the relative time preference measures to explain relative differences in alcohol use rates, I first normalize the measures of β as Z-scores, then append them to a typical rational addiction equation such as $D_t = C + \gamma_1 D_{t-1} + \gamma_2 D_{t+1} + \gamma_3 P_t + \varepsilon_t$ where D_t denotes drinking at time t and P denotes the price of alcohol. The two standard econometric problems to overcome in a rational addiction estimate are (i) skewness in the distribution of addiction in the population and (ii) endogeneity of leads and lags of addictive consumption. To cope with skewness, I adopt a two-part estimation strategy employing an initial probit for any alcohol use followed by estimates of heavy drinking among the sample of drinkers. To cope with endogeneity I adopt a two-stage least squares approach using as instruments leads and lags of the real beer tax. The real beer tax data which is used as the price variable is available by state for 1979–94 and is described in detail in Chaloupka and Wechsler (1995).

Table 7.6 indicates that more patience (high β) is significantly related to both any alcohol use and among drinkers to the measure of the number of days of drunkenness in the past 30 days. The three columns on the far right of Table 7.6 append to the rational addiction equation variable to control for other elements that are correlated with by β the very nature of its construction. Recall that β is computed according to equation (7.15) as a linear combination of personal characteristics such as age, schooling, gender, and so on plus an individual specific fixed effect that is computed by maximum likelihood. Appending the personal characteristics offers assurance that the effects found in Table 7.6 are not simply the effects of

Table 7.6. Rational addiction estimates of the relationship between drinking and the discount rate

	Probit	OLS	2SLS	Probit	OLS	2SLS
Dependent variable	Any drinking last month (1989)	Days drank > 6 last month (1989)	Days drank > 6 last month (1989)	Any drinking last month (1989)	Days drank > 6 last month (1989)	Days drank > 6 last month (1989)
Z score of discount Rate (β)	−0.043	−0.186	−0.308	−0.041	−0.314	−0.462
	(−2.062)**	(−1.567)	(−1.926)*	(−1.876)*	(−2.517)**	(−2.765)***
Any drinking last month (1984)	0.684			0.606		
	(14.688)***			(12.708)***		
Any drinking last month (1994)	0.616			0.559		
	(13.950)			(12.416)***		
Days drank > 6 last month (1984) §		0.283	−0.277		0.261	−0.283
		(16.323)***	(−1.272)		(14.747)***	(−1.274)
Days drank > 6 in last month (1994) §		0.355	0.565		0.343	0.591
		(22.364)***	(2.618)***		(21.582)***	(2.928)***
Real beer tax (1989)	−0.121	−0.195	−0.593	−0.075	−0.218	−0.528
	(−3.065)***	(−0.786)	(−1.625)	(−1.789)*	(−0.856)	(−1.512)
Age (Years)				−0.008	−0.079	−0.045
				(−0.836)	(−1.342)	(−0.545)
Highest grade (Years)				0.048	−0.004	0.0169
				(4.885)***	(−0.064)	(0.229)
Married = 1				−0.226	−1.026	−1.160
				(−5.290)***	(−4.135)***	(−3.341)***
Female = 1				−0.431	−1.338	−2.741
				(−10.143)***	(−5.168)***	(−2.897)***
Black = 1				−0.219	0.1983	−0.380
				(−4.344)	(0.628)	(−0.747)
Lived with father in 1979				−0.0408956	−0.344	−0.719
				(−0.885)	(−1.241)	(−1.801)*
Religious attendance				−0.005	−0.120	−0.278
				(−0.414)	(−1.577)	(−2.071)**
Constant	−0.164	2.853	5.827 (2.492)**	−0.043	6.922	9.753
	(−3.199)***	(12.380)***		(−0.141)	(3.792)***	(2.739)***
Adj. or Pseudo-R^2	0.0917	0.2853	0.0313	0.1209	0.2968	0.0637
N	5118	2801	2277	5118	2801	2277

Notes

§ Denotes endogenous variables in 2SLS models. Instruments for 2SLS models are annual real beer taxes from 1979 to 1994.

* P < 0.10.

** P < 0.05.

*** P < 0.01.

these potential confounders.

5 DISCUSSSION

The finding of an aging effect on time preference leads to the possibility of dynamic inconsistency in planning one's consumption path. Finding that the measure of time preference is an independent predictor of both drinking and drunkenness suggests that life-cycle shifts in time preference are important for the study of health behavior. If adolescents fail to account for the likelihood that they will become more patient with age, they could make decisions that would have been rational had their rates of time preference remained constant, but which lead to regret in the face of life-cycle changes in time preference.

6 CONCLUSION

I have expanded and refined a method pioneered by Viscusi and Moore (1989) to examine the response of subjects to various offers to trade their survival for money in the labor market. Because I demonstrate that the estimates obtained in this way depend critically upon the assumption of perfect risk perception, I do not share their conclusion that this method leads to unbiased estimates of the absolute rate of time preference in a population. I do believe that measuring and parameterizing these trades is a promising strategy for the study of relative differences in risky decision making between subjects in a population. Although the measures obtained in this manner confound both time preference and the ability to accurately perceive fatality risks, this confounding is neither conceptually nor empirically unappealing. Both factors are cognitive responses to contingent states of the world that dampen the full consideration of possibilities other than the present moment.

The investigation found that subjects become more patient with aging and that patience is independently correlated with less drinking and less drunkenness among drinkers. The presence of an aging effect on the discount rate leads to the possibility of dynamic inconsistency in planning intertemporal consumption paths. The fact that a 'self' that starts down a consumption path could differ in an unforeseeable way from one's future 'self' can lead to tragedy when the goods consumed have addictive or irreversibly harmful properties.

NOTES

1 The discount rate β is defined as ratio $\beta = [\beta^{t+1}U(X_{t+1})]/[\beta^{t}U(X_{t})]$ where $X_t = X_{t+1}$ is the same quantity of a good consumed at either time t or time $t+1$ and $U(\,)$ is a utility function mapping consumption at various dates to utility. The rate of time preference is defined as $-\log(\beta)$. Having no time preference is when the value of future satisfaction and the value of present satisfaction are equal in which case $\beta = 1$ and time preference $= 0$. Infinite time preference is when the subject does not value the future at all in which case $\beta = 0$ and time preference $\to \infty$.

2 A notable exception is Uzawa's demonstration that intertemporal models with discount functions that depend on the level of consumption require the assumption that β would fall with consumption (Uzawa 1968). To assume otherwise would lead to a degenerate case in which wealth accumulation approached infinity. Uzawa's assumption is counterintuitive to Blanchard and Fisher who suggest that one would expect that the wealthy have more future-oriented time preference, $\beta \to 1$ (Blanchard and Fischer 1989).

3 Adam Smith is credited with the original observation that wages and danger are related. According to Smith, 'In trades which are known to be very unwholesome, the wages of labour are always remarkably high' (Smith 1776, p.123). Interestingly, the notion that risk attitude is different among adolescents also appears to originate with Smith in precisely the context of occupational choice. In Book 1 he writes, 'The contempt of risk and the presumptuous hope of success, are in no period of life more active than at the age at which young people chose their professions . . . . A tender mother, among the inferior ranks of people, is often afraid to send her son to school at a sea-port town, lest the sight of the ships and the conversation and adventures of the sailors should entice him to go to sea' (pp. 122–3).

REFERENCES

Ainslie, G. and N. Haslam (1992), 'Hyperbolic discounting', in G. Loewenstein (ed.), *Choice over Time*, New York: Russell Sage Foundation, pp. 57–92.

Altonji, J.G. (1987), 'Do wages rise with job seniority', *Review of Economic Studies*, **54**: 437–59.

Becker, G., M. Grossman and K.M. Murphy (1990), *An Empirical Analysis of Cigarette Addiction*, Cambridge, MA: National Bureau of Economic Research.

Becker, G.S., M. Grossman and K.M. Murphy (1991), 'Rational addiction and the effect of price on consumption', *American Economic Review*,

81(2): 237–41.

Becker, G.S. and C.B. Mulligan (1997), 'The endogenous determination of time preference', *Quarterly Journal of Economics*, **August**: 729–58.

Becker, G.S. and K.M. Murphy (1988), 'A theory of rational addiction', *Journal of Political Economy*, **96**(4): 675–700.

Behrman, J., R.A. Pollak and P. Taubman (1995), *From Parent to Child*, Chicago: University of Chicago Press.

Blanchard, O. and S. Fischer (1989), *Lectures on Macroeconomics*, Cambridge, MA: MIT Press.

Bryk, A. and S.W. Raudenbush (1992), *Hierarchical Linear Models*, London: Sage Publications.

Cairns, J.A. and M.M. van der Pol (1997), 'Saving future lives: a comparison of three discounting models', *Health Economics*, **6**(4): 341–50.

Chaloupka, F.J. and H. Wechsler (1995), *The Impact of Price, Availability, and Alcohol Control Policies on Binge Drinking in College*, Cambridge, MA: National Bureau of Economic Research.

Daniel, K. (1995), 'The marriage premium', in M. Tommasi and K. Ierulli (eds), *The New Economics of Human Behavior*, New York: Cambridge University Press, pp. 92–112.

England, P. (1992), *Comparable Worth: Theories and Evidence*, New York: Aldine.

England, P., L.L. Reid and B.S. Kilbourne (1996), 'The effect of the sex composition of jobs on starting wages in an organization: findings from the NLSY', *Demography*, **33**(4): 511–21.

Fuchs, V.R. (1982), 'Time preference and health', in V.R. Fuchs (ed.), *Economic Aspects of Health*, Chicago: University of Chicago Press.

Grossman, M. (1972), 'On the concept of health capital and the demand for health', *Journal of Political Economy*, **80**: 223–55.

Grossman, M., F. Chaloupka, H. Saffer and A. Laixuthai (1994), 'Effects of alcohol price policy on youth: a summary of economic research', *Journal of Research on Adolescence*, **4**(2): 347–64.

Grossman, M., F.J. Chaloupka and I. Sirtalan (1996), *An Empirical Analysis of Alcohol Addiction: Results from the Monitoring the Future Panels*, Cambridge, MA: National Bureau of Economic Research.

Kahn, S. and K. Lang (1988), 'Efficient estimation of structural hedonic systems', *International Economic Review*, **29**(1): 157–66.

Kahneman, D. and A. Tversky (1979), 'Prospect theory: an analysis of decision under risk', *Econometrica*, **47**: 263–91.

Leigh, J.P. and A.M. Gill (1991), 'Do women receive compensating wages for risks of dying on the job?', *Social Science Quarterly*, **72**(4): 727–37.

Loewenstein, G. (1996), 'Out of control: visceral influences on behavior', *Organizational Behavior and Human Decision Processes*, **65**(3): 272–92.

Loewenstein, G. and D. Prelec (1992), 'Anomalies in intertemporal choice: evidence and an interpretation', *Quarterly Journal of Economics*, **107**(2): 573–97.

Moore, M.J. and W.K. Viscusi (1988), 'The quantity-adjusted value of life', *Economic Inquiry*, **31**: 369–88.

Moore, M.J. and W.K. Viscusi (1990), 'Models for estimating discount rates for long-term health risks using labor market data', *Journal of Risk and Uncertainty*, **3**(4): 381–401.

Orphanides, A. (1994), 'Rational addiction with learning and regret', *Journal of Political Economy*, **103**(4): 739–58.

Ribar, D.C. (1994), 'Teenage fertility and high school completion', *The Review of Economics and Statistics*, **76**: 413–24.

Schultz, T.P. (1988), 'Education investments and returns', in H. Chenery and T.N. Srinivasan (eds), *Handbook of Development Economics*, New York: North-Holland: **1**: 543–630.

Smith, A. (1776), *The Wealth of Nations*, Chicago: University of Chicago Press.

Strotz, R.H. (1956), 'Myopia and inconsistency in dynamic utility maximization', *Review of Economic Studies*, **23**: 165–80.

Thaler, R. (1981), 'Some empirical evidence on dynamic inconsistency', *Economics Letters*, **8**: 201–7.

Thaler, R. and S. Rosen (1976), 'The value of saving a life: evidence from the labor market', in N.E. Terleckyj (ed.), *Household Production and Consumption*, New York: National Bureau of Economic Research, pp. 265–98.

Uzawa, H. (1968), 'Time preference, the consumption function and optimum asset holdings', in J.N. Wolfe (ed.), *Value, Capital, and Growth: Papers in Honour of Sir John Hicks*, Edinburgh: University of Edinburgh Press, pp. 485–504.

Viscusi, W.K. (1993), 'The value of risks to life and health', *Journal of Economic Literature*, **31**: 1912–46.

Viscusi, W.K., W.A. Magat and J. Huber (1987), 'An investigation of the rationality of consumer valuations of multiple health risks', *Rand Journal of Economics*, **18**(4): 465–79.

Viscusi, W.K. and M.J. Moore (1989), 'Rates of time preference and valuations of the duration of life', *Journal of Public Economics*, **38**(3): 297–317.

PART III

Costs of Substance Use

8. The labor productivity costs of smoking in the United States

John A. Rizzo

1 INTRODUCTION

Cigarette smoking has been a major public health concern in the United States for more than a generation. Approximately 48 million Americans, or 26.5 percent of the adult population, were estimated to be smokers as of 1992 (US Department of Health and Human Services 1994a). Per capita cigarette consumption among adults aged 18 years and above is 2493 per annum (US Department of Health and Human Services 1994b). Smoking is widely understood to be a leading cause of mortality in the United States; it is considered responsible for an estimated 400,000 deaths annually (Sims 1994).

Deaths are but one of the social costs of smoking. Smoking also involves significant morbidity from emphysema, cardiovascular disease, and lung cancers, increasing healthcare costs substantially. Research linking smoking and these adverse health outcomes is well known (Peto et al. 1994), and a number of studies have documented the adverse effects of smoking on healthcare costs (Miller et al. 1998; Adams 1994; Lynch and Hopkins 1996; Schumacher 1996; Shopland et al. 1996; Fielding 1985; Oster et al. 1984).

Given the adverse health consequences of smoking, there is good reason to suspect that smoking could have important effects on labor productivity, as well. These costs may occur in several ways. First, smoking may increase unemployment by making subjects too ill to work. Second, among those able to work, smoking may have debilitating effects that cause workers to incur more sick days. For jobs requiring physical exertion, it is also likely that smoking lowers performance. Finally, smoking-related deaths among working-age individuals entail productivity costs due to lost work years.

Studies of the labor market effects of smoking have focused largely upon job absenteeism. The results of this literature are equivocal, with some studies pointing to large effects and others to considerably smaller ones (Leigh 1995; Fielding 1985; Kristein 1983). Leigh (1995) estimated the smoking/job absenteeism relationship adjusting for selection effects associated with the decisions to smoke and work. He found that the economic impact of job absenteeism is likely to be substantially less than was previously thought.

In contrast to research on the smoking/absenteeism relationship, there is very little evidence on the implications of smoking for employment. Levine et al. (1995), examining data from the National Longitudinal Survey of Youth, found little evidence that smoking was related to employment status. That study was confined to a sample of young workers, however. It has remained unclear whether smoking would be seen to affect employment among a more nationally representative sample of individuals.

Following previous work, this study quantifies the labor productivity costs to the US economy associated with smoking. Although we focus on the effect of smoking on employment status and job absenteeism, on-the-job labor productivity effects associated with smoking and other illnesses are likely to matter as well. Data limitations have generally precluded calculation of this dimension of labor productivity, although recent work has begun to assess the on-the-job productivity effects of depression (Berndt et al. 1996). Although the on-the-job productivity effects of smoking may be quite important, no data relating smoking status to on-the-job productivity are available. Productivity losses from premature death due to smoking are also likely to be substantial. Calculating such effects requires additional assumptions as to what the long-term employment of smokers would have been had they not expired, and how the economy adjusts in the long term to employment shortfalls from workers who die because of smoking. These are important issues for further work, but they lie beyond the scope of the present study.

2 METHODS

In this analysis, the labor productivity costs of smoking were hypothesized to occur because smoking increases the probability of being unemployed and, among employed individuals, increases disability days lost from work. The basic strategy of the analysis was to estimate the productivity costs of being unemployed and, among those individuals who are employed, additional productivity costs from incurring increased disability days due to smoking. Productivity costs of being unemployed were estimated using multivariate models determining the effects of smoking on the probability of being unemployed. This was combined with information on annual earnings to obtain expected productivity losses from unemployment due to smoking. To obtain productivity losses due to disability days, models were developed relating smoking to the number of work disability days. These multivariate results were used to estimate the numbers of days lost from work per annum due to smoking. This calculation was combined with earnings information to arrive at the productivity losses from work disability days.

2.1 Data Sources

The data for the statistical analyses in this study were taken from the National Medical Expenditure Survey (NMES). Collected by the Agency for Health Care Policy and Research, NMES provides information on health status, healthcare utilization and cost, work, disability, and sociodemographic characteristics for a nationally representative sample of the non-institutionalized civilian population of the United States in 1987 (US Department of Health and Human Services 1991). It is a widely used data source among health economists and health services researchers, having been employed to investigate the determinants of healthcare utilization and labor productivity outcomes (for example, Deb and Trivedi 1997; Rubinstein et al. 1997; Vistnes 1997; Rizzo et al. 1996, 1998) and related issues. Productivity models generated using the NMES data are combined with information on earnings of males and females to estimate labor productivity costs.

The data collected through NMES are available on a number of Public Use Tapes. The present analysis used the following NMES data tapes: (i) Population Characteristics and Utilization Data (Public Use Tape no. 13) and (ii) Health Status Questionnaire and Access to Care Supplement Data (Public Use Tape no. 9). For selected outcomes, such as healthcare utilization and disability days, respondents were queried at quarterly intervals for a period of one year. These responses were then aggregated to arrive at annual figures. Health and functional status, as well as information on acute and chronic conditions, were ascertained using the Health Status Questionnaire, generally during the first round of the surveys. Sociodemographic characteristics were obtained at the initial screening interview.

The NMES survey has a complex sampling design, involving sample stratification, clustering, and oversampling of certain subgroups, such as persons having difficulties with activities of daily living. As a result, all statistical analyses performed are adjusted for these effects using variables provided in NMES for these purposes.

2.2 Empirical Models

Labor productivity costs have typically been assessed in terms of disability days and employment status (Vistnes 1997; Rizzo et al. 1996, 1998). These are the measures considered here. Separate estimates are provided for males and females. This is common practice in the labor economics literature, and reflects evidence suggesting that the determinants of employment status and other labor market outcomes differ between men and women (Killingsworth 1983). We also stratify the sample according to age. The rationale for doing so is that younger individuals have on average been smoking for shorter periods of time than older subjects, and as a result, may experience less adverse labor productivity effects from smoking. 'Young' cohorts consist of individuals aged 18–40; 'old' cohorts consist of subjects aged 40–64. Thus our analysis considers four groups: males aged 18–40; males aged 40–64; females aged 18–40; and females aged 40–64.

Employment effects

A key issue in estimating the effects of smoking is which sample is relevant to include in the study. An important question here is how to treat 'unemployed' persons. Economists define the unemployed as the stock of individuals who are not currently working, but who are either moving to a new job or searching for work but unable to find it. Together with employed workers, these individuals are considered to be in the labor force.

In contrast, retired individuals would be considered out of the labor force and hence not among the unemployed. Depending on the specific question asked, one may or may not wish to exclude people who are unemployed because they are not in the labor force (for example, retired individuals). In the case of smoking, however, it is entirely possible that some subjects are no longer in the labor force because of their smoking behavior. To the extent that this is true, one should include such subjects in the study. Thus, we used a broader measure of unemployment than is typically used by economists, including subjects such as retirees who would typically be considered to be out of the labor force. This enabled us to capture the extent to which smoking causes people to be unemployed by forcing them to leave the labor force entirely.

The dependent variable measuring employment status included the general population of working-age individuals (for example, those 18 to 64 years old). We used this as the dependent variable in multivariate logistic regression models of the form:

$$Pr\,(EMPLOYED = 1) = F(HISMOKE, LOSMOKE, FORSMOKE, \text{SUBJECT}), \qquad (8.1)$$

where

EMPLOYED = A binary variable indicating whether or not the subject is employed
HISMOKE = A binary variable indicating whether the subject smokes at least one pack per day
LOSMOKE = A binary variable indicating whether the subject smokes less than one pack per day
FORSMOKE = A binary variable indicating whether the subject is a former smoker
SUBJECT = A vector of subject-specific characteristics (age, race, educational attainment, comorbidities, risk-taking behavior)

Disability days

The disability days calculations were confined to the population of employed individuals between the ages of 18 and 64. The disability day indicator is a binary variable (*DISDAY*) indicating whether the individual had missed any days from work during a one-year period due to illness or disability. In a preliminary analysis, we estimated a two-part model for disability days (Leung and Yu 1996). The first part used *DISDAY* to estimate the propensity to incur disability days. The second part estimated actual disability days, conditional on missing at least one. We found little evidence that smoking status affected conditional disability. Instead, the effects of smoking appeared to be concentrated on the propensity to miss work. Hence, for ease of exposition, we focused the multivariate modeling effort on the propensity to miss work and assumed that conditional days lost do not vary by smoking status. Thus we estimated multivariate logistic regressions of the form:

$$Pr\,(DISDAY = 1) = F(HISMOKE, LOSMOKE, FORSMOKE, \text{SUBJECT}). \qquad (8.2)$$

2.3 Specification Issues

Unless one believes that the propensity to smoke is determined by genetic factors that are randomly distributed in the population, smoking is a choice variable, and hence including it as an explanatory variable raises endogeneity concerns. One potential source of bias is that smokers may be less willing to reveal their smoking status on surveys due to the negative connotations associated with this behavior. If some smokers were erroneously coded as non-smokers, this would bias against finding that smoking has adverse labor productivity consequences, since some of the adverse labor productivity effects of smoking would be blended in with the labor productivity calculations for non-smokers. This bias is not a major concern, however, because it leads to conservative estimates of the impact of smoking.

More serious are biases that have the potential to overstate the adverse economic impacts of smoking. One possibility is that stressful life events, such as becoming unemployed or incurring work disability days, cause people to begin smoking. Failure to control for these 'reverse causation' effects would lead to an overestimate of the true impact of smoking on employment and work disability days. According to this view, the estimated association of smoking with employment (disability days) would reflect in part an effect of transient unemployment (disability days) on transient smoking behavior. This effect is unlikely to be important, however, because the vast majority of smokers began smoking in their youth, hence smoking is a long-term phenomenon, not a transient one. According to the NMES data, fully 95 percent of smokers started smoking between the ages of 13 and 25.

Another potential source of bias stems from the omission of potentially important explanatory variables that might be correlated with both smoking status and the economic outcomes of interest. Health status measures quickly come to mind. It is natural to want to control for such measures, because they are quite likely to affect both employment and work disability days. On the other hand, correlations between smoking status and, say, lung cancer, most likely reflect the impact of smoking on lung cancer, not the other way around (if seems far-fetched indeed to posit that individuals begin to smoke upon learning that they have contracted lung cancer).

In this view, including diseases that smoking is known to cause as explanatory variables may 'rob' smoking status of some of its true impacts on labor market outcomes. In any event, we estimated models which included indicators for ten major diseases (cancer, heart disease, atherosclerosis, hypertension, prior heart attack, prior stroke, diabetes, arthritis, rheumatism, and chronic back ache) and an indicator for obesity, and contrasted these with models that excluded such health status indicators. The estimated impact of smoking was insensitive to the inclusion or exclusion of these health indicators. Because these health indicators are themselves strongly related to employment outcomes, however, we elected to retain these measure in the estimates reported here.

It is curious, however, that including heart disease and cancer – the two most prominent health risks of smoking – did not appreciably diminish the estimated impact of smoking on either employment or work disability days.

Incentives to retire due to the timing of social security benefits may also lead to bias. In particular, many people tend to retire at age 62–63 when their social security benefits start. To check on the importance of this effect, we re-estimated the models for males (females) aged 40 and above, excluding males (females) aged 62 and over. For males, the estimated effects of smoking were quite similar to those reported in the text. The female cohort exhibited weaker smoking effects. As will be seen below, however, the labor productivity costs associated with older female smokers is very small even when subjects aged 62 and above are included. Hence, it does not appear that this source of bias is an important one.

Smoking-specific differences in risk-taking behavior may also have confounded the results. Research suggests that smokers are more tolerant of risk than is the average individual (Barsky et al. 1997). If risk-taking behavior is correlated with smoking and injury, failure to control for such behavior could lead to biased estimates of the labor productivity effects of smoking. Fortunately, the NMES database includes information on subjects' attitudes toward risk-taking behaviors. Specifically, subjects were asked to gauge the extent to which they were more than average risk takers (the allowed responses were disagree strongly, disagree somewhat, agree somewhat, agree strongly, and uncertain). Using this information, we appended a variable measuring the degree of subjects' risk-taking behavior (*TAKERISK*) to equations (8.1) and (8.2). The estimated impacts of smoking were little affected by the inclusion of this variable, suggesting that differences in risk-taking behavior between smokers and non-smokers is not an important source of bias. As with any multivariate specification, there is the potential that other important factors may have been omitted. For example, the NMES database includes no information on alcohol consumption, which is likely to be correlated with smoking behavior. Other omitted variables problems might stem from unobserved variations in job type and quality of education.[1] Thus, the results presented below should be viewed with this limitation in mind.

In principle, instrumental variables estimation offers a solution to each of these problems. One might, for example, use cigarette taxes in different states to identify exogenous variations in smoking behavior. Unfortunately, geographic indicators needed to link the data to state cigarette tax rates are unavailable in the NMES database in order to maintain respondents' confidentiality. Moreover, there are no variables in the NMES data that appear to be suitable instruments for identifying smoking behavior. The lack of good instruments, and the growing literature suggesting that weak instruments may introduce serious bias (Staiger and Stock 1997; Bound et al. 1995; Nelson and Startz 1990), persuaded us to forgo instrumental variables estimation.

3 RESULTS

3.1 Descriptive Statistics

Descriptive statistics for the variables used in the multivariate analyses are provided in table 8.1. The probability of being employed was higher for males than for females, while the propensity to incur a work disability day was lower. A higher percentage of males were heavy smokers (that is, a pack or more per day). The table also reveals that a substantial fraction of males and females were former smokers. Males appear more prone to engaging in risk-taking behavior, as indicated by their higher mean scores for *TAKERISK*. Otherwise values appear to be similar across gender cohorts of like age.

3.2 Determinants of Employment Status

Multivariate models were specified to determine the effects of smoking on employment status for males (Table 8.2) and females (Table 8.3). Turning first to the results for males, it is evident that smoking had a strong, negative, and highly significant impact on employment among older (that is, 40 to 64 years of age) males. Moreover, this negative impact is greatest among current smokers. However, former smokers were also substantially less likely to work than were non-smokers. Among younger males, heavy smokers (that is, a pack or more per day) were significantly less likely to be employed.

Most other explanatory variables were estimated precisely, and the results tended to be in the direction one might expect. For both young and old male cohorts, employment followed a life-cycle effect, first increasing with age and then declining. Better-educated individuals were more likely to be employed. Among the older male cohort, the higher number of chronic conditions (that is, a higher value for *NUMCHRON*) was associated with a lower likelihood of employment, while obesity was associated with lower employment probabilities among younger males.

The results for women revealed substantially more modest effects of smoking on employment. More education was again associated with a

Table 8.1 Names, descriptions, and mean values of variables used in the study

	Dependent name	Males < 40 (n = 3550)	Males ≥ 40 (n = 2716)	Females < 40 (n = 3229)	Females ≥ 40 (n = 2259)
Dependent variables					
EMPLOYED	Binary variable (BV) = 1 if subject employed else = 0	0.92	0.85	0.76	0.62
DISDAY[1]	BV = 1 if subject incurred work disability day else = 0	0.40	0.36	0.49	0.43
SMOKING STATUS					
HISMOKE[2]	BV = 1 if subject smokes 1 or more packs per day else = 0	0.22	0.26	0.17	0.18
LOSMOKE[2]	BV = 1 if subject smokes less than 1 pack per day else = 0	0.11	0.08	0.14	0.10
FORSMOKE[2]	BV = 1 if subject is a former smoker else = 0	0.18	0.38	0.15	0.22
Demographics					
BLACK	BV = 1 if subject is black else = 0	0.09	0.07	0.11	0.09
AGE	Subject's age in years	29.61	50.66	29.21	51.25
AGESQ	Square of subject's age	909.11	2620.85	886.45	2683.33
TAKERISK[3]	Extent to which subject is a risk taker	2.83	2.36	2.21	1.91
NUMCHRON[4]	Number of chronic conditions subject has	0.37	1.09	0.45	1.26
OBESE[5]	BV = 1 if subject is obese else = 0	0.10	0.17	0.10	0.19
HSGRAD[6]	BV = 1 if subject is high school grad else = 0	0.39	0.33	0.41	0.44
SOMECOLL[6]	BV = 1 if subject attended college but did not graduate else = 0	0.22	0.18	0.24	0.17
COLLGRAD[6]	BV = 1 if subject is a college graduate else = 0	0.15	0.12	0.13	0.08
GRADSCHL[6]	BV = 1 if subject attended graduate school else = 0	0.09	0.14	0.07	0.07

Notes

1 The mean value for *DISDAY* is the mean among the sample of employed males (females). All other means pertain to the full samples of males and females, including employed and unemployed persons.

2 Non-smokers are the excluded reference group.

3 *TAKERISK* is a categorical value ranging between 1 and 5. A response equal to 1 indicates that the subject strongly disagrees that he or she is an above-average risk taker. A value of 5 indicates that the subject strongly believes that he or she is an above-average risk taker.

4 The chronic conditions are: arthritis, chronic back ache, cancer, diabetes, atherosclerosis, rheumatism, prior heart attack, heart disease, hypertension, and prior stroke.

5 Obesity is defined as a body mass index greater than 30.

6 Subjects having less than high school educations constitute the excluded reference group.

Table 8.2 Logistic regression model of employment status – males

Variable	Parameter estimate	Standard error	*t*-statistic	Odds ratio
		Males < 40 ($n = 3550$)		
INTERCEPT	–2.43	1.56	1.56	–
HISMOKE	–0.38	0.16	2.39**	0.68
LOSMOKE	–0.13	0.23	0.56	0.88
FORSMOKE	0.19	0.22	0.88	1.21
BLACK	–1.30	0.19	6.82***	0.27
AGE	0.26	0.11	2.31**	1.29
AGESQ	–0.004	0.02	1.83	1.00
TAKERISK	0.02	0.05	0.38	1.02
NUMCHRON	–0.10	0.08	1.25	0.90
OBESE	–0.86	0.21	4.14***	0.42
HSGRAD	0.78	0.16	4.81***	2.17
SOMECOLL	1.87	0.22	8.45***	6.49
COLLGRAD	3.06	0.50	6.08***	21.34
GRADSCHL	2.31	0.58	3.97***	10.03
		Males ≥ 40 ($n = 2716$)		
INTERCEPT	–14.01	4.01	3.50***	–
HISMOKE	–1.19	0.23	5.18***	0.31
LOSMOKE	–1.19	0.23	5.13***	0.30
FORSMOKE	–0.72	0.20	3.58***	0.49
BLACK	–0.93	0.16	5.91***	0.39
AGE	0.73	0.16	4.70***	2.08
AGESQ	–0.01	0.001	5.31***	0.99
TAKERISK	0.14	0.05	2.78***	1.15
NUMCHRON	–0.36	0.04	8.43***	0.70
OBESE	–0.09	0.15	0.65	0.91
HSGRAD	0.52	0.13	4.05***	1.69
SOMECOLL	0.71	0.20	3.62***	2.04
COLLGRAD	1.02	0.26	3.93***	2.78
GRADSCHL	1.93	0.38	5.11***	6.88

Notes

*** Statistically significant at the 1 percent level, two-tailed test.

** Statistically significant at the 5 percent level, two-tailed test.

Table 8.3 Multivariate model of employment status—females

Variable	Parameter estimate	Standard error	*t*-statistic	Odds ratio
		Females < 40 (n = 4305)		
INTERCEPT	3.54	0.92	3.87***	–
HISMOKE	–0.18	0.12	1.42	0.84
LOSMOKE	–0.12	0.12	0.96	0.89
FORSMOKE	–0.22	0.11	2.04**	0.80
BLACK	–0.30	0.12	2.47**	0.74
AGE	–0.21	0.07	3.25***	0.81
AGESQ	0.03	0.001	0.003***	1.00
TAKERISK	0.02	0.04	0.56	1.02
NUMCHRON	–0.11	0.06	1.88	0.90
OBESE	–0.58	0.12	5.03***	0.56
HSGRAD	0.85	0.11	8.06***	2.34
SOMECOLL	1.69	0.12	13.83***	5.44
COLLGRAD	1.76	0.17	10.19***	5.79
GRADSCHL	2.45	0.27	8.98***	11.59
		Females ≥ 40 (n = 3305)		
INTERCEPT	–5.74	2.54	2.26**	–
HISMOKE	–0.09	0.14	0.63	0.92
LOSMOKE	0.23	0.13	1.81	1.26
FORSMOKE	–0.03	0.10	0.30	0.97
BLACK	0.06	0.11	0.05	1.01
AGE	0.30	0.10	3.01***	1.35
AGESQ	–0.003	0.001	3.64***	1.00
TAKERISK	0.01	0.03	0.42	1.01
NUMCHRON	–0.20	0.03	6.09***	0.82
OBESE	0.0003	0.11	0.003	1.00
HSGRAD	0.49	0.10	4.81***	1.63
SOMECOLL	0.95	0.13	7.30***	2.60
COLLGRAD	1.18	0.18	6.41***	3.24
GRADSCHL	1.76	0.23	7.52***	5.81

Notes

*** Statistically significant at the 1 percent level, two-tailed test.

** Statistically significant at the 5 percent level, two-tailed test.

higher probability of employment, and among younger females, blacks are less likely to be employed.

3.3 Determinants of the Propensity to Miss Work

Tables 8.4 and 8.5 show the impact of smoking on the propensity to miss work for males and females, respectively. Here the results for men and women are more similar. For both young males and females, heavy smokers were substantially more likely to incur work disability days than were non-smokers. Light smokers were also significantly more likely to miss work than were non-smokers. Among older male workers, former smokers were significantly more likely to miss work.

3.4 Smoking and Employment Status

To gain a better sense of the magnitude of the relationship between smoking status and employment, we used the estimated coefficients from the models in Tables 8.2 and 8.3 to compute average employment rates according to smoking status. These results are provided in Table 8.6. As the table indicates, older males who are heavy smokers or light smokers were more than 10 percentage points less likely to be employed than were non-smokers, other factors being equal. Older male former smokers were 5.5 percentage points less likely to be employed. The relationship between smoking status and employment is considerably smaller in other age/gender cohorts.

The precise reasons for the gender variation in the relationship between smoking status and employment is unclear. Conceivably, smoking may have a more important effect on employment among males because their jobs require more physical exertion, on average, and smoking may thus inhibit their ability to perform this work. Men may be heavier smokers, as well. For example, within the class of heavy smokers, the NMES data indicate that a higher fraction of men (43 percent) than women (32 percent) were very heavy smokers (two or more packs per day).

3.5 Smoking and the Propensity to Miss Work

Table 8.7 uses the results in Tables 8.4 and 8.5 to compute the relationships between smoking status and the propensity to miss work. As the table indicates, smoking has non-trivial effects on work disability; among both males and females, heavy smokers were substantially more likely to incur a work disability day than were non-smokers. In every cohort, light smokers and former smokers were also more likely to incur a

Table 8.4 Logistic regression model of propensity to miss work – employed males

Variable	Parameter estimate	Standard error	*t*-statistic	Odds ratio
		Employed males < 40 (n = 3229)		
INTERCEPT	–1.07	1.13	0.95	–
HISMOKE	0.39	0.12	3.30***	1.47
LOSMOKE	0.28	0.13	2.12**	1.33
FORSMOKE	0.07	0.12	0.59	1.08
BLACK	–0.24	0.13	1.89	0.79
AGE	0.04	0.08	0.55	1.04
AGESQ	–0.001	0.001	0.69	1.00
TAKERISK	–0.04	0.04	1.08	0.96
NUMCHRON	0.28	0.06	4.26***	1.32
OBESE	0.21	0.12	1.67	1.23
HSGRAD	0.02	0.11	0.18	1.02
SOMECOLL	0.09	0.11	0.85	1.09
COLLGRAD	0.30	0.16	1.93	1.36
GRADSCHL	–0.001	0.17	0.004	1.00
		Employed males ≥ 40 (n = 2259)		
INTERCEPT	0.40	2.97	0.13	–
HISMOKE	0.23	0.14	1.65	1.26
LOSMOKE	0.10	0.20	0.51	1.11
FORSMOKE	0.33	0.13	2.62***	1.39
BLACK	–0.33	0.13	2.48**	0.72
AGE	–0.03	0.12	0.24	0.97
AGESQ	0.00004	0.001	0.03	1.00
TAKERISK	–0.02	0.04	0.62	0.98
NUMCHRON	0.30	0.04	7.47***	1.35
OBESE	0.16	0.13	1.20	1.18
HSGRAD	–0.31	0.14	2.17**	0.73
SOMECOLL	0.04	0.17	0.22	1.04
COLLGRAD	–0.03	0.16	0.21	0.97
GRADSCHL	–0.10	0.17	0.60***	0.91

Notes

*** Statistically significant at the 1 percent level, two-tailed test.

** Statistically significant at the 5 percent level, two-tailed test.

Table 8.5 Logistic regression model of propensity to miss work – employed females

Variable	Parameter estimate	Standard error	*t*-statistic	Odds ratio
		Employed females < 40 (n = 3194)		
INTERCEPT	–1.50	1.14	1.32	–
HISMOKE	0.30	0.12	2.45**	1.35
LOSMOKE	0.33	0.11	2.99***	1.39
FORSMOKE	0.07	0.11	0.65	1.07
BLACK	–0.20	0.10	1.91	0.82
AGE	0.10	0.08	1.23	1.10
AGESQ	–0.002	0.001	1.52	1.00
TAKERISK	–0.07	0.04	1.95	0.93
NUMCHRON	0.44	0.07	6.60***	1.55
OBESE	0.32	0.14	2.32**	1.38
HSGRAD	0.27	0.14	1.89	1.31
SOMECOLL	0.30	0.13	2.23**	1.34
COLLGRAD	0.56	0.16	3.43***	1.75
GRADSCHL	0.54	0.17	3.24***	1.72
		Employed females ≥ 40 (n = 1994)		
INTERCEPT	2.76	2.72	1.01	–
HISMOKE	0.23	0.14	1.62	1.26
LOSMOKE	0.06	0.17	0.39	1.07
FORSMOKE	0.12	0.13	0.97	1.13
BLACK	–0.22	0.13	1.66	0.81
AGE	–0.12	0.11	1.15	0.88
AGESQ	0.001	0.001	0.97	1.00
TAKERISK	–0.02	0.05	0.39	0.98
NUMCHRON	0.28	0.04	6.35***	1.33
OBESE	0.28	0.14	2.04**	1.32
HSGRAD	0.10	0.16	0.64	1.11
SOMECOLL	0.29	0.17	1.73	1.33
COLLGRAD	0.26	0.22	1.21	0.30
GRADSCHL	0.37	0.21	1.73	1.45

Notes

*** Statistically significant at the 1 percent level, two-tailed test.

** Statistically significant at the 5 percent level, two-tailed test.

Table 8.6 Smoking and employment status

Cohort	Percent employed			
	Males < 40	Males ≥ 40	Females < 40	Females ≥ 40
Heavy smokers	90.7	81.6	75.0	61.4
Light smokers	92.4	81.6	76.0	67.8
Former smokers	92.0	86.5	74.3	62.7
Non-smokers	93.2	92.0	77.9	63.3

Table 8.7 Smoking and the propensity to miss work

Cohort	Percent missed work			
	Males < 40	Males ≥ 40	Females < 40	Females ≥ 40
Heavy smokers	43.8	34.9	55.0	49.8
Light smokers	41.1	32.1	55.7	45.7
Former smokers	36.2	37.1	49.5	47.1
Non-smokers	34.6	30.1	47.8	44.2

work disability day than were non-smokers.

3.6 Individual Labor Productivity Costs of Smoking

What do the adverse employment and work disability effects of smoking imply in terms of labor productivity costs? Using the results from the multivariate models described above,[2] as well as information on employee earnings and fringe benefits from the *Statistical Abstract of the United States* (1998), we computed financial losses from decreased employment and more disability days as a result of smoking. These results, summarized in Table 8.8, should be interpreted as the expected incremental costs for an individual who smokes relative to a non-smoker.

The results in Table 8.8 confirm that the productivity costs of smoking are high. For males aged 40–64 who smoke a pack or more per day, annual labor productivity costs from decreased employment opportunities and increased work disability days averaged $4359; the

Table 8.8 Individual labor productivity costs of smoking (annual costs, $)

Cohort	Employment costs	Disability day costs	Employment costs	Disability day costs	Employment costs	Disability day costs	Employment costs	Disability day costs
	Males < 40		Males ≥ 40		Females < 40		Females ≥ 40	
Heavy smokers	1026	106	4269	90	955	78	626	81
Light smokers	328	75	4269	37	626	86	–1482	22
Former smokers	493	18	2258	131	1185	18	198	42

corresponding figure for older males who smoke less than a pack per day was nearly as large at $4306, and for former smokers, $2389. Labor productivity costs for women and for younger men were smaller, although still substantial.

3.7 Total Labor Productivity Costs from Unemployment and Disability Days

Because a large proportion of working-age individuals smoke, the aggregate annual productivity costs are formidable. Applying population values for the United States using NMES weights, and using the costs per smoker from Table 8.8, the aggregate annual productivity costs from unemployment and disability days due to smoking totaled $65 billion per year (see Table 8.9). These costs were disproportionately concentrated among older males. At $43.7 billion per year, these individuals alone accounted for 67 percent of the estimated productivity costs, even though they represent only 20 percent of our sample.

4 DISCUSSION

Previous work points to increased job absenteeism, rather than unemployment, as the main adverse labor productivity consequence of smoking. The results of this study are in sharp contrast to earlier findings. Although we find that smoking has a statistically significant effect on job absenteeism that is non-trivial in magnitude, these costs are small in relation to the unemployment costs of smoking. Our findings with respect to employment also stand in contrast to earlier work.

What factors can account for the discrepancy between the strong effects on smoking that we observe and earlier research reporting only weak effects? A likely explanation is that the earlier study by Levine et al. (1995) considered only young workers, many of whom had not been smoking for long enough to experience substantial adverse effects on their health. Our findings suggest that labor productivity costs from smoking are substantially smaller among younger male cohorts relative to older ones. In contrast, smoking had more adverse effects on the employment of younger females. Disentangling age- and gender-specific differences in the labor productivity effects of smoking would be a useful direction for further work.

This study identifies large variations in labor productivity costs by gender and age. Such variations may be informative for identifying subgroups of the population where labor productivity costs are likely to

Table 8.9 Aggregate labor productivity costs of smoking (annual costs, $bn)

Cohort	Employment costs	Disability day costs	Employment costs	Disability day costs	Employment costs	Disability day costs	Employment costs	Disability day costs
	Males < 40		Males ≥ 40		Females < 40		Females ≥ 40	
Heavy smokers	5.95	0.62	20.07	0.42	3.82	0.31	1.75	0.23
Light smokers	0.98	0.23	5.99	0.04	2.00	0.28	–2.52	0.03
Former smokers	2.47	0.09	16.26	0.94	4.38	0.07	0.63	0.13
Total	9.40	0.94	42.32	1.40	10.20	0.66	–0.14	0.39
Grand total $65.17 bn								

be highest, and in directing smoking cessation or related programs at these cohorts. Based on the results of this analysis, it appears that the adverse labor productivity effects of smoking are concentrated among males aged 40 to 64. Work-related smoking cessation programs and related interventions may be particularly effective in preventing labor productivity losses if they are directed at these groups.[3] At the same time, the adverse labor productivity effects among former smokers we document suggests that smoking cessation programs may not be able to restore workers to pre-smoking productivity levels.

Overall, we estimate that the employment and job absenteeism costs of smoking are extremely large, at approximately $65 billion per year. This figure is almost as large as recent estimates of the aggregate medical costs of smoking at $72.7 billion per year (Miller et al. 1998).

Estimating the impacts of smoking is an inexact science. Our non-experimental design and our inability to eliminate all concerns about endogeneity in the smoking variables suggest that these findings must be viewed with caution. Nevertheless, even if our results overstate the labor productivity effects of smoking by 100 percent, the actual cost is still too large to be overlooked.

NOTES

1. As a rough gauge of the likely importance of these additional sources of bias, we compared results for smoking in the models reported in the text to simpler models that included only smoking variables. If smoking effects decline precipitously in the more comprehensive models, this might suggest that including additional important omitted variables would cause further declines. The estimated effects of smoking for males aged 40 and above were remarkably stable, whether we used the simpler model or the more comprehensive one. This is significant, given that this cohort alone accounts for two-thirds of the labor productivity losses associated with smoking. Among younger males and females, the estimated effects of smoking showed sharper declines when we compared the simpler models to the more comprehensive ones reported in the text. Collectively, these results suggest that the strong majority of our productivity cost estimates are not seriously biased, but we cannot exclude the possibility that a significant minority of costs among younger cohorts may be overstated. We thank an anonymous reviewer for suggesting this approach for gauging potential bias.
2. Specifically, we used the logistic regression coefficients from the models reported in Tables 8.2–8.5 to obtain predicted values of the propensity to smoke and incur work disability days for different smoking cohorts.

[3] Because the adverse impacts of smoking cumulate over time, however, preventive efforts to reduce smoking in the young may be quite effective as well. We thank an anonymous reviewer for calling this point to our attention.

REFERENCES

Adams M.L. (1994), 'The public health impact and economic cost of smoking in Connecticut – 1989', *Connecticut Medicine*, **58**(4): 195–8.

Barsky, R., F. Juster, M. Kimball and M. Shapiro (1997), 'Preference parameters and behavioral heterogeneity: an experimental approach in the health and retirement study', *Quarterly Journal of Economics*, **12**(2): 537–79.

Berndt, E.R., S.N. Finkelstein, P.E. Greenberg, A. Keith, M.B. Keller and J. Russell (1996), 'Workplace performance from chronic depression and its treatment', Working Paper, Massachusetts Institute of Technology.

Bound, J., D. Jaeger and R. Baker (1995), 'Problems with instrumental variables estimation when the correlation between the instruments and the endogenous explanatory variable is weak', *Journal of the American Statistical Association*, **90**(430): 443–50.

Deb, P. and P. Trivedi (1997), 'Demand for medical care by the elderly: a finite mixture approach', *Journal of Applied Econometrics*, **12**(3): 313–36.

Fielding, J. (1985), 'Smoking: health effects and control', *New England Journal of Medicine*, **331**(8): 491–8.

Killingsworth, M.R. (1983), *Labor Supply*, New York: Cambridge University Press.

Kristein, M. (1983), 'How much can business expect to profit from smoking cessation?', *Preventive Medicine*, **12**: 358–81.

Leigh, J.P. (1995), 'Smoking, self-selection, and absenteeism', *The Quarterly Review of Economics and Finance*, **35**(4): 365–86.

Leung, S.F. and S. Yu (1996), 'On the choice between sample selection and two-part models', *Journal of Econometrics*, **72**(1–2): 197–229.

Levine, P.B., T.A. Gustafson and A.D. Velenchik (1995), 'More bad news for smokers? The effects of cigarette smoking on wages', National Bureau of Economic Research Working Paper No. 5270, September.

Lynch T.A. and R.S. Hopkins (1996), 'Estimating tobacco-related health care and mortality costs in Florida', *Journal of the Florida Medical Association*, **83**(2): 128–33.

Miller, L.S., X. Zhang, D.P. Rice and W. Max (1998), 'State estimates of total medical expenditures attributable to smoking – 1993', *Public*

Health Reports, **113**(5): 447–58.

Nelson, C. and R. Startz (1990), 'The distribution of the instrumental variables estimator and its *t*-ratio when the instrument is a poor one', *Journal of Business*, **63**(Part 2): S125–S140.

Oster, G., G.A. Colditz and N.L. Kelly (1984), 'The economic costs of smoking and the benefits of quitting for individual smokers', *Preventive Medicine*, **13**: 377–89.

Peto, R., A. Lopez, J. Boreham, M. Thun and C. Heath (1994), *Mortality from Smoking in Developed Countries 1950–2000*, New York: Oxford University Press.

Rizzo, J., T. Abbott and M. Berger (1998), 'Labor productivity costs of chronic back ache in the United States', *Medical Care*, **36**: 1471–88.

Rizzo, J., T. Abbott and S. Pashko (1996), 'Labor productivity effects of prescribed medicines for chronically ill workers', *Health Economics*, **5**: 249–65.

Rubinstein, L., E. Chrischelles and M. Voelker (1997), 'The impact of Parkinson's disease on health status, health expenditures, and productivity estimates from the National Medical Expenditure Survey', *PharmacoEconomics*, **12**(4): 486–98.

Schumacher, C. (1996), 'Smoking attributable mortality and economic costs in Alaska 1992–1994', *Alaska Medicine*, **38**(1): 13–17.

Shopland, D.R., A.M. Hartman, J.T. Gibson, M.D. Muller, L.G. Kessler and W.R. Lynn (1996), 'Cigarette smoking among U.S. adults by state and region: estimates from the current population survey, *Journal of the National Cancer Institute*, **88**(23): 1748–58.

Sims, J. (1994), 'Tobacco: the leading cause of death', *Journal of the Florida Medical Association*, **81**: 818–21.

Staiger, D. and J. Stock (1997), 'Instrumental variables estimation with weak instruments', *Econometrica*, **65**(3): 557–86.

US Department of Commerce (1998), *Statistical Abstract of the United States*.

US Department of Health and Human Services, Public Health Service, Agency for Health Care Policy and Research (1991), *National Medical Expenditure Survey* (Public Use Tapes Nos 9 and 13), Rockville, MD.

US Department of Health and Human Services, Public Health Service, Centers for Disease Control and Prevention (1994a), 'Smoking among adults – United States, 1992, and changes in the definition of current cigarette smoking', *Morbidity and Mortality Weekly Report*, **43**(19): 342–46.

US Department of Health and Human Services, Public Health Service, Centers for Disease Control and Prevention (1994b), 'Surveillance for selected tobacco-use behaviors – United States, 1900–1994', *Morbidity*

and Mortality Weekly Report, **43**(SS-3): 6–7.
Vistnes, J. (1997), 'Gender differences in days lost from work due to illness', *Industrial and Labor Relations Review*, **50**(2): 304–23.

9. Alcohol and drug use: risk factors for unintended pregnancy

Robert Kaestner and Theodore Joyce

1 INTRODUCTION

Planning and controlling fertility is an issue that has always affected society and continues to do so even today at a time when there is access to relatively reliable, although costly, means of contraception. What makes fertility control so problematic is the uncertainty inherent in the process. Even the most reliable contraceptive methods have a positive failure rate and the practice of a consistent and effective contraceptive regime is obviously not an easy task, as evidenced by the number of unintended pregnancies that occur each year. More importantly, the occurrence of an unintended pregnancy creates financial and emotional hardships for women and families who have to decide whether to terminate the pregnancy or have another child. Each choice involves significant costs and the consequences of any decision may be profound.

The magnitude of the problem should not be underestimated. In 1995, there were 1.2 million unintended births of which approximately 374,000 were estimated to be unwanted – a woman did not want to have any more children in her lifetime. In addition, there were 1.4 million abortions in 1995.[1] Thus, in just one year, imperfect fertility control resulted in 374,000 more children than desired, and families incurred the monetary and psychological costs associated with 1.4 million abortions. These figures imply billions of dollars of loss to families and do not even include the costs associated with 850,000 births that were mistimed – a woman wanted a child, but at a later date.

Unintended pregnancy also creates a variety of social problems since children born as a result of unintended pregnancies are at greater risk of dying in infancy, of being abused as a child, and of suffering lasting developmental deficits (Brown and Eisenberg 1995). Unintended pregnancy also divides our society as evidenced by the vitriolic public debate over abortion, and is related to a variety of social issues such as teenage childbearing and welfare dependence since unintended pregnancy is concentrated among the young, poor and unmarried. The serious consequences of unintended pregnancy make understanding the causes of unintended pregnancy an important research issue.

One potential cause of unintended pregnancy is substance use. For example, Poole et al. (1997) reported that among a group of low-income women in Birmingham, Alabama, those who reported their pregnancy to be unintended had higher levels of prenatal drug and alcohol use than did those who reported their pregnancy to be intended. Alcohol and drug use affects a person's physical, psychological and emotional functioning and can alter behavior in ways that may result in an unintended pregnancy. For example, alcohol and drug use may decrease inhibition and lead to more unplanned sexual encounters that lead to increased incidence of unprotected sex and unintended pregnancy. The relationship between substance use and unintended pregnancy may be particularly important for teenagers and young adults since the majority of these people are unmarried, sexually active and experimenting with drugs and alcohol. Teenagers and young adults are also an interesting group because of their high rates of unintended pregnancy. Data from the 1995 National Survey of Family Growth (NSFG) indicate that in 1994, approximately 78 percent of all pregnancies and 66 percent of all births to teenage (< 20) women were unintended (Henshaw 1998).[2]

Previous research on the effects of substance use on sexual activity has not adequately controlled for unmeasured influences that may confound estimates of the causal effect of substance use. Therefore, it is still unknown whether substance use is simply correlated with unintended pregnancy or a cause of unintended pregnancy. This point is effectively made by Leigh and Stall (1993) who note that many studies that found substance use to be correlated with sexual behavior also found cigarette smoking to be significantly correlated with sexual behavior. It is hard to argue, however, that smoking is a cause of sexual behavior and its outcomes (for example, unintended pregnancy), although it may indicate a certain type of personality that is associated with this behavior.

In this study, we investigate the relationship between alcohol and drug use and unintended pregnancy among young adult women. Specifically, we use data in the National Longitudinal Survey of Youth (NLSY) to test whether substance use is associated with an unintended birth among women between the ages of 19 and 32. We also investigate the effect of substance use on contraception use to test the robustness of our findings related to unintended pregnancy. The goal of this study is to estimate the causal effect of substance use on unintended pregnancy. Toward this end we exploit the longitudinal data in the NLSY and data on drug and alcohol prices to account for the influence of unmeasured determinants of unintended pregnancy that may be correlated with substance use.

2 RELATED RESEARCH

There have been no studies that directly examined the effect of substance use on unintended pregnancy. This is surprising since unintended pregnancy is one of the two most important adverse outcomes of risky sexual behavior, the other being sexually transmitted disease. However, two prior studies examined the relationship between substance use and premarital pregnancy and another investigated the relationship between substance use and out-of-wedlock birth. Since 78 percent of all pregnancies and 58 percent of all births to never married women are unintended, these studies come closest to examining the question posed by this analysis.

In addition to these studies, many researchers have investigated the relationship between substance use and risky sexual practices such as early onset of sexual intercourse and engaging in unprotected sex.[3] The vast majority of these studies have found a positive relationship between substance use and risky sexual behavior. In general, these studies have two major weaknesses. First, many of them used non-representative samples such as students at one or two high schools, or students in one metropolitan area. Thus, the results of these studies may not be applicable to other localities as the relationship between substance use and sexual practices may differ across cities or regions. Second, most of these studies failed to control for a variety of family background and personal factors that may confound estimates of the relationship between substance use and sexual practices.

Past studies that come closest to examining the effect of substance use on unintended pregnancy are those that look at the effect of substance use on premarital pregnancy and out-of-wedlock birth. There are three such studies: two by Denise Kandel and her colleagues and one by Kaestner (1998). The study by Kaestner is primarily descriptive. He used cross-sectional data to measure the statistical association between prior drug and alcohol use and the incidence of being an unmarried woman with a child; he also used longitudinal data to examine the effect of prior drug and alcohol use on the probability of having an out-of-wedlock birth. Kaestner included an extensive set of control variables in the model including family background measures, cognitive achievement scores, other personal attributes and area characteristics of the social and economic environment. He found that drug use was a significant predictor of being an unwed mother and of having an out-of-wedlock birth.

Yamaguchi and Kandel (1987) examined the effect of drug use on the hazard rate for premarital pregnancy among a sample of New York State high school students. Yamaguchi and Kandel found that use of other illicit drugs besides marijuana was significantly related to an increased likelihood of experiencing a premarital pregnancy. They also found, however, that the effect of other illicit drugs besides marijuana was approximately the same for current and former users of illicit drugs, suggesting that the effect may be due to unobserved person-specific factors associated with both drug use and premarital pregnancy. Surprisingly, Yamaguchi and Kandel found no effect of marijuana use on the hazard rate of premarital pregnancy. In a similar study, Mensch and Kandel (1992) examined the effect of drug use on the hazard rate for premarital pregnancy using data from the NLSY. Findings from this study indicated that prior use of other illicit drugs besides marijuana had a significant impact on the premarital pregnancy hazard. Prior use of marijuana had no effect on the premarital pregnancy hazard rate. It is surprising that both of these studies by Kandel and her colleagues found an effect of other illicit drug use on premarital pregnancy, but did not find an effect of marijuana use on the incidence of premarital pregnancy. The prevalence of other illicit drug use is quite low, making it difficult to detect significant effects.

The two studies by Kandel and her colleagues were carefully done and provide preliminary evidence that drug use and unintended (that is, premarital) pregnancy are causally related. The two studies, however, have several limitations. First, both studies used samples that are not representative of the national population. Second, both studies have methodological weaknesses. Yamaguchi and Kandel (1987) estimated the parameters of a continuous time exponential hazard function that restricts the hazard to be time independent. This methodology assumes that conditional on covariates, the probability of a premarital pregnancy in each period is the same regardless of the length of time the individual has been at risk of pregnancy. This is a strong assumption that may have biased estimates. Probably the most important limitation of the studies by Kandel and colleagues, however, is that neither of the studies adequately controls for unmeasured heterogeneity: unobserved factors that vary across women and are correlated with fertility outcomes such as premarital pregnancy.

In summary, the review of the literature has clearly revealed that substance use and sexual activity, and the outcomes of such activity, are positively related among teenagers and young adults. Thus, it appears that the popular slogan ‘sex, drugs and rock and roll’ has some scientific basis.

The remaining unanswered question is whether substance use causes risky sexual behavior and unintended pregnancy. It may be the case that substance use and such behaviors and outcomes are manifestations of a common personality type. The difference is crucial for the design of public policy. On the one hand, if substance use and risky sexual practices are both the result of a common personality trait, then public policies addressing either issue should focus on factors that affect this common trait. On the other hand, if substance use adversely affects sexual practices and causes unintended pregnancy, then an appropriate public policy would be to find ways to reduce substance use among teens and young adults.

3 UNINTENDED PREGNANCY AND SUBSTANCE USE

3.1 Behavioral Model of Unintended Pregnancy

Our model of pregnancy intentions is derived from an argument similar to that presented by Michael and Willis (1975) in their analysis of contraception. Suppose that, without any cost and with perfect certainty, a woman can choose the optimal number and timing of her children. Under these circumstances, a woman can achieve her maximum level of utility. Now suppose that the woman's fertility choices are constrained by costly and imperfect fertility control. Given these additional constraints, a woman will choose an efficient fertility control (that is, contraception) strategy that will yield an optimal expected number of children. In other words, she will adopt a particular method of contraception and plan to have the number of children that this contraceptive method and her rate of sexual activity yield. Due to the uncertainty of fertility control, however, the actual number of births a woman has will be above or below the number she expects or plans to have. Moreover, the greater the degree of uncertainty (or the cost of reducing uncertainty), the larger will be the variation in the number of actual births from the expected, or desired, number of births.

As noted by Michael and Willis (1975), this simple behavioral model leads to a natural definition of unwanted births: an unwanted birth is one that raises family size above the optimal number. The key feature of this simple model is that the definition of unwanted births stems from the uncertainty of fertility control. In addition, this definition of unwanted births is based on deviations of actual births from some target number of births. Thus, factors that affect the target number of births may also affect the number of unwanted births. For example, Michael and Willis constructed a model in which the variance (uncertainty) of births increases with the mean number of births. Thus, uncertainty and the number of unwanted births increase with the number of planned children: families that plan to have more children will also have more unintended pregnancies.

This simple model is not intended to accurately portray the complexity of a woman's decision to describe her pregnancy as unintended. Rather, it is useful because it contains an interesting prediction: namely that factors affecting the expected or planned number of births will also affect the variance of births and thus the number of unwanted births. Therefore, researchers interested in the effect of substance use on unintended pregnancy need to control for variables that affect both substance use and the expected number of children. For example, academic achievement or educational attainment may affect a woman's substance use and her desired (that is, planned) family size. Failure to control for this and other characteristics, some of which are often unmeasured, may lead to biased estimates of the effect of substance use on unintended pregnancy. This point underlies our main criticism of previous research that it has failed to adequately control for both measured and unmeasured factors that are likely to confound estimates of the effect of substance use on unintended pregnancy.

3.2 Substance Use and Unintended Pregnancy

Substance use may affect the incidence of unintended pregnancy in a number of ways, most of which focus on the relationship between substance use and the uncertainty of fertility control. One of the most obvious ways that substance use may affect unintended pregnancy is if substance use leads to early initiation of sexual activity. Given that most contraceptive methods have a non-zero failure rate, early initiation of sexual activity will necessarily increase the likelihood of having a pregnancy, which among teens implies that the pregnancy will be unintended in 78 percent of the cases (Henshaw 1998). Similar reasoning implies that substance use may increase the risk of unintended pregnancy because it affects the timing and incidence of marriage. Kaestner (1997) showed that drug use is associated with a later age of first marriage and greater marital instability. Thus, substance use may increase the time at risk for having an unintended pregnancy by causing a delay in the age of marriage. Substance use may also affect unintended pregnancy through its effect on the frequency of sexual activity and the number of sexual partners. Research has shown that contraceptive use among teens and young adults is greatest when sexual activity is planned and when sexual partners have developed a close relationship (Zabin and Hayward 1994). Substance use may impair judgment and lead to more unplanned sexual activity with a larger number of sexual partners, or it may influence partner selection that in turn affects communication between partners and contraceptive use. These possibilities may increase the incidence of unintended pregnancy. Finally, substance use may cause an unintended pregnancy if its use affects the efficacy of contraception. The efficacy of contraception may be affected by improper application of a given method or by poor choice of methods (for example, no method).

4 RESEARCH DESIGN

4.1 Individual Fixed-effects Model

We begin with a model that relates recent substance use to the probability of having an unintended pregnancy in the two-year period following the survey date that substance use information was collected. For example, we examine the effect of substance use at the time of the 1984 interview on the probability of having an unintended pregnancy during the two-year period following the date of the 1984 interview. The two-year period was chosen due to data considerations and is discussed in more detail below. Algebraically, the model may be represented as follows:

$$U_{i(t+1)} = \alpha_i + \lambda_1 Drug_{it} + X_{it}\beta + v_{i(t+1)}, \qquad (9.1)$$

where U is an indicator of whether woman i in period t had an unintended pregnancy, *Drug* is a measure, or measures, of substance use (drug and alcohol use), X is a vector of control variables such as education, income, family background, attitudes toward sex, religion and other factors that may affect the incidence of pregnancy and pregnancy intentions, and v is an error term.

There are four points to note about equation (9.1). First, the dependent variable represents a dichotomy between having an unintended pregnancy versus not having an unintended pregnancy. Women who have an intended pregnancy and those who did not get pregnant are in the latter group. This classification is appropriate since not having a pregnancy is evidence of successful fertility control and is equivalent to having an intended pregnancy, which is also an indicator of successful fertility control.

Second, the specification of equation (9.1) relates recent substance use to a subsequent outcome (that is, unintended pregnancy) of sexual behavior. This is necessitated by the data since we do not have a precise history of substance use or sexual activity. Our strategy, however, is appropriate since substance use does not necessarily have to immediately precede sexual activity for it to affect the incidence of unintended pregnancy. Substance use may influence the pattern of communication between partners that has been shown to be an important determinant of contraceptive use. For example, substance use may influence partner selection. The upshot is that substance use may cause unintended pregnancy even if it does not immediately precede sexual activity. Moreover, we develop several measures of substance use that separate users into casual users and more involved users. Since more involved users have a more continuous pattern of substance use, we would expect these measures of substance use to have larger effects than measures of casual substance use. If, however, both types of substance use measures are found to have an effect and there is an absence of a dose response effect, this would be evidence of an omitted variable that confounds the relationship between substance use and unintended pregnancy.

Third, our analysis ignores the influence of substance use on unintended pregnancy that works through its effect on the early onset of sexual activity. In this model, we are examining the incidence of unintended pregnancy during a specific period of time, not the incidence of the first unintended pregnancy.

Finally, equation (9.1) includes a separate intercept parameter (α_i) for each individual. This specification of the model indicates that there are unmeasured person-specific factors that affect the incidence of unintended pregnancy. These unmeasured factors are time-invariant as illustrated by the lack of a time subscript in equation (9.1). Examples of such factors are the respondent's efficiency using contraceptive methods and psychological costs of contraception. The importance of this parameter is that it controls for factors that may confound estimates of the effect of substance use on the incidence of unintended pregnancy if these unmeasured factors are also correlated with substance use.

We hypothesized that substance use may be related to unintended pregnancy because of its effect on the frequency of sexual activity and use of contraception. Thus, we also examine the effect of substance use on an outcome that combines sexual abstinence and contraception use. We refer to this outcome as contraception since abstinence may be considered a form of contraception (that is, fertility control). The motivation for this analysis stems from a desire to check the robustness of our findings related to unintended pregnancy.

The hypothesized correspondence between our two outcome measures, unintended pregnancy and contraception, may not be mechanical. Theoretically, unintended pregnancy depends not only on the incidence of pregnancy, which is mechanically related to sexual activity and contraception, but also on attitudes. For example, two women, one who is a substance user and one who is not, may both use the same amount of contraception, but when confronted with a contraceptive failure have different attitudes toward the pregnancy. Perhaps the woman who is a substance user will view the pregnancy as unwanted because of a reluctance to accept adult social roles (Yamaguchi and Kandel 1987). This scenario would lead to the finding that substance use has an effect on unintended pregnancy, but not on contraception use. Alternatively, these two women may use different amounts of contraception and have different attitudes toward a pregnancy. This scenario would lead to the finding of a significant effect of substance use on contraception, but perhaps no effect on unintended pregnancy. The upshot of this discussion is that while unintended pregnancy and contraception are linked, they are not representations of the same outcome and substance use may have different effects on each outcome.

We specify a model of contraception use similar to equation (9.1):

$$C_{it} = \delta_i + \gamma_1 Drug_{it} + X_{it}\Gamma + n_{it}\,. \tag{9.2}$$

The only new symbol in equation (9.2) is C, which indicates whether woman i in year t used contraception during sexual intercourse or abstained from sexual intercourse in the month prior to the interview.

One of the primary impediments of obtaining causal estimates of the effect of substance use on unintended pregnancy is the presence of unmeasured person-specific effects. To address this issue, we examine the effect of changes in substance use on changes in the incidence of unintended pregnancy. The advantage of this empirical strategy, which is referred to as the fixed-effects model, is that it eliminates the effect of unmeasured, time-invariant person-specific effects. The fixed-effects specification of equation (9.1) is given by

$$U_{i(t+2)} - U_{i(t+1)} = \alpha_1(Drug_{i(t+1)} - Drug_{it}) + (X_{i(t+1)} - X_{it})\beta + v_{i(t+2)} - v_{i(t+1)}\,. \tag{9.3}$$

The important feature of equation (9.2) is that the individual person-specific intercept (α_i) has been eliminated by examining changes in the incidence of unintended pregnancy. The fixed-effects model is an improvement over the simple cross-sectional model, although it may still yield biased estimates. The reason for this is that there may be some time-varying factors that have been omitted from the model (not included in X) that are correlated with both substance use and unintended pregnancy.

Omission of these variables, however, also affects the cross-sectional model of equation (9.1). Thus, the fixed-effects model is the preferred specification. Similar estimates for contraception use are not obtained because of data limitations described below.

We obtain estimates of equation (9.3) using two statistical methodologies: maximum likelihood logit regression and ordinary least squares (OLS) regression. Given the dichotomous nature of the dependent variable, it is appropriate to use maximum likelihood procedures, which under certain conditions yield unbiased and efficient estimates. Chamberlain (1980) provides the details for estimating equation (9.3) using maximum likelihood procedures. An important point to note about this procedure, however, is that it only uses observations that change pregnancy outcomes over time: women who experienced an unintended pregnancy in the first period (1985–86), but did not experience an unintended pregnancy in the second period (1989–90); and women who did not experience an unintended pregnancy in the first period, but who did experience an unintended pregnancy in the second period. Women who had the same unintended pregnancy outcome in both periods, either always unintended or never unintended, are dropped from the analysis.

In the current application, there may be many women who drop out of the sample because they did not experience changes in the incidence of unintended pregnancy. This may be problematic since these women may have changed their pattern of substance use during this period. Thus, dropping these observations from the analysis entails a loss of information about the relationship between substance use and unintended pregnancy. To test whether the estimates are sensitive to this potential problem, we also obtain estimates of the model using OLS. The OLS procedure uses all the observations and is quite similar to Chamberlain's (1984) random effects probit model.[4] Estimates obtained by OLS are consistent, but not efficient. To correct for heteroskedasticity, we follow the method proposed by White (1980) to calculate consistent estimates of the standard errors.

4.2 Instrumental Variables Model

The fixed-effects model is a valuable approach and in many cases provides more credible estimates of causal effects than simple cross-sectional models. There are, however, disadvantages associated with this approach. One of the problems associated with the fixed-effects model is that it may exacerbate statistical problems associated with measurement error. Another problem is that there is often insufficient variation over time in important explanatory variables that preclude obtaining precise estimates of the effect of these variables. Both problems may be present in the current application, particularly with regard to substance use.

An alternative procedure that preserves the causal interpretation of the parameter estimates is instrumental variables (IV). An IV procedure theoretically eliminates the correlation between substance use and unmeasured person-specific determinants of unintended pregnancy. The reason for this is that the IV procedure consists of replacing actual substance use, which may be partly determined by these unmeasured person-specific factors (for example, risk taking), with drug and alcohol use predicted by the price of these substances. The key point to understand is that predicted drug use varies across individuals only because of variation in the prices of drugs and alcohol and not because of variation in the quantity of unmeasured person-specific factors that also determine unintended pregnancy. Thus, predicted drug use and the unmeasured person-specific factor are theoretically uncorrelated. We illustrate the IV model with respect to the dependent variable unintended pregnancy:

$$U_{ij(t+1)} = \alpha_i + \alpha_1 \hat{Drug}_{jt} + X_{ijt}\beta + \delta_j + v_{ij(t+1)}, \tag{9.4}$$

$$Drug_{ijt} = \pi_1 + \pi_2 Price_{jt} + X_{it}\rho + \sigma_j + \upsilon_{it}. \tag{9.5}$$

Equation (9.5) represents the first stage of the model and illustrates that individual substance use depends on the prices of drugs and alcohol and all other exogenous determinants of unintended pregnancy. The explanatory variables in equation (9.5) are referred to as instruments because they are used to create an instrumental variable, predicted drug use. Note that the price of drug use does not vary according to individual i, but only by geographic (for example, state) area j and time t. Thus, the only independent variation in predicted drug use is from state and time variation in drug prices (see subscript in equation (9.4)). The second stage of the model is given by equation (9.4). In this equation, unintended pregnancy depends on the instrumental variable, predicted drug use and other exogenous determinants of unintended pregnancy including dummy variable (σ_j) that measures the influence of unobserved geographic-specific determinants of unintended pregnancy. Again, the important aspect of this model is that the use of an instrumental variable eliminates the correlation between unmeasured person-specific effects (α_i) and substance use.[5]

The efficacy of the IV model depends on two conditions: how well prices of drugs and alcohol predict substance use and whether the price of drugs and alcohol are determinants of unintended pregnancy and contraception use (that is, exclusion restrictions). Taking up the latter point first, there appears to be little justification for the hypothesis that the price of drugs and alcohol are predictors of unintended pregnancy or contraception use holding constant the quantity of drugs and alcohol. Thus, the exclusion of prices from equation (9.4) is reasonable. The more important point is whether the price of drugs and alcohol are powerful enough predictors of substance use so that precise estimates of the effects of substance use on unintended pregnancy can be obtained. Research by Bound et al. (1995) has shown that weak instruments will result in biased IV estimates. Previous research by Grossman et al. (1998) and Grossman and Chaloupka (1998) has shown that drug and alcohol prices are significant predictors of drug and alcohol consumption. Therefore, we believe that our implementation of the IV procedure is on firm footing. To estimate the IV model, we use ordinary least squares and follow the approach of Heckman and MaCurdy (1985).

5 DATA

The data used in this analysis are the youth cohort of the National Longitudinal Survey of Labor Market Experiences (NLSY). The NLSY is a national probability sample of young adults who were between the ages of 14 and 21 in 1979, the first year of the survey (Center for Human Resource Research 1994). The respondents have been interviewed on a yearly basis since that time. The NLSY is an excellent data source highly suited to our purposes. First, it is a large nationally representative sample, originally comprising 12,686 youths, approximately half of whom are women. The retention rate for the survey has been extremely high, 91 percent of the eligible population as of 1993.[6] In addition to the large female sample, the NLSY has obtained information for 10,042 children born to mothers by 1994. Second, the NLSY contains information about all of the variables of interest including pregnancy intentions for all births and pregnancies up to 1992, contraception use, substance use and an extensive set of personal and family characteristics.

Data availability forces us to limit our sample to respondents to the 1984 and 1988 surveys. These are the only two years of the survey that contain the requisite information on substance use that are relevant, although information about both alcohol and drug use was obtained in three years: 1984, 1988 and 1994. We chose not to use information from the 1994 survey because in 1994, the average age of women in the NLSY is 33. Women of this age have the lowest rates of unintended pregnancy and low rates of substance (drug) use. For example, approximately 2.2 percent of women used cocaine in the past year at the time of the 1994 survey. Thus, there is relatively little variation in our dependent variable, unintended pregnancy, and our explanatory variable of interest, substance use. This lack of variation makes it difficult to detect statistically significant effects, particularly in the context of the fixed-effects and IV methodologies.

5.1 Substance Use

In 1984 and 1988, the NLSY gathered information about a respondent's lifetime and current use of marijuana and cocaine, and information about the respondent's recent alcohol consumption.[7] From this information we develop several measures of a respondent's alcohol and drug use. Guiding the construction of these variables is the desire to separate women who are regular and involved users of alcohol and drugs from women who are casual users. This approach does not stem from a normative belief about casual use of alcohol and drugs, but rather from the practical demands of the empirical analysis and a belief that unintended pregnancy is most likely to be associated with relatively heavy substance use.

In all models, we include one measure of alcohol use and one measure of drug use as opposed to an extensive set of drug and alcohol variables. We require a parsimonious characterization of drug and alcohol use because of the statistical methodologies we employ. The IV procedure requires that we replace actual drug and alcohol with their predicted values. In each case, the same set of instruments is used to predict drug and alcohol use. Thus, predicted drug and alcohol use are expected to be highly correlated and this collinearity between the two measures of substance use makes it difficult to obtain precise estimates of the effect of substance use on unintended pregnancy. Including a more extensive set of drug and alcohol variables only exacerbates the problem. A restricted set of substance use measures is also advantageous in the context of the fixed-effects model. The precision and consistency of the estimates improves when right-hand-side variables are well measured and when they have significant variation over time. In sum, a more parsimonious specification can increase the variation and reduce measurement error, particularly in regard to drug use.

We construct several measures of drug use according to the responses to questions about current, past and age of first use of marijuana and cocaine. We use the following definitions to separate women according to their drug use:

- *Definition* 1 A woman is a drug user if she has used either marijuana or cocaine in the past year.
- *Definition* 2 A woman is a drug user if she has used either marijuana or cocaine in the past year and the combined frequency of use is at least five times per year. Frequency of use per year is calculated from information about the age of first use and the frequency of lifetime use.
- *Definition* 3 A woman is a drug user if she has used both marijuana and cocaine in the last year.
- *Definition* 4 A woman is a drug user if she has used both marijuana and cocaine in the past year and the combined frequency of use is at least five times per year. Frequency of use per year is calculated from information about the age of first use and the frequency of lifetime use.

We use each of these definitions in our analysis to test the sensitivity of the results to the different ways of characterizing drug use.

Information about alcohol use is less extensive. The NLSY contains information about the number of drinks in the past month and the frequency of heavy drinking. Accordingly, we construct only two different measures of alcohol use: the number of alcoholic drinks in the past month and the frequency of having six or more drinks at one time in the past month.[8] Again, we use each of these measures in our analysis to test the sensitivity of our findings to different definitions of alcohol consumption.

5.2 Pregnancy Intentions and Contraception Use

The NLSY also contains detailed information about the number and timing of pregnancies to female respondents. For each pregnancy, information about the intendedness of the pregnancy was collected and the questions in the NLSY closely parallel those in the National Survey of Family Growth (NSFG). For each pregnancy, a woman is asked a series of five questions about the wantedness of the pregnancy either during the pregnancy or at the time of the first interview after the pregnancy. As of 1992, pregnancy intentions were obtained during pregnancy for 28.9 percent of the cases. For the remaining pregnancies, the response was obtained *ex post*, in the vast majority of cases less than one year after the birth of the child. The breakdown of the intendedness responses is as follows: 59.8 percent wanted, 30.2 percent mistimed, and 10.0 percent unwanted. These figures lie between those of two other national surveys that contain information on pregnancy intentions for women at about the same period: the 1988 National Survey of Family Growth and the 1988 National Maternal and Infant Health Survey.

Using the information about pregnancy intentions we construct a dichotomous dependent variable that equals one if a woman had an unintended pregnancy during the two-year period following the interview and zero otherwise. As noted earlier, a woman who is not sexually active or who does not get pregnant is categorized as not having an unintended pregnancy. The key issue is whether the woman was successful at regulating her fertility and abstinence and effective contraceptive use is defined as a successful fertility control outcome.

We also examine the effect of alcohol and drug use on the use of contraception in the month prior to the interview. We define a dichotomous variable equal to one if a woman abstained from sex during the prior month or if she always used a contraceptive method other than withdrawal and zero otherwise. This definition of contraception use is somewhat unorthodox because it includes abstinence. However, as we previously noted, we expect substance use to influence the incidence of unintended pregnancy primarily through its effect on the frequency of sexual activity, on the number of sexual partners and contraceptive use. Thus, our definition of contraception use combines the frequency of sexual activity and contraception use and is consistent with our behavioral model.

The analysis of contraceptive use differs from unintended pregnancy since we are examining whether current drug and alcohol use affects current contraceptive practices. For this outcome, however, we limit the analysis to 1984 due to problems with the survey questions pertaining to contraception use in 1988. In 1984, women were first asked whether they were sexually active in the last month. If they answered yes to this question, they were then asked whether they used contraception. Based on these two questions we were able to construct the dependent variable we are interested in, namely whether a woman took action to control her fertility. We treat abstinence as another form of fertility control.[9] In 1988, however, all women were asked whether they used contraception even if they were not sexually active. Included in the possible responses to this question was 'abstinence'. Thus, women who were not sexually active had to choose this response to indicate the absence of sexual activity. Only 3 percent of the sample chose the 'abstinence' response, a figure that is extremely low according to other surveys. For example, a recent national survey of sexual practices reported that 12 percent of women of similar age to those in the NLSY indicate that they have not had sexual intercourse in the last year (Michael et al. 1994). These figures strongly suggest that there may be a significant amount of mis-reporting of contraception use in the 1988 NLSY. Therefore, we did not use this information.

5.3 Other Variables

One criticism of many previous studies is that they do not control for many factors besides substance use that may affect pregnancy intentions. This is problematic since variables such as education, income and parity may all affect the incidence of unintended pregnancy and be correlated with substance use. In this regard, the NLSY is a data set that is extremely well suited to study pregnancy intentions since it contains an extensive amount of information about the respondent. In this study, we use a large set of explanatory variables including:

- Demographic characteristics of the woman – age, race, ethnicity, education, marital status, number and ages of children, and health status.
- Family background characteristics – mother's education, family structure at age 14, and religiosity.
- Attitudes, expectations and psychological indices – locus of self-control scale, self-esteem scale, desired number of children, expectations about marriage, attitude toward marriage and work.
- Labor market experience and income.
- Social and economic indicators of the respondent's county of residence.
- Cognitive achievement test scores.

An important point to note about many of these variables is that they are measured well before the 1984 interview. For example, information about a respondent's attitudes, expectations, psychological state of mind, cognitive achievement and family background was obtained at the time of the 1979 and 1980 interviews. These variables are clearly exogenous since they occur long before the measurement of fertility outcomes.

6 RESULTS

6.1 Descriptive Analysis

Table 9.1 shows descriptive information about the substance use, incidence of unintended pregnancy and personal characteristics of the women in the sample. The sample is divided into two racial/ethnic groups:

non-Black, non-Hispanic women and Black and Hispanic women. In addition, means were calculated separately by whether a woman had an unintended pregnancy during the two-year period between the 1984 and

Table 9.1 Substance use and personal characteristics by unintended pregnancy, 1984 NLSY

	Non-Black, Non-Hispanic sample		Black and Hispanic sample	
Variable	Unintended pregnancy	No unintended pregnancy	Unintended pregnancy	No unintended pregnancy
Drug and alcohol use				
Past year use of cocaine *or* marijuana	0.346*	0.286	0.292*	0.210
Past year cocaine *or* marijuana use: yearly frequency of use ≥ 5	0.232	0.200	0.173	0.134
Past year cocaine *and* marijuana use	0.088	0.076	0.051	0.037
Past year cocaine *and* marijuana use: yearly frequency of use ≥ 5	0.088	0.075	0.047	0.037
Number of alcoholic drinks past month	15.912*	12.603	7.719	6.363
Other selected variables				
Contraception use in last month	0.744*	0.840	0.736*	0.801
Two-parent family at age 14	0.684*	0.771	0.490*	0.578
Mother's years of education	11.36	11.67	9.691	9.687
Desired number of children	2.566	2.556	2.518	2.421
Index of self-esteem	32.21	32.18	31.69	32.00
AFQT percentile score	47.05*	51.09	23.28	25.42
Never married	0.434	0.500	0.632	0.646
High school education	0.496	0.443	0.510*	0.431
More than high school education	0.306*	0.411	0.252*	0.364
Proportion of time in labor force last year	0.550*	0.649	0.421*	0.506
Number of observations (%)	228 (8.4)	2479 (91.6)	253 (13.0)	1688 (87.0)

Notes: Drug and alcohol use is measured at the time of the 1984 interview. Unintended pregnancy is measured over a two-year interval following the 1984 survey. Women who did not get pregnant during this period are considered not to have had an unintended pregnancy. An asterisk next to a number indicates a statistically significant ($p < 0.05$) difference between the means.

1986 interviews. All other variables are measured at the time of the 1984 interview or earlier (for example, AFQT (Armed Forces Qualifying Test) percentile score measured in 1980).

The figures in the top half of Table 9.1 show that drug and alcohol use is greater among women who subsequently experience an unintended pregnancy than among women who did not have an unintended pregnancy. This pattern is found for every measure of substance use and is consistent with previous studies that show a positive correlation between substance use and risky sexual behavior. Few of the differences, however, are statistically significant. Among the sample of non-Black, non-Hispanic women, only differences related to past year use of marijuana or cocaine and alcohol use are significant. In the case of Black and Hispanic women, the only significant difference in substance use relates to past year use of cocaine or marijuana. The figures in Table 9.1 also indicate that substance use is greater among non-Black, non-Hispanic women than among Black and Hispanic women, a result found in other surveys of substance use among young adults.

The positive relationship between substance use and unintended pregnancy observed in the top half of Table 9.1 suggests that drug use may be a cause of unintended pregnancy. However, as we have noted repeatedly, such evidence cannot be used to make causal inferences, as there may be a common determinant of both behaviors. In fact, figures in the bottom half of the table are consistent with such a hypothesis. These figures indicate that women who had an unintended pregnancy differ from women who did not have an unintended pregnancy in several significant ways besides substance use. For both racial/ethnic groups, women who had an unintended pregnancy:

- were less likely to use contraception in the last month,
- were more likely to come from a single-parent family,
- have lower levels of education, and
- have spent less time in the labor market in the last year

than women who did not have an unintended pregnancy. These differences in personal characteristics between the two groups raise the possibility that the observed relationship between substance use and sexual behavior and its outcomes is the result of confounding influences. For example, both unintended pregnancy and substance use may stem from problems associated with growing up in a single-parent family. Thus, while the figures in the top half of Table 9.1 are suggestive of a positive relationship between substance use and unintended pregnancy, the figures in the bottom half suggest that a causal interpretation is not warranted.

Below, we explore the effect of substance use on unintended pregnancy in a multivariate context.

We have hypothesized that substance use may affect the incidence of unintended pregnancy through its effect on contraceptive use and the frequency of sexual activity. Given the positive relationship between substance use and unintended pregnancy in Table 9.1, we may also expect to find that substance use is positively related to sexual activity and/or contraception. Accordingly, we have constructed a measure of contraception that includes abstinence (that is, sexual activity) and examined the relationship between substance use and this outcome. In Table 9.2, we present mean substance use by contraception status and the presentation of the table is similar to that of Table 9.1.

Surprisingly, the figures in Table 9.2 indicate that there is little difference in substance use by contraception status for non-Black, non-Hispanic women. This finding contrasts with the results in Table 9.1, which indicated a positive relationship between substance use and unintended pregnancy. Among the sample of Black and Hispanic women, however, there is a significant difference in substance use between women that use contraception and those that do not. Finally, the figures in Table 9.2 indicate that there are even greater differences in personal characteristics between women that do and do not use contraception than between women who had and did not have an unintended pregnancy.

The evidence in Tables 9.1 and 9.2 is mixed. While there is some indication that substance use is positively related to unintended pregnancy, the relationship is not particularly strong. Moreover, there are other observed differences among women that may confound the relationship between substance use and unintended pregnancy. Next, we present the results from a multivariate analysis of the effects of substance use on unintended pregnancy. In this analysis, we use statistical methods to address the issue of confounding due to both measured and unmeasured determinants of unintended pregnancy.

6.2 Multivariate Analysis

Unintended pregnancy

Estimates of the effect of drug and alcohol use on the incidence of unintended pregnancy among non-Black, non-Hispanic women are listed in Table 9.3. A variety of estimates are presented and the table is organized as follows:

- cross-sectional, maximum-likelihood logistic estimates were obtained for 1984 and 1988 (columns 1, 2, 4 and 5);

Table 9.2 Substance use and personal characteristics by contraceptive use, 1984 NLSY

Variable	Non-Black, Non-Hispanic sample		Black and Hispanic sample	
	No contraception in past month	Contraception in past month	No contraception in past month	Contraception in past month
Drug and alcohol use				
Past year use of cocaine *or* marijuana	0.302	0.292	0.297*	0.205
Past year cocaine *or* marijuana use: yearly frequency of use ≥ 5	0.218	0.202	0.207*	0.125
Past year cocaine *and* marijuana use	0.077	0.079	0.052	0.036
Past year cocaine *and* marijuana use: yearly frequency of use ≥ 5	0.075	0.078	0.052	0.035
Number of alcoholic drinks past month	13.39	12.882	10.55*	5.665
Other selected variables				
Two-parent family at age 14	0.721*	0.773	0.486*	0.587
Mother's years of education	11.15*	11.76	9.285*	9.811
Desired number of children	2.574	2.552	2.395	2.456
Index of self-esteem	31.49*	32.29	31.37*	32.14
AFQT percentile score	42.00*	52.63	19.28*	26.82
Never married	0.265*	0.544	0.550*	0.680
High school education	0.463	0.441	0.460*	0.435
More than high school education	0.266*	0.433	0.211*	0.390
Proportion of time in labor force last year	0.583*	0.652	0.421*	0.513
Number of observations (%)	441 (16.8)	2188 (83.2)	387 (20.8)	1475 (79.2)

Notes: Drug and alcohol use is measured at the time of the 1984 interview. Contraception use refers to past month and is defined to include abstinence; those who abstained from sexual activity are defined as using contraception. An asterisk next to a number indicates a statistically significant ($p < 0.05$) difference between the means.

- cross-sectional, ordinary least squares IV estimates were obtained for 1984 and 1988 (columns 3 and 6);[10]
- fixed-effects estimates were obtained using OLS (column 7) and maximum likelihood logistic regression (column 8).

To test whether the estimates were sensitive to model specification, we obtained two sets of cross-sectional logit estimates that differ depending

Table 9.3 Estimates of the effect of drug and alcohol use on the incidence of unintended pregnancy, Non-Black, Non-Hispanic sample

Variable	1984 Logit-model 1	1984 Logit-model 2	1984 OLS IV-model 2	1988 Logit-model 1	1988 Logit-model 2	1988 OLS IV-model 2	Fixed effects OLS-model 2	Fixed effects Logit-model 2
Past year use of cocaine *or* marijuana	0.110	0.067	−0.268	0.109	−0.068	0.330	−0.014	−0.265
	(0.161)	(0.165)	(0.251)	(0.227)	(0.240)	(0.333)	(0.015)	(0.344)
Number of drinks past month	0.006*	0.006*	0.004	0.005 +	0.005 +	0.002	0.001*	0.021*
	(0.003)	(0.003)	(0.004)	(0.003)	(0.003)	(0.004)	(0.0002)	(0.009)
Past year cocaine *or* marijuana use:	−0.042	−0.120	−0.574	0.349	0.183	0.543	−0.027	−0.470
frequency of use ≥ 5	(0.181)	(0.187)	(0.596)	(0.242)	(0.255)	(0.351)	(0.017)	(0.385)
Number of drinks past month	0.007*	0.007*	0.007	0.004	0.004	0.002	0.001*	0.021*
	(0.003)	(0.003)	(0.007)	(0.003)	(0.003)	(0.004)	(0.0003)	(0.009)
Past year cocaine *and* marijuana use	−0.070	−0.170	0.300	0.580 +	0.516	1.590	−0.035	−0.561
	(0.269)	(0.277)	(0.354)	(0.319)	(0.331)	(0.946)	(0.021)	(0.491)
Number of drinks past month	0.007*	0.007*	0.002	0.004	0.003	−0.002	0.001*	0.022*
	(0.003)	(0.003)	(0.004)	(0.003)	(0.003)	(0.006)	(0.0003)	(0.009)
Past year cocaine *and* marijuana use:	−0.019	−0.108	0.261	0.590 +	0.527	1.094	−0.036	−0.505
frequency of use ≥ 5	(0.267)	(0.276)	(0.332)	(0.329)	(0.341)	(0.609)	(0.022)	(0.494)
Number of drinks past month	0.006*	0.007*	0.002	0.004	0.003	0.001	0.001*	0.022*
	(0.003)	(0.003)	(0.004)	(0.003)	(0.003)	(0.004)	(0.0003)	(0.009)
Number of observations	2707			2573			2304	253
Mean of dependent variable	0.084			0.053			−0.028	0.372

Notes: Model 1 includes: family background measures (religious affiliation, mother's education, presence of magazines, newspapers and library card, family structure at age 14), personal characteristics measured in 1979–80 (index of self-esteem, locus of control scale, AFQT percentile score, desired number of children, indicator of traditional values, number of illegal acts), age at interview, region of residence, and urban density. Model 2 includes all variables in Model 1 and: educational attainment, indicator of Aid to Families with Dependent Children (AFDC) program participation in last year, labor force participation in past year, marital status, number of children, number of pregnancies. In fixed-effects models, family background measures, characteristics measured in 1979–80, and region and urban density are omitted since these variables have no variation over time. Standard errors are in parentheses. * indicates p-value < 0.05, + indicates p-value < 0.10.

on which control variables were included in the model (for example, columns 1 and 2). The notes to Table 9.3 list the variables included in each model, but basically, one set of estimates is obtained using a set of control variables that are clearly exogenous (not determined by either substance use or sexual behavior) and another using less plausibly exogenous controls (for example, marital status). Finally, in each column, we show four sets of estimates obtained from separate analyses that differ according to which measure of drug use was included in the model. For example, the first row of Table 9.3 lists the estimates of the effect of alcohol and drug use, where drug use is defined as past year use of marijuana or cocaine. Similarly, the second row in the table lists the estimates of the effect of alcohol and drug use, where drug use is defined as past year use of marijuana or cocaine and an average annual frequency of use of five.

We begin our discussion of the results with the estimates obtained using the sample of women drawn from the 1984 wave of the NLSY (columns 1 through 3). In this year, respondents had a mean age of 23.[11] The cross-sectional logistic estimates indicate that alcohol use is positively associated with the incidence of unintended pregnancy. The estimates associated with alcohol use are statistically significant and relatively small in magnitude. For example, the logistic estimate of 0.007 implies that a woman who had 12 drinks in the last month has a 10 percent greater likelihood of having an unintended pregnancy than does a woman who does not drink.[12] The median number of drinks in the sample is approximately six. The cross-sectional logistic estimates also indicate that drug use has no effect on the incidence of unintended pregnancy, as none of the estimates associated with drug use are statistically significant.

We also obtained estimates of the effect of drug and alcohol use on unintended pregnancy by means of an IV procedure. In this analysis, we replace actual drug and alcohol use with their predicted values. The key aspect of this analysis is that predicted drug and alcohol use are not correlated with unmeasured determinants of unintended pregnancy since drug and alcohol use were predicted using the price of these substances. Variation in the prices of drug and alcohol use does not depend on individual characteristics. We obtained the estimates using OLS regression and the estimates are listed in column 3 of Table 9.3. Since they are from an OLS regression, the magnitudes associated with the coefficients are not directly comparable to the logistic estimates also presented in Table 9.3.

In general, the IV procedure did not yield reliable information as the estimates are imprecisely measured as evidenced by their large standard errors: the standard errors are almost always larger than the estimates. In addition, the IV estimates of the effect of drug and alcohol use are large in magnitude compared to the logistic estimates, a fact that also undermines their credibility. For example, the 0.004 IV estimate associated with alcohol use indicates that a woman who has 12 drinks a month has a 48 percent (0.048/0.084) greater likelihood of having an unintended pregnancy than does a woman who does not drink. It is unfortunate that the IV procedure did not produce more credible estimates since theoretically, these estimates are preferred.

Empirically, the quality of the IV estimates depends critically on the adequacy of the instruments used to predict the endogenous variable, which in this case is substance use. We used three instruments to predict drug and alcohol use: the state-specific price of cocaine derived from the Drug Enforcement Administration's System to Retrieve Information from Drug Evidence (STRIDE), the state-specific beer tax taken from the Brewers' Almanac and the minimum legal drinking age in the respondent's state. We also used one-year leads and lags of the cocaine prices and beer tax. Marijuana prices are not available, but there is considerable evidence that cocaine, marijuana and alcohol are related in consumption (Saffer and Chaloupka 1999). Thus, variation in cocaine and alcohol prices should explain variation in marijuana consumption. The imprecision of the IV estimates suggests that the instruments we used were not sufficiently correlated with substance use to obtain credible IV estimates of the effect of substance use on unintended pregnancy. Therefore, we do not place much emphasis on these estimates and present them for purposes of completeness.

Estimates obtained using the 1988 wave of the NLSY are also listed in Table 9.3. Since the NLSY is a panel, the women in the sample are approximately four years older at the time of the 1988 survey. The cross-sectional logistic estimates (columns 4 and 5) indicate that both alcohol and drug use are positively associated with unintended pregnancy. The estimates, however, are in most instances only marginally ($p<0.20$) significant. In addition, the results associated with drug use indicate that only the measures of more involved use are positively associated with unintended pregnancy. The logistic estimates of the effect of alcohol are between 0.003 and 0.005 depending on which measure of drug use is included in the model. These estimates suggest that 12 additional drinks per month increase the probability of an unintended pregnancy by between 3 and 6 percent. Estimates of the effect of drug use are mostly positive and excluding the estimates associated with the broadest measure of drug use (row 1) are between 0.18 and 0.59. These estimates indicate that women who use drugs have a probability of having an unintended pregnancy that is 17 to 55 percent higher than women who do not use drugs. There also appears to be a dose–response relationship since the measures of drug use that indicate more involved use have a larger effect than measures that include casual users.

The final set of estimates listed in Table 9.3 is the fixed-effects estimates (columns 7 and 8). These estimates are obtained using the difference in individual outcomes and characteristics between 1984 and 1988. The fixed-effects estimation strategy accounts for unmeasured individual characteristics that may confound the relationship between substance use and unintended pregnancy. Estimates were obtained using OLS and logistic regression. The sample for the logistic regression is greatly reduced, however, because only those women who experience a change in unintended pregnancy between the two years are used in the analysis (Chamberlain 1980).

Both sets of fixed-effects estimates indicate that alcohol use is positively and significantly related to unintended pregnancy. The magnitudes of the estimates are larger than the cross-sectional estimates previously reported. In this case, 12 additional drinks per month increase the likelihood of an unintended pregnancy by approximately 17 percent. The fixed-effects estimates of the effect of drug use are never statistically significant, although in each case they are negative and relatively large. The negative fixed-effects estimates contrast with the positive cross-sectional logistic estimates.

Table 9.4 contains estimates of the effect of substance use on unintended pregnancy for Black and Hispanic women and is organized in a similar way as Table 9.3. Few estimates are statistically significant. The estimates of the effect of alcohol use are small and statistically insignificant. This is true for the logistic estimates in 1984, 1988 and the fixed-effects estimates. Therefore, it does not appear that alcohol use is associated with unintended pregnancy for this group of women. Estimates of the effect of drug use on unintended pregnancy are in the vast majority of cases statistically insignificant, but the cross-sectional logistic estimates are all positive and relatively large in magnitude. The lack of statistical significance may be due to inadequate statistical power caused by the relatively small sample size and the low incidence of unintended pregnancy and drug use. The lack of statistical power may obscure a true drug effect. However, the fixed-effects estimates of the effect of drug use are negative and sometimes statistically significant. Based on this evidence, we conclude that drug use does not have a systematic effect on unintended pregnancy for Black and Hispanic women.

Contraception

We hypothesized that substance use may be related to unintended

Table 9.4 Estimates of the effect of drug and alcohol use on the incidence of unintended pregnancy, Black and Hispanic sample

	1984			1988			Fixed effects	
Variable	Logit-Model 1	Logit-Model 2	OLS IV-Model 2	Logit-Model 1	Logit-Model 2	OLS IV-Model 2	OLS-Model 2	Logit-Model 2
Past year use of cocaine *or* marijuana	0.352*	0.288 +	0.393	0.250	0.108	–0.299	0.013	0.134
	(0.167)	(0.172)	(0.358)	(0.245)	(0.250)	(0.236)	(0.026)	(0.289)
Number of drinks past month	0.000	0.000	–0.006	–0.001	–0.001	–0.005	0.0003	0.001
	(0.004)	(0.004)	(0.008)	(0.004)	(0.004)	(0.005)	(0.0005)	(0.008)
Past year cocaine *or* marijuana use:	0.181	0.111	0.380	0.081	–0.099	–0.456	–0.088*	–0.830*
frequency of use ≥ 5	(0.203)	(0.209)	(0.492)	(0.302)	(0.309)	(0.353)	(0.031)	(0.352)
Number of drinks past month	0.002	0.001	–0.008	0.000	–0.000	–0.001	0.0005	0.003
	(0.004)	(0.004)	(0.011)	(0.004)	(0.004)	(0.006)	(0.0005)	(0.008)
Past year cocaine *and* marijuana use	0.260	0.172	–0.061	0.470	0.333	–0.555	–0.092*	–0.412
	(0.336)	(0.344)	(0.547)	(0.409)	(0.416)	(0.430)	(0.046)	(0.477)
Number of drinks past month	0.002	0.001	–0.001	–0.001	–0.001	–0.002	0.0004	0.001
	(0.004)	(0.004)	(0.007)	(0.004)	(0.004)	(0.006)	(0.0005)	(0.008)
Past year cocaine *and* marijuana use:	0.165	0.072	–0.132	0.475	0.331	–0.659	–0.120*	–0.645
frequency of use ≥ 5	(0.346)	(0.355)	(0.521)	(0.432)	(0.438)	(0.515)	(0.049)	(0.522)
Number of drinks past month	0.002	0.002	–0.000	–0.000	–0.001	–0.002	0.0003	0.001
	(0.004)	(0.004)	(0.007)	(0.004)	(0.004)	(0.006)	(0.0005)	(0.008)
Number of observations	1941			1813			1609	309
Mean of dependent variable	0.130			0.084			–0.049	0.372

Note: See notes to Table 9.3.

pregnancy because of its effect on the frequency of sexual activity and use of contraception. In this section we explicitly test this hypothesis and present the results from analysis of substance use on an outcome that combines sexual activity and contraception. We refer to this outcome as contraception since abstinence may be considered a form of contraception (that is, fertility control). The motivation for this analysis stems from a desire to check the robustness of our findings related to unintended pregnancy. For example, we found that among non-Black, non-Hispanic women, alcohol use was associated with a greater incidence of unintended pregnancy. Therefore, we would expect to find that alcohol use is associated with less contraception as currently defined – either greater frequency of sexual activity and/or less use of contraception. Similarly, among the sample of Black and Hispanic women, substance use was statistically unrelated to unintended pregnancy. Thus, we would expect that substance use would be unrelated to contraception.

Table 9.5 lists the estimates of the effect of substance use on contraception. It is organized in a similar fashion to Tables 9.3 and 9.4, although since there was only one year of data it was not possible to obtain fixed-effects estimates. The cross-sectional logistic estimates (columns 1 and 2) associated with the non-Black, non-Hispanic sample indicates that alcohol use is associated with less contraception, although only a few of the estimates are statistically significant. This finding is consistent with earlier findings that showed a positive relationship between alcohol use and unintended pregnancy. There is no evidence, however, to suggest that drug use is associated with contraception for non-Black, non-Hispanic women. While the findings related to alcohol use appear to be consistent with earlier findings, the cross-sectional nature of the analysis prevents a causal interpretation of such results. We note that these cross-sectional estimates are subject to the criticism that some unmeasured variables may be confounding the relationship between alcohol use and use of contraception including abstinence. To address the issue of causality, we obtained instrumental variables estimates. The IV estimates in Table 9.5, however, are plagued by the same empirical problems noted in regard to Tables 9.3 and 9.4: the instruments used to predict substance use were not sufficiently correlated with substance use to obtain precise estimates. Therefore, we shall not discuss them and again present them only for purposes of completeness.

Table 9.5 also contains the estimates of the effect of substance use on contraception for the sample of Black and Hispanic women. The cross-sectional logistic estimates (columns 4 and 5) of the effect of both alcohol and drug use are negative and statistically significant. The magnitudes of the effect of alcohol are relatively small. A woman who has 12 drinks per

Table 9.5 Effect of drug and alcohol use on contraception in last month maximum likelihood logit estimates, 1984 sample

Variable	Non-Black, Non-Hispanic sample			Black and Hispanic sample		
	Logit-Model 1	Logit-Model 2	OLS IV-Model 2	Logit-Model 1	Logit-Model 2	OLS IV-Model 2
Past year use of cocaine *or* marijuana	−0.097 (0.114)	−0.161 (0.121)	−0.462 (0.409)	−0.361* (0.137)	−0.461* (0.144)	−0.041 (0.361)
Number of drinks past month	−0.001 (0.002)	−0.003 (0.003)	0.004 (0.006)	−0.011* (0.003)	−0.012* (0.003)	−0.004 (0.009)
Past year cocaine *or* marijuana use: frequency of use ≥ 5	−0.107 (0.129)	−0.096 (0.136)	−0.826 (0.818)	−0.449** (0.161)	−0.469** (0.169)	0.134 (0.450)
Number of drinks past month	−0.001 (0.002)	−0.004 (0.002)	0.008 (0.008)	−0.010** (0.003)	−0.012** (0.003)	−0.007 (0.011)
Past year cocaine *and* marijuana use	0.049 (0.198)	−0.005 (0.209)	0.195 (0.440)	−0.356 (0.254)	−0.423 (0.261)	−0.205 (0.592)
Number of drinks past month	−0.001 (0.002)	−0.004 + (0.002)	0.001 (0.005)	−0.012** (0.003)	−0.013** (0.003)	−0.003 (0.008)
Past year cocaine *and* marijuana use: frequency of use ≥ 5	0.081 (0.201)	0.013 (0.212)	0.232 (0.421)	−0.397 (0.255)	−0.453 + (0.262)	−0.180 (0.554)
Number of drinks past month	−0.001 (0.002)	−0.004 + (0.002)	0.001 (0.005)	−0.012** (0.003)	−0.013** (0.003)	−0.003 (0.008)
Number of observations	3084			2106		
Mean of dependent variable	0.823			0.783		

Notes
See notes to Table 9.3.
* = p-value < 0.05.
** = p-value < 0.01.

month is approximately 11 percent more likely not to use contraception than is a woman who does not drink. In contrast, the drug effects are relatively large. A woman who used both cocaine and marijuana in the past year is approximately 30 percent more likely not to use contraception.

The large drug effects, however, need to be interpreted with caution for two reasons. First, they are inconsistent with previous results that showed no relationship between drug use and unintended pregnancy. This suggests that (Black and Hispanic) women who use drugs are less likely to use contraception than women who do not use drugs, and consequently they are more likely to experience a pregnancy. However, women who use drugs do not view this additional pregnancy as unintended. This combination of results may obtain if women who use drugs wanted larger families than women who did not use drugs, but the desired number of children is being held constant in the analysis. Thus, it is difficult to easily reconcile the different findings associated with Tables 9.4 and 9.5. A second reason to be cautious is the absence of a dose–response effect. Use of marijuana *or* cocaine in the past year has the same effect as use of marijuana *and* cocaine combined with significant frequency of use of these substances. The latter measure of drug use should identify relatively involved users and the estimate associated with it should be larger than the estimate associated with the measure of more casual use. The absence of such a dose–response effect suggests that there may be an omitted factor correlated with drug use and contraception use. Cross-sectional estimates in Table 9.4 indicated that drug use had relatively large, although insignificant, effects on unintended pregnancy among Black and Hispanic women. Fixed-effect estimates, however, showed the opposite, suggesting that there were important omitted personality traits that were confounding the relationship between drug use and unintended pregnancy. We believe that the omitted variable problem may also be confounding estimates in Table 9.5, but are prevented from testing this hypothesis due to data limitations.

7 CONCLUSIONS

Unintended pregnancy is a serious social problem. A recent Institute of Medicine (IOM) report entitled *The Best Intentions: Unintended Pregnancy and the Well-Being of Children and Families* (Brown and Eisenberg 1995), concludes that 'the consequences of unintended pregnancy are serious, imposing appreciable burdens on children, women, men and families' (p.1). Policies directed at reducing unintended pregnancy, the report continues, would reduce the risk of adverse outcomes for infants and children. The committee on unintended pregnancy therefore, 'urges, first and foremost, that the nation adopt a new social norm: All pregnancies should be intended' (p. 3). To this end, it recommends 'a multifaceted, long-term campaign to (1) educate the public about the major social and public health burdens of unintended pregnancy and (2) stimulate a comprehensive set of activities at national, state, and local levels to reduce such pregnancies' (p. 4).

Although not mentioned in the IOM report, one potential cause of unintended pregnancy may be substance use. In this study we have investigated this question by examining the effect of drug and alcohol use on the incidence of unintended pregnancy and contraception use. Our study provides the first direct evidence of the effect of substance use on unintended pregnancy. It is related to previous studies that examined the effect of substance use on the determinants of unintended pregnancy (for example, sexual activity and contraception use), although we examined a slightly older group than previous studies. Importantly, ours is one of the few studies that worried about causality.

We carried out this analysis using data on a nationally representative sample of young adults between the ages of 19 and 32 drawn from the National Longitudinal Survey of Youth. Our empirical analysis included both descriptive and multivariate analyses of the relationship between substance use and unintended pregnancy. We also paid particular attention to the issue of causality and used statistical methods appropriate for obtaining causal estimates of the effect of substance use on unintended pregnancy. These methods included the fixed-effects and IV methodology. Unfortunately, the IV methodology did not prove useful as estimates obtained by this method were imprecisely measured and unreliable. The fixed-effects estimates, however, were more informative and provided evidence that in some cases were consistent with cross-sectional estimates, but in other cases failed to confirm the cross-sectional estimates. Since the fixed-effects estimates are theoretically preferable, we emphasize them in our conclusions. In addition to using appropriate statistical procedures to address the issue of causality, we also included an extensive set of family background measures and personal characteristics to control for the influence of these factors on our outcomes of interest.

The results of our analyses indicated the following:

- alcohol consumption decreased the use of contraception among non-Black, non-Hispanic women;
- alcohol consumption increased the incidence of unintended pregnancy among non-Black, non-Hispanic women;
- drug use had no statistically significant effect on contraception or unintended pregnancy for non-Black, non-Hispanic women;
- alcohol and drug use had no statistically significant effect on unintended pregnancy for Black and Hispanic women; and
- alcohol and drug use had a strong negative association with contraception use in cross-sectional analyses for Black and Hispanic women.

The last bulleted result warrants a caveat. The strong negative association between substance use and contraception use among Black and Hispanic women is, in our opinion, not particularly credible. This result is inconsistent with the findings related to substance use and unintended pregnancy and the absence of a dose–response effect in regard to drug use leads us to conclude that this result is primarily due to confounding from an omitted factor.

Our results are somewhat inconsistent with previous studies that have tended to show a stronger relationship between substance use and the determinants of unintended pregnancy. This is true whether we consider the simple descriptive analyses presented in Tables 9.1 and 9.2 or the multivariate analyses in Tables 9.3 through 9.5. Two reasons may explain the difference. First, our sample consists of older persons. The mean age of our sample was 23 in 1984 and 27 in 1988. Second, we examine the effect of substance use on outcomes that depend on use of contraception and sexual activity. Previous studies have examined these outcomes separately. Moreover, separate analyses may lead researchers to conclude incorrectly that substance use leads to more risky sex if substance use is associated with less contraception, but also less sexual activity. For example, a typical analysis will look at contraception only among those who are sexually active and find that substance use is negatively related to use of contraception. Accordingly, they conclude that substance use increases risky sex. However, substance use may be related to sexual activity, and may increase abstinence. Perhaps substance use makes it more difficult to find a partner because of the stigma associated with such use, or substance use may dampen motivation and cause a decrease in efforts to find partners. In this case, substance use may have no effect on unintended pregnancy or a measure of contraception that includes abstinence.

In conclusion, our study has found that alcohol use increases the incidence of unintended pregnancy and decreases the use of contraception among non-Black, non-Hispanic women. This result suggests that public policies aimed at reducing alcohol consumption among young adults will reduce unintended pregnancy and the adverse consequences associated with it. The evidence we have presented also provides support for programs that target the link between alcohol use and sexual behavior. Whether any particular program should be implemented or expanded, however, ultimately relies on whether it is cost effective, but our results suggest that such programs have a legitimate and valid basis.

NOTES

1. These figures are derived from data presented in Henshaw (1998) and Forrest and Singh (1990). To estimate the number of unwanted births, we used the

distribution of pregnancy intention status reported in Forrest and Singh.

2 Unintended pregnancy is also prevalent among women aged 20 to 24. In 1994, 59 percent of all pregnancies and 39 percent of all births were unintended among this group of women. These figures represent a decline in the percentages of unintended pregnancies and births since 1988, but are similar to percentages in 1982 (Forrest and Singh 1990; Forrest 1994).

3 See Harvey and Beckman (1986); Yamaguchi and Kandel (1987); Mott and Haurin (1988); Elliot and Morse (1989); Kandel (1989); Biglan et al. (1990); Ensminger (1990); Hingson et al. (1990); Leigh (1990); Rosenbaum and Kandel (1990); Gold et al. (1991, 1992); Gold and Skinner (1992); Orr et al. (1991); Shafer and Boyer (1991); Mensch and Kandel (1992); Strunin and Hingson (1992); Leigh (1993); Leigh and Stall (1993); Shafer et al. (1993); Cooper et al. (1994); Laumann et al. (1994); Lowry et al. (1994); Senf and Price (1994); Donovan and McEwan (1995); de Gaston et al. (1995); Graves and Leigh (1995); Harvey and Spigner (1995); Fergusson and Lynskey (1996); Fortenberry et al. (1997); Jakobsen et al. (1997); Kaestner (1997, 1998); and Kowaleski-Jones and Mott (1998). This list excludes studies that describe sexual behavior among specific groups of substance abusers such as alcoholics and intravenous drug users.

4 OLS methods in this application are very similar to Chamberlain's random effects probit model. This can be illustrated as follows:

$$Y_{it} = \alpha_i + \beta X_{it} + v_{it} \qquad (9.i)$$
$$Y_{i(t-1)} = \alpha_i + \beta X_{i(t-1)} + v_{i(t-1)} \qquad (9.ii)$$
$$\alpha_i = \pi_1 X_{it} + \pi_2 X_{i(t-1)} \qquad (9.iii)$$

Chamberlain (1984) suggests substituting (9.iii) into (9.i) and (9.ii) to yield:

$$Y_{it} = (\beta + \pi_1) X_{it} + \pi_2 X_{i(t-1)} + v_{it} \qquad (9.iv)$$
$$Y_{i(t-1)} = \pi_1 X_{it} + (\beta + \pi_2) X_{i(t-1)} + v_{i(t-1)} \qquad (9.v)$$

The next step is to estimate (9.iv) and (9.v) using maximum likelihood probit methods and to impose cross-equation restrictions to obtain an estimate of β. In the linear model, we can subtract (9.iv) from (9.v) to derive the standard fixed-effects model that uses first differences of the data.

5 Also note that the IV procedure produces unbiased estimates when there is a time-varying person-specific effect as long as predicted drug use is not correlated with this time-varying factor. Since variation in predicted drug use comes from variation in prices, which is expected to be uncorrelated with person-specific factors, the IV estimate is unbiased even in this case.

6 The eligible population includes those respondents who were not intentionally dropped from the sample. In 1985, the NLSY dropped a subsample of military

participants and in 1991, dropped a subsample of disadvantaged white youths.

7 The 1984 survey contained the most extensive set of questions related to drug use, including questions about the use of a variety of illicit drugs. In 1988 and 1992, the drug-use section of the survey was restricted to marijuana and cocaine use.

8 Most studies use five or more drinks as a measure of heavy alcohol use, but the NLSY questionnaire used six or more drinks as a threshold. Therefore, data limitations force us to use this higher threshold.

9 In this analysis we omitted women who were pregnant at the time of interview.

10 Based on the results from the OLS regressions, we decided it was not worthwhile to pursue other estimation strategies. We comment more on this later in the text.

11 We tested whether the effect of substance use differed by age but the results indicated that there were no significant differences by age.

12 The marginal effect of alcohol on the probability of unintended pregnancy is calculated based on the following approximation: $b\ [P(1-P)]$ where b is the coefficient (0.007) and P is the mean probability of unintended pregnancy (0.084).

REFERENCES

Biglan A., C.W. Metzler, R. Wirt, D. Ary, J. Noell, L. Ochs, C. French and D. Hood (1990), 'Social and behavioral factors associated with high-risk sexual behavior among adolescents', *Journal of Behavioral Medicine*, **13**: 245–61.

Bound J., D.A. Jaeger and R.M. Baker (1995), 'Problems with instrumental variables estimation when the correlation between the instruments and the endogenous explanatory variables is weak', *Journal of the American Statistical Association*, **90**: 443–50.

Brown S.S. and L. Eisenberg (eds) (1995), *The Best Intentions: Unintended Pregnancy and the Well-being of Children and Families*, Washington, DC: National Academy Press.

Center for Human Resource Research, Ohio State University (1994), *NLS Handbook*, Columbus, OH: Ohio State University.

Chamberlain, G. (1980), 'Analysis of covariance with qualitative data', *Review of Economic Studies*, **47**: 225–38.

Chamberlain G. (1984), 'Panel data', in Z. Griliches and M.D. Intriligator (eds), *Handbook of Econometrics*, Vol. II, Amsterdam: North-Holland, pp. 1248–318.

Cooper M.L., R.S. Peirce and R.F. Huselid (1994), 'Substance use and sexual risk taking among black adolescents and white adolescents',

Health Psychology, **13**: 251–62.

de Gaston J.F., L. Jensen and S. Weed (1995), 'A closer look at adolescent sexual activity', *Journal of Youth and Adolescence*, pp. 465–77.

Donovan C. and R. McEwan (1995), 'A review of the literature examining the relationship between alcohol use and HIV-related sexual risk-taking in young people', *Addiction*, **90**: 319–28.

Elliott, D.S. and B.J. Morse (1989), 'Delinquency and drug use as risk factors in teenage sexual activity', *Youth & Society*, **21**: 32–60.

Ensminger, M.E. (1990), 'Sexual activity and problem behaviors among black, urban adolescents', *Child Development*, **60**: 2032–46.

Fergusson, D.M. and M.T. Lynskey (1996), 'Alcohol misuse and adolescent sexual behaviors and risk taking', *Pediatrics*, **98**: 91–6.

Forrest, J.D. (1994), 'Preventing unwanted pregnancy: the role of hormonal contraceptives', *American Journal of Obstetrics and Gynecology*, **170**: 485–9.

Forrest, J.D. and S. Singh (1990), 'The sexual and reproductive behavior of American women, 1982–1988', *Family Planning Perspectives*, **22**(5): 206–14.

Fortenberry J.D., D.P. Orr, B.P. Katz, E.J. Brizendine and M.J. Blythe (1997), 'Sex under the influence: a diary self-report study of substance use and sexual behavior among adolescent women', *Sexually Transmitted Diseases*, **24**: 313–21.

Gold, R.S., A. Karmiloff–Smith, M.J. Skinner and J. Morton (1992), 'Situational factors and thought processes associated with unprotected intercourse in heterosexual students', *AIDS Care*, **4**: 305–23.

Gold, R.S. and M.J. Skinner (1992), 'Situational factors and thought processes associated with unprotected intercourse in young gay men', *AIDS*, **6**: 1021–30.

Gold, R.S., M.J. Skinner, P.J. Grant and D.C. Plummer (1991), 'Situational factors and thought processes associated with unprotected intercourse in gay men', *Psychology and Health*, **5**: 259–78.

Graves, K.L. and B.C. Leigh (1995), 'The relationship of substance use to sexual activity among young adults in the United States', *Family Planning Perspectives*, **27**: 18–33.

Grossman, M. and F. J. Chaloupka (1998), 'A rational addiction model of cocaine use', *Journal of Health Economics*, **17**: 427–74.

Grossman, M., F.J. Chaloupka and I. Sirtalan (1998), 'An empirical analysis of alcohol addiction: results from the Monitoring the Future panels', *Economic Inquiry*, **36**(January): 39–48.

Harvey, S.M. and L.J. Beckman (1986), 'Alcohol consumption, female sexual behavior and contraceptive use', *Journal of Studies on Alcohol*, **47**: 327–32.

Harvey, S.M. and C. Spigner (1995), 'Factors associated with sexual behavior among adolescents: a multivariate analysis', *Adolescence*, **30**(118): 253–64.

Heckman, J.J. and T. MaCurdy (1985), 'A simultaneous linear probability model', *Canadian Journal of Economics*, **18**: 27–37.

Henshaw, S.K. (1998), 'Unintended pregnancy in the United States', *Family Planning Perspectives*, **30**: 24–9.

Hingson, R.W., L. Strunin, B.M. Berlin and T. Heeren (1990), 'Beliefs about AIDS, use of alcohol and drugs, and unprotected sex among Massachusetts adolescents', *American Journal of Public Health*, **80**: 295–99.

Jakobsen, R., J. Rise, H. Aas and N. Anderssen (1997), 'Noncoital sexual interactions and problem behavior among young adolescents: the Norwegian Longitudinal Health Behavior Study', *Journal of Adolescence*, **20**: 71–83.

Kaestner, R. (1997), 'The effects of cocaine and marijuana use on marriage and marital stability', *Journal of Family Issues*, **18**(2): 145–73.

Kaestner, R. (1998), 'Drug use, culture and welfare incentives: correlates of family structure and out-of-wedlock birth', *Eastern Economic Journal*, **24**: 395–416.

Kandel, D.B. (1989), 'Issues of sequencing of adolescent drug use and other problem behaviors', *Journal of Drug Issues*, **53**: 55–76.

Kowaleski-Jones, L. and F.L. Mott (1998), 'Sex, contraception and childbearing among high-risk youth: do different factors influence males and females?', *Family Planning Perspectives*, **30**(4): 163–9.

Laumann, E.O., J.H. Gagnon, R.T. Michael and S. Michaels (1994), *The Social Organization of Sexuality: Sexual Practices in the United States*, Chicago: University of Chicago Press.

Leigh, B.C. (1990), 'Alcohol and unsafe sex: an overview of research and theory', *Alcohol, Immunomodulation, and AIDS*, pp. 35–46.

Leigh, B.C. (1993), Alcohol consumption and sexual activity as reported with a diary technique', *Journal of Abnormal Psychology*, **102**: 490–93.

Leigh, B.C. and R. Stall (1993), 'Substance use and risky sexual behavior for exposure to HIV: issues in methodology, interpretation, and prevention', *American Psychologist*, **48**: 1035–45.

Lowry, R., D. Holzman, B.I. Truman, L. Kann, J.L. Collins and L.J. Kolbe (1994), 'Substance use and HIV-related sexual behavior among US high school students: are they related?', *American Journal of Public Health*, **84**: 1116–20.

Mensch, B. and D.B. Kandel (1992), 'Drug use as a risk factor of premarital teen pregnancy and abortion in a national sample of young white women', *Demography*, **29**(3): 409–29.

Michael, R.T., J.H. Gagnon, E.O. Laumann and G. Kolata (1994), *Sex in America: A Definitive Survey*, New York: Little, Brown & Company.

Michael, R.T. and R.J. Willis (1975), 'Contraception and fertility: household production under uncertainty', in Nestor E. Terleckyj (ed.), *Household Production and Consumption*, New York: Columbia University Press, pp. 27–93.

Mott, F.L. and R.J. Haurin (1988), 'Linkages between sexual activity and alcohol and drug use among American adolescents', *Family Planning Perspectives*, **20**(3): 107–15.

Orr, D.P., M. Beiter and G. Ingersoll (1991), 'Premature sexual activity as an indicator of psychosocial risk', *Pediatrics*, **87**: 141–7.

Poole, V.L., L.V. Klerman, J.S. Flowers and R.L. Goldenberg (1997), 'Pregnancy intendedness and maternal behavior in a low-income, high risk population', *Journal of Nursing Science*, **2**: 133–41.

Rosenbaum, E. and D. Kandel (1990), 'Early onset of adolescent sexual behavior and drug involvement', *Journal of Marriage and the Family*, **52**: 783–98.

Saffer, H. and F.J. Chaloupka (1999), 'The demand for illicit drugs', *Economic Inquiry*, **37**: 401–11.

Senf, J.H. and C.Q. Price (1994), 'Young adults, alcohol and condom use: what is the connection?', *Journal of Adolescent Health*, **15**: 238–44.

Shafer, M.A. and C.B. Boyer (1991), 'Psychosocial and behavioral factors associated with risk of sexually transmitted diseases, including human immunodeficiency virus infection among urban high school students', *Journal of Pediatrics*, **119**: 826–33.

Shafer, M.A., J.F. Hilton, M. Ekstrand, J. Keogh, L. Gee and L. Digiorgio-Haag (1993), 'Relationship between drug use and sexual behaviors and the occurrence of sexually transmitted diseases among high-risk male youth', *Sexually Transmitted Diseases*, **30**: 307–13.

Strunin L. and R. Hingson (1992), 'Alcohol, drugs, and adolescent sexual behavior', *International Journal of Addictions*, **27**: 129–46.

White, Halbert (1980), 'A heteroscedasticity-consistent covariance matrix estimator and a direct test for heteroscedasticity', *Econometrica*, **48**: 149–70.

Yamaguchi, K. and D.B. Kandel (1987), 'Drug use and other determinants of premarital pregnancy and its outcome: a dynamic analysis of competing life events', *Journal of Marriage and the Family*, **49**(2): 257–70.

Zabin, L.S. and S.C. Hayward (1994), *Adolescent Sexual Behavior and Childbearing*, New York: Sage.

Mensch, [illegible] and [illegible] Kandel [illegible] (1988), [illegible] in [illegible] *Public Health* [illegible] (1), [illegible].

10. Substance use and workplace attendance

Michael T. French, Alphonse G. Holtmann, Kerry Anne McGeary and Gary A. Zarkin*

1 INTRODUCTION

Although it is well documented that drug use lowers physical and emotional capabilities (for example, Chait et al. 1985; Herning et al. 1989; and Yesavage et al. 1985), economic studies have found somewhat conflicting relationships between substance use and earnings (for example, Buchmueller and Zuvekas 1998; Gill and Michaels 1992; Register and Williams 1992; Kandel and Davies 1990; Mullahy and Sindelar 1989, 1991; French et al. 1998). Surprisingly, some studies have found a positive association between substance use and earnings (for example, Berger and Leigh 1988; Kaestner 1993, 1994; French and Zarkin 1995; Heien 1996; Zarkin et al. 1998a). While it is difficult to reconcile a positive relationship between substance use and earnings, plausible hypotheses may be consistent with the insignificant results. First, it is possible that substance use may affect physical and emotional abilities, but these factors may not be important determinants of workers' productivity in some workplace situations. Second, substance use may affect productivity, but employers may be unable to adjust workers' wages (at least in the short run) to reflect performance changes. Wages are complex in many organizations and it may take several months or years before employers recognize that a worker has a substance use problem. Finally, it is possible that existing statistical models and data sets are not well suited to uncovering the influence of substance use on wages or productivity. Kaestner (1998) and French et al. (1998) provide recent and detailed reviews of the literature on substance use and earnings.

Rather than estimating the association between substance use and wages or earnings, this study used data from two worksites (hospital and school district) to analyse the direct impact of substance use on two factors related to worker productivity: the number of days during the past year that an employee was absent from work (full absenteeism) and the number of days during the past year that an employee either arrived late to work or left early from work (partial absenteeism). Substance use was measured by three variables related to cigarette smoking, alcohol use, and illicit drug use. Focusing on attendance rather than wages, our primary hypothesis was that substance use negatively influenced workplace attendance, which was directly related to worker productivity. To our knowledge, this is one of the few studies to investigate empirically the relationships between substance use and workplace attendance (see also, French et al. 1998; Kandel and Davies 1990).

2 EMPIRICAL MODEL

Substance users may be less productive per hour and they may be unable to supply as many hours per year to the labor market as non-substance users (Kaestner 1993; Mullahy and Sindelar 1996; Zarkin et al. 1998b). Substance use can also negatively affect the amount of human capital investment an individual makes, leading to a reduction in educational attainment, which in turn has a profound impact on occupational choice (Cook and Moore 1993). This situation would be especially true if heavy substance use or substance abuse began during an individual's late teens or twenties, a period of intensive human capital investment.

These considerations suggest that no simple and direct way exists to portray the relationship between substance use and workplace attendance. Because of these complexities and data constraints, our analysis involved a reduced-form labor market model based on standard human capital theory (for example, Mincer 1974; French and Zarkin 1995, 1998; French et al. 1998; French and Zarkin 1998). To determine the relationships between various measures of substance use and employee attendance, we estimated separate equations for women and men because it is well documented that women have higher absenteeism rates and different labor market behavior relative to men (Kandel and Davies 1990; Mullahy and Sindelar 1996; Kaestner 1994). Attendance was measured by (i) the number of full days an individual reported being absent from work and (ii) the number of days that the individual reported arriving late to work or leaving early from work. Both measures applied to the previous 12 months.[1]

The final specifications included the two attendance variables and separate equations for the number of cigarettes smoked per day in the last 12 months, the number of alcoholic drinks consumed in the last 12 months, and a dichotomous variable for any illicit drug use in the last 12 months.[2] Thus, we report results from six regressions for female employees and six regressions for male employees. Separate regressions were estimated for each substance use measure because of strong multicollinearity among these variables. Nevertheless, we also examined comorbidity effects of multiple substance use by including all three measures in the same specification. The comorbidity results are reported after the core set of findings. In general, we believe that workplace attendance can be described by the following relationship:

$$A_i = f(\boldsymbol{X}_i, OCC_i, W_i, YR_i, H_i, SU_i) \tag{10.1}$$

where A_i is a measure of annual absenteeism for individual i (that is, days absent from work, days arrived to work late or left work early), $\boldsymbol{X}_i$ is a vector of demographic variables (for example, age, race, education), OCC_i represents indicator variables for different occupations (for example, management/professional, service), W_i represents measures for work status and individual 'exposure' effects (for example, full-time status, weeks worked), YR_i represents dummy variables for survey year (that is, 1996 and 1997), H_i is an indicator variable for the hospital worksite, and SU_i is a measure for substance use (either smoking, drinking, or illicit drug use).

The self-reported attendance measures were based on full days of absenteeism (full absenteeism) and days arriving late or leaving early (partial absenteeism). Both attendance measures were reported categorically by respondents and then converted to continuous measures by taking the midpoint of the categories.

Since both measures of attendance are non-negative count variables, it is best to estimate these relationships with a technique that explicitly deals with the discrete nature of the dependent variables rather than ordinary least squares (OLS) (Greene 1997; Long 1997). However, the traditional Poisson count data models restrict variance to be equal to the conditional mean. In situations where the variance is not equal to the conditional mean (for example, overdispersion), the negative binomial technique is more appropriate. We tested for overdispersion in every equation and rejected the Poisson technique in favor of the negative binomial technique in all cases (StataCorp. 1999).

Another factor must be considered when estimating count variable models such as full and partial absenteeism. The number of counts or events for any individual is conditional on the exposure period over which events can be recorded. If the exposure period is identical for all individuals (for example, number of days absent during the previous week for full-time workers) then no correction in the model is necessary. In our example, however, both measures of absenteeism during the past year were conditional on the number of weeks worked during the past 12 months and work status (that is, full time or part time). Following Hausman et al. (1984) in their analysis of research and development (R&D) expenditures and patents, we controlled for exposure by including the log of weeks worked and a dummy variable for full-time work in the negative binomial models. Thus, the resulting analysis allows for both 'exposure' effects and 'overdispersion' in the data.

3 SAMPLE AND DATA

The data for this analysis were collected in three annual and independent cross-sections beginning in 1995 as part of a larger study to design, implement, and evaluate a new employee assistance program (EAP) outreach intervention. Approximately 600 employees were randomly and anonymously selected each year (1995, 1996, and 1997) from the roster of all employees at two worksites in a midwestern community. Upon their selection, the employees were asked to complete a confidential questionnaire on workplace policies, practices, and perceptions. The respondents also answered questions regarding personal characteristics, job performance and earnings, and their use of cigarettes, alcohol, and illicit drugs. The questionnaires were administered by a survey research professional from the Research Triangle Institute (RTI) who was unaffiliated with either worksite. All respondents were guaranteed anonymity. Participation was voluntary, each respondent was given a small gift certificate, and they were eligible for a $500 cash lottery. The survey took about 30 minutes to complete and the overall response rate was greater than 80 percent at both worksites.[3]

Worksite 1 is a non-profit hospital with approximately 2600 full- and part-time workers. Some employees work at various satellite clinics or home health locations, but most employees are located at the main hospital. Worksite 2 is a relatively large school district with about 3800 full- and part-time employees. School district employees are scattered around the city and county in various schools, administrative facilities, and maintenance facilities. The school district employs a wide range of workers, including teachers, administrators, bus drivers, and clerical staff. The final sample size for the present study was 1759 observations, including 1358 females and 401 males.

The type of sensitive information from these self-reported data is rarely found in public-use data sets. In particular, employees were asked about their frequency and quantity of alcohol consumption, the number of cigarettes they smoked per day, and whether they had used any illicit drug (marijuana, cocaine, crack, heroin, and other narcotics) during the last 12 months. These measures, of course, are imprecise indicators of abuse or dependence, but they have often been used in empirical studies of substance use, and the unit of measure is easily understood (Buchmueller and Zuvekas 1998; French et al. 1998; Heien 1996; Zarkin et al. 1998a, 1998b). Participants were also asked numerous questions concerning their work habits and attendance. Although there are well-understood limitations to using self-reported data, these data offer a unique opportunity to explore the influence of substance use on workplace behaviour.

4 RESULTS

Descriptive statistics for all variables used in the empirical models are reported in Table 10.1. Several characteristics of the sample are worth noting. Approximately 23 percent of the total sample is male, which is not surprising for a hospital and a school district. Men were significantly older, more educated, and more likely to be non-white. Women had fewer years of tenure on the job than men, and they had more days absent from work.[4] It is also noteworthy that over 50 percent of the employees were managers or professionals. Although the sample characteristics are not typical of most workplace settings, they may be generalized to important service industries where women dominate the labor force such as nursing homes, childcare centers, hospitals, and school districts.

Table 10.1 also shows that smoking and illicit drug use did not differ significantly across genders, but men consumed significantly more alcoholic drinks than women during the past year. Specifically, men at these worksites had 169 drinks during the past year and women had only 70 drinks, on average. A slightly larger percentage of men used illicit drugs during the past year, but the average prevalence across both genders was only 4.4 percent.

The regression results for females are reported in Table 10.2. While we anticipated a negative relationship between attendance and both alcohol consumption and drug use, the negative and significant relationship between cigarette smoking and attendance was unexpected. To our knowledge, such findings are unique. Although researchers have known about the health problems associated with smoking, cigarette smoking has never been considered an important factor related to the productivity of workers.[5] It is also noteworthy that cigarette smoking was positively and

Table 10.1 Variable means for demographics, job characteristics, and substance use, by gender

Variable	Females (N = 1,358)	Males (N = 401)	Total (N = 1,759)
Demographics			
Age**	40.3415	43.0228	40.9511
Non-white (yes = 1, no = 0)**	0.1359	0.2231	0.1565
Highest grade completed (years)**	14.7906	15.5275	14.9591
Married (yes = 1, no = 0)	0.7101	0.7494	0.7185
Currently attending school (yes = 1, no = 0)	0.1665	0.1633	0.1666
Occupations			
Management/professional*	0.5299	0.5919	0.5444
Technical support	0.0942	0.0806	0.0911
Administrative support**	0.1360	0.0025	0.1049
Service	0.1009	0.1184	0.1054
Transportation	0.0314	0.0831	0.0430
Other	0.1076	0.1235	0.1112
Survey measures			
1995 wave (yes = 1, no = 0)	0.2084	0.2170	0.2090
1996 wave (yes = 1, no = 0)	0.4131	0.3965	0.4096
1997 wave (yes = 1, no = 0)	0.3785	0.3865	0.3814
Hospital worksite (yes = 1, no = 0)**	0.5965	0.3167	0.5352
Labor market measures			
Weeks worked	44.0275	43.4829	43.9177
Worked full-time**	0.7537	0.9322	0.7950
Days arrived late or left work early	2.2273	2.1218	2.2313[a]
Days absent due to illness or accident**	2.7601	2.4082	2.7025[b]
Substance use measures			
Number of cigarettes per day, past 12 months	3.3869	2.9949	3.2972
Number of drinks past 12 months**	69.8356	168.8351	92.6358
Illicit drug use past 12 months (yes = 1, no = 0)	0.0390	0.0560	0.0443

Notes

* Statistically significant difference in variable means between males and females, $p \leq 0.10$.

** Statistically significant difference in variable means between males and females, $p \leq 0.05$.

[a] Relative to the full sample, partial absenteeism was higher for smokers (2.8367) and drug users (3.5333), but lower for drinkers (2.2175). In addition, partial absenteeism was slightly higher at the hospital worksite (2.3194) relative to the school district worksite (2.1305).

[b] Relative to the full sample, full absenteeism was higher for smokers (3.7060) and drug users (3.6757), but lower for drinkers (2.6499). In addition, full absenteeism was higher at the school district worksite (3.0037) relative to the hospital worksite (2.4392).

Table 10.2 Regression coefficient estimates for females (N=*1358*)

Independent variables	Late/early days			Absent days		
	Equation 1	Equation 2	Equation 3	Equation 4	Equation 5	Equation 6
Number of cigarettes per day, past 12 months	0.0147**	–	–	0.0143**	–	–
Number of drinks past 12 months	–	0.0006**	–	–	0.0001	–
Illicit drug use past 12 months	–	–	0.4148*	–	–	0.1148
Age	0.0568*	0.0759**	0.0505*	–0.0495**	–0.0363	–0.0370
Age^2	–0.0008**	–0.0011**	–0.0007**	0.0006**	0.0004	0.0004
Non-white	0.3937**	0.6094**	0.3514**	0.2911**	0.3262**	0.2709**
Highest grade completed	0.0104	–0.0079	–0.0116	–0.0251	–0.0345*	–0.0400*
Married	–0.0510	–0.0655	–0.0410	–0.0150	–0.0662	–0.0406
Attending school	–0.0643	–0.0325	–0.0694	–0.1478	–0.2017**	–0.1741*
Management/professional	–0.3307**	–0.2340	–0.2744*	–0.1100	–0.1574	–0.0947
Technical support	–0.0033	0.0585	–0.0363	–0.0454	–0.0901	–0.0809
Administrative support	–0.0785	–0.0042	–0.0740	–0.1187	–0.1768	–0.1381
Service	–0.2256	–0.1440	–0.1298	–0.0620	0.0038	0.0087
Transportation	–0.0609	–0.7359**	–0.2100	0.0857	0.0086	0.0709
Ln(weeks worked)	0.1675	0.1101	0.1217	0.4021**	0.3912**	0.3657**
Worked full-time	0.3264**	0.3902**	0.3021**	–0.0738	–0.0281	–0.0399
1996 wave	–0.0169	–0.0487	–0.0186	0.0276	0.0315	0.0606
1997 wave	0.0620	0.0560	0.0835	0.0452	0.0885	0.0755
Hospital worksite	0.0531	0.0013	0.0514	–0.3171**	–0.2964**	–0.2980**
Constant	–1.0050	–0.9054	–0.4194	1.1078*	1.1414*	1.2356**
Log likelihood	–2348.31	–2209.72	–2335.84	–2598.21	–2438.19	–2599.04
Likelihood ratio $\chi^2(17)$	51.51**	62.22**	39.82**	71.29**	61.06**	55.88**

Notes
* Coefficient estimate is statistically different from zero, $p \leq 0.10$.
** Coefficient estimate is statistically different from zero, $p \leq 0.05$.

significantly related to both days absent and days arriving late to work or leaving early. The regression coefficients for alcohol consumption and drug use were positive for women, but not significant in the days absent regressions. Perhaps the most important finding of this research was that arriving to work late or leaving work early was significantly related to smoking, drinking, and drug use among women. Since few studies have the data to examine partial absenteeism as we did here, this finding is both important and original.

Some of the other regression coefficients in Table 10.2 provide important information as well. Partial absenteeism was a concave function of age, but full absenteeism was a convex function, for the female sample. This result suggests that older workers were more punctual in their arrival and departure times, but they also had more full days absent due to illness or injury relative to younger workers. Full-time work status was positive and significant in the partial absenteeism equations, but negative and insignificant in the full absenteeism equations. This result is plausible because part-time workers tend to have more flexibility in arrival and departure times relative to full-time workers. As expected, log of weeks worked was positively related to absenteeism in all equations (statistically significant in the full absenteeism equations) implying that longer 'exposure' to the workplace setting led to more absenteeism events. It is also notable that race was related to attendance for women at these two worksites. Specifically, the regression coefficients for 'non-white' women were positive and significant in all regressions reported in Table 10.2. In addition, education and schooling were related to days absent, but not days arriving late or leaving early. Finally, female employees at the hospital reported significantly less days absent relative to female employees at the school district.

The regression coefficients for men are reported in Table 10.3. One immediate observation is that the patterns between substance use and attendance are subtler for men relative to women. For example, smoking, alcohol use, and illicit drug use were significantly related to partial absenteeism at the 90 percent level. Smoking was significantly related to full absenteeism at the 95 percent level, and illicit drug use was significant at the 90 percent level. Again, it appears that smoking was more strongly related to workplace attendance than drinking or illicit drug use. Few of the other variables in Table 10.3 were significantly related to days absent or late/early days.[6]

It is interesting to note that days absent, as estimated for females and males and reported in Tables 10.2 and 10.3, was significantly lower in the hospital compared to the school district. Another curious finding was that men who were working in transportation-related jobs were less likely to

Table 10.3 Regression coefficient estimates for males (N=*401*)

Independent variables	Late/early days			Absent days		
	Equation 1	Equation 2	Equation 3	Equation 4	Equation 5	Equation 6
Number of cigarettes per day, past 12 months	0.0195*	–	–	0.0195**	–	–
Number of drinks past 12 months	–	0.0004*	–	–	−9.92e−07	–
Illicit drug use past 12 months	–	–	0.6160*	–	–	0.5842*
Age	0.0923*	0.0851	0.0857	0.0584	0.0552	0.0652
Age^2	−0.0014	−0.0013	−0.0014	−0.0008	−0.0007	−0.0008
Non-white	0.3577	0.3570	0.2918	0.2637	0.1811	0.2359
Highest grade completed	0.0654	0.0053	0.0394	−0.0802*	−0.1056**	−0.1098**
Married	0.1275	0.0127	0.1183	0.0865	0.0391	0.0628
Attending school	−0.3587	−0.2738	−0.3227*	−0.0221	−0.0758	−0.0905
Management/professional	−0.1073	−0.0086	−0.2146	−0.0630	−0.1675	−0.1309
Technical support	0.3488	0.3744	0.2521	0.2175	0.1910	0.1452
Administrative support	0.9262	0.7329	0.7417	0.1232	0.0264	0.0957
Service	−0.0035	−0.3857	−0.1970	−0.0860	−0.2982	−0.2455
Transportation	0.3233	0.4425	0.5102	−0.7932**	−0.7165**	−1.0028**
Ln(weeks worked)	−0.3507	−0.1360	−0.1209	0.2917	0.4811**	0.4064*
Worked full-time	0.7040	0.5248	0.7349*	−0.2237	−0.1331	−0.2466
1996 wave	0.0235	0.0961	0.0634	0.1157	0.1359	0.1089
1997 wave	−0.1263	−0.0345	0.0048	−0.1393	−0.0670	−0.0965
Hospital worksite	−0.0373	−0.1573	−0.1586	−0.5428**	−0.6581**	−0.6445**
Constant	−0.9564	−0.5488	−1.2299	0.2755	0.0781	0.2634
Log likelihood	−690.72	−650.47	−683.41	−722.82	−689.81	−709.93
Likelihood ratio $\chi^2(17)$	21.99	21.25	22.27	36.34**	29.63**	37.10**

Notes

* Coefficient estimate is statistically different from zero, $p \leq 0.10$.

** Coefficient estimate is statistically different from zero, $p \leq 0.05$.

report days absent. Finally, the effect of substance use on attendance did not differ greatly for women and men, but illicit drug use may be a greater problem for men. This similarity in results, especially for smoking, was somewhat surprising because men and women had different attendance rates and different substance use patterns.

The final set of results pertains to specifications with all three measures of substance use included in the same equations. Again, separate equations were estimated for each attendance measure, by gender. Table 10.4 shows that, qualitatively, the estimates for smoking, drinking, and drug use were generally similar to those reported in Tables 10.2 and 10.3, but the magnitude and the significance levels were generally lower. However, the null hypothesis that the three substance-use measures were jointly equal to zero was rejected for every specification. Furthermore, smoking continued to appear as the most significant predictor of attendance for both males and females. The coefficient estimate for drug use in the full absenteeism specification (males) was the only other substance-use coefficient that was individually significant from zero. These findings imply that, even after controlling for multiple substance-use (comorbidity), smoking, drinking, and drug use were (jointly) significantly related to full and partial absenteeism. And, smoking had a significant individual effect on absenteeism for both genders.[7]

5 SUMMARY

Based on our analysis of data from two service organizations, we conclude that smoking, drinking, and illicit drug use were significantly related to both partial and full workplace attendance, which are directly observable and important measures of productivity. In addition, controlling for the comorbidity effects of multiple substance use did not appreciably alter the direction of the substance-use estimates, and all three estimates were jointly significant. Considering the medical literature on the adverse effects of alcoholism and drug abuse (for example, Chait et al. 1985; Herning et al. 1989; Yesavage et al. 1985), it was not particularly surprising to learn that drinking and illicit drug use were negatively related to attendance. However, smoking was a significant predictor of both full and partial absenteeism, regardless of gender. This result was interesting and somewhat surprising because smoking is not normally associated with absenteeism. Nevertheless, the strong association between smoking and absenteeism is intuitively plausible given the health risks attributed to heavy and long-term smoking. We encourage future research to further test the relationships between

Table 10.4 Regression coefficient estimates for females (N = 1358) and males (N = 401): comorbidity

Independent variables	Females		Males	
	Late/early days	Absent days	Late/early days	Absent days
Number of cigarettes per day, past 12 months	0.0121**	0.0135**	0.0196*	0.0158*
Number of drinks past 12 months	0.0004	−0.00002	0.0003	−0.0002
Illicit drug use past 12 months	0.1729	−0.0093	0.5330	0.6807**
χ^2 (3) Joint significance	10.4100**	10.9500**	8.5000**	6.9000*
Age	0.0852**	−0.0382	0.0552	0.0496
Age^2	−0.0012**	0.0004	−0.0010	−0.0006
Non-white	0.5102**	0.3155**	0.4007	0.1870
Highest grade completed	−0.0058	−0.0220	0.0441	−0.0856*
Married	−0.0718	−0.0390	0.0260	0.0069
Attending school	0.0039	−0.1683*	−0.3148	−0.0743
Management/professional	−0.2391	−0.1506	0.0396	−0.1041
Technical support	0.0641	−0.0574	0.5724	0.2376
Administrative support	0.0008	−0.1414	0.8285	0.1516
Service	−0.1767	−0.0339	−0.2260	−0.2735
Transportation	−0.7578**	0.0192	0.6243	−0.9475**
Ln(weeks worked)	0.1416	0.3850**	−0.1990	0.4506**
Worked full-time	0.3834**	−0.0527	0.9549**	−0.1966
1996 wave	−0.0603	0.0072	0.0690	0.0752
1997 wave	0.0416	0.0769	−0.1137	−0.1311
Hospital worksite	−0.0142	−0.2974**	−0.1437	−0.6610**
Constant	−1.2608	0.9810	−0.8094	−0.0153
Log likelihood	−2157.16	−2383.25	−636.28	−670.14
Likelihood ratio χ^2(17)	65.95**	65.80**	27.33*	37.76**

Notes

* Coefficient estimate is statistically different from zero, $p \leq 0.10$.

** Coefficient estimate is statistically different from zero, $p \leq 0.05$.

smoking and absenteeism with larger and more representative data sets.

Several methodological and data limitations associated with the research should be noted. First, all data were self-reported, which raises questions about respondent honesty and recall. Harrison and Hughes (1997) have examined the reliability of self-reported data in this context and the results were quite good. Second, substance use is a behavioral choice that is probably endogenous in the attendance regressions. Unfortunately, data limitations precluded statistical corrections for this potential endogeneity bias. Third, the results demonstrated that substance use was significantly related to attendance, but one cannot conclude that substance use *causes* attendance problems. We were not able to estimate a causal model. Finally, the data apply to employees at two service organizations, a hospital and a school district. Additional research with a different data set is necessary to determine whether the findings can be generalized to other workplace settings and employees.

Although the empirical model was straightforward and the data were not nationally representative, these findings are interesting and important because workplace attendance and substance use have never been explored in this fashion. Indeed, very few data sets have detailed information on smoking, drinking, and drug use. Furthermore, absenteeism is usually included in surveys as 'days absent from work' (that is, full absenteeism). To our knowledge, this is the first study to analyse the relationships between substance use and days arriving late or leaving early (that is, partial absenteeism).

In summary, these findings suggest that substance use may be significantly related to workplace attendance because attendance is a directly observable measure of productivity and poor attendance is one of the first signs of a troubled employee. Unlike indirect measures of productivity such as wages or earnings, attendance will often change soon after a substance use problem materializes. Other directly observable measures of productivity include workplace accidents, incidents, and grievances. Perhaps future studies of substance use and workplace productivity should concentrate more on directly observable and straightforward measures of performance rather than indirect measures such as wages or earnings.

NOTES

* Financial assistance for this study was provided by the National Institute on Alcohol Abuse and Alcoholism through a grant to the Research Triangle Institute (grant No. 1R01 AA10318) and a subcontract to the University of Miami. Additional financial support was provided by a grant from the National Institute on Drug Abuse (grant No. 1R01 DA11506). The authors received numerous helpful suggestions from Hwei-Lin Chuang, Michael Dennis, Michael

Grossman, Chee-Ruey Hsieh, Helena Salomé, participants at the Taipei International Conference on Health Economics, and two anonymous referees. Finally, editorial assistance from Carmen Martinez and Silvana Zavala improved the chapter.

1 In addition to continuous measures of absenteeism, we also created dichotomous measures for above-average full and partial absenteeism. These specifications were then estimated using probit. Since the probit results were qualitatively similar to the negative binomial findings, we only report the negative binomial estimates in this chapter.

2 We also experimented with dichotomous measures for problem drinking and heavy smoking. Since the dichotomous measures produced results that were qualitatively similar to those reported here, we focused on the continuous measures of smoking and drinking because the continuous measures offer more information across the full sample of workers.

3 A copy of the survey instrument is available upon request from Michael French, University of Miami, 1801 NW 9th Avenue, third floor, Miami, FL33136, USA.

4 Relative to the full sample, partial absenteeism was higher for smokers (2.8367) and drug users (3.5333), but lower for drinkers (2.2175). In addition, partial absenteeism was slightly higher at the hospital worksite (2.3194) relative to the school district worksite (2.1305). Alternatively, relative to the full sample, full absenteeism was higher for smokers (3.7060) and drug users (3.6757), but lower for drinkers (2.6499). In addition, full absenteeism was higher at the school district worksite (3.0037) relative to the hospital worksite (2.4392).

5 In an earlier version of this chapter, an anonymous referee correctly pointed out that cigarette smoking may be significantly related to one or more omitted variables in the attendance regressions, causing an exaggeration of the magnitude and significance of the smoking effect. For example, smoking may be related to family problems or health problems, both of which could be interfering with attendance. Of course, this omitted variable bias could be working through alcohol use and drug use as well.

6 It should be noted that the goodness of fit measures (likelihood ratio, $\chi^2(17)$) for the partial absenteeism regressions for males were not significant at conventional levels.

7 In addition to the main effects of smoking, drinking, and drug use on absenteeism, we also tested for interaction effects. The null hypothesis that the interaction terms were jointly equal to zero could not be rejected in any of the specifications. These results are not reported in the tables, but the full set of regression output is available on request from Michael French, University of Miami, 1801 NW 9th Avenue, third floor, Miami, FL33136, USA.

REFERENCES

Berger, M.C. and J.P. Leigh (1988), 'The effect of alcohol use on wages', *Applied Economics*, **20**: 1343–51.

Buchmueller, T.C. and S.H. Zuvekas (1998), 'Drug use, drug abuse, and labour market outcomes', *Health Economics*, **7**: 229–45.

Chait, L.D., M.W. Fischman and C.R. Schuster (1985), '"Hangover" effects the morning after marijuana smoking', *Drug and Alcohol Dependence*, **15**: 229–38.

Cook, P.J. and M.J. Moore (1993), 'Drinking and schooling', *Journal of Health Economics*, **12**: 411–29.

French, M.T. and G.A. Zarkin (1995), 'Is moderate alcohol use related to wages? Evidence from four worksites', *Journal of Health Economics*, **14**: 319–44.

French, M.T. and G.A. Zarkin (1998), 'Mental health, absenteeism, and earnings at a large manufacturing worksite', *Journal of Mental Health Policy and Economics*, **1**: 161–72.

French, M.T., G.A. Zarkin and L.J. Dunlap (1998), 'Illicit drug use, absenteeism, and earnings at six U.S. worksites', *Contemporary Economic Policy*, **16**: 334–46.

Gill, A.M. and R.J. Michaels (1992), 'Does drug use lower wages?', *Industrial and Labor Relations Review*, **45**: 419–34.

Greene, W.H. (1997), *Econometric Analysis*, Englewood Cliffs, NJ: Prentice-Hall.

Harrison, L. and A. Hughes (1997), '*The Validity of Self-reported Drug Use: Improving the Accuracy of Survey Estimates*', National Institute on Drug Abuse Research Monograph 167, NIH Publication No. 97-4147, Rockville, MD.

Hausman, J., B.H. Hall and Z. Griliches (1984), 'Econometric models for count data with an application to the patents–R&D Relationship', *Econometrica*, **52**: 909–38.

Heien, D.M. (1996), 'Do drinkers earn less?', *Southern Economic Journal*, **63**: 60–8.

Herning, R.I., B.J. Glover, B.S. Koeppl and J.H. Jaffe (1989), 'Cocaine and workplace performance: inferences from clinical studies', National Institute on Drug Abuse Conference on Drugs in the Workplace.

Kaestner, R. (1993), 'The effect of illicit drug use on the labor supply of young adults', *Journal of Human Resources*, **29**: 126–55.

Kaestner, R. (1994), 'New estimates of the effect of marijuana and cocaine use on wages', *Industrial and Labor Relations Review*, **47**: 454–70.

Kaestner, R. (1998), 'Illicit drug use and labor market outcomes: a review of economic theory and its empirical implications', *Journal of Drug Issues*, **28**: 663–80.

Kandel, D.B. and M. Davies (1990), 'Labor force experience of a national sample of young men', *Youth and Society*, **21**: 411–45.

Long, J.S. (1997), *Regression Models for Categorical and Limited Dependent Variables*, Thousand Oaks, CA: Sage Publications.

Mincer, J. (1974), *Schooling, Experience, and Earnings*, New York: National Bureau of Economic Research.

Mullahy, J. and J.L. Sindelar (1989), 'Lifecycle effects of alcoholism on education, earnings, and occupation', *Inquiry*, **26**: 272–82.

Mullahy, J. and J.L. Sindelar (1991), 'Gender differences in labor market effects of alcoholism', *American Economic Association Papers and Proceedings*, **81**(2): 161–5.

Mullahy, J. and J. Sindelar (1996), 'Employment, unemployment, and problem drinking', *Journal of Health Economics*, **15**: 409–34.

Register, C.A. and D.R. Williams (1992), 'Labor market effects of marijuana and cocaine use among young men', *Industrial and Labor Relations Review*, **45**: 435–48.

StataCorp. (1999), *Stata Statistical Software*: *Release 6.0*, College Station, TX: Stata Corporation.

Yesavage, J.A., V.O. Leirer, M. Denari and L.E. Hollister (1985), 'Carry-over effects of marijuana intoxication on aircraft pilot performance: a preliminary report', *American Journal of Psychiatry*, **142**: 1325–9.

Zarkin, G.A., M.T. French, T.A. Mroz and J.W. Bray (1998a), 'Alcohol use and wages: new results from the national household survey on drug abuse', *Journal of Health Economics*, **17**: 53–68.

Zarkin, G.A., T.A. Mroz, J.W. Bray and M.T. French (1998b), 'The relationship between substance use and labor supply for young men', *Labour Economics*, **5**: 385–409.

PART IV

Criminal Violence and Substance Use

11. Alcohol regulation and violence on college campuses

Michael Grossman and Sara Markowitz*

1 INTRODUCTION

This chapter is a contribution to the literature on the effects of alcohol regulation on the adverse consequences of alcohol abuse. Previous research has considered such outcomes as cirrhosis mortality (Cook and Tauchen 1982; Saffer 1991); motor vehicle accident mortality (Saffer and Grossman 1987; Chaloupka et al. 1993; Ruhm 1996); failure to complete college (Cook and Moore 1993a); and drunk driving (Kenkel 1993; Sloan et al. 1995). These studies have found that increases in the price of alcohol, which various levels of government regulate via taxation, lead to reductions in the adverse outcomes just mentioned.

Our study focuses on the effects of variations in alcoholic beverage prices among states of the United States on violence on college campuses. The principal hypothesis tested is that the incidence of violence is negatively related to the price of alcohol. This hypothesis is derived from two well-established relationships: the positive relationship between alcohol and violence and the negative relationship between the use of alcohol and its price. The data employed in the study are the 1989, 1990, and 1991 Core Alcohol and Drug Surveys of College Students. Combined, these surveys contain almost 120,000 college students from approximately 200 colleges and universities throughout the United States. They contain measures of the use of alcohol and the adverse consequences of its use. These adverse consequences include the following indicators of violence: getting in trouble with the police, residence hall, or other college authorities; damaging property or pulling a fire alarm; getting into an argument or a fight; and taking advantage of another person sexually or having been taken advantage of sexually. Our principal finding is that the incidence of each of these four acts of violence is inversely related to the price of beer in the state in which the student attends college.

2 BACKGROUND

By July 1988, each state of the United States had enacted legislation barring persons under the age of 21, many of whom are college students, from purchasing and consuming alcohol. Despite this legislation, consumption of alcohol by underage youths hardly has been eliminated. Approximately 73 percent of all high school seniors consumed alcohol in the past year in 1996 and 30 percent engaged in binge drinking (consumption of five or more drinks in a row) in the past two weeks in that year (Johnston et al. 1997). In 1993, 81 percent of underage college students consumed alcohol in the past year and 45 percent engaged in binge drinking in the past two weeks (Chaloupka and Wechsler 1996). The almost annual occurrence of the death of at least one fraternity pledge due to alcohol poisoning is a stark reminder of the extent and serious consequences of alcohol abuse on college campuses.

The role played by alcohol in violence is well known. The National Institute on Alcohol Abuse and Alcoholism deemed this relationship of sufficient importance to issue a conference volume dealing with it in 1993 (Martin 1993). Alcohol is present in a large proportion of violent events, including between one-half and two-thirds of all homicides and serious assaults involving adults and adolescents and many reported instances of family violence (Wolfgang 1958; Viscusi 1986; Pernanen 1981, 1991, 1993; Cordilia 1985; Cook and Moore 1993b; Fagan 1993a, 1993b). The Bureau of Justice Statistics (1988, 1998) highlights this relationship in more detail. About half of the inmates in surveys conducted by the BJS in the late 1980s and in the 1990s drank an average of one ounce or more of alcohol daily, while only one-tenth of the adult population consumed this quantity. Over 20 percent of inmates were consuming the equivalent of nine ounces of 80 proof liquor or eight cans of beer daily during the year before the crime. Probationers and inmates reported consuming the equivalent of between nine and 15 beers during a period of up to eight hours prior to the crime.

Alcohol is more prevalent in violent crimes than in other crimes. In 1997, about 45 percent of state prisoners convicted of assault or murder had used alcohol just before committing the crime (BJS 1999). On the other hand, about 37 percent of burglars and 27 percent of drug offenders (those convicted of possession or distribution) used alcohol just prior to the crime for which they were convicted.

There is no general agreement in the literature concerning the nature of the causality implied by the positive association between alcohol and violence. Theories range from simple pharmacological effects to the complex interaction of endocrinological, neurobiologic, environmental, social and cultural determinants (Goldstein 1985; Reiss and Roth 1993). For example, there may exist a psychopharmacological relationship in which alcohol can alter behavior by increasing excitability and/or boosting courage (Pernanen 1981; Fagan 1993a). Under this theory, people may be more likely to commit a violent act when under the influence of alcohol than they would otherwise. A second theory proposes that alcohol affects the brain in such a way that people misinterpret social cues with the result of violent reactions (Collins and Schlenger 1988). A third theory asserts that people's reactions to alcohol follow what society has taught them to believe it does. For example, in the United States, people are taught that alcohol and drug use may cause people to lose their inhibitions and/or release violent tendencies, and thus users cannot be blamed fully for their actions. In other words, drunkenness may give people an excuse for aberrant behavior, despite whether or not actual pharmacological effects exist (Gelles and Cornell 1990).

The theories just summarized indicate that the statistical association between drinking and violence does not necessarily reflect causality from alcohol consumption to violence. The relationship may be due to reverse causality or to differences in one or more 'third variables' that affect both violence and alcohol use in the same direction. Reverse causality results when the decision to engage in violent acts stimulates drinking to provide an excuse or to provide courage. The third variable explanation points to such factors as a risk-seeking personality or a social environment that encourages deviant behavior (Fagan 1993b).

Prior to the early 1990s, economists had contributed little to the phenomenon of alcohol-related violence. Cook and Moore (1993b) point out that this can be explained on empirical and theoretical grounds. Empirically, economists often are reluctant to focus on relationships in which the direction and degree of causality appear to be difficult to establish. Theoretically, economists typically assume rational behaviour, but this assumption may not hold in the case of alcohol-related violence.

Cook and Moore (1993b) proceed to argue that the rational economic model can be applied to alcohol-related violence and that this approach has in fact been adopted by researchers in other disciplines (for example, Pernanen 1991). Thus, consider a man who deliberately abuses his wife or child to control their behaviour or to increase his share in family resources along the lines of an economic model of domestic violence proposed by Long et al. (1983) and by Tauchen et al. (1991). The actual cost of this action is lower if the abuser expects that his victims will attribute his actions to alcohol rather than directly hold him responsible. In the former case, the victims may be more likely to forgive the abuser. Alcohol can also lower the perceived costs of violence, many of which occur in the future. Heavy alcohol consumption is likely to increase the discount factor that potential offenders apply to future costs. Thus, it may make the commission of a violent act more likely. Cook and Moore (1993b) also refer to a model proposed by several economists in which consumers have stable but inconsistent short-run and long-run preferences (for example, Schelling 1978; Thaler and Shefrin 1981). Excessive alcohol consumption raises the costs of self-management and makes it more likely that decisions will be dominated by the preferences of the myopic doer rather than by the far-sighted planner.

Although it is not mentioned by Cook and Moore, the rational addiction model developed by Becker and Murphy (1988) and expanded by Becker et al. (1991) can also be used to justify an economic approach to alcohol-related violence. In the Becker–Murphy model, rational utility-maximizing consumers may become addicted to the consumption of harmful goods such as cigarettes, illegal drugs, and alcohol consumption. In their framework, consumers are rational or farsighted in the sense that they anticipate the expected future consequences of their current actions. They choose to consume these goods because the marginal benefit of current consumption exceeds the expected future marginal costs. These goods are addictive if an increase in past consumption raises current consumption because it raises the marginal benefit of current consumption by more than it raises the expected future marginal costs. Becker and Murphy also show that a myopic model of addiction – one in which consumers ignore the future consequences of their current actions – is a special case of their general approach to addiction. The key point to note is that alcohol-related violence can be viewed as an anticipated or unanticipated consequence of the addictive consumption of excessive amounts of alcohol.

The importance of the economic models of violence summarized by Cook and Moore and the Becker–Murphy addiction model is that they all contain demand functions for alcohol in which the quantity of alcohol demanded by an individual is negatively related to its price and to other exogenous determinants such as income and tastes or preferences. Chaloupka and Saffer (1992), Cook and Moore (1993b), and Markowitz and Grossman (1998, 2000) have used this approach to estimate reduced-form violence equations that result when alcohol consumption, an endogenous variable in a structural violence equation, is replaced by its determinants. Both Chaloupka and Saffer (1992) and Cook and Moore (1993b) investigate the effects of variations in beer tax rates among states of the United States on various crime rates from the Federal Bureau of Investigation's Uniform Crime Reports (UCR) in a time series of state cross-sections for the period 1975 through 1990 (Chaloupka and Saffer) and for the period 1979 through 1987 (Cook and Moore). Both include the violent crimes of murder, rape, assault, and robbery; while Chaloupka and Saffer also consider burglary, larceny, and motor vehicle theft. Cook and Moore adopt a fixed-effects specification in which the only regressors other than the beer tax are dichotomous variables for each state except one and each year except one. Saffer and Chaloupka adopt a more fully specified model of the determinants of crime. Both studies find that increases in beer tax rates lead to statistically significant reductions in most of the crime rates. For example, Chaloupka and Saffer predict that a doubling of the federal beer tax would reduce murders by 3 percent, rapes by 3 percent, robberies by 4.7 percent, and burglaries and thefts by 1.3 percent each. Cook and Moore estimate that a 10 percent increase in the state beer tax rate would reduce murder and assaults by 0.3 percent each, rapes by 1.3 percent, and robbery by 0.9 percent.

Markowitz and Grossman (1998) use the 1976 National Family Violence Survey to examine the effects of variations in state beer tax rates on the incidence and amount of severe and overall violence directed at children by parents. Acts of severe violence include kicking, biting or hitting with fist; hitting or trying to hit with something; beating up the child; threatening with a gun or knife; or using a knife or gun. Overall violence includes these behaviors as well as the minor acts of violence of throwing something at the child and pushing, grabbing or shoving the child. Markowitz and Grossman find that a 10 percent increase in the beer tax will reduce the probability of severe violence by 2.3 percent, the probability of overall violence by 1.2 percent, and the number of violent acts by parents who commit these acts by 1.6 percent. By pooling data from the 1985 and 1976 National Family Violence Surveys with a set of state dummies, Markowitz and Grossman (2000) show that the negative tax effects are not due to unobserved state factors.

3 ANALYTICAL FRAMEWORK

We adopt the framework employed in our previous studies (Markowitz and Grossman, 1998, 2000) to generate reduced-form equations for acts of violence committed by students on college campuses. Our framework is sufficiently broad to accommodate cases in which the violence caused by alcohol consumption or excessive consumption yields negative utility and cases in which violence or the power, control, or other outcome that it produces is a positive source of utility. In the former case the negative consequences can be anticipated or unanticipated. If they are anticipated, the positive marginal utility of alcohol consumption must outweigh the negative marginal utility of violence. If the consequences are unanticipated, alcohol consumption can be positive even if this condition is not satisfied. Whether the consequences are anticipated or unanticipated, by the law of the downward-sloping demand function, an increase in the price of alcohol causes a reduction in consumption and a reduction in violence.[1]

The above ideas are formalized in a three-equation econometric model. The first equation is a structural equation for violence:

$$v = v\,(a, e, \mathbf{x}). \tag{11.1}$$

Here v is a measure of violence, e represents law enforcement variables that affect the expected penalty for committing violent acts, a is alcohol consumption, and $\mathbf{x}$ is a vector of demographic, socioeconomic, and personal characteristics. Some of the members of the $\mathbf{x}$ vector, such as a risk-seeking personality or a social environment that encourages deviant behavior, are not observed. The second equation is a demand function for alcohol:

$$a = a(p, \mathbf{y}), \tag{11.2}$$

where p is the price of alcohol and $\mathbf{y}$ is a vector of other determinants of consumption, one of whose members is income. Note the variables in the $\mathbf{x}$ and $\mathbf{y}$ vectors may or may not be identical. Substituting equation (11.2) into equation (11.1), one obtains a reduced-form violence equation:

$$v = v\,(p, \mathbf{x}, \mathbf{y}, e). \tag{11.3}$$

We estimate the demand function and the reduced-form violence equation by ordinary least squares (OLS). Our focus is on the third equation and on the coefficient of the price of alcohol in that equation. In addition we estimate equation (11.1), the structural violence equation, in which alternative acts of violence depend on alcohol consumption – an endogenous right-hand-side variable. We estimate this equation by two-stage least squares (TSLS) for two reasons. First, the vectors $\mathbf{x}$ and $\mathbf{y}$ may share common unobserved variables. Second, as noted in Section 2, the relationship between alcohol consumption and violence may be due in part to reverse causality from violence to consumption. In either case, the disturbance term in the equation is correlated with observed alcohol consumption. Identification is achieved in the context of the TSLS approach by imposing the restriction that the price of alcohol should have no impact on violence with alcohol consumption held constant.

4 DATA AND EMPIRICAL IMPLEMENTATION

Data on criminal behavior on college campuses, alcohol consumption, and individual student characteristics come from the 1989, 1990, and 1991 Core Alcohol and Drug Surveys of College Students (hereafter termed the Core Surveys), conducted by the University of Southern Illinois's Core Institute (a Center for Alcohol and Drug Studies) and described in detail by Presley et al. (1993, 1995) and by Presley et al. (1996). Each of the three surveys contains approximately 50,000 college students. Taken together, 238 different colleges from 46 states are represented in the three surveys. These are colleges receiving two-year grants from the Fund for the Improvement of Postsecondary Education (FIPSE) of the US Department of Education to establish substance abuse programs. Student demographics at these colleges are similar to those of American colleges and universities generally. The Core Institute requested that FIPSE colleges administer the Core Survey on their campuses prior to the establishment of the substance abuse program using representative sampling techniques. The survey focuses on the use of alcohol and illegal drugs and on the consequences of this use.

For reasons of confidentiality, the only information on the college available to us is the state in which it is located. Moreover, the information on student and family background characteristics (described below) is limited. Therefore, to control for unmeasured factors and to avoid distorting trends, we restrict the sample to colleges in one of the 29 states that was in the 1989 survey.[2] These states accounted for 80 percent of the population of the United States in 1990. Our final sample contains 122,416 students from 191 colleges and universities.

Definitions, means, and standard deviations of all variables employed in the regressions in Section 5 are given in Table 11.1. Dichotomous indicators of the incidence of four alternative types of violent behaviour due to drinking or illegal drug use in the past year are employed as outcomes in linear probability regression models.[3] They are: getting in trouble with the police, residence hall, or other college authorities (termed trouble); damaging property, pulling a fire alarm, and so on (termed damage); getting into an argument or a fight (termed fight); and taking advantage of another person sexually or having been taken advantage of sexually (termed sexual advantage). Their incidence rates are 12.3 percent for trouble, 7.5 percent for damage, 31.2 percent for fight, and 14.3 percent for sexual advantage.[4] Some behaviors in the first category (trouble) may be more appropriately categorized as mischief rather than as crime, and the first two outcomes (trouble and damage) do not necessarily involve violent behavior. We use the term violence to describe

Table 11.1 Definitions, means and standard deviations of variables (n = 120,864 except where otherwise indicated)

Variable	Definition	Mean, standard deviation
Trouble[a]	Dichotomous variable that equals 1 if respondent had been in trouble with police, residence hall, or other college authorities due to drinking or drug use in the past year	0.123, 0.329 (*n* = 115,752)
Damage[a]	Dichotomous variable that equals 1 if respondent had damaged property, pulled fire alarm, etc. due to drinking or drug use in the past year	0.075, 0.264 (*n* = 115,471)
Fight[a]	Dichotomous variable that equals 1 if respondent got into an argument or fight due to drinking or drug use in the past year	0.312, 0.463 (*n* = 115,061)
Sexual advantage[a]	Dichotomous variable that equals 1 if respondent had been taken advantage of sexually or had taken advantage of another sexually due to drinking or drug use in the past year	0.143, 0.350 (*n* = 86,801)
Number of drinks[a]	Average number of drinks consumed in a week. (A drink is a bottle of beer, a glass of wine, a wine cooler, a shot glass of liquor, or a mixed drink)	4.709, 8.734 (*n* = 118,177)
Real beer price	Real annual beer price in 1982–1984 dollars	2.488, 0.219
Real income	State real per capita income	10,079.710, 1048.430
Number of licensed outlets per capita	State per capital number of retail outlets licensed to sell beer, wine, or spirits in a state	0.002, 0.001
Marijuana decriminalization	Dichotomous variable that equals 1 if respondent resides in a state in which incarceration and heavy fines are not penalties for most marijuana possession offenses	0.432, 0.495
Mormon	Percentage of the state population who are Mormon	1.839, 8.189
Southern Baptist	Percentage of the state population who are Southern Baptist	3.984, 6.251
Protestant	Percentage of the state population who are Protestant	21.028, 9.125
Catholic	Percentage of the state population who are Catholic	22.255, 12.182
Jewish	Percentage of the state population who are Jewish	2.392, 2.619
Age	Respondent's age	22.913, 6.935
Sophomore	Dichotomous variable that equals 1 if respondent is a sophomore	0.229, 0.417
Junior	Dichotomous variable that equals 1 if respondent is a junior	0.186, 0.385

Table 11.1 Definitions, means and standard deviations of variables (n = 120,864 except where otherwise indicated) (cont.)

Variable	Definition	Mean, standard deviation
Senior	Dichotomous variable that equals 1 if respondent is a senior	0.181, 0.382
Graduate student	Dichotomous variable that equals 1 if respondent is seeking a graduate or professional degree	0.058, 0.232
Non-matriculated	Dichotomous variable that equals 1 if respondent is not seeking a degree	0.027, 0.160
Black	Dichotomous variable that equals 1 if respondent is black, non-Hispanic	0.050, 0.215
Hispanic	Dichotomous variable that equals 1 if respondent is Hispanic	0.048, 0.210
Other race	Dichotomous variable that equals 1 if respondent is of another race/ethnicity	0.076, 0.261
Female	Dichotomous variable that equals 1 if respondent is female	0.589, 0.473
Married	Dichotomous variable that equals 1 if respondent is married	0.134, 0.339
Divorced	Dichotomous variable that equals 1 if respondent is divorced	0.042, 0.199
Part-time student	Dichotomous variable that equals 1 if respondent attends school part time	0.140, 0.343
Works full time	Dichotomous variable that equals 1 if respondent works full time	0.134, 0.336
Works part time	Dichotomous variable that equals 1 if respondent works part time	0.460, 0.492
Lives in on-campus housing	Dichotomous variable that equals 1 if respondent lives in on-campus housing	0.357, 0.479
Lives in a fraternity/sorority	Dichotomous variable that equals 1 if respondent lives in a fraternity or sorority	0.017, 0.131
On-campus residence unknown	Dichotomous variable that equals 1 if respondent lives in on-campus housing, but type of housing is unknown	0.210, 0.407
Mother has alcohol/drug problems	Dichotomous variable that equals 1 if respondent's mother had alcohol or drug problems	0.054, 0.227
Father has alcohol/drug problems	Dichotomous variable that equals 1 if respondent's father had alcohol or drug problems	0.159, 0.366
1990	Dichotomous indicator for survey year 1990	0.271, 0.445
1991	Dichotomous indicator for survey year 1991	0.261, 0.439

Note: [a] Mean and standard deviation based on a sample that excludes unknown values.

all four behaviors because the simple correlations among them, which range from 0.23 to 0.36, are high relative to the simple correlations among other variables in the data. Moreover, persons who break laws governing non-violent behaviour may be more likely to break laws governing violent behavior.

Due to the way in which the violence questions are worded, respondents are supposed to be reporting behavior caused by the use of alcohol or illegal drugs. This increases the value of these behaviors in assessing the effects of changes in the cost of alcohol on violence but decreases their value in assessing the overall contribution of alcohol abuse to violence. Of course, violence can be caused by more than one factor, and alcohol is present in a large proportion of violent and non-violent criminal events as indicated in Section 1. Thus, on balance the benefits of wording the questions in this manner may outweigh the costs.[5]

Most of the victims of sexual advantage are females, and most of the perpetrators are males. The sample size for the sexual advantage outcome is much smaller than the sample sizes for the other three outcomes because the question was asked exactly as it appears in Table 11.1 in 1989. In 1991 taking advantage of another person sexually and being taken advantage of sexually by another person were reported as separate items. In 1990 approximately 11 percent of the sample were asked the new question, while the rest were asked the old question. The data that we received from the Core Institute did not contain the responses to the old question. For 1990 and 1991 we created a single indicator of sexual advantage that equals one if at least one of the two separate indicators equals one. Note that gender-specific regressions did not indicate differences in slope coefficients.

Alcohol consumption is given by the average number of drinks consumed in a week. The mean value is 4.71 drinks per week and 7.85 drinks per week for the 60 percent of the sample that reported a positive number of drinks per week. This figure does not imply that 40 percent of the sample were abstainers because roughly 85 percent of the students consumed alcohol in the past year. These numbers suggest that 25 percent of the respondents consumed some alcohol in the past year but less than one drink per week.[6]

Alcohol consumption in the Core also can be measured by the incidence of binge drinking in the past two weeks (consumption of five or more drinks in a row) and by the number of such occasions. Forty percent of students engage in this behavior. The mean number of occasions is 1.28 for the whole sample and 3.19 for bingers. The incidence of binge drinking and the number of occasions are highly correlated with the number of drinks per week ($r = 0.530$ and $r = 0.734$, respectively). We do not use them as alternative measures of consumption because the violence outcomes pertain to the past year. Preliminary estimates that did employ them were very similar to the results presented in Section 5.

Student characteristics employed as independent variables in the regressions include age; class year (sophomore, junior, senior, graduate student, or non-matriculated student); race/ethnicity (Black non-Hispanic, Hispanic, or other); gender; marital status (married or divorced); part-time student status; work status (full-time or part-time); and type of residence (on-campus housing but not in a fraternity or sorority, fraternity/sorority, or on-campus but type unknown). The only parental variables are indicators that the mother has alcohol/drug problems and that the father has alcohol/drug problems.[7] Finally, all models include dichotomous variables for the years 1990 and 1991.

The price of alcohol is given by the real price of beer in 1982–84 dollars in the state in which the college is located. The price of beer is selected because beer is the most heavily consumed alcoholic beverage and because beer is the beverage of choice among college students. The money price of beer is taken from the *Inter-city Cost of Living Index*, published quarterly by the American Chamber of Commerce Researchers Association (ACCRA various years) for between 250 and 300 cities. The specific beer price collected by ACCRA is the price of a six-pack (six12-ounce cans) of Budweiser or Miller Light.[8] In addition to obtaining information on the prices of a variety of consumer goods, the ACCRA constructs a city-specific cost of living for each city with an average for all cities in a given quarter and year equal to one.

The Core Surveys were conducted during the fall semesters of 1989, 1990, and 1991. Since the violence outcomes pertain to the previous year, the beer price in the survey year is given as a four-quarter average of the prices in the first two quarters of the survey year and the last two quarters of the previous year. Before averaging, each quarterly price is converted to a real price by dividing it by a quarter- and city-specific cost of living index. This index is the ACCRA city-specific cost of living index multiplied by the quarterly Bureau of Labor Statistics' consumer price index (CPI) for the US as a whole (1982–84 = 1). Quarterly state prices are then computed as population weighted averages of city prices, and annual prices are obtained by averaging these prices over the four relevant quarters.

In interpreting the results in Section 5, one should bear in mind that the real price of beer is subject to measurement error for a variety of reasons. The price data pertain to the state in which the respondent attends college rather than to the city in which the college is located. In addition, the cost of living index reflects expenditure patterns of midmanagement (middle-income) households. These patterns may differ from those of college students. Random measurement error in an independent variable biases its coefficient and *t*-ratio toward zero. Thus, the price coefficients and associated *t*-ratios in Section 5 are conservative lower-bound estimates. With regard to the *t*-ratios, a factor that goes in the opposite direction is that conventional standard errors on which they are based do not take account of possible correlations among disturbances terms of students in the same college. Given positive correlations in these disturbance terms, *t*-ratios based on robust or Huber (1967) standard errors are smaller than the conventional or unadjusted *t*-ratios. If there is no measurement error in price and positive correlations among disturbance terms, unadjusted *t*-ratios are overstated, but this is not necessarily the case in the presence of measurement error.

We report both conventional and Huber *t*-ratios in the tables in the next section. In computing the latter, we use the college as the grouping factor. In the text we use conventional *t*-ratios in assessing statistical significance because we think that measurement error in the price is an important phenomenon. We realize, however, that the reader's views of this issue may differ from ours and provide enough information to allow him or her to evaluate significance based on Huber *t*-ratios.

Several other state-specific variables are included in some of the regression models. State real per capita income in 1982–84 dollars is a proxy for the student's income or his or her family income. If alcohol consumption or excessive consumption has a positive income elasticity, an increase in income should lead to more violence. A factor that goes in the opposite direction is that income may be positively correlated with the opportunity cost of the time spent in violence. Money per capita income by state is taken from the Bureau of Economic Analysis (various years). It is deflated by a state- and year-specific cost of living index obtained by multiplying the quarterly ACCRA cost of living index by the CPI for the US, obtaining population weighted averages at the state level, and then averaging over the four relevant quarters. The use of state income as a proxy for student's family income may be less valid for out-of-state students than for other students. Since there is no information on state of residence, the estimated income parameters should be interpreted with caution.

The per capita number of outlets that are licensed to sell alcoholic beverages for consumption on the premises, off the premises, or on and off the premises is a negative correlate of the amount of travel time required to purchase alcohol and should have positive effects on consumption and violence. The measure pertains to 1992 and is taken from Jobson Publishing Corporation (1993).

Violent behavior may depend on the use of illegal drugs as well as on the use of alcohol. The nature of the relationship, however, is ambiguous for reasons discussed in Markowitz and Grossman (1998, 2000). Since we focus on reduced-form violence equations, illegal drug prices rather than quantities are the relevant regressors.[9] Between 1976 and 1978, eleven states decriminalized the possession of small amounts of marijuana. This results in a lower full price of consuming marijuana in these states. We include a dichotomous variable that identifies students who attend colleges in these states. The sign of the coefficient of this variable is ambiguous. It depends on whether alcohol and marijuana are substitutes or complements. It also depends on the sign of the effect of marijuana consumption on violence and, if the effect is positive, on its magnitude relative to the magnitude of the alcohol effect. The decriminalization indicator is taken from the Bureau of Justice Statistics (1985).

'Drinking sentiment' may play a potential role in the endogenous determination of alcoholic beverage prices, alcohol consumption, and violence. This factor refers to cultural and taste factors that may either encourage or discourage alcohol consumption. For example, anti-drinking sentiment should be relatively widespread in states in which those religious groups that oppose the use of alcohol, such as Mormons and Southern Baptists, are prevalent. These states may enact high excise tax rates on beer as part of the political process. In this situation the price coefficients that emerge from regressions that omit drinking sentiment overstate in absolute value the true parameters.[10] To account for drinking sentiment, the percentages of the state population who are Mormons, Southern Baptists, Catholics, Protestants (excluding Mormons and Southern Baptists), and Jewish are included in one specification of the model. The omitted category pertains to the percentage of the population with no religion.

For several reasons, caution should be exercised in interpreting the regressions that include the religion variables. First, our estimates pertain to college students who may play a much smaller role in the political process determining prices and taxes than older adults. Second, an individual's drinking sentiment is the key measure that determines his or her consumption of alcohol. With this variable held constant, there is little reason why state sentiment should have an impact on consumption. A student's sentiment toward alcohol may be reflected quite well by the decision to live in a fraternity/sorority and by parental alcohol behavior. Thus, the price effects are not necessarily biased by the omission of the religion variable.[11]

For 1990 the religion variables except for the Jewish percentage are taken from Bradley et al. (1992). For 1989 and 1991, they are taken from interpolations and extrapolations of state-specific logarithmic time trends between 1980 and 1990. The 1980 data are reported by Quinn et al. (1982). The Jewish percentage is taken from the Bureau of Economic Analysis (various years).

Law enforcement variables, which affect the expected penalties for committing violent acts, are not available. This creates no biases as long as enforcement is not correlated with measured determinants. There is little reason to expect a correlation between campus-level enforcement and state-level measures of the price and availability of alcohol. But enforcement may vary with alcohol consumption. This point should be kept in mind when the structural estimates are presented.

5 EMPIRICAL RESULTS

Table 11.2 contains reduced-form violence regressions for the probability of getting into trouble with the police, residence hall, or other college authorities (trouble) and for the probability of damaging property, pulling a fire alarm, and so on (damage). Table 11.3 contains similar regressions for the probability of an argument or fight (fight) and for the probability of having been taken advantage of sexually or having taken advantage of another person sexually (termed sexual advantage). Table 11.4 contains reduced-form demand functions for the number of drinks of alcohol in a week. Three models are estimated for each of these five outcomes. In the first model, the only state-specific variable is the real beer price. In the second, real per capita income and the per capita number of outlets that are licensed to sell alcohol are added as regressors. In the third, the five religion measures are included.

The most important result in these three tables is that the beer price coefficients are always negative and are significant in 14 of the 15 regressions. The only exception pertains to the sexual advantage regression that includes the religion variables. This finding is consistent with the hypothesis that an increase in the cost of alcohol lowers violence because it lowers alcohol consumption. The beer price effects are reduced in absolute value when the other state-specific variables are included. In general these reductions are largest when the religion variables are employed as regressors. The ratio of the price coefficient in model 1 to the corresponding coefficient in model 3 is 1.04 for trouble, 1.64 for damage, 1.29 for fight, 7.75 for sexual advantage, and 1.25 for the number of drinks.

The coefficient of real per capita income is positive in all models except when damage is the outcome and the religion variables are held

Table 11.2 Reduced-form violence estimates (trouble, damage)

	Trouble (*n* = 115,752)			Damage (*n* = 115,471)		
	(1)	(2)	(3)	(1)	(2)	(3)
Real beer price	−0.025	−0.023	−0.024	−0.018	−0.019	−0.011
	(−5.48)	(−4.93)	(−4.34)	(−4.91)	(−5.12)	(−2.45)
	[−1.28]	[−1.10]	[−1.00]	[−2.07]	[−2.19]	[−0.97]
Real income		0.00001	0.00001		0.000001	−0.0000002
		(7.87)	(4.22)		(0.89)	(−0.21)
		[2.42]	[1.39]		[0.36]	[−0.10]
Number of licensed outlets per capita		0.107	6.509		5.798	8.890
		(0.08)	(3.62)		(5.17)	(6.13)
		[0.02]	[0.99]		[2.01]	[2.76]
Marijuana decriminalization		0.0001	−0.001		0.002	−0.0003
		(0.03)	(−0.40)		(1.28)	(−0.19)
		[0.01]	[−0.11]		[0.51]	[−0.09]
Mormon			0.0001			−0.00003
			(0.69)			(−0.24)
			[0.23]			[−0.13]
Southern Baptist			−0.001			−0.0001
			(−3.70)			(−0.56)
			[−1.15]			[−0.25]
Protestant			0.001			0.001
			(7.68)			(5.62)
			[2.20]			[2.36]
Catholic			0.001			0.001
			(8.93)			(8.20)
			[2.23]			[3.06]
Jewish			−0.003			0.001
			(−5.77)			(1.36)
			[−1.36]			[0.54]
Age	−0.003	−0.003	−0.003	−0.002	−0.002	−0.002
	(−13.62)	(−13.86)	(−14.00)	(−12.80)	(−12.74)	(−12.74)
	[−13.71]	[−13.91]	[−14.24]	[−11.63]	[−11.87]	[−12.14]
Sophomore	0.002	0.001	0.002	−0.001	−0.001	−0.0001
	(0.68)	(0.57)	(0.90)	(−0.60)	(−0.37)	(−0.06)
	[0.40]	[0.34]	[0.57]	[−0.44]	[−0.28]	[−0.05]
Junior	−0.009	−0.010	−0.011	−0.002	−0.002	−0.002
	(−3.32)	(−3.60)	(−3.97)	(−0.93)	(−0.71)	(−0.93)
	[−2.06]	[−2.27]	[−2.57]	[−0.65]	[−0.51]	[−0.68]
Senior	−0.032	−0.032	−0.034	−0.011	−0.011	−0.012
	(−10.82)	(−10.94)	(−11.45)	(−4.65)	(−4.48)	(−4.99)
	[−6.44]	[−6.35]	[−6.73]	[−2.76]	[−2.71]	[−3.14]
Graduate student	−0.052	−0.054	−0.051	−0.026	−0.026	−0.024
	(−11.14)	(−11.57)	(−10.81)	(−6.96)	(−6.91)	(−6.51)
	[−7.56]	[−7.83]	[−6.82]	[−5.49]	[−5.22]	[−4.71]
Non-matriculated	−0.010	−0.012	−0.010	0.002	0.002	0.002
	(−1.54)	(−1.80)	(−1.53)	(0.47)	(0.45)	(0.45)
	[−1.76]	[−2.06]	[−1.64]	[0.49]	[0.49]	[0.49]
Black	−0.076	−0.075	−0.071	−0.047	−0.049	−0.048
	(−17.23)	(−16.92)	(−16.05)	(−13.34)	(−13.89)	(−13.38)
	[−12.98]	[−12.46]	[−11.85]	[−14.11]	[−13.48]	[−13.34]
Hispanic	−0.041	−0.042	−0.034	−0.026	−0.026	−0.023
	(−8.98)	(−9.20)	(−7.46)	(−7.22)	(−7.26)	(−6.31)
	[−6.98]	[−7.28]	[−5.70]	[−7.01]	[−7.19]	[−5.84]

Table 11.2 Reduced-form violence estimates (trouble, damage) (cont.)

	Trouble (*n* = 115,752)			Damage (*n* = 115,471)		
	(1)	(2)	(3)	(1)	(2)	(3)
Other race	−0.054	−0.054	−0.048	−0.038	−0.039	−0.035
	(−14.82)	(−14.68)	(−13.05)	(−13.04)	(−13.03)	(−11.93)
	[−10.67]	[−11.20]	[−10.29]	[−11.17]	[−11.33]	[−10.51]
Female	−0.100	−0.099	−0.100	−0.109	−0.109	−0.110
	(−50.03)	(−49.88)	(−50.18)	(−68.08)	(−68.07)	(−68.64)
	[−21.42]	[−21.56]	[−22.76]	[−25.52]	[−25.63]	[−26.57]
Married	−0.048	−0.048	−0.047	−0.032	−0.032	−0.031
	(−13.42)	(−13.23)	(−12.90)	(−11.18)	(−11.10)	(−10.53)
	[−12.55]	[−12.66]	[−12.76]	[−14.27]	[−14.81]	[−14.51]
Divorced	−0.013	−0.013	−0.012	0.002	0.003	0.003
	(−2.44)	(−2.33)	(−2.24)	(0.48)	(0.57)	(0.78)
	[−2.66]	[−2.53]	[−2.42]	[0.50]	[0.59]	[0.79]
Part-time student	−0.003	−0.003	−0.002	−0.003	−0.003	−0.003
	(−0.83)	(−0.91)	(−0.69)	(−1.27)	(−1.21)	(−1.13)
	[−0.77]	[−0.83]	[−0.62]	[−1.30]	[−1.26]	[−1.19]
Works full time	−0.035	−0.035	−0.035	−0.019	−0.019	−0.019
	(−10.33)	(−10.37)	(−10.32)	(−6.90)	(−6.94)	(−7.04)
	[−7.71]	[−7.70]	[−7.77]	[−6.19]	[−6.21]	[−6.28]
Works part time	−0.029	−0.029	−0.030	−0.012	−0.011	−0.012
	(−13.87)	(−14.07)	(−14.42)	(−7.00)	(−6.80)	(−6.99)
	[−7.11]	[−7.33]	[−7.76]	[−4.50]	[−4.45]	[−4.78]
Lives in on-campus housing	0.047	0.048	0.045	0.004	0.004	0.001
	(19.46)	(19.71)	(18.70)	(2.08)	(1.91)	(0.56)
	[6.55]	[6.58]	[6.14]	[0.98]	[0.91]	[0.29]
Lives in a fraternity/sorority	0.077	0.081	0.081	0.087	0.086	0.087
	(10.57)	(11.03)	(11.07)	(14.79)	(14.70)	(14.85)
	[4.81]	[5.28]	[5.51]	[4.75]	[4.78]	[4.93]
On-campus residence unknown	0.006	0.006	0.009	−0.006	−0.005	−0.004
	(1.95)	(2.11)	(3.07)	(−2.28)	(−2.21)	(−1.63)
	[0.97]	[1.07]	[1.58]	[−1.60]	[−1.59]	[−1.25]
Mother has alcohol/drug problems	0.025	0.024	0.026	0.027	0.027	0.027
	(5.82)	(5.79)	(6.12)	(7.84)	(7.87)	(8.06)
	[5.02]	[4.97]	[5.40]	[6.51]	[6.55]	[6.67]
Father has alcohol/drug problems	0.025	0.025	0.026	0.019	0.019	0.020
	(9.70)	(9.61)	(9.76)	(9.21)	(9.23)	(9.37)
	[9.34]	[9.29]	[9.32]	[8.68]	[8.71]	[8.84]
1990	−0.020	−0.019	−0.019	0.003	0.004	0.003
	(−7.55)	(−7.14)	(−7.00)	(1.41)	(1.91)	(1.35)
	[−1.95]	[−1.86]	[−1.98]	[0.51]	[0.74]	[0.59]
1991	−0.007	0.003	0.001	0.003	0.004	0.003
	(−3.00)	(1.11)	(0.46)	(1.45)	(1.89)	(1.20)
	[−0.93]	[0.35]	[0.16]	[0.69]	[0.84]	[0.63]
R-squared	0.059	0.060	0.062	0.059	0.059	0.061
F-statistic	316.905	283.417	246.448	313.744	278.728	239.908

Note: *t*-statistics in parentheses, Huber *t*-statistics in square brackets, and intercepts not shown.

Table 11.3 Reduced-form violence estimates (fight, sexual advantage)

	Fight (n = 115,061)			Sexual advantage (n = 86,801)		
	(1)	(2)	(3)	(1)	(2)	(3)
Real beer price	–0.045	–0.045	–0.035	–0.031	–0.028	–0.004
	(–7.08)	(–7.00)	(–4.59)	(–5.59)	(–4.97)	(–0.63)
	[–1.61]	[–1.64]	[–1.02]	[–2.72]	[–2.42]	[–0.33]
Real income		0.00001	0.00001		0.000004	0.00001
		(9.13)	(5.65)		(2.78)	(3.45)
		[2.19]	[1.65]		[1.23]	[2.07]
Number of licensed outlets per capita		15.252	21.198		1.735	7.102
		(7.77)	(8.36)		(1.04)	(3.16)
		[1.51]	[2.09]		[0.46]	[1.71]
Marijuana decriminalization		0.004	–0.002		0.004	–0.004
		(1.50)	(–0.70)		(1.72)	(–1.35)
		[0.35]	[–0.19]		[0.78]	[–0.73]
Mormon			–0.0003			–0.0001
			(–1.18)			(–0.56)
			[–0.34]			[–0.43]
Southern Baptist			0.0001			–0.001
			(0.29)			(–3.01)
			[0.07]			[–1.65]
Protestant			0.002			0.001
			(11.11)			(3.80)
			[2.64]			[1.97]
Catholic			0.002			0.001
			(13.41)			(3.20)
			[2.72]			[1.97]
Jewish			0.0004			0.003
			(0.56)			(4.70)
			[0.14]			[2.02]
Age	–0.009	–0.009	–0.009	–0.004	–0.004	–0.004
	(–29.94)	(–30.09)	(–30.15)	(–14.09)	(–14.16)	(–14.20)
	[–25.43]	[–25.64]	[–26.43]	[–13.33]	[–13.43]	[–13.45]
Sophomore	0.006	0.007	0.008	–0.003	–0.003	–0.002
	(1.55)	(1.78)	(2.26)	(–1.02)	(–1.02)	(–0.74)
	[0.96]	[1.11]	[1.44]	[–0.76]	[–0.77]	[–0.55]
Junior	0.012	0.012	0.010	–0.014	–0.015	–0.014
	(2.99)	(3.05)	(2.49)	(–4.03)	(–4.13)	(–3.90)
	[1.50]	[1.57]	[1.32]	[–3.25]	[–3.31]	[–3.26]
Senior	0.011	0.011	0.007	–0.018	–0.019	–0.019
	(2.63)	(2.76)	(1.78)	(–4.95)	(–5.01)	(–5.05)
	[1.19]	[1.26]	[0.86]	[–3.59]	[–3.59]	[–3.70]
Graduate student	–0.070	–0.072	–0.067	–0.041	–0.042	–0.040
	(–10.57)	(–10.94)	(–10.21)	(–6.97)	(–7.11)	(–6.77)
	[–5.87]	[–5.97]	[–5.22]	[–5.35]	[–5.40]	[–4.81]
Non-matriculated	0.001	–0.001	–0.001	–0.005	–0.006	–0.006
	(0.14)	(–0.15)	(–0.15)	(–0.61)	(–0.70)	(–0.78)
	[0.12]	[–0.13]	[–0.12]	[–0.55]	[–0.62]	[–0.72]
Black	–0.163	–0.168	–0.164	–0.059	–0.059	–0.056
	(–26.37)	(–26.98)	(–26.22)	(–11.15)	(–11.11)	(–10.41)
	[–15.57]	[–15.43]	[–15.09]	[–7.07]	[–7.16]	[–6.64]

Table 11.3 Reduced-form violence estimates (fight, sexual advantage) (cont.)

	Fight (n = 115,061)			Sexual advantage (n = 86,801)		
	(1)	(2)	(3)	(1)	(2)	(3)
Hispanic	−0.082 (−12.81) [−7.11]	−0.084 (−13.10) [−7.12]	−0.073 (−11.33) [−5.46]	−0.029 (−5.05) [−4.27]	−0.030 (−5.18) [−4.39]	−0.024 (−4.23) [−3.73]
Other race	−0.144 (−27.93) [−17.13]	−0.144 (−27.77) [−16.88]	−0.134 (−25.71) [−16.70]	−0.044 (−9.36) [−8.05]	−0.044 (−9.47) [−8.16]	−0.041 (−8.64) [−7.77]
Female	−0.022 (−7.99) [−4.34]	−0.022 (−7.83) [−4.27]	−0.025 (−8.90) [−5.08]	−0.001 (−0.50) [−0.31]	−0.001 (−0.44) [−0.27]	−0.002 (−0.98) [−0.64]
Married	−0.114 (−22.34) [−18.19]	−0.112 (−22.05) [−19.05]	−0.108 (−21.16) [−18.96]	−0.070 (−15.66) [−18.68]	−0.069 (−15.48) [−18.22]	−0.067 (−14.98) [−17.30]
Divorced	−0.035 (−4.53) [−3.96]	−0.033 (−4.31) [−3.66]	−0.030 (−3.94) [−3.27]	0.007 (1.06) [0.83]	0.008 (1.16) [0.91]	0.009 (1.29) [0.99]
Part-time student	−0.008 (−1.73) [−1.36]	−0.008 (−1.73) [−1.36]	−0.007 (−1.45) [−1.12]	−0.007 (−1.71) [−1.67]	−0.007 (−1.67) [−1.60]	−0.008 (−1.87) [−1.80]
Works full time	−0.008 (−1.75) [−1.43]	−0.009 (−1.87) [−1.52]	−0.010 (−1.98) [−1.62]	−0.001 (−0.21) [−0.18]	−0.001 (−0.15) [−0.12]	−0.001 (−0.33) [−0.27]
Works part time	−0.009 (−3.02) [−1.47]	−0.009 (−2.93) [−1.47]	−0.010 (−3.26) [−1.75]	−0.005 (−1.85) [−1.42]	−0.005 (−1.79) [−1.41]	−0.005 (−1.84) [−1.51]
Lives in on-campus housing	0.001 (0.21) [0.07]	0.001 (0.22) [0.07]	−0.007 (−1.98) [−0.68]	0.021 (7.29) [4.34]	0.021 (7.36) [4.36]	0.017 (5.90) [4.00]
Lives in a fraternity/sorority	0.166 (16.18) [8.48]	0.170 (16.50) [8.98]	0.171 (16.70) [9.86]	0.073 (7.58) [5.72]	0.073 (7.59) [5.79]	0.072 (7.54) [6.02]
On-campus residence unknown	0.002 (0.39) [0.17]	0.003 (0.67) [0.30]	0.007 (1.58) [0.72]	0.009 (2.02) [1.69]	0.009 (1.99) [1.66]	0.009 (2.05) [1.77]
Mother has alcohol/drug problems	0.052 (8.71) [7.38]	0.052 (8.72) [7.45]	0.054 (9.13) [7.83]	0.054 (10.37) [10.47]	0.054 (10.32) [10.48]	0.054 (10.37) [10.44]
Father has alcohol/drug problems	0.052 (13.96) [14.09]	0.051 (13.91) [14.06]	0.052 (14.17) [14.47]	0.042 (12.77) [11.58]	0.041 (12.73) [11.57]	0.042 (12.85) [11.77]
1990	−0.029 (−7.89) [−1.63]	−0.026 (−6.76) [−1.47]	−0.028 (−7.33) [−1.80]	0.006 (1.10) [0.95]	0.008 (1.34) [1.04]	−0.001 (−0.20) [−0.14]
1991	−0.022 (−6.61) [−1.66]	−0.004 (−1.12) [−0.27]	−0.009 (−2.26) [−0.70]	−0.005 (−1.98) [−1.01]	0.000004 (0.001) [0.00]	0.0002 (0.07) [0.05]
R-squared	0.063	0.064	0.068	0.029	0.029	0.030
F-statistic	338.811	303.887	272.181	110.989	98.579	86.554

Note: *t*-statistics in parentheses, Huber *t*-statistics in square brackets, and intercepts not shown.

Table 11.4 Demand equations (n = *118,177*)

	Average number of drinks per week		
	(1)	(2)	(3)
Real beer price	−1.762 (−15.24) [−2.35]	−1.864 (−15.88) [−2.44]	−1.408 (−10.14) [−1.57]
Real income		0.0003 (10.14) [2.18]	0.0003 (8.74) [2.11]
Number of licensed outlets per capita		545.125 (15.22) [2.88]	797.742 (17.26) [3.41]
Marijuana decriminalization		0.063 (1.21) [0.20]	0.062 (1.06) [0.21]
Mormon			0.015 (3.50) [0.88]
Southern Baptist			0.015 (2.67) [0.57]
Protestant			0.030 (8.52) [1.70]
Catholic			0.060 (20.22) [3.75]
Jewish			0.010 (0.76) [0.12]
Age	−0.054 (−10.19) [−5.55]	−0.054 (−10.25) [−5.61]	−0.053 (−10.00) [−5.53]
Sophomore	0.053 (0.78) [0.47]	0.094 (1.38) [0.87]	0.140 (2.07) [1.30]
Junior	0.443 (6.02) [2.71]	0.478 (6.50) [3.01]	0.444 (6.04) [2.95]
Senior	0.594 (7.83) [2.82]	0.629 (8.27) [3.05]	0.543 (7.16) [2.81]
Graduate student	−0.438 (−3.63) [−2.04]	−0.471 (−3.91) [−2.16]	−0.376 (−3.12) [−1.60]
Non-matriculated	0.664 (3.91) [2.30]	0.613 (3.61) [2.29]	0.610 (3.60) [2.35]
Black	−3.250 (−28.68) [−16.60]	−3.449 (−30.24) [−14.89]	−3.367 (−29.49) [−15.29]

Table 11.4 Demand equations (n = *118,177*) (*cont.*)

	Average number of drinks per week		
	(1)	(2)	(3)
Hispanic	−1.786	−1.814	−1.653
	(−15.21)	(−15.43)	(−13.98)
	[−10.00]	[−10.68]	[−9.49]
Other race	−2.444	−2.427	−2.269
	(−26.10)	(−25.85)	(−24.07)
	[−13.32]	[−13.55]	[−13.34]
Female	−3.923	−3.915	−3.970
	(−76.32)	(−76.23)	(−77.37)
	[−23.72]	[−24.00]	[−25.30]
Married	−1.903	−1.875	−1.789
	(−20.45)	(−20.15)	(−19.23)
	[−11.98]	[−12.82]	[−12.25]
Divorced	0.166	0.208	0.264
	(1.17)	(1.47)	(1.86)
	[0.62]	[0.77]	[0.97]
Part-time student	−0.114	−0.109	−0.092
	(−1.33)	(−1.27)	(−1.08)
	[−0.84]	[−0.84]	[−0.71]
Works full time	−0.827	−0.850	−0.868
	(−9.35)	(−9.62)	(−9.85)
	[−4.99]	[−5.25]	[−5.44]
Works part time	−1.232	−1.213	−1.225
	(−22.78)	(−22.44)	(−22.71)
	[−8.42]	[−8.54]	[−8.97]
Lives in on-campus housing	1.175	1.159	1.010
	(18.93)	(18.66)	(16.19)
	[3.99]	[3.96]	[3.73]
Lives in a fraternity/sorority	6.175	6.204	6.274
	(32.82)	(32.96)	(33.39)
	[6.07]	[6.21]	[6.54]
On-campus residence unknown	−0.202	−0.173	−0.102
	(−2.67)	(−2.29)	(−1.35)
	[−1.01]	[−0.87]	[−0.52]
Mother has alcohol/drug problems	0.922	0.931	0.968
	(8.42)	(8.51)	(8.86)
	[5.33]	[5.40]	[5.61]
Father has alcohol/drug problems	0.573	0.573	0.589
	(8.41)	(8.41)	(8.68)
	[6.82]	[6.80]	[6.92]
1990	−0.311	−0.223	−0.271
	(−4.66)	(−3.25)	(−3.92)
	[−0.79]	[−0.58]	[−0.77]
1991	−0.050	0.312	0.268
	(−0.82)	(4.36)	(3.62)
	[−0.16]	[0.97]	[0.98]
R-squared	0.100	0.102	0.107
F-statistic	568.390	513.464	454.585

Note: *t*-statistics in parentheses, Huber *t*-statistics in square brackets, and intercepts not shown.

constant and significant except in the damage equations. The coefficient of the number of licensed outlets is positive except when trouble is the outcome and the religion variables are not held constant and is significant in each case in which it is positive except in the trouble equation. There is little evidence that marijuana decriminalization has an impact on violence or alcohol consumption.

The effects of the religion variables do not show a consistent pattern and are difficult to interpret. For example, an increase in the percentage of the population who are Mormons or Southern Baptists increases alcohol consumption rather than reduces it. The coefficients of these two variables do not have stable signs in the violence equations. The Mormon coefficient is positive in the trouble regression and negative in the damage, fight, and sexual advantage regression. The Southern Baptist coefficient is negative except when fight is the outcome. The Protestant and Catholic coefficients are consistently positive and significant, but it is not clear whether these are true effects or effects of variables correlated with these two measures. The Jewish measure is usually positive and insignificant. On balance, we prefer the models that exclude the religion variables. We realize, however, that the reader may have different views on this issue, and we give equal weight to models that include and exclude the religion variables in summarizing the magnitudes of the price effects below.

Many of the student characteristics are important determinants of alcohol consumption and violence. We want to call attention to the differentials associated with living in a fraternity/sorority or in having a mother or father with alcohol/drug problems. Students who reside in a fraternity/sorority have approximately six more drinks per week than students who live off-campus and have approximately five more drinks per week than students who reside in a dormitory. The presence of a mother with alcohol/drug problems is associated with one extra drink per week and the presence of a father is associated with slightly more than one-half extra drink per week. The coefficients of these three variables always are positive and significant in the violence equations.

Table 11.5 contains price, income, and outlet elasticities of the five outcomes considered in Tables 11.2, 11.3, and 11.4 at the sample means. The price elasticity of the number of drinks of alcohol ranges between –0.74 and –0.98 with a mean of –0.89.[12] This estimate is in the range of those in the published literature for young adults. Grossman et al. (1998) report a price elasticity of –0.65 for the number of drinks in the past year for persons between the ages of 19 and 27, not all of whom are in college.[13] Kenkel (1993) estimates a price elasticity of –2.24 for the number of days in the past year on which a person between the ages of 18 and 21 had five or more drinks.[14] Our income elasticity of the number

Table 11.5 Price, income, and outlet elasticities

	Beer price and individual characteristics	Beer price, marijuana decriminalization, income, outlets, and individual characteristics	Beer price, marijuana decriminalization, income, outlets, religion, and individual characteristics
Trouble			
Price	–0.500	–0.457	–0.477
Income		0.733	0.444
Number of outlets		0.002	0.124
Damage			
Price	–0.590	–0.624	–0.354
Income		0.108	–0.029
Number of outlets		0.180	0.276
Fight			
Price	–0.360	–0.362	–0.281
Income		0.474	0.330
Number of outlets		0.115	0.159
Sexual advantage			
Price	–0.532	–0.485	–0.076
Income		0.289	0.414
Number of outlets		0.028	0.116
Number of drinks			
Price	–0.931	–0.985	–0.744
Income		0.638	0.619
Number of outlets		0.271	0.397

of drinks of 0.63 is substantial, but the income measure employed in the regressions may be a poor proxy for the student's command of resources. The outlet elasticity of alcohol consumption of 0.33 is much smaller than the price or income elasticities.

The elasticity of each of the four violence outcomes with respect to the beer price is –0.48 for trouble, –0.52 for damage, –0.33 for fight, and –0.36 for sexual advantage. Consider an exactly identified model in which the beer price is the only variable omitted from the structural violence equation. In this model, the implied elasticity of violence with respect to alcohol consumption is 0.54 for trouble, 0.58 for damage, 0.37 for fight, and 0.40 for sexual advantage.

Table 11.6 contains actual estimates of structural violence equations by TSLS for trouble and damage, and Table 11.7 contains similar estimates for fight and sexual advantage. The number of drinks of alcohol is treated as an endogenous variable in these estimates. The three models for each outcome correspond to the three models in Tables 11.2 and 11.3. In model 1 the beer price is the only instrument for alcohol consumption (the only variable included in the first stage but excluded from the second stage). In models 2 and 3, the instruments are the beer price and the number of outlets. The treatment of income is somewhat controversial. If income affects violence solely through alcohol consumption, it should be excluded from the second stage. We include it to capture omitted endogenous and exogenous factors that may determine violence. Similar comments can be made with regard to such student characteristics as residence in a fraternity/sorority and the presence of a parent with alcohol/drug problems.

Alcohol consumption has a positive and significant coefficient in all 12 models in Tables 11.6 and 11.7. According to the Wu (1973) *F*-test, the consistency of OLS estimation of the structure is rejected in four cases but accepted in eight cases at the 5 percent level. Therefore, it is worth considering both the OLS and the TSLS elasticity of each of the violence outcomes with respect to alcohol consumption. These are shown in Table 11.8. The TSLS elasticity is 0.40 for trouble, 0.63 for damage, 0.39 for fight, and 0.33 for sexual abuse. The corresponding OLS elasticities are 0.48, 0.58, 0.27, and 0.30. These elasticities do not dramatically differ from each other or from those that are implied by the exactly identified model that was described above.

In summary our results are consistent with a causal mechanism in which the price of alcohol affects violence because it affects the consumption of alcohol. These results do not indicate whether violence is an anticipated or unanticipated consequence of alcohol consumption. They also do not indicate whether alcohol consumption is treated by students as an input to facilitate violent behavior or as an anticipated negative consequence that is outweighed by the positive benefits derived from its consumption. What they do suggest is that alcohol regulatory variables may influence the general level of violence.

Table 11.6 Two-stage least squares structural violence estimates (trouble, damage)

	Trouble (n = 113,553)			Damage (n = 113,275)		
	(1)	(2)	(3)	(1)	(2)	(3)
Number of drinks	0.014	0.007	0.010	0.010	0.010	0.010
	(5.90)	(3.83)	(5.78)	(5.17)	(7.38)	(6.88)
	[1.97]	[0.95]	[1.83]	[3.65]	[4.62]	[4.47]
Real income		0.00001	0.000003		−0.000002	−0.000003
		(8.32)	(2.73)		(−2.77)	(−3.71)
		[3.12]	[1.13]		[−1.93]	[−2.67]
Marijuana decriminalization		0.001	−0.001		0.001	−0.001
		(0.57)	(−0.54)		(0.84)	(−0.71)
		[0.17]	[−0.20]		[0.56]	[−0.47]
Mormon			−0.00002			−0.0002
			(−0.17)			(−1.70)
			[−0.07]			[−1.50]
Southern Baptist			−0.001			−0.0002
			(−5.73)			(−1.11)
			[−1.89]			[−0.81]
Protestant			0.001			0.0003
			(5.69)			(3.33)
			[1.84]			[2.18]
Catholic			0.0004			0.0001
			(3.18)			(1.28)
			[0.98]			[0.81]
Jewish			−0.003			0.0004
			(−6.16)			(1.01)
			[−1.94]			[0.71]
Age	−0.002	−0.003	−0.002	−0.002	−0.002	−0.002
	(−8.46)	(−11.20)	(−10.47)	(−8.07)	(−8.62)	(−8.67)
	[−4.64]	[−5.55]	[−6.42]	[−7.60]	[−8.66]	[−9.05]
Sophomore	0.001	0.001	0.001	−0.002	−0.002	−0.002
	(0.45)	(0.57)	(0.50)	(−0.96)	(−0.95)	(−0.88)
	[0.30]	[0.36]	[0.34]	[−0.76]	[−0.75]	[−0.69]
Junior	−0.016	−0.013	−0.016	−0.007	−0.007	−0.007
	(−5.30)	(−4.52)	(−5.54)	(−2.74)	(−2.84)	(−2.94)
	[−3.08]	[−2.56]	[−3.66]	[−2.25]	[−2.28]	[−2.43]
Senior	−0.040	−0.035	−0.039	−0.017	−0.017	−0.017
	(−12.35)	(−11.58)	(−12.91)	(−6.51)	(−6.97)	(−7.19)
	[−6.48]	[−5.99]	[−7.70]	[−4.95]	[−5.25]	[−5.47]
Graduate student	−0.046	−0.051	−0.047	−0.022	−0.022	−0.021
	(−10.08)	(−11.07)	(−10.28)	(−5.98)	(−5.84)	(−5.74)
	[−8.05]	[−7.56]	[−7.69]	[−6.31]	[−6.11]	[−5.77]
Non-matriculated	−0.020	−0.016	−0.016	−0.004	−0.004	−0.004
	(−2.96)	(−2.40)	(−2.48)	(−0.75)	(−0.70)	(−0.68)
	[−2.81]	[−2.37]	[−2.67]	[−0.82]	[−0.79]	[−0.79]
Black	−0.029	−0.053	−0.036	−0.015	−0.014	−0.014
	(−3.29)	(−7.52)	(−5.07)	(−2.06)	(−2.53)	(−2.47)
	[−1.25]	[−2.34]	[−1.96]	[−1.59]	[−1.85]	[−1.83]
Hispanic	−0.015	−0.029	−0.016	−0.008	−0.007	−0.006
	(−2.46)	(−5.42)	(−2.95)	(−1.54)	(−1.65)	(−1.32)
	[−1.12]	[−2.13]	[−1.48]	[−1.26]	[−1.38]	[−1.09]

Table 11.6 Two-stage least squares structural violence estimates (trouble, damage) (cont.)

	Trouble (n=113,553)			Damage (n=113,275)		
	(1)	(2)	(3)	(1)	(2)	(3)
Other race	−0.020	−0.038	−0.025	−0.014	−0.014	−0.013
	(−3.00)	(−6.98)	(−4.55)	(−2.58)	(−3.14)	(−2.90)
	[−1.18]	[−2.25]	[−1.93]	[−2.04]	[−2.46]	[−2.23]
Female	−0.044	−0.074	−0.059	−0.070	−0.070	−0.071
	(−4.57)	(−10.38)	(−7.96)	(−9.06)	(−12.28)	(−11.83)
	[−1.57]	[−2.71]	[−2.62]	[−6.23]	[−7.18]	[−7.38]
Married	−0.021	−0.035	−0.028	−0.013	−0.013	−0.013
	(−3.57)	(−7.19)	(−5.87)	(−2.79)	(−3.30)	(−3.29)
	[−1.46]	[−2.53]	[−2.64]	[−2.36]	[−2.81]	[−2.84]
Divorced	−0.014	−0.013	−0.013	0.001	0.001	0.002
	(−2.62)	(−2.39)	(−2.53)	(0.34)	(0.31)	(0.42)
	[−2.98]	[−2.82]	[−2.92]	[0.47]	[0.43]	[0.56]
Part-time student	−0.002	−0.002	−0.001	−0.002	−0.002	−0.002
	(−0.52)	(−0.61)	(−0.42)	(−0.91)	(−0.87)	(−0.84)
	[−0.57]	[−0.64]	[−0.45]	[−1.05]	[−1.00]	[−0.96]
Works full time	−0.024	−0.031	−0.027	−0.010	−0.010	−0.010
	(−5.95)	(−8.27)	(−7.22)	(−3.23)	(−3.41)	(−3.45)
	[−3.30]	[−4.15]	[−4.13]	[−3.04]	[−3.28]	[−3.23]
Works part time	−0.012	−0.022	−0.018	0.0002	0.001	0.0001
	(−3.44)	(−7.44)	(−6.02)	(0.07)	(0.26)	(0.05)
	[−1.35]	[−2.51]	[−2.46]	[0.05]	[0.19]	[0.04]
Lives in on-campus housing	0.030	0.039	0.034	−0.008	−0.008	−0.009
	(7.84)	(12.41)	(11.32)	(−2.61)	(−3.29)	(−3.74)
	[3.02]	[4.07]	[4.30]	[−1.86]	[−2.24]	[−2.54]
Lives in a fraternity/sorority	−0.005	0.043	0.020	0.029	0.027	0.028
	(−0.33)	(3.41)	(1.58)	(2.22)	(2.63)	(2.69)
	[−0.12]	[0.99]	[0.56]	[1.54]	[1.55]	[1.47]
On-campus residence unknown	0.004	0.006	0.007	−0.006	−0.007	−0.006
	(1.45)	(1.88)	(2.49)	(−2.70)	(−2.80)	(−2.55)
	[0.88]	[1.05]	[1.51]	[−2.44]	[−2.57]	[−2.38]
Mother has alcohol/drug problems	0.013	0.019	0.017	0.018	0.018	0.018
	(2.76)	(4.41)	(3.87)	(4.77)	(5.01)	(5.12)
	[1.72]	[2.66]	[2.61]	[3.98]	[4.22]	[4.34]
Father has alcohol/drug problems	0.018	0.022	0.020	0.014	0.014	0.015
	(6.39)	(8.17)	(7.52)	(6.25)	(6.59)	(6.65)
	[3.74]	[4.83]	[5.16]	[5.65]	[6.36]	[6.48]
1990	−0.012	−0.015	−0.013	0.009	0.010	0.009
	(−4.18)	(−5.46)	(−4.68)	(4.05)	(4.36)	(3.84)
	[−1.58]	[−1.83]	[−1.85]	[2.75]	[2.97]	[2.66]
1991	−0.005	0.003	−0.0002	0.005	0.002	0.002
	(−1.90)	(0.99)	(−0.07)	(2.38)	(1.15)	(0.70)
	[−0.76]	[0.36]	[−0.03]	[1.68]	[0.76]	[0.46]
R-squared	0.065	0.065	0.068	0.064	0.065	0.066
F-statistic	344.887	313.102	276.554	338.922	312.916	267.296
Wu F-ratio	0.513	11.676	1.263	0.122	0.415	0.211

Note: Asymptotic t-statistics in parentheses, Huber t-statistics in square brackets, and intercepts not shown. For Wu F-test, critical values of $F(1, \infty)$ are 3.84 at 5 percent and 6.64 at 1 percent.

Table 11.7 Two-stage least squares structural violence estimates (fight, sexual advantage)

	Fight (n = 112,888)			Sexual advantage (n = 85,856)		
	(1)	(2)	(3)	(1)	(2)	(3)
Number of drinks	0.026	0.026	0.025	0.014	0.009	0.007
	(7.49)	(10.59)	(10.00)	(5.67)	(4.69)	(3.23)
	[2.94]	[3.41]	[3.88]	[2.91]	[2.93]	[2.15]
Real income		0.00001	0.000002		0.000003	0.000003
		(4.36)	(1.35)		(2.63)	(2.25)
		[1.54]	[0.55]		[1.49]	[1.43]
Marijuana decriminalization		0.002	−0.004		0.004	−0.005
		(0.73)	(−1.45)		(1.73)	(−1.67)
		[0.26]	[−0.58]		[0.96]	[−1.01]
Mormon			−0.001			−0.0003
			(−3.64)			(−1.49)
			[−1.67]			[−1.16]
Southern Baptist			−0.0003			−0.001
			(−1.02)			(−2.75)
			[−0.36]			[−1.92]
Protestant			0.001			0.0005
			(7.96)			(3.00)
			[2.90]			[1.95]
Catholic			0.001			0.00005
			(3.36)			(0.24)
			[1.09]			[0.17]
Jewish			0.00002			0.003
			(0.03)			(4.39)
			[0.01]			[2.48]
Age	−0.007	−0.007	−0.007	−0.003	−0.003	−0.003
	(−20.93)	(−22.93)	(−22.99)	(−9.42)	(−10.98)	(−11.12)
	[−11.71]	[−12.09]	[−14.59]	[−7.47]	[−10.29]	[−9.68]
Sophomore	0.004	0.004	0.005	−0.003	−0.003	−0.003
	(1.15)	(1.04)	(1.28)	(−0.90)	(−0.93)	(−1.02)
	[0.82]	[0.73]	[0.94]	[−0.71]	[−0.72]	[−0.81]
Junior	0.001	0.0001	−0.001	−0.018	−0.017	−0.017
	(0.24)	(0.03)	(−0.24)	(−5.02)	(−4.84)	(−4.68)
	[0.14]	[0.02]	[−0.15]	[−4.92]	[−4.26]	[−4.28]
Senior	−0.004	−0.004	−0.006	−0.024	−0.022	−0.022
	(−0.78)	(−0.97)	(−1.35)	(−6.15)	(−5.88)	(−5.81)
	[−0.42]	[−0.51]	[−0.88]	[−5.37]	[−4.70]	[−4.57]
Graduate student	−0.059	−0.060	−0.058	−0.034	−0.038	−0.038
	(−9.04)	(−9.33)	(−8.97)	(−5.85)	(−6.46)	(−6.56)
	[−6.30]	[−6.66]	[−6.15]	[−4.71]	[−5.54]	[−5.21]
Non-matriculated	−0.015	−0.016	−0.016	−0.014	−0.011	−0.011
	(−1.57)	(−1.75)	(−1.72)	(−1.65)	(−1.36)	(−1.30)
	[−1.12]	[−1.29]	[−1.32]	[−1.50]	[−1.23]	[−1.24]
Black	−0.081	−0.079	−0.079	−0.013	−0.028	−0.032
	(−6.34)	(−7.97)	(−7.77)	(−1.31)	(−3.33)	(−3.61)
	[−2.68]	[−2.97]	[−3.59]	[−0.78]	[−2.07]	[−2.24]
Hispanic	−0.033	−0.034	−0.027	−0.003	−0.012	−0.013
	(−3.86)	(−4.49)	(−3.55)	(−0.45)	(−1.84)	(−1.94)
	[−1.72]	[−1.89]	[−1.81]	[−0.30]	[−1.63]	[−1.75]

Table 11.7 Two-stage least squares structural violence estimates (fight, sexual advantage) (cont.)

	Fight (n = 112,888)			Sexual advantage (n = 85,856)		
	(1)	(2)	(3)	(1)	(2)	(3)
Other race	−0.081	−0.081	−0.076	−0.009	−0.021	−0.024
	(−8.49)	(−10.55)	(−9.74)	(−1.24)	(−3.18)	(−3.52)
	[−3.61]	[−3.96]	[−4.46]	[−0.75]	[−2.42]	[−2.89]
Female	0.078	0.079	0.076	0.054	0.036	0.026
	(5.70)	(7.95)	(7.25)	(5.34)	(4.29)	(2.81)
	[2.23]	[2.64]	[2.85]	[2.81]	[2.89]	[1.98]
Married	−0.065	−0.064	−0.062	−0.042	−0.051	−0.053
	(−7.76)	(−9.29)	(−9.29)	(−6.19)	(−8.48)	(−8.82)
	[−3.66]	[−4.12]	[−4.86]	[−4.06]	[−6.90]	[−7.72]
Divorced	−0.037	−0.036	−0.035	0.006	0.007	0.007
	(−4.89)	(−4.81)	(−4.56)	(0.86)	(1.01)	(1.10)
	[−3.99]	[−3.91]	[−3.62]	[0.75]	[0.87]	[0.91]
Part-time student	−0.005	−0.006	−0.004	−0.005	−0.006	−0.007
	(−1.19)	(−1.24)	(−0.96)	(−1.32)	(−1.36)	(−1.64)
	[−1.01]	[−1.05]	[−0.80]	[−1.33]	[−1.35]	[−1.62]
Works full time	0.015	0.015	0.014	0.010	0.007	0.004
	(2.60)	(2.86)	(2.74)	(2.17)	(1.43)	(0.96)
	[1.53]	[1.81]	[1.96]	[1.46]	[1.15]	[0.81]
Works part time	0.023	0.023	0.022	0.012	0.007	0.004
	(4.47)	(5.46)	(5.04)	(3.07)	(1.83)	(0.96)
	[1.90]	[2.38]	[2.79]	[1.77]	[1.41]	[0.77]
Lives in on-campus housing	−0.030	−0.030	−0.033	0.005	0.011	0.010
	(−5.69)	(−6.77)	(−7.78)	(1.28)	(2.98)	(2.73)
	[−2.43]	[−2.80]	[−3.53]	[0.77]	[2.05]	[2.04]
Lives in a fraternity/sorority	0.015	0.016	0.019	−0.015	0.016	0.028
	(0.66)	(0.93)	(1.05)	(−0.80)	(0.98)	(1.61)
	[0.27]	[0.34]	[0.45]	[−0.45]	[0.74]	[1.18]
On-campus residence unknown	−0.0003	−0.0001	0.002	0.004	0.006	0.007
	(−0.08)	(−0.03)	(0.52)	(0.94)	(1.34)	(1.57)
	[−0.05]	[−0.02]	[0.32]	[0.82]	[1.18]	[1.33]
Mother has alcohol/ drug problems	0.029	0.029	0.031	0.041	0.045	0.047
	(4.48)	(4.70)	(4.99)	(7.30)	(8.30)	(8.53)
	[2.63]	[2.99]	[3.36]	[6.91]	[8.54]	[8.37]
Father has alcohol/ drug problems	0.038	0.037	0.038	0.034	0.037	0.038
	(9.30)	(9.79)	(9.92)	(9.81)	(10.90)	(11.12)
	[6.33]	[6.96]	[7.21]	[8.14]	[9.12]	[9.62]
1990	−0.015	−0.014	−0.015	0.014	0.013	0.004
	(−3.61)	(−3.49)	(−3.62)	(2.38)	(2.23)	(0.67)
	[−1.22]	[−1.16]	[−1.42]	[1.78]	[1.50]	[0.40]
1991	−0.017	−0.009	−0.013	−0.004	−0.001	−0.001
	(−5.05)	(−2.58)	(−3.55)	(−1.65)	(−0.38)	(−0.43)
	[−1.95]	[−1.00]	[−1.53]	[−1.07]	[−0.25]	[−0.30]
R-squared	0.068	0.069	0.073	0.029	0.030	0.031
F-statistic	358.383	333.723	297.701	113.045	105.672	92.117
Wu F-ratio	5.443	11.276	9.678	1.419	0.099	0.893

Note: Asymptotic t-statistics in parentheses, Huber t-statistics in square brackets, and intercepts not shown. For Wu F-test, critical values of $F(1,\infty)$ are 3.84 at 5 percent and 6.64 at 1 percent.

Table 11.8 Elasticities of violence with respect to number of drinks

	Beer price and individual characteristics	Beer price, marijuana decriminalization, income, outlets, and individual characteristics	Beer price, marijuana decriminalization, income, outlets, religion, and individual characteristics
Trouble			
Two-stage least squares	0.544	0.254	0.397
Ordinary least squares	0.477	0.477	0.476
Damage			
Two-stage least squares	0.629	0.642	0.628
Ordinary least squares	0.585	0.585	0.583
Fight			
Two-stage least squares	0.388	0.391	0.384
Ordinary least squares	0.269	0.269	0.266
Sexual advantage			
Two-stage least squares	0.457	0.304	0.236
Ordinary least squares	0.304	0.304	0.302

NOTES

* This chapter was presented at a session entitled Economic Aspects of Substance Use and Abuse at the Taipei International Conference on Health Economics organized by the Institute of Economics, Academia Sinica in Taipei, Taiwan, March 25–26, 1999. A preliminary version was presented at the 1998 meeting of the American Economic Association. Research for the study was supported by grant number 1 R01 AA10817 from the National Institute on Alcohol Abuse and Alcoholism (NIAAA) to the National Bureau of Economic Research (NBER). We are indebted to Rob Lyerla, formerly Assistant Director of the Core Institute of Southern Illinois University, for giving us permission to acquire the Core Surveys with state identifiers and to Jeffrey R. Cashin, currently Assistant Director of the Core Institute, for creating our data diskettes. We also are indebted to Philip J. Cook, Andrew M. Jones, Donald S. Kenkel, Henry Saffer, an anonymous reviewer, and participants of the two conferences at which the chapter was presented for helpful comments and suggestions. This chapter has

not undergone the review accorded official NBER publications; in particular, it has not been submitted for approval by the Board of Directors. Any opinions expressed are those of the authors and not those of NIAAA or NBER.

1 If the consequences are anticipated and have monetary penalties, the quantity of alcohol demand and the amount of violence depend on these penalties as well as on the price of alcohol. A model in which violence is a positive source of utility formalizes the notion that the decision to engage in violent acts can stimulate alcohol consumption because consumption raises productivity or lowers the cost of violence. Here we assume that violence is produced by two endogenous inputs: alcohol consumption and the own time of the perpetrator. For more details, see Markowitz and Grossman (1998, 2000).

2 The states included are Alaska, California, Colorado, Connecticut, Florida, Georgia, Illinois, Indiana, Iowa, Louisiana, Maryland, Massachusetts, Michigan, Minnesota, Missouri, Montana, Nebraska, New Hampshire, New York, North Carolina, Ohio, Oregon, Pennsylvania, South Carolina, Texas, Utah, Virginia, Washington, and West Virginia. Maine and New Jersey are omitted because the price of beer was missing for these two states in 1989.

3 Given the large sample size, little is gained by fitting logit or probit models. The number of occasions of each type of violence in the past year also is reported, but we have not yet exploited this information.

4 Each rate was computed after deleting observations with missing values. The same comment applies to the mean value of the number of drinks of alcohol in a week in Table 11.1.

5 One caveat to the above argument pertains to a situation in which violence that does not involve alcohol is positively related to the price of alcohol. This case is extremely unlikely. If, however, it does occur, price may have no effect on all types of violence even if it has a negative effect on alcohol-related violence. The more likely case is the one that we implicitly assume: no relationship between price and violence not involving alcohol.

6 Respondents could not indicate that they consumed alcohol but consumed less than one drink per week in answering the question pertaining to drinks per week.

7 Except for type of residence, the small number of missing values for the variables just listed are replaced by sample means. A change in the questions determining type of residence between 1989 and 1990 generated a large number of cases in which a student lived on-campus, but it could not be determined whether the residence was a dormitory or a fraternity/sorority.

8 Prior to the fourth quarter of 1989, the brands of beer were Budweiser and Schlitz. Prices for quarters prior to the fourth quarter of 1989 were adjusted based on the trend in the mean ACCRA beer price for the US as a whole between the third and fourth quarters of 1989 relative to the trend in the US beer price index reported by the Bureau of Labor Statistics.

9 The Core Surveys contain information on the use of marijuana, cocaine, and

other illegal drugs. They are relevant endogenous regressors in the structural violence equation, but we have not yet exploited these variables.

10 The bias could go in the other direction if states in which pro-drinking sentiment is widespread (anti-drinking sentiment is weak) and alcohol consumption is large enact higher beer taxes because the taxation of beer is an attractive source of revenue.

11 We limit the number of state-specific regressors because Markowitz and Grossman (1998, 2000) report that such additional determinants of alcohol consumption and violence as restrictions on alcohol advertising, permission of beer sales by grocery stores, the percentage of the state's population residing in counties that prohibit the sale of alcohol, and the price of cocaine have little impact on the outcomes they consider. Clearly, measures that vary by state alone are likely to be collinear. Thus, the degree of multicollinearity in the data is reduced by curtailing the number of state-specific regressors.

12 In the remainder of this section, all elasticities mentioned in the text are averages of those that emerge from the three alternative models employed for a given dependent variable.

13 The Grossman et al. indicator of the number of drinks in the past year is measured subject to error because it is computed as the product of the number of drinking occasions in the past year and the number of drinks consumed on a typical occasion. The latter is inferred from the response to a question concerning how often the respondent drinks enough to feel pretty high. For this reason and others, their dependent variable is not entirely comparable to our dependent variable.

14 This is an average of the separate estimates that Kenkel reports for males and females. When we employ the number of days in the past two weeks on which an individual consumed five or more drinks in a row as an outcome, we obtain a price elasticity of –0.78.

REFERENCES

American Chamber of Commerce Researchers Association (ACCRA) (various years), *Inter-city Cost of Living Index*, Louisville, KY: ACCRA.

Becker, Gary S., Michael Grossman and Kevin M. Murphy (1991), 'Rational addiction and the effect of price on consumption', *American Economic Review*, **81**(2), May: 237–41.

Becker, Gary S. and Kevin M. Murphy (1988), 'A theory of rational addiction', *Journal of Political Economy*, **96**(4), August: 675–700.

Bradley, Martin R., Norman M. Green, Jr., Dale E. Jones, Mac Lynn and Lou McNeil (1992), *Churches and Church Membership in the United*

States 1990, Atlanta, GA: Glenmary Research Center.

Bureau of Economic Analysis, US Department of Commerce (various years), *Survey of Current Business*.

Bureau of Justice Statistics (BJS), US Department of Justice (1985), *Sourcebook of Criminal Justice Statistics 1984*, Washington, DC: US Government Printing Office.

Bureau of Justice Statistics (BJS), US Department of Justice (1988), *Report to the Nation on Crime and Justice*, 2nd edn, NCJ-105506, March.

Bureau of Justice Statistics (BJS), US Department of Justice (1998), *Alcohol and Crime*, NCJ-168632, April.

Bureau of Justice Statistics (BJS), US Department of Justice (1999), *Substance Abuse and Treatment, State and Federal Prisoners, 1997*, NCJ-172871, January.

Chaloupka, Frank J. and Henry Saffer (1992), 'Alcohol, illegal drugs, public policy, and crime', Presented at the annual meeting of the Western Economic Association, San Francisco, California, July.

Chaloupka, Frank J., Henry Saffer and Michael Grossman (1993), 'Alcohol-control policies and motor-vehicle fatalities', *Journal of Legal Studies*, **22**(1), January: 161–86.

Chaloupka, Frank J. and Henry Wechsler (1996), 'Binge drinking in college: the impact of price, availability, and alcohol control policies', *Contemporary Economic Policy*, **14**(4), October: 112–24.

Collins, James J. and William Schlenger (1988), 'Acute and chronic effects of alcohol use on violence', *Journal of Studies on Alcohol*, **49**(6): 516–21.

Cook, Phillip J. and Michael J. Moore (1993a), 'Drinking and schooling', *Journal of Health Economics*, **12**(4), December: 411–30.

Cook, Phillip J. and Michael J. Moore (1993b), 'Economic perspectives on reducing alcohol-related violence', in Martin (ed.), pp. 193–211.

Cook, Philip J. and George Tauchen (1982), 'The effect of liquor taxes on heavy drinking', *Bell Journal of Economics*, **13**(2), Autumn: 379–90.

Cordilia, Ann (1985), 'Alcohol and property crime: exploring the causal nexus', *Journal of Studies on Alcohol*, **46**(2): 161–71.

Fagan, Jeffrey (1993a), 'Interactions among drugs, alcohol, and violence', *Health Affairs*, **12**(4), Winter: 65–79.

Fagan, Jeffrey (1993b), 'Set and setting revisited: influences of alcohol and illicit drugs on the social context of violent events', in Martin (ed.), pp. 161–92.

Gelles, Richard J. and Claire P. Cornell (1990), *Intimate Violence in Families*, Newbury Park, CA: Sage Publications.

Goldstein, Paul J. (1985), 'The drugs/violence nexus: a tripartite conceptual model', *Journal of Drug Issues*, **15**, Fall: 493–506.

Grossman, Michael, Frank J. Chaloupka and Ismail Sirtalan (1998), 'An empirical analysis of alcohol addiction: results from the Monitoring the Future panels', *Economic Inquiry*, **36**(1), January: 39–48.

Huber, Peter J. (1967), 'The behavior of maximum likelihood estimates under nonstandard conditions', in *Fifth Berkeley Symposium on Mathematical Statistics and Probability*, Berkeley, CA: University of California Press, pp. 221–33.

Jobson Publishing Corporation (1993), *Licensed Beverage Marketing & Merchandising Fact Book 1993*, New York: Jobson Publishing Corporation.

Johnston, Lloyd D., Patrick M. O'Malley and Jerald G. Bachman (1997), *National Survey Results on Drug Use from Monitoring the Future Study, 1975–1996*, Rockville, MD: National Institute on Drug Abuse.

Kenkel, Donald S. (1993), 'Drinking, driving, and deterrence: the effectiveness and social costs of alternative policies', *Journal of Law and Economics*, **36**(2), October: 877–913.

Long, Sharon K., Ann D. Witte and Patrice Karr (1983), 'Family violence: a microeconomic approach', *Social Science Research*, **12**: 363–92.

Markowitz, Sara and Michael Grossman (1998), 'Alcohol regulation and domestic violence towards children', *Contemporary Economic Policy*, **15**(3), July: 309–20.

Markowitz, Sara and Michael Grossman (2000), 'The effects of beer taxes on physical child abuse', *Journal of Health Economics*, **19**(2), March: 271–82.

Martin, Susan E. (ed.) (1993), *Alcohol and Interpersonal Violence: Fostering Multidisciplinary Perspectives*, National Institute on Alcohol Abuse and Alcoholism Research Monograph 24, NIH Publication No. 93-3496, Washington, DC: US Government Printing Office.

Pernanen, Kai (1981), 'Theoretical aspects of the relationship between alcohol use and crime', in James J. Collins (ed.), *Drinking and Crime: Perspectives on the Relationship between Alcohol Consumption and Criminal Behavior*, New York: Guilford Press, pp. 1–69.

Pernanen, Kai (1991), *Alcohol in Human Violence*, New York: Guilford Press.

Pernanen, Kai (1993), 'Alcohol-related violence: conceptual models and methodological issues', in Martin (ed.), pp. 37–70.

Presley, Cheryl A., Philip W. Meilman and Rob Lyerla (1993), *Alcohol and Drugs on American College Campuses*, Vol. I: 1989–91, Carbondale, IL: Southern Illinois University Core Institute.

Presley, Cheryl A., Philip W. Meilman and Rob Lyerla (1995), *Alcohol and Drugs on American College Campuses*, Vol. II: 1990–92, Carbondale, IL: Southern Illinois University Core Institute.

Presley, Cheryl A., Philip W. Meilman, Jeffrey R. Cashin and Rob Lyerla (1996), *Alcohol and Drugs on American College Campuses*, Vol. III: 1991–93, Carbondale, IL: Southern Illinois University Core Institute.

Quinn, Bernard, Herman Anderson, Martin Bradley, Paul Goetting and Peggy Shriver (1982), *Churches and Church Membership in the United States 1980*, Atlanta, GA: Glenmary Research Center.

Reiss, Albert J. Jr. and Jeffrey E. Roth (eds) (1993), *Understanding and Preventing Violence*, Washington, DC: National Academy Press.

Ruhm, Christopher J. (1996), 'Alcohol policies and highway fatality rates', *Journal of Health Economics*, **15**(4), August: 435–54.

Saffer, Henry (1991), 'Alcohol advertising bans and alcohol abuse: an international perspective', *Journal of Health Economics*, **10**(1), May: 65–79.

Saffer, Henry and Michael Grossman (1987), 'Beer taxes, the legal drinking age, and youth motor vehicle fatalities', *Journal of Legal Studies*, **16**(2), June: 351–74.

Schelling, Thomas C. (1978), 'Egonomics, or the art of self-management', *American Economic Review*, **68**(2), May: 291–4.

Sloan, Frank A., Bridget A. Reilly and Christopher Schenzler (1995), 'Effects of tort liability and insurance on heavy drinking and drinking and driving', *Journal of Law and Economics*, **38**(1), April: 49–78.

Tauchen, Helen V., Ann Dryden Witte and Sharon K. Long (1991), 'Domestic violence: a nonrandom affair', *International Economic Review*, **32**(2), May: 491–511.

Thaler, Richard H. and H.M. Shefrin (1981), 'An economic theory of self-control', *Journal of Political Economy*, **89**(2), April: 392–406.

Viscusi, W. Kip (1986), 'Market incentives for criminal behavior', in Richard B. Freeman and Henry J. Holzer (eds), *The Black Youth Employment Crisis*, Chicago: University of Chicago Press, pp. 301–46.

Wolfgang, Marvin E. (1958), *Patterns in Criminal Behavior*, New York: John Wiley & Sons.

Wu, De-Min (1973), 'Alternative tests of independence between stochastic regressors and disturbances', *Econometrica*, **41**(4), July: 733–50.

12. Substance abuse control and crime: evidence from the National Household Survey of Drug Abuse

Henry Saffer[*]

1 INTRODUCTION

Alcohol and illicit drugs impose significant costs on society and on the individual users. These costs include increased crime, health problems, and employment problems. Because of these considerable costs, government, at all levels, has made alcohol and illicit drug control an important priority. According to the Bureau of Justice Statistics (BJS 1998), in 1997 Americans experienced about 35 million criminal victimizations, which was the lowest number in the 24 years that these data have been collected. These victimizations included over 9 million personal crimes and 27 million property crimes. The BJS (1997) reports that about 3 million violent crimes occur each year in which victims perceive the offender to have been drinking at the time of the offense. Among those victims, who provided information about the offender's use of alcohol, about 35 percent of the victimizations involved an offender who had been drinking. Two-thirds of victims, who suffered violence by a current or former spouse, boyfriend, or girlfriend, reported that alcohol had been a factor. Among spouse victims, three out of four incidents were reported to have involved an offender who had been drinking. In addition, an estimated 31 percent of stranger victimizations, where the victim could determine the absence or presence of alcohol, were perceived to be alcohol related. For about one in five violent victimizations involving perceived alcohol use by the offender, victims also reported they believed the offender to have been using drugs as well.

Data from the BJS (1998) also indicate that among the 5.3 million convicted offenders under the jurisdiction of corrections agencies in 1996, nearly 2 million, or about 36 percent, were estimated to have been drinking at the time of the offense. About 1.3 million of these alcohol-involved offenders were sentenced to probation and more than 200,000 to parole. Jail inmates' self-reported alcohol consumption equaled about 11 beers, and prisoners drank the equivalent of 15 beers during a period of up to 8 hours prior to the crime. The highest overall consumption prior to the offense was reported by state prisoners serving time after conviction for a property offense.

2 SUBSTANCE ABUSE AND CRIME

There is general agreement in the literature that the consumption of alcohol is linked to various criminal behaviors. Why alcohol is linked to crime, or whether both alcohol consumption and crime are outcomes related to a common third factor remains a controversial subject. There is less agreement on the co-occurrence of illicit drug use and criminal behaviors. This may be the result of differences in the psychopharmacological effects of the various illicit drugs in use. The estimation procedures employed in this chapter rely on reduced-form models which eliminate the problem of joint causality between substance use and criminal behaviors. The models presented link the policy variables, drug control spending and beer taxes directly to criminal behavior.

There are a few prior studies by economists that examine the effects of alcohol and illicit drug prices and control policies on various crime-related outcomes.[1] These studies rely on a variety of data and methods and generally show that higher alcohol prices reduce both violent and property crimes. The effect of higher drug prices is generally found to have no effect on crimes of violence. However, there is some evidence that drug use is correlated with income-producing crime.

Two prior studies use pooled cross-section, time-series data. Chaloupka and Saffer (1992) employed a time series of cross-sections for the states of the US and Washington, DC from 1975 through 1990. They examined the effect of beer taxes and marijuana decriminalization on ten alternative measures of crime. Their results show that increased beer taxes reduce murder, rape, robbery, burglary, larceny and motor vehicle theft. The only crime unresponsive to higher taxes is assault. Decriminalization of marijuana is generally estimated to have a positive impact on the various crime rates, with the exception of the murder rate. Cook and Moore (1993) employed a time series of 48 state cross-sections from 1979 through 1988. They examined the effect of beer taxes on homicide, rape, robbery and assault rates. They conclude that increased beer taxes reduce those crimes with the strongest effects on rape and robbery.

Three studies use micro data to examine the relationship between substance abuse control and violence in families. Markowitz (forthcoming) employs data from the 1985 National Family Violence Survey. She estimates the effect of alcohol prices on violence against spouses. Her results show that higher alcohol prices reduce violence against wives, but the evidence of an effect on husbands is mixed. Markowitz and Grossman (1998) employ data from the 1976 Physical Violence in American Families Survey. They estimate the effect of state beer taxes and illicit drug prices on violence against children. They find that higher beer taxes reduce violence against children, but that drug prices have no effect. Markowitz and Grossman (2000) expand the prior study to include both the 1976 and 1985 Physical Violence in American Families Survey. They estimate gender-specific effects of state beer taxes and illicit drug prices on violence against children. They find that increased beer taxes will reduce the incidence of violence against children committed by women, but have no effect on the incidence of such violence committed by men. They find no effect of drug prices.

Another study examines the effect of substance abuse policy on violence among college students. Grossman and Markowitz (1999) employ the 1989, 1990 and 1991 Core Alcohol and Drug Surveys of College Students to examine the effects of the price of beer on four measures of violence: (i) any trouble with police or authorities, (ii) damage to property, (iii) fighting and (iv) taking sexual advantage, or being taken advantage of sexually. They find that increases in the price of beer reduce all four measures of violence among college students.

Corman and Mocan (forthcoming) employ time-series data for New York City from 1970 to 1996 to examine the effect of the number of police officers and number of arrests on the number of murders, assaults, robberies, burglaries, grand larcenies and auto thefts. They also examine the effect of drug use on the incidence of these crimes. They find that an increase in the number of police reduces robbery and burglary, an increase in arrests reduces murder, robbery, burglary and motor vehicle theft, and drug use is related to robbery and burglary.

3 THEORETICAL MODEL

The economic models of criminal behavior developed by Becker (1968, 1974), Tauchen et al. (1991), Chaloupka and Saffer (1992), and Cook and Moore (1993) imply the following structural equation for criminal acts (C):

$$C = C(E, A, D, \mathbf{Y}, U). \qquad (12.1)$$

Here E represents law enforcement, A is alcohol consumption, D is illicit drug consumption, $\mathbf{Y}$ is a vector of other observed factors that affect the benefits and costs of crime such as income, employment status and wages, and years of formal schooling completed, and U stands for unobserved individual or environmental determinants that affect deviant behavior.

Consumer demand theory provides a demand for alcohol equation and a demand for illicit drugs equation. The demand function for alcohol is:

$$A = A\ (P_A, \mathbf{Y}, U), \tag{12.2}$$

where the variable P_A is the price of alcohol.[2] The market for illicit drugs is more complex than the market for alcohol due to the effect of drug control on supply and demand. The prices of illicit drugs reflect almost entirely the expected sanctions resulting from use or possession of the substance. These expected sanctions vary by community. Actual drug production and distribution costs are virtually an irrelevant component of the retail price (Reuter 1988). Increases in expected sanctions reduce demand and reduce supply. The net effect of expected sanctions is a reduction in equilibrium quantity but an uncertain effect on equilibrium price. The effect of expected sanctions on price depends on whether demand or supply is more affected. The reduced form of drug demand and supply, which solves for equilibrium quantity is:

$$D = D\ (C_D, \mathbf{Y}, U), \tag{12.3}$$

where C_D is expected sanctions for illicit drug possession or use.[3] Substitution of equations (12.2) and (12.3) into equation (12.1) yields a reduced-form equation for crime:

$$C = C\ (P_A, CD, E, \mathbf{Y}, U). \tag{12.4}$$

An increase in the price of alcohol, or an increase in expected sanctions could reduce crime. In the case of illicit drugs and income crimes, the relationships may be different. If the increase in expected sanctions raised the price of illicit drugs, users with an inelastic demand for illicit drugs would face increased drug expenditures. If these users financed their drug expenditures with income crime then an increase in expected sanctions would increase the level of income crime committed by these users. For individuals who finance their drug use from legal employment, lower drug use may have no effect on income crime. Alcohol price may affect income crime if criminals drink shortly before committing income crimes to increase their courage (Cordilia 1985). Alternatively, alcohol use may serve as a deterrent to income crimes by raising the probability that the offender will be caught (Chaloupka and Saffer 1992).

The equation to be estimated is the reduced-form equation (12.4). Estimation of the reduced-form equation avoids the bias which would occur if the structural equation (12.1) were estimated. In this structural equation, unobserved factors that determine violence and crime may also determine alcohol and drug use. Hence A and D are correlated with U in the structural equation, introducing bias.

4 THE DATA SET

A data set derived from the 1991 National Household Survey on Drug Abuse (NHSDA) was employed for estimation. The 1991 survey has about 32,000 observations, which is important since a large sample increases the number of observed criminal outcomes. The NHSDA is a cross-sectional survey of the US household population aged 12 or older and contains information on socioeconomic characteristics as well as data on criminal behavior. These surveys exclude residents of non-institutional group quarters (that is, college dormitories) and exclude residents of institutional group quarters (that is, prisons). Also excluded are those people with no permanent residence (that is, homeless and residents in transient hotels). Less than 2 percent of the population is excluded. The excluded 2 percent may have a higher percentage of substance abusers than the included 98 percent.

Five dichotomous dependent variables have been defined. Each variable is equal to one if, during the past year, the respondent has engaged in the activity described by the variable name. The first variable is arrested, which is positive if the respondent was arrested. The arrest variable may understate crime to the extent that criminals commit multiple crimes or are successful in avoiding arrest. Arrest may also overstate crime to the extent that innocent individuals are arrested. The second variable is defined as property crime and is positive if the respondent reports stealing anything of value, including a car, or breaking into a house. The third variable is property damage which is positive if the respondent damaged someone else's property. The fourth variable is defined as use of force and is equal to one if the respondent used force, including use of a weapon, to commit a crime. The fifth variable is defined as illicit drug selling and is positive if the respondent sold illicit drugs. Although these variables are self-reported, studies such as Hindelang et al. (1981) find that self-reported data and official data are very similar.

The price of alcohol is measured by the state tax on beer. Excise tax data are the most reliable price data available. Beer tax data were chosen since beer is the most popular alcoholic beverage among offenders.[4] The beer tax variable is defined as the sum of the federal and state excise tax rates on a case of 24 12-ounce containers of beer and is deflated by the national consumer price index (CPI) (1982–84 base year). State excise tax rates were taken from the Beer Institute, *Brewer's Almanac*. These data were appended, by state, to each record in the 1991 NHSDA.

Expected sanctions are measured by per capita illicit drug control expenditures. These data, for 1991, were taken from *State and Local Spending on Drug Control Activities* prepared by the Office of National Drug Control Policy (ONDCP 1993). These data were collected as part of a special survey on drug control done by the US Bureau of the Census. The data are estimates of expenditure on drug control only. These data were appended, by state, to the data taken from the NHSDA. Drug control expenditures include spending on police activities, judicial activities, prosecution and legal services, public defense, corrections, other criminal justice activities, education and treatment.[5] Prosecution and legal services include the criminal justice activities of the attorneys general, district attorneys and other departments which have the full power to prosecute drug violation cases. Public defense includes court paid fees to individually retained counsel, fees paid by the court to court appointed counsel, government contributions to private legal aid societies and the expenses of established public defender office or program. Treatment includes expenditures for hospital facilities directly operated by state or local government and for payments to private facilities. Education includes expenditures by state and local government for elementary and secondary school drug education. The drug control expenditure variable was divided by state population. It is also important to measure the effect of drug control expenditure on crime since these expenditures can be controlled directly by policy choice. These data were appended by state to each record in the NHSDA.

Additional economic and demographic variables have been defined with the data in the NHSDA. These include total personal income from all sources including wages, self-employment, social security, public assistance, child support and other pension income. Income is a continuous variable measured in 1983 dollars. The demographic variables are indicators of age, race, gender and marital status. Age and age-squared variables were included to allow for differential age effects. A dichotomous variable equal to one if the individual reports that they are Black has also been defined. A similar variable was defined for Hispanics. A dichotomous variable equal to one if the individual is male has also been defined. A variable for married has also been defined. There were a number of missing values for this variable. Rather than deleting these observations or omitting this variable, the missing values were estimated. A probit regression using the non-missing marriage data as the dependent variable with income, age, education, race and ethnicity as independent variables was estimated.[6] This equation was used to predict the values of the marriage variable for the missing observations. Table 12.1 provides the means and summary definitions of all of the variables.

5 REGRESSION RESULTS

The regression results are presented in Tables 12.2–6 with one table for each independent variable. In each table, three alternative specifications are presented. Each specification includes the same set of demographic variables and either: (i) drug control expenditure, (ii) the beer tax or (iii) both drug control expenditure and the beer tax. These three specifications are repeated for individuals under age 21. All of the regressions in Tables 12.2–6 are estimated as probits with robust standard errors.[7] The estimates are probits since the dependent variables are all dichotomous. The robust standard errors are used to correct for dependence across individuals within the same group. The individual's state of residence is used as the grouping variable in the computation of these standard errors.

In Tables 12.2–6, each specification includes one or both policy variables. In all tables, the sign, magnitude and significance of each policy variable and all other independent variables are unaffected by the inclusion or omission of the other policy variables. This suggests that the policy variables have no collinearity problems with the other variables and that neither policy variable introduces any bias due to endogeneity.[8]

For the entire sample, the results for the policy variables show that increased drug control reduces arrests, property damage, and drug sales. The exception is property crimes and use of force. Since none of the respondents is homeless or living in institutions, they may pay for their drugs from legal employment. This could result in drug control having no effect on property crime in this data set. The lack of an effect on violence may be due to the psychopharmacology of most illicit drugs. Increased beer taxes are shown to reduce arrests, property crime, property damage and use of force. The exception is drug sales. Perhaps individuals who sell drugs tend to prefer drugs over beer and are thus unresponsive to higher beer taxes. The effect of the policy variables on arrests is generally consistent with their effects on the other dependent variables. This suggests that the arrest data are also a good measure of crime.

Table 12.1 Weighted means from the 1991 National Household Survey of Drug Abuse

Variables	Definition and mean
Arrest	A dichotomous variable equal to one if the individual was arrested for breaking the law in the past 12 months. $\mu = 0.019$ $\mu^* = 0.041$
Property crime	A dichotomous variable equal to one if the individual engaged in theft or broke into a house in the past 12 months. $\mu = 0.048$ $\mu^* = 0.175$
Property damage	A dichotomous variable equal to one if the individual damaged someone else's property in the past 12 months. $\mu = 0.022$ $\mu^* = 0.102$
Use of force	A dichotomous variable equal to one if the individual used force or a weapon to obtain something from another person in the past 12 months. $\mu = 0.005$ $\mu^* = 0.014$
Sold drugs	A dichotomous variable equal to one if the individual sold illegal drugs in the past 12 months. $\mu = 0.009$ $\mu^* = 0.027$
Drug control	The sum of spending on police, courts, prosecution, public defense, corrections education in schools about illicit drugs and spending on drug treatment, and miscellaneous other spending for drug-related offenses as a percent of state population. $\mu = 0.060$ $\mu^* = 0.057$
Beer tax	Tax on beer. $\mu = 1.954$ $\mu^* = 1.997$
Real income	Total personal income in thousands of 1983 dollars. $\mu = 11.838$ $\mu^* = 2.233$
Education	Total years of schooling completed. $\mu = 12.200$ $\mu^* = 9.386$
Male	A dichotomous variable equal to one for males. $\mu = 0.479$ $\mu^* = 0.511$
Marital status	A dichotomous variable equal to one if married. $\mu = 0.569$ $\mu^* = 0.074$
Age	A continuous variable measuring age. $\mu = 40.760$ $\mu^* = 16.130$
Agesq	Square of Age. $\mu = 2014.770$ $\mu^* = 266.837$
Hispanic	A dichotomous variable equal to one if an individual self-reports that they are Hispanic. $\mu = 0.080$ $\mu^* = 0.110$
Black	A dichotomous variable equal to one if an individual self-reports that they are Black. $\mu = 0.117$ $\mu^* = 0.155$

Note: Final sample size when missing values were excluded is 30,821 for the complete sample and 10,551 for the youth sample. All data are weighted. *Mean for under age 21.

Table 12.2 Regression results: dependent variable – arrest

Specification	Overall population			Under age 21*		
	1	2	3	4	5	6
Drug control spending	−2.6056 (−2.40)	–	−2.4926 (−2.38)	−1.8723 (−1.74)	–	−1.6623 (−1.65)
Beer tax	–	−0.0320 (−3.16)	−0.0303 (−2.66)	–	−0.0627 (−4.44)	−0.0639 (−4.27)
Real income	−0.0103 (−2.41)	−0.0106 (−2.41)	−0.0104 (−2.48)	0.0104 (1.07)	0.0104 (1.06)	0.0094 (0.96)
Education	−0.0357 (−3.59)	−0.0347 (−3.26)	−0.0355 (−3.50)	−0.0841 (−3.30)	−0.0853 (−3.30)	−0.0856 (−3.35)
Male	0.5812 (16.04)	0.5753 (15.39)	0.5828 (15.93)	0.5377 (14.74)	0.5459 (14.67)	0.5444 (14.76)
Married	−0.5007 (−10.11)	−0.4826 (−9.49)	−0.5002 (−10.08)	−0.5640 (−2.26)	−0.5643 (−2.21)	−0.5729 (−2.25)
Age	0.0825 (6.84)	0.0802 (6.78)	0.0822 (6.81)	1.0579 (4.97)	1.0743 (5.01)	1.0688 (5.03)
Age squared	−0.0013 (−7.04)	−0.0012 (−6.99)	−0.0013 (−6.99)	−0.0281 (−4.50)	−0.0285 (−4.56)	−0.0283 (−4.55)
Hispanic	0.0656 (1.02)	0.0229 (0.41)	0.0689 (1.16)	0.0668 (0.97)	0.0369 (0.67)	0.0687 (1.14)
Black	0.0731 (1.59)	0.0615 (1.66)	0.0906 (2.12)	0.0876 (1.28)	0.0889 (1.47)	0.1225 (1.89)
Constant	−2.6121 (−14.97)	−2.6859 (−17.13)	−2.5619 (−14.54)	−10.8317 (−6.34)	−10.9775 (−6.32)	−10.8349 (−6.41)
No. of observations	30,821	31,386	30,821	10,551	10,711	10,551

Note: All specifications are estimated as probit. Calculated standard errors are robust. Standard normal z values are in parentheses. *Ages less than 21.

For the sample of individuals under age 21, the results for the policy variables show that increased drug control reduces arrests, property damage, and drug sales. Increased beer taxes are shown to reduce arrests, property crime and property damage. These results are the same as in the entire sample with the exception of use of force. Table 12.7 reports the elasticities for both the entire sample and for the sample restricted individuals to under age 21. The elasticities for youth are generally larger than for the total sample. The largest increase is the effect of beer taxes on arrests. This may reflect both a greater price sensitivity of youth and the enforcement of minimum age laws for the purchase of alcohol. Drug

Table 12.3 Regression results: dependent variable – property crime

Specification	Overall population			Under age 21*		
	1	2	3	4	5	6
Drug control spending	−0.5029 (−0.57)	–	−0.4040 (−0.48)	−0.5469 (−0.65)	–	−0.4660 (−0.58)
Beer tax	–	−0.0372 (−3.70)	−0.0382 (−3.89)	–	−0.0325 (−2.33)	−0.0344 (−2.55)
Real income	−0.0061 (−2.44)	−0.0058 (−2.54)	−0.0062 (−2.60)	0.0120 (2.14)	0.0123 (2.13)	0.0114 (2.00)
Education	0.0174 (1.94)	0.0178 (1.89)	0.0177 (1.94)	0.0534 (3.39)	0.0503 (2.90)	0.0527 (3.26)
Male	0.3101 (10.71)	0.3111 (10.96)	0.3126 (10.82)	0.3093 (10.77)	0.3148 (11.07)	0.3131 (11.02)
Married	−0.3402 (−7.64)	−0.3343 (−7.67)	−0.3383 (−7.54)	−0.3774 (−2.80)	−0.3741 (−2.77)	−0.3734 (−2.75)
Age	−0.0565 (−6.51)	−0.0573 (−6.86)	−0.0572 (−6.66)	0.8854 (11.72)	0.8846 (11.71)	0.8897 (11.44)
Age squared	0.0003 (3.53)	0.0003 (3.74)	0.0003 (3.66)	−0.0295 (−12.59)	−0.0294 (−12.64)	−0.0296 (−12.43)
Hispanic	−0.1418 (−3.26)	−0.1463 (−4.14)	−0.1354 (−3.34)	−0.1400 (−3.20)	−0.1463 (−3.73)	−0.1367 (−3.38)
Black	−0.0950 (−1.42)	−0.0973 (−1.71)	−0.0747 (−1.25)	−0.1473 (−2.05)	−0.1522 (−2.44)	−0.1278 (−1.88)
Constant	−0.4143 (−4.01)	−0.3694 (−3.85)	−0.3465 (−3.22)	−7.9783 (−13.06)	−7.9335 (−13.61)	−7.9590 (−12.76)
No. of observations	31,762	32,354	31,762	10,841	11,011	10,841

Note: All specifications are estimated as probit. Calculated standard errors are robust. Standard normal *z* values are in parentheses. *Ages less than 21.

Table 12.4 Regression results: dependent variable – property damage

Specification	Overall population			Under age 21*		
	1	2	3	4	5	6
Drug control spending	−1.6654 (−1.75)	–	−1.5833 (−1.69)	−2.2579 (−2.44)	–	−2.1637 (−2.39)
Beer tax	–	−0.0275 (−2.75)	−0.0272 (−2.89)	–	−0.0308 (−2.11)	−0.0298 (−2.44)
Real income	−0.0074 (−1.80)	−0.0076 (−1.91)	−0.0075 (−1.88)	0.0073 (1.04)	0.0067 (0.94)	0.0067 (0.93)
Education	−0.0074 (−0.92)	−0.0077 (−0.91)	−0.0073 (−0.88)	0.0265 (1.44)	0.0192 (0.95)	0.0254 (1.36)
Male	0.4350 (12.48)	0.4379 (12.90)	0.4370 (12.73)	0.4438 (12.64)	0.4478 (13.08)	0.4466 (13.03)
Married	−0.4351 (−6.95)	−0.4171 (−6.85)	−0.4342 (−6.89)	−0.0485 (−0.35)	−0.0365 (−0.26)	−0.0474 (−0.34)
Age	−0.0440 (−2.94)	−0.0440 (−2.98)	−0.0442 (−2.95)	0.9011 (7.72)	0.9094 (7.82)	0.9030 (7.65)
Age squared	0.0001 (0.27)	0.0001 (0.27)	0.0001 (0.28)	−0.0297 (−8.76)	−0.0297 (−8.81)	−0.0297 (−8.70)
Hispanic	−0.1178 (−1.69)	−0.1484 (−2.80)	−0.1150 (−1.74)	−0.0952 (−1.22)	−0.1417 (−2.50)	−0.0940 (−1.26)
Black	−0.0242 (−0.45)	−0.0342 (−0.68)	−0.0090 (−0.18)	−0.1150 (−2.14)	−0.1308 (−2.88)	−0.0980 (−2.08)
Constant	−0.6761 (−4.89)	−0.7250 (−5.58)	−0.6305 (−4.41)	−8.2918 (−9.14)	−8.4314 (−9.41)	−8.2610 (−8.95)
No. of observations	31,762	32,254	31,762	10,841	11,011	10,841

Note: All specifications are estimated as probit. Calculated standard errors are robust. Standard normal z values are in parentheses. *Ages less than 21.

Table 12.5 Regression results: dependent variable – use of force

Specification	Overall population			Under age 21*		
	1	2	3	4	5	6
Drug control spending	–0.3050 (–0.54)	–	–0.2623 (–0.49)	–0.1303 (–0.19)	–	–0.0845 (–0.12)
Beer tax	–	–0.0178 (–1.98)	–0.0174 (–1.91)	–	–0.0191 (–1.36)	–0.0190 (–1.33)
Real income	0.0003 (0.03)	0.0002 (0.02)	0.0002 (0.02)	0.0249 (2.27)	0.0291 (2.66)	0.0246 (2.23)
Education	–0.0469 (–2.61)	–0.0447 (–2.52)	–0.0467 (–2.58)	–0.0973 (–3.69)	–0.0994 (–3.77)	–0.0977 (–3.68)
Male	0.4736 (4.72)	0.4710 (4.84)	0.4751 (4.75)	0.5138 (6.00)	0.5121 (6.09)	0.5158 (6.01)
Married	–0.3549 (–5.00)	–0.3120 (–3.92)	–0.3538 (–4.93)	–0.4022 (–1.88)	–0.4009 (–1.90)	–0.4006 (–1.89)
Age	0.0252 (1.34)	0.0217 (1.17)	0.0245 (1.30)	1.0691 (6.78)	1.1338 (6.89)	1.0712 (6.77)
Age squared	–0.0006 (–1.79)	–0.0006 (–1.69)	–0.0006 (–1.75)	–0.0316 (–6.23)	–0.0337 (–6.39)	–0.0317 (–6.24)
Hispanic	–0.0443 (–0.51)	–0.0409 (–0.52)	–0.0423 (–0.50)	0.0319 (0.35)	0.0382 (0.47)	0.0328 (0.37)
Black	0.2051 (2.97)	0.2134 (3.33)	0.2160 (3.01)	0.1928 (1.89)	0.1975 (1.96)	0.2046 (1.92)
Constant	–2.3445 (–12.57)	–2.3061 (–13.28)	–2.3100 (–12.38)	–10.5581 (–8.24)	–11.0085 (–8.35)	–10.5440 (–8.21)
No. of observations	31,762	32,354	31,762	10,841	11,011	10,841

Note: All specifications are estimated as probit. Calculated standard errors are robust. Standard normal *z* values are in parentheses. *Ages less than 21.

Table 12.6 Regression results: dependent variable – sold drugs

Specification	Overall population			Under age 21*		
	1	2	3	4	5	6
Drug control spending	−1.4673 (−2.41)	–	−1.4030 (−2.35)	−2.1171 (−2.07)	–	−2.0862 (−2.13)
Beer tax	–	−0.0201 (−1.45)	−0.0170 (−1.18)	–	−0.0100 (−0.57)	−0.0073 (−0.42)
Real income	−0.0104 (−2.69)	−0.0100 (−2.83)	−0.0104 (−2.73)	0.0216 (3.02)	0.0243 (3.42)	0.0216 (3.04)
Education	−0.0090 (−0.87)	−0.0077 (−0.73)	−0.0089 (−0.85)	−0.0531 (−2.59)	−0.0504 (−2.42)	−0.0532 (−2.59)
Male	0.4561 (10.44)	0.4484 (10.41)	0.4566 (10.45)	0.3180 (4.40)	0.3235 (4.51)	0.3183 (4.40)
Married	−0.4980 (−7.56)	−0.4603 (−6.89)	−0.4956 (−7.59)	−0.3209 (−1.44)	−0.3089 (−1.41)	−0.3192 (−1.44)
Age	0.0655 (2.57)	0.0627 (2.51)	0.0647 (2.56)	1.7531 (9.72)	1.7331 (9.75)	1.7557 (9.70)
Age squared	−0.0013 (−2.80)	−0.0012 (−2.78)	−0.0013 (−2.80)	−0.0496 (−9.67)	−0.0491 (−9.74)	−0.0496 (−9.66)
Hispanic	−0.1644 (−2.24)	−0.1903 (−3.02)	−0.1625 (−2.24)	−0.0695 (−0.72)	−0.1158 (−1.45)	−0.0695 (−0.72)
Black	0.0774 (1.31)	0.0861 (1.52)	0.0874 (1.46)	0.1004 (1.68)	0.0858 (1.45)	0.1051 (1.64)
Constant	−2.7738 (−10.21)	−2.7976 (−10.54)	−2.7388 (−10.51)	−16.7388 (−11.53)	−16.6742 (−11.69)	−16.7488 (−11.50)
No. of observations	31,762	32,354	31,762	10,841	11,011	10,841

Note: All specifications are estimated as probit. Calculated standard errors are robust. Standard normal z values are in parentheses. *Ages less than 21.

Table 12.7 Elasticities

	Arrest	Property crime	Use of force	Property damage	Sold drugs
Drug control (overall pop)	–0.23			–0.10	–0.10
Drug control (under age 21)	–0.18			–0.24	–0.22
Beer tax (overall pop)	–0.08	–0.10	–0.05	–0.05	
Beer tax (under age 21)	–0.21	–0.10		–0.10	

Note: Elasticities for the full sample are computed using regression specification 3. Elasticities for the under age 21 sample are computed using regression specification 6.

control and beer taxes have about twice the effect on reducing property damage by youth than for the entire sample.

For the entire sample the other independent variables are fairly consistent with prior expectations. Higher income generally has a negative and significant effect on all crime outcome variables. The exception is use of force which is unrelated to income. These results are consistent with Corman and Mocan (forthcoming) who find that poverty increases crime. Increased education also has a negative effect on crime with the exception of property damage and drug sales. Men consistently commit more crimes and individuals who are married consistently commit less crime. Age generally has a negative effect on crime. Hispanics commit less crime, with the exception of use of force. Blacks generally commit more crimes involving use of force and are arrested more, but commit fewer property crimes.

For one sample under age 21, the other independent variables are somewhat different. Higher income generally has no effect on arrests and property damage but has a positive effect on property crimes, use of force and drug selling. This may reflect a positive income effect on the demand for substances for youth in families with higher incomes. Increased education also has a negative effect on arrests, use of force and drug selling. Males commit more crimes and youths who are married generally commit less crimes. For youths, age generally has a positive effect on crime. Hispanic youths have about the same levels of crime as the general population. Black youths generally commit more crimes involving use of force and are arrested more, but commit fewer property crimes.

6 CONCLUSIONS

The results in this chapter show that increased drug control spending and increased beer taxes can reduce crime. When the sample is restricted to individuals under age 21, the magnitude of the effects generally increases. These estimated effects are consistent with similar measures estimated in other studies.

There is a small but increasing empirical literature which employs a variety of data and consistently finds that substance abuse control reduces crime. The estimation results produced in this study, as in any other study, should be considered in the context of the limitations of the data. These limitations include unmeasured individual specific characteristics, omitted enforcement data and measurement error in the self-reported crime data. The significance of this study is as another contribution to the literature on the effects of substance abuse control on crime. When all of these studies are viewed together, in spite of their individual limitations, there is clear evidence that substance abuse policies reduce crime. Policy makers, when considering the social costs and benefits of increased alcohol prices, should add reduced crime as an additional social benefit. While drug use is widely condemned, its illicit status eliminates taxation as a control option. The options for drug control mostly involve outlays of public money. Policy makers should consider the reduction in crime and other benefits of drug control expenditures against the opportunity cost of these outlays.

NOTES

* The author would like to thank Dhaval Dave for research assistance and the seminar participants at the Taipei International Conference on Health Economics, held in Taipei, Taiwan, March 1999, for helpful comments. This project was supported by grant no. 1 RO1 AA 10817 from the National Institute on Alcoholism and Alcohol Abuse.

1. There is a large literature written by criminologists on the relationship between drug use and crime. See Harrison (1992) for a review of this literature.
2. The price of drugs may also affect the demand for alcohol. This effect is included in the reduced-form crime equation through the drug enforcement variable.
3. The price of alcohol may also affect the demand for illicit drugs. This effect is

included in the reduced-form crime equation through the alcohol price variable.

4 Meaningful wine and distilled spirits taxes are only available for states which permit the sale of all alcoholic beverages in licensed establishments.

5 The other category primarily includes state-level spending on coordinating councils and commissions.

6 This equation used age, income, education, Hispanic and Black as independent variables. All variables were highly significant. All variables were positive except Black. The regression correctly predicted 73 percent of the known values.

7 Also known as White or Huber standard errors.

8 Total law enforcement data are also available and were included in the preliminary regressions. This variable produced a positive coefficient on several crime measures. This was probably due to endogeneity between crime and total law enforcement. Since there is no way of identifying a separate enforcement equation, this variable was dropped from the final regressions. The omission of total law enforcement may result in an overstatement of the effects of the included policy variables.

REFERENCES

Becker, Gary S. (1968), 'Crime and punishment: an economic approach', *Journal of Political Economy*, **76**(2), March/April: 169–217.

Becker, Gary S. (1974), 'A theory of social interactions', *Journal of Political Economy*, **82**(6), November/December: 1063–93.

Beer Institute (1993), *Brewer's Almanac*, New York: United States Brewers Foundation.

Bureau of Justice Statistics (BJS) (1997), *National Crime Victimization Survey*, Washington, DC: US Department of Justice.

Bureau of Justice Statistics (BJS) (1998), *Alcohol and Crime*, Washington, DC: US Department of Justice.

Chaloupka, Frank J. and Henry Saffer (1992), 'Alcohol, illegal drugs, public policy, and crime', Presented at the annual meeting of the Western Economic Association, San Francisco, California, July.

Cook, P.J. and M.J. Moore (1993), 'Economic perspectives on reducing alcohol-related violence', in S.E. Martin (ed.), *Alcohol and Interpersonal Violence: Fostering Multidisciplinary Perspectives*, National Institute on Alcohol Abuse and Alcoholism Research Monograph 24, NIH Publication No. 93–3496, Washington, DC: US Government Printing Office.

Cordilia, Ann (1985), 'Alcohol and property crime: exploring the causal nexis', *Journal of Studies on Alcohol*, **46**(2): 161–71.

Corman, H. and Naci Mocan (forthcoming), 'A time series analysis of crime, drug abuse and deterrence in New York City', *American Economic Review*.

Grossman, Michael and Sara Markowitz (1999), 'Alcohol regulation on college campuses', manuscript, National Bureau of Economic Research.

Harrison, Lana D. (1992), 'The drug-crime nexus in the USA', *Contemporary Drug Problems*, **19**(2), Summer: 203–46.

Hindelang, Michael J., Travis Hirschi and Joseph G. Weis (1981), *Measuring Delinquency*, Beverly Hills, CA: Sage.

Markowitz, Sara (forthcoming) 'The price of alcohol, wife abuse, and husband abuse', *Southern Economic Journal*.

Markowitz, Sara and Michael Grossman (1998), 'Alcohol regulation and domestic violence towards children', *Contemporary Economic Policy*, **16**(3), July: 309–20.

Markowitz, Sara and Michael Grossman (2000), 'The effects of beer taxes on physical child abuse', *Journal of Health Economics*, **19**(2), March: 271–82.

Office of National Drug Control Policy (ONDCP) (1993), *State and Local Spending on Drug Control Activities: Report from the National Survey of State and Local Governments*, Washington, DC: Office of National Drug Control Policy.

Reuter, Peter (1988), 'Quantity illusions and paradoxes of drug interdiction: federal intervention into vice policy', *Law and Contemporary Problems*, **51**(1), Winter: 233–52.

Tauchen, Helen V., Ann Dryden Witte and Sharon K. Long (1991), 'Domestic violence: a nonrandom affair', *International Economic Review*, **32**(2), May: 491–511.

US Department of Commerce, Economics and Statistics Administration (1993, 1994), *Statistical Abstract of the United States*, Washington, DC: US Government Printing Office.

13. Criminal violence and alcohol beverage control: evidence from an international study

Sara Markowitz*

1 INTRODUCTION

Violent crime is a serious social problem faced by almost all nations around the world. Studies from many different countries show that there is a well-established link between alcohol consumption and violence (see Miczek et al. 1994, for a complete review of the literature). When studying criminal violence, there are two aspects of the drinking/violence relationship that must be addressed. The first is the relationship between alcohol consumption by the perpetrator and his or her propensity towards violence, while the second focuses on the alcohol consumption of the potential victim, which may put him or her at a higher risk for victimization.

Focusing first on the perpetrator's alcohol consumption, many studies show a direct link between alcohol use and criminal violence. For example, the Bureau of Justice Statistics (1988) reports that in the United States, about 60 percent of all persons convicted of assault had been drinking just prior to the crime. By contrast, about 40 percent of burglars and 30 percent of drug offenders used alcohol just prior to the crimes that they had committed. Other studies of crime outside the United States find similar results. Using samples of violent and non-violent Scottish prisoners, Myers (1982, 1986) finds that violent offenders were more likely to have consumed alcohol at the time of the offence than non-violent offenders. Roslund and Larson (1979) find that 68 percent of violent offenders in Sweden were intoxicated when committing crimes as compared to 38 percent of non-violent offenders. It is important to note that these studies do not establish causality from drinking to violence, rather they highlight an association between the two behaviors.

Some studies have revealed that it is not only the criminals who consume alcohol prior to committing crimes, but the victim's consumption behavior may inadvertently put him or her at risk. According to the 'lifestyle' theory of victimization, 'persons who drink extensively or go "cruising" for social activity, especially at night, are at higher risk for assault because such behavior often occurs at bars, parties, and other places where victimization risk is heightened' (Sampson and Lauritsen, 1994, p. 32). Drinking may also lower guardianship potential which can lead to increased victimization risk of assault and other personal crimes such as rape and robbery. In fact, many studies have shown a high prevalence of alcohol in both the offender and the victims of aggression. For example, Johnson et al. (1978) examine a sample of rapes in Winnipeg, Canada from 1966 to 1975. They find that in 72 percent of the cases, alcohol was used by the victim and/or offender, with alcohol being used by both the victim and the offender in 39 percent of the cases. Alcohol was used by the victim only (and not by the offender) in 9 percent of the cases and by the offender only in 24 percent of the cases. In studies on homicides, Virkkunen (1974) shows that alcohol was present in both victims and murderers in Helsinki from 1963 to 1968, and Lindqvist (1986) finds that in Sweden from 1970 to 1980, 47 percent of both the murderers and victims were intoxicated during the attack.

In addition to the well-established link between alcohol consumption and violence, alcohol consumption has been shown to be negatively related to the price of alcoholic beverages. (See, for example, Kenkel 1993; Leung and Phelps 1993; Manning et al. 1995; and Grossman et al. 1998.) Given these two relationships, the purpose of this chapter is to examine the direct relationship between the price of alcohol and the incidence of criminal violence. This study focuses on prices rather than consumption as a potential tool to reduce violence since the easiest way for governments to achieve reductions in consumption is to increase the price through tax increases.

The data come from the 1989 and 1992 International Victimization Surveys. The respondents were asked if they had been victims of three types of violent crime in the past year: robbery, assault, and sexual assault (female respondents only). This is the first study to relate alcoholic beverage prices to criminal violence in an international framework. One advantage of using a cross-country analysis is that there are much larger variations in prices and crime rates than in a within country analysis. Results of this study show that higher alcoholic beverage prices lead to lower incidences of all three types of violent crime in models where country fixed effects are not included. Results from models which include country fixed effects are not reliable.

2 LITERATURE REVIEW

There have been very few studies relating the determinates of alcohol consumption to the incidence of criminal violence. Cook and Moore (1993) and Chaloupka and Saffer (1992) both examine the effects of alcohol prices on a time series of aggregate state crime rates in the United States. In particular, both sets of authors look at rates of murder, rape, assault, and robbery. Cook and Moore model criminal offenses as a function of alcohol consumption and the socioeconomic and demographic characteristics of a state's population. Chaloupka and Saffer expand the model to include drug consumption and law enforcement as variables affecting crime rates. Alcohol consumption (as well as drug consumption in Chaloupka and Saffer) is treated as endogenous and is determined by price, availability, sentiment towards drinking, and laws designed to curtail consumption. Both sets of authors choose to address the endogeneity by using a reduced-form model where a specific crime rate is a function of the state excise tax on beer and other demographic variables. Chaloupka and Saffer also include variables that may affect the availability of alcohol such as the minimum legal drinking age and the percentage of a state's population living in dry counties. Results of both studies indicate that increasing the tax on beer reduces most types of violent crimes (with the exception of assault) while the effects of the availability and control measures used by Chaloupka and Saffer are mixed.

Other evidence on the effects of alcohol consumption and availability on crime rates comes from Scandinavian studies. One study by Lenke (1975) shows that there is a high statistical correlation between rates of violent crime and per capita alcohol consumption in several Scandinavian countries during the 1960–73 period. In addition, Lenke (1975) and Takala (1973) look at changes in alcohol prices, incidence of strikes by employees of liquor stores, and introduction of new sales points (that is, selling beer in grocery stores) to explain changes in violent crime rates. Both studies show that violent crimes decrease when alcohol is less available.

Finally, studies of the effects of higher alcohol prices on other types of violence include studies on child abuse (Markowitz and Grossman 1998a and 2000), spousal abuse (Markowitz 2000) and violence on college campuses (Grossman and Markowitz 1999). These studies all show that increasing the price of alcohol is an effective way to reduce the incidence of violence.

This current project expands on the existing literature by focusing on criminal victimization, as reported by the victims, in a cross-country framework. The studies cited above by Cook and Moore, and by Chaloupka and Saffer use US state-level data from the Uniform Crime Reports. One advantage of using individual-level data over aggregate-level data is that the characteristics of the victim can be controlled for. Aggregate-level data presents another problem in that often the sources of data, such as the Uniform Crime Reports, only include crimes that had been reported to the police. In the United States, for example, the 1994 National Crime Victimization Survey estimates that less than half (41.6 percent) of violent crimes were reported to police. The use of aggregate data may cause the price coefficient in the reduced-form equation to be biased because of measurement error. If this measurement error is random, the only effect would be to raise the standard errors of the coefficients on all the independent variables. However, if crime is systematically underreported and correlated with the price of alcohol then the coefficient on price would be biased. Such a situation might occur if people in areas with low alcoholic beverage prices consume more, live in areas with higher crime rates, and are less likely to report crimes to the police, perhaps because of perceived police inaction or lack of trust in the police.

3 ANALYTICAL FRAMEWORK

As mentioned above, the many studies on crime and drinking do not establish a direction of causality from alcohol consumption to violence. In fact, there is no general agreement in the existing literature on the direction of the causality. One prominent theory is that alcohol use does promote violence through a pharmacological mechanism that alters behavior (Pernanen 1981 and Fagan 1993). This theory states that alcohol use causes violence. A competing theory proposes that violence may cause alcohol consumption in that people who plan on being violent may drink in order to give themselves courage or an excuse for the behavior (Fagan 1990 and Cordilia 1985).[1] Finally, a third theory states that alcohol and violence are both outcomes of an unobserved third factor, for example, a risk-taking personality (Fagan 1990). As discussed below, these competing theories are not problematic for the analytical framework.

The analytical framework is derived from the economic models of crime developed by Becker (1968), Chaloupka and Saffer (1992) and Cook and Moore (1993). Criminal violence is determined by both the actions of the perpetrator and the victim. Taking into account the drinking habits and personal characteristics of both the potential criminal and victim gives the following equation for violence:

$$V_i = v\,(A_i, A_j, E, Y_i, Y_j, U_i, U_j). \tag{13.1}$$

Equation 13.1, termed the structural violence equation, shows that the probability of being a victim of a violent crime (V_i) is a function of the alcohol consumption of the individual, A_i, who is the potential victim, the alcohol consumption of other individuals (A_j) who can be strangers or acquaintances and are potential perpetrators, law enforcement variables (E), and other observed factors of individuals (Y_i, Y_j) which affect the propensity towards crime or victimization such as age, gender, income, and employment status. Unobserved individual-level factors (U_i, U_j) which influence the probability of violent crime are also included.

Alcohol consumption by either party can be expressed as a demand function:

$$A = a\,(P_A, Y, U), \tag{13.2}$$

where P_A is the full price of alcohol, and Y and U are individual characteristics that may determine consumption. These sets of characteristics may be the same ones that determine violence. The full price of alcohol reflects both the monetary price of alcohol and other costs of obtaining the substance, such as time and travel costs.

Substituting equation 13.2 into equation 13.1 gives a reduced-form estimate for violence:

$$V_i = v\,(P_A, E, Y_i, Y_j, U_i, U_j). \tag{13.3}$$

Given that the crimes examined in this study are crimes of personal contact, the victim and the criminal will be located in close proximity and thus face the same price of alcohol. Equation 13.3 cannot be fully estimated empirically because data on crimes typically have characteristics on either the perpetrator or the victim, but not both. In light of this, a modified version of equation 13.3 serves as the basis for estimation in this chapter where incidents of victimization are observed:

$$V_i = v\,(P_A, Y_i, e), \tag{13.4}$$

where e is an error term that contains E, Y_j, U_j, and U_i.[2] A negative sign on the price coefficient indicates that an increase in the price of alcohol will lead to a reduction in violence. This reduction in violence is a result of decreased consumption by both the potential victim and the perpetrator.[3]

Using country-specific fixed effects will help control for some of the unmeasured characteristics in the error term. However, omitting individual characteristics of either the perpetrator or the victim should not be problematic so long as these variables are uncorrelated with the price of alcohol, the variable of interest in this chapter.

In estimating equation 13.4, the direction of causality between alcohol and violence is not a problem because consumption is substituted out of the equation. If alcohol causes violence then the coefficient on the price of alcohol will be negatively related to violence. If violence causes consumption, then changing consumption through prices would have no measurable effect on violence and the coefficient on the price in the reduced form would reflect this. If, however, there is an unmeasured third factor that determines both consumption and violence, then so long as the price is uncorrelated with this third factor, estimating equation 13.3 will produce unbiased estimates of the effect of price on violence. (See Cook and Moore 1993 for a further discussion of these issues.)

4 DATA

The data come from the 1989 and 1992 cross-sections of the International Victimization Survey conducted by the Dutch Ministry of Justice. These surveys are random samples of individuals aged 16 and older, and are designed to measure the experience of crime and crime-related issues in a variety of countries around the world. The 1989 survey consists of responses from approximately 2000 individuals in each of 14 countries, while the 1992 survey has respondents from 18 countries. Not all countries in the surveys are used because of the lack of corresponding alcohol control variables, and the same country is not necessarily included in both years. There are eight countries that appear in both survey years: Australia, Belgium, Canada, Finland, the Netherlands, Spain, the United Kingdom, and the United States. The 1989 survey also includes France, Germany, Japan, Norway, and Switzerland, while the 1992 survey includes Italy, New Zealand, and Sweden.

4.1 Dependent Variables

Three questions in the International Victimization Surveys focus on violent crimes. First, respondents are asked about robbery or attempted robbery in the past year. Specifically, the question asks if anyone has taken something from the respondent by using force or threatening them, or did anyone try to do so. About 0.9 percent of the sample were victims of robbery in 1988 and 1.2 percent were victims in 1991. The second question asks about assault. In other words, had the respondent been personally attacked or threatened by someone in a way that really frightened them, either at home, or elsewhere, such as in a pub, the street, at school, on public transportation, in cinemas, on the beach, or at one's workplace. In 1988, 2.9 percent of respondents were victims of assault while 3.2 percent were victims in 1991. The third dependent variable focuses on sexual assault against women only. The question on sexual assault reads,

> People sometimes grab, touch or assault others for sexual reasons in a really offensive way. This can happen inside one's house or elsewhere, for instance, in a pub, the street, at school, on public transportation, in cinemas, on the beach, or at one's workplace. Has anyone done this to you?

In 1988, 2.5 percent of women were victims of sexual assault and in 1991, 2.2 percent of women were victims.

Table 13.1 shows rates of violence by year and country. Notice that Japan has no reported cases of robbery in 1988. Finding no robberies in a sample of 2411 Japanese individuals is quite likely because Japan has very low crime rates in general. Dolan and Worden (1994) find that in 1989, Japan experienced 1.3 robberies per 100 000 population, as compared with 48.6 for West Germany, 65.8 for Britain, and 233.0 for the United States. These data come from the United Nations Survey of Crime Trends and Operations of Criminal Justice Systems, which gives rates of crimes that are reported to the police. These robbery figures are much lower than the rates presented in Table 13.1 because the International Victimization Surveys include attempted crimes and crimes which are not necessarily reported to authorities. In fact, in the International Victimization Surveys, less than half (43 percent) of the respondents who admitted to having been robbed reported the robbery to the police.

Even though the levels of crime vary widely between the UN survey and the data presented here, the ranking of countries by crime rates is very similar in both surveys. For example, Spain, the US, and Canada rank first, second, and third for the most robberies per capita in 1988 in both the UN survey and the International Victimization Survey, whereas Finland ranks near the bottom and Japan is last. Similar ranks hold for robbery in the 1991 surveys. Canada and the US also consistently rank at the top of the list for assault while Italy and Japan rank at the bottom. The rankings for sexual assault vary widely between the surveys primarily because of inconsistent reporting methodologies across countries.

Table 13.1 Mean rates of violence by year and country

Country	Year	Number of observations	Robbery	Assault	Sexual assault	Price of alcohol	Tax on alcohol
Australia	1988	2012	0.006	0.048	0.069	1.526	0.446
	1991	2006	0.011	0.042	0.032	1.627	0.547
Belgium	1988	2060	0.009	0.020	0.012	0.413	0.015
	1991	1485	0.009	0.017	0.011	0.456	0.016
Canada	1988	2074	0.013	0.044	0.041	1.301	0.264
	1991	2152	0.012	0.049	0.037	1.315	0.307
Finland	1988	1025	0.004	0.025	0.005	1.454	1.122
	1991	1655	0.009	0.039	0.030	1.526	1.085
France	1988	1502	0.005	0.021	0.012	0.466	0.099
Germany	1988	5274	0.008	0.035	0.034	0.576	0.129
Italy	1991	2024	0.013	0.007	0.016	0.419	0.044
Japan	1988	2411	0.000	0.005	0.011	4.087	0.456
Netherlands	1988	2000	0.007	0.035	0.025	0.522	0.214
	1991	2000	0.010	0.029	0.023	0.533	0.192
New Zealand	1991	2048	0.005	0.047	0.027	0.631	0.304
Norway	1988	1009	0.005	0.028	0.018	1.962	1.037
Spain	1988	2041	0.029	0.031	0.023	0.290	0.159
	1991	1634	0.032	0.019	0.013	0.312	0.205
Sweden	1991	1707	0.004	0.026	0.012	1.461	0.764
Switzerland	1988	1000	0.002	0.009	0.012	2.176	0.088
United Kingdom	1988	6013	0.005	0.018	0.014	2.522	0.610
	1991	2001	0.009	0.034	0.019	2.585	0.554
United States	1988	1996	0.019	0.052	0.045	0.768	0.184
	1991	1501	0.015	0.044	0.024	0.837	0.202
All countries	1988	30,417	0.009	0.029	0.025	1.453	0.345
	1991	20,213	0.012	0.032	0.022	1.085	0.382

4.2 Independent Variables

Two different measures are used to represent the price of alcohol. The first is the price of one ounce of pure alcohol expressed in real (1992 = 1) US dollars and the second is the tax on one ounce of pure alcohol expressed in real US dollars. Including the tax on alcohol, besides providing an alternative measure of price, will provide a direct estimate of the ability of governments to affect violence rates through tax increases. Actual prices and taxes on alcohol by country are not available but household expenditures on alcohol, total tax revenue, and consumption data are available. The price and the tax on alcohol for each country are constructed by the following formulas:

$$P = E/(C*PPP*D), \tag{13.5}$$

and

$$T = R/(C*PPP*D), \tag{13.6}$$

where E is per capita expenditures on all alcoholic beverages expressed in the national currency, R is per capita tax revenue from alcohol expressed in the national currency, C is the sum of per capita consumption of the pure alcohol from beer, wine and liquor in a country, PPP is purchasing power parity (national currency per US dollar), and D is the GDP deflator for the United States.[4] This is the same procedure used by Saffer (1991) to calculate the price of alcohol in OECD countries. Total tax revenue (R) is reported as the sum of excise taxes, duties on monopolies, specific customs duties and special taxes on catering establishments. The consumption of alcohol includes sake for Japan and cider for England and Switzerland. Expenditures on alcohol, tax revenues from alcoholic beverages, the GDP deflator and the purchasing power parity all come from the OECD Health Data 1997 data base. Consumption data come from the Brewers Association of Canada's, *Alcoholic Beverage Taxation and Control Policies* (1997).

Table 13.1 shows there is much variation in the price and tax on alcohol among countries. However, the constructed prices of alcohol can differ among countries because of variations in consumption shares, rather than from actual price differences. If, for example, two countries face the same price for liquor, but the share of total consumption for liquor is higher in one country, then the constructed price will differ because of the consumption differences. In order to control for this problem, the percentage of total consumption from wine and liquor for each country are included in all models. Including the percentage of total consumption also allows the models to control for countries which are predominately beer or wine drinking, and thus control for some of the unobserved sentiment towards consumption.[5]

Three other alcohol control variables are included in the models in order to account for country-specific factors that may affect the availability or full price of alcohol. All three variables come from *Alcoholic Beverage Taxation and Control Policies* (Brewers Association of Canada 1997). The first variable is the legal blood alcohol level indicative of impaired or drunk driving. Higher legal blood alcohol levels may result in more consumption (and more violence) because higher blood alcohol levels make it harder to penalize drivers for driving while intoxicated. That is, the expected costs of drunk driving are lower with higher blood alcohol levels. Higher blood alcohol levels may also be indicative of more tolerance towards drinking in a nation. Legal blood alcohol levels range from practically zero (Japan has no tolerance for drunk driving) to 0.10. The majority of countries have levels of 0.05 or 0.08. The second variable is a dichotomous indicator for alcohol advertising. This variable equals 1 if a country bans beer, wine and liquor advertising on television or radio.[6] Five of the 16 countries in the surveys have implemented this ban. Advertising of alcohol can affect either total consumption or brand choice decisions, although Saffer (1991) shows that quantity consumed is lower in countries which ban broadcast advertising of alcoholic beverages. Finally, the minimum legal drinking age for purchase of beer or wine is included. In some countries, the minimum legal drinking age differs for consumption on-premise (in a bar or restaurant) or off-premise. In these cases, the age used is an average of the minimum legal ages for on- and off-premise. Minimum legal drinking ages generally range from ages 16 to 21, but Belgium had no minimum age for off-premise consumption.

Per capita disposable income in real US dollars for each country is included in all models because this variable may control for some substitution in consumption of different quality beer, liquors and wines. That is, as people get richer, they may substitute high-quality alcohol for the cheaper brands. Such a substitution would result in higher total consumer expenditures on alcohol and thus, a higher calculated price. The calculated tax is less subject to this problem since most countries collect both excise taxes and *ad valorem* taxes. Per capita disposable income comes from the OECD Health Data 1997 data base.

Other variables which account for characteristics of the respondent and the locational characteristics of the respondent are also included.

Specifically, all models include the respondent's gender, age, a dichotomous indicator for whether the respondent's income is higher than the country's median income, and employment status (part-time worker, unemployed, student, or other occupation which includes individuals who are retired, in the armed services or are homemakers). The number of days per year the respondent goes out in the evening for recreational purposes (to a pub, restaurant, cinema or to see friends) is also included. This variable is important in that people who are out late at night may be more likely to be victims of crime. The National Research Council (1993, p. 146) notes that 'nighttime activity outside the home' is the social behavior most highly associated with violent victimization in the United States. This same source cites similar results in Canadian and British surveys. Finally, a dummy for 1991 and the size of the town that the respondent lives in are also included in all models. Any missing values on the individual level variables are replaced with year and country-specific means. An alternative strategy would be to delete the incomplete observations. This strategy gives results very similar to those presented here.

5 ESTIMATION

The probability of being a victim of violent crime is estimated using probit techniques. Tables 13.2, 13.3, and 13.4 show the results for robbery, assault, and sexual assault against females, respectively. Each table contains four models. Columns 1 and 2 use the calculated price of alcohol while columns 3 and 4 include the tax on alcohol. Columns 1 and 3 are otherwise identical in that each includes a price of alcohol, the other three regulatory variables (the legal blood alcohol level, the indicator for the ban of alcohol advertising on radio and television, and the minimum legal drinking age), and the individual characteristics. The models in columns 2 and 4 include country fixed effects, and thus are limited to the set of countries that are included in both years of the survey.[7] The advertising ban and minimum legal drinking age cannot be included in the models with the country dummies because the values of variables do not change over the two years of the survey.

The fixed-effects models are important because these models can capture the unobserved effects of culture on crime and drinking in each country. Japan, for instance, has a very low crime rate because of emphasis on family honor. In addition, reliable criminal justice data such as expenditures on law enforcement are not available for many countries. Omitting the fixed effects can result in biases in the included variables if

Table 13.2 Probability of being a victim of violent crime: robbery

	All countries (1)	Only countries in both years (2)	All countries (3)	Only countries in both years (4)
Price	−0.127 (−4.14) ***−0.002***	0.154 (0.08) ***0.003***		
Tax			−0.263 (−2.50) ***−0.005***	−1.191 (−0.62) ***−0.026***
Percentage of consumption from wine	0.293 (1.84) ***0.005***	0.921 (0.23) ***0.020***	0.361 (2.23) ***0.007***	−2.175 (−0.35) ***−0.047***
Percentage of consumption from liquor	1.513 (3.85) ***0.028***	0.439 (0.11) ***0.009***	1.962 (5.23) ***0.038***	0.576 (0.15) ***0.012***
Blood alcohol level	6.362 (4.65) ***0.117***	0.350 (0.08) ***0.008***	6.651 (4.96) ***0.127***	−1.615 (−0.36) ***−0.035***
Advertising prohibited	−0.234 (−3.37) ***−0.004***		−0.195 (−2.86) ***−0.003***	
Minimum legal drinking age	−0.009 (−0.94) ***−0.0002***		−0.017 (−1.80) ***−0.0003***	
Per capita income	−0.027 (−3.20) ***−0.0005***	−0.035 (−0.66) ***−0.001***	−0.034 (−3.62) ***−0.001***	−0.027 (−0.57) ***−0.001***
Female	−0.075 (−2.02) ***−0.001***	−0.115 (−2.70) ***−0.003***	−0.074 (−2.00) ***−0.001***	−0.114 (−2.67) ***−0.003***
Age	−0.010 (−7.63) ***−0.0002***	−0.014 (−9.14) ***−0.0003***	−0.010 (−7.61) ***−0.0002***	−0.014 (−9.11) ***−0.0003***
High income	−0.025 (−0.62) ***−0.0005***	−0.025 (−0.54) ***−0.001***	−0.024 (−0.61) ***−0.0005***	−0.026 (−0.56) ***−0.001***
Frequency goes out	0.0005 (3.34) ***0.00001***	0.001 (3.10) ***0.00001***	0.0005 (3.33) ***0.00001***	0.001 (3.13) ***0.00001***
Town size	0.090 (8.48) ***0.002***	0.089 (6.77) ***0.002***	0.093 (8.86) ***0.002***	0.088 (6.77) ***0.002***

Table 13.2 Probability of being a victim of violent crime: robbery (cont.)

	All countries (1)	Only countries in both years (2)	All countries (3)	Only countries in both years (4)
1991	0.111	0.047	0.140	0.060
	(2.45)	(0.41)	(3.19)	(0.70)
	0.002	***0.001***	***0.003***	***0.001***
Part-time work	−0.068	−0.044	−0.069	−0.044
	(−0.91)	(−0.52)	(−0.93)	(−0.52)
	−0.001	***−0.001***	***−0.001***	***−0.001***
Unemployed	0.039	0.011	0.039	0.009
	(0.76)	(0.17)	(0.76)	(0.14)
	0.001	***0.0002***	***0.001***	***0.0002***
Student	0.072	0.087	0.072	0.084
	(0.82)	(0.84)	(0.83)	(0.82)
	0.001	***0.002***	***0.002***	***0.002***
Other occupation	0.083	0.147	0.073	0.140
	(1.19)	(1.77)	(1.06)	(1.66)
	0.002	***0.004***	***0.002***	***0.003***
Australia		−0.766		0.131
		(−0.51)		(0.09)
		−0.009		***0.003***
Belgium		−0.357		−0.135
		(−0.34)		(−0.17)
		−0.006		***−0.003***
Canada		−0.435		−0.208
		(−0.49)		(−0.64)
		−0.007		***−0.004***
Finland		−0.661		0.497
		(−0.57)		(0.28)
		−0.008		***0.018***
Netherlands		−0.465		−0.202
		(−0.53)		(−0.28)
		−0.007		***−0.004***
Spain		−0.300		0.633
		(−0.18)		(0.30)
		−0.005		***0.026***
United Kingdom		−0.858		0.182
		(−0.26)		(0.14)
		−0.012		***0.004***
Chi-squared on country dummies		5.136		10.682
		[0.643]		[0.153]
N	50,542	33,585	50,542	33,585

Note: *T*-statistics in parentheses, marginal effects in italics, *p*-values in square brackets for chi-squared test, and intercept not shown.

Table 13.3 Probability of being a victim of violent crime: assault

	All countries (1)	Only countries in both years (2)	All countries (3)	Only countries in both years (4)
Price	−0.120 (−6.60) ***−0.007***	1.224 (0.99) ***0.074***		
Tax			−0.213 (−3.42) ***−0.012***	−2.023 (−1.57) ***−0.123***
Percentage of consumption from wine	−1.160 (−9.80) ***−0.063***	8.438 (3.43) ***0.513***	−1.203 (−9.38) ***−0.066***	3.178 (0.78) ***0.193***
Percentage of consumption from liquor	−0.521 (−2.15) ***−0.028***	3.228 (1.42) ***0.196***	−0.120 (−0.50) ***−0.007***	3.355 (1.47) ***0.204***
Blood alcohol level	0.984 (1.23) ***0.053***	5.175 (1.80) ***0.314***	2.166 (2.84) ***0.119***	0.389 (0.13) ***0.024***
Advertising prohibited	0.071 (1.79) ***0.004***		0.138 (3.62) ***0.008***	
Minimum legal drinking age	0.029 (4.49) ***0.002***		0.016 (2.66) ***0.001***	
Per capita income	−0.015 (−2.60) ***−0.001***	−0.137 (−3.71) ***−0.008***	−0.023 (−3.37) ***−0.001***	−0.150 (−4.54) ***−0.009***
Female	−0.091 (−3.69) ***−0.005***	−0.080 (−2.75) ***−0.005***	−0.091 (−3.68) ***−0.005***	−0.079 (−2.71) ***−0.005***
Age	−0.015 (−16.98) ***−0.001***	−0.015 (−14.15) ***−0.001***	−0.015 (−17.02) ***−0.001***	−0.015 (−14.12) ***−0.001***
High income	−0.066 (−2.54) ***−0.004***	−0.045 (−1.44) ***−0.003***	−0.066 (−2.52) ***−0.004***	−0.046 (−1.46) ***−0.003***
Frequency goes out	0.001 (5.77) ***0.00003***	0.001 (5.03) ***0.00004***	0.001 (5.75) ***0.00003***	0.001 (5.03) ***0.00004***
Town size	0.051 (7.06) ***0.003***	0.045 (5.01) ***0.003***	0.058 (8.10) ***0.003***	0.045 (5.03) ***0.003***

Table 13.3 Probability of being a victim of violent crime: assault (cont.)

	All countries (1)	Only countries in both years (2)	All countries (3)	Only countries in both years (4)
1991	−0.009 (−0.30) ***−0.0005***	0.019 (0.27) ***0.001***	0.031 (1.06) ***0.002***	0.066 (1.21) ***0.004***
Part-time work	0.012 (0.27) ***0.001***	0.010 (0.19) ***0.001***	0.013 (0.30) ***0.001***	0.007 (0.14) ***0.0004***
Unemployed	−0.036 (−1.04) ***−0.002***	−0.038 (−0.92) ***−0.002***	−0.033 (−0.96) ***−0.002***	−0.039 (−0.96) ***−0.002***
Student	0.088 (1.53) ***0.005***	0.092 (1.33) ***0.006***	0.084 (1.46) ***0.005***	0.086 (1.25) ***0.006***
Other occupation	0.003 (0.07) ***0.0002***	0.014 (0.26) ***0.001***	−0.010 (−0.21) ***−0.001***	0.006 (0.11) ***0.0004***
Australia		−2.231 (−2.40) ***−0.047***		−0.162 (−0.18) ***−0.009***
Belgium		−1.183 (−1.67) ***−0.033***		−1.337 (−2.62) ***−0.035***
Canada		−1.179 (−2.10) ***−0.035***		−0.409 (−2.02) ***−0.019***
Finland		−1.847 (−2.54) ***−0.036***		0.559 (0.49) ***0.053***
Netherlands		−1.029 (−1.70) ***−0.032***		−1.046 (−2.25) ***−0.033***
Spain		−3.346 (−2.94) ***−0.057***		−2.499 (−1.88) ***−0.047***
United Kingdom		−3.555 (−1.72) ***−0.137***		−0.271 (−0.32) ***−0.014***
Chi-squared on country dummies		60.496 [0.000]		78.557 [0.000]
N	50,464	33,521	50,464	33,521

Note: *T*-statistics in parentheses, marginal effects in italics, *p*-values in square brackets for chi-squared test, and intercept not shown.

they are correlated with the country-level unobservables. However, in order to include the country dummies, it is necessary to limit the sample to only the eight countries which appear in both years of the survey. Hence, models are presented both with the larger sample of all countries, and with the smaller sample that includes the country dummies.

Each table lists the probit coefficients first, the *t*-statistic on the coefficients in parentheses, and the marginal effects of the coefficients in italics. The marginal effects shown for the dummy variables are calculated by $\Phi(\mathbf{X}_1 b) - \Phi(\mathbf{X}_0 b)$, where Φ is the cumulative normal density, and $\mathbf{X}_0$ and $\mathbf{X}_1$ are vectors of the means of the independent variables except that the value of the dummy variable of interest equals 0 and 1, respectively. Marginal effects for continuous variables are calculated at the means of the independent variables.

In using a set of alcohol regulatory variables, one must be concerned with the potential problems of omitted variable bias and multicollinearity. Including all the relevant control variables, as shown in Tables 13.2–4, may lead to multicollinearity. This problem would arise if countries which have high anti-drinking sentiment impose higher taxes on alcohol and place more restrictions on availability. Omitting the regulatory variables, however, may lead to omitted variable bias if the regulatory measures are predictors of violence. Models were tested without the blood alcohol level, the advertising ban, and the minimum legal drinking age, but the results were very similar to those presented in Tables 13.2–4.

It should be cautioned that the prices of alcohol contain measurement error for two reasons. The first is simply that the price and tax are calculated, rather than observed directly, and second, individuals are assigned country-specific prices rather than area-specific prices. Random measurement error in an independent variable biases its coefficient and *t*-ratio towards zero. Thus, the price coefficients and associated *t*-ratios are considered conservative lower-bound estimates.[8]

6 RESULTS

The results of the reduced-form equations are presented in Tables 13.2–4. Table 13.2 shows the effects of the alcohol regulatory variables and individual characteristics on the probability of being a victim of robbery. Beginning with the models that include the price (columns 1 and 2), the results show that the price coefficient is negative and statistically significant only in the model which excludes the country dummies (column 1).[9] Once the country dummies are added, the price coefficient becomes positive and insignificant. A serious problem with the models

Table 13.4 Probability of being a victim of violent crime: sexual assault against women

	All countries (1)	Only countries in both years (2)	All countries (3)	Only countries in both years (4)
Price	−0.116 (−4.22) ***−0.004***	1.282 (0.66) ***0.044***		
Tax			−0.331 (−3.28) ***−0.011***	−3.278 (−1.60) ***−0.113***
Percentage of consumption from wine	−0.719 (−4.33) ***−0.024***	8.334 (2.00) ***0.289***	−0.859 (−4.72) ***−0.029***	−0.142 (−0.02) ***−0.005***
Percentage of consumption from liquor	−1.775 (−4.94) ***−0.060***	−8.599 (−1.90) ***−0.298***	−1.523 (−4.29) ***−0.052***	−8.428 (−1.86) ***−0.291***
Blood alcohol level	−2.907 (−2.37) ***−0.099***	6.194 (1.33) ***0.215***	−1.997 (−1.76) ***−0.068***	−0.318 (−0.07) ***−0.011***
Advertising prohibited	−0.148 (−2.38) ***−0.004***		−0.089 (−1.45) ***−0.003***	
Minimum legal drinking age	0.063 (6.18) ***0.002***		0.055 (5.76) ***0.002***	
Per capita income	0.010 (1.11) ***0.0003***	−0.127 (−2.23) ***−0.004***	−0.003 (−0.28) ***0.000***	−0.140 (−2.64) ***−0.005***
Age	−0.025 (−16.57) ***−0.001***	−0.026 (−14.12) ***−0.001***	−0.025 (−16.50) ***−0.001***	−0.026 (−14.09) ***−0.001***
High income	−0.111 (−2.82) ***−0.004***	−0.140 (−2.93) ***−0.005***	−0.112 (−2.86) ***−0.004***	−0.141 (−2.95) ***−0.005***
Frequency goes out	0.001 (5.00) ***0.00003***	0.001 (3.93) ***0.00003***	0.001 (5.10) ***0.00003***	0.001 (3.98) ***0.00003***
Town size	0.064 (5.90) ***0.002***	0.060 (4.36) ***0.002***	0.070 (6.54) ***0.002***	0.059 (4.31) ***0.002***
1991	−0.103 (−2.17) ***−0.003***	−0.188 (−1.54) ***−0.006***	−0.061 (−1.35) ***−0.002***	−0.136 (−1.41) ***−0.005***

Table 13.4 Probability of being a victim of violent crime: sexual assault against women (cont.)

	All countries (1)	Only countries in both years (2)	All countries (3)	Only countries in both years (4)
Part-time work	0.038	0.089	0.041	0.086
	(0.72)	(1.36)	(0.77)	(1.33)
	0.001	***0.003***	***0.001***	***0.003***
Unemployed	−0.098	−0.065	−0.092	−0.066
	(−1.94)	(−1.05)	(−1.83)	(−1.06)
	−0.003	***−0.002***	***−0.003***	***−0.002***
Student	−0.001	0.006	0.0001	−0.003
	(−0.01)	(0.06)	(0.001)	(−0.03)
	−0.00002	***0.0002***	***0.000003***	***−0.0001***
Other occupation	−0.245	−0.243	−0.273	−0.257
	(−3.21)	(−2.58)	(−3.59)	(−2.71)
	−0.007	***−0.007***	***−0.008***	***−0.007***
Australia		−3.990		−1.103
		(−2.53)		(−0.76)
		−0.041		***−0.018***
Belgium		−3.169		−3.100
		(−2.82)		(−3.53)
		−0.030		***−0.029***
Canada		−1.080		−0.140
		(−1.20)		(−0.44)
		−0.018		***−0.004***
Finland		−1.417		2.107
		(−1.22)		(1.16)
		−0.018		***0.382***
Netherlands		−1.653		−1.389
		(−1.76)		(−1.83)
		−0.021		***−0.020***
Spain		−3.924		−2.123
		(−2.16)		(−0.99)
		−0.038		***−0.024***
United Kingdom		−4.640		−0.484
		(−1.40)		(−0.36)
		−0.131		***−0.013***
Chi-squared on country dummies		70.081		89.504
		[0.000]		[0.000]
N	27,251	18,322	27,251	18,322

Note: *T*-statistics in parentheses, marginal effects in italics, *p*-values in square brackets for chi-squared test, and intercept not shown.

that include the country dummies is that they suffer from multicollinearity in that the price is highly correlated with the country dummies. The *r*-squared from a regression of the price on the country dummies is 0.99 indicating that the country dummies explain practically all of the variation in the price. Adding a set of variables which are highly correlated with an existing variable can result in wide swings in the magnitude, sign and significance of the variable.

Columns 3 and 4 show the results of the reduced-form violence equation with the tax included rather than the price. The results of the tax coefficient are very similar to that of the price. Without the country dummies (column 3) the coefficient on the tax is negative and significant indicating that an increase in the tax on alcohol will lower the probability of being a victim of robbery. However, once the country dummies are added, the coefficient on the tax remains negative, but becomes statistically insignificant. As with the price, most of the variation in the tax variable can be explained by the country dummies. The *r*-squared from a regression of the tax on the country dummies is 0.99.

The models in columns 1 and 3 also include other alcohol regulatory variables. The results indicate that higher legal blood alcohol levels will lead to more robbery, while prohibitions on advertising will lead to less robbery. The coefficient on the legal minimum legal drinking age is negative as expected. However, it is only statistically significant at the 10 percent level when the tax is included (column 3). The blood alcohol level is the only regulatory variable included with the country dummies (see columns 2 and 4). Here, increases in the blood alcohol level have no effect on the probability of robbery.

Some of the individual characteristics affect the likelihood of being a victim of robbery. Women and older people are less likely to be victims, while people who go out frequently at night or who live in large communities are more likely to be victims. Employment status and income have no effects on the probability of being robbed. These results hold both with the price and the tax included.

In Table 13.3, the probability of being assaulted is the dependent variable. The conclusions are strikingly similar to the models where robbery is the dependent variable. When the price or tax is included with the full set of countries, the coefficient is negative and significant (columns 1 and 3). When the country dummies are added (columns 2 and 4), the coefficient on the price becomes positive and insignificant, and the coefficient on the tax becomes negative and insignificant.

In columns 1 and 3 of Table 13.3, while both the advertising and minimum legal drinking age coefficients are statistically significant, neither displays the anticipated sign. However, the blood alcohol level is positive as expected, and is statistically significant in column 3 when the tax is included. Next, the same individual characteristics which affect the probability of robbery also affect the probability of being assaulted. Women and older people are less likely to be victims, while people who go out frequently at night and people who live in large communities are more likely to be victims. Employment status has no effect on the probability of being assaulted, but in the models with all countries included (columns 1 and 3), having income higher than the median for the country is associated with a lower probability of assault. This finding does not remain statistically significant once the country dummies are included.

Finally, Table 13.4 shows the results of the probability of females being victims of sexual assault. As with robbery and assault, increases in both measures of the price of alcohol will serve to reduce the probability of sexual assault against women when the country dummies are excluded (columns 1 and 3). The ability of the other alcohol regulatory variables to reduce the probability of sexual assault is unclear. Only the coefficient on the prohibition of advertising has the anticipated sign, and this is only significant in column 1. The blood alcohol level and the minimum legal drinking age are statistically significant, but the sign is not in the anticipated direction. Including the country dummies makes the coefficient on the blood alcohol level insignificant.

The individual characteristics that affect the probability of sexual assault are the same as those that affect both robbery and assault. In addition, high income is associated with a lower probability of sexual assault, and this result holds across all models. Finally, women who report occupation as other (which includes homemakers, retirees, and women in the armed services) or are unemployed (when the country dummies are excluded) have a lower probability of being sexually assaulted as compared to other women who work full time, part time, or are students.

7 DISCUSSION

Using data from the 1989 and 1992 International Victimization Surveys, this chapter shows some evidence that increasing the price of alcohol can be an effective policy tool in reducing violent crime. That is, rates of robbery, assault, and sexual assault against women can be lowered by increasing either the price of alcoholic beverages or by increasing the tax on alcoholic beverages. Controlling for country fixed effects does not allow for precise estimates of the price or tax on the probability of violence because of severe collinearity between the price measures and the country dummies. Clearly, a longer time series or different measures of the price of alcohol would be needed in order to separate out the effects of country-level unobservables from the price measures.

Estimates from models which exclude country fixed effects reveal that the magnitude of increases in the price of alcohol in reducing crime may be very small. Elasticities are calculated by multiplying the marginal effect of the coefficient to the ratio of the average price to the average crime rate. A one percent increase in the calculated price of alcohol will lead to a 0.27 percent decrease in the probability of robbery, a 0.30 percent decrease in the probability of assault, and a 0.21 percent decrease in the probability of sexual assault. Similarly, a one percent increase in the calculated tax on alcohol will cause the probabilities of robbery, assault, and sexual assault to fall by 0.19 percent, 0.25 percent, and 0.16 percent, respectively.

Other regulatory variables may have some negative effects on crime. However, the conclusions are not consistent across the different types of violent crime. Lower legal blood alcohol levels, advertising bans, and higher minimum legal drinking ages will lower the probability of robbery. Lower legal blood alcohol levels may also reduce the probability of assault, but neither advertising bans nor higher minimum legal drinking ages will reduce the probability of assault or sexual assault against women.

NOTES

* This chapter was presented at the Allied Social Sciences Associating meeting in New York, NY, January 3–5, 1999 and at the Taipei International Conference on Health Economics organized by the Institute of Economics, Academia Sinica in Taipei, Taiwan, March 25–26, 1999. I would like to thank Phil Cook, Michael Grossman, Ya-Chen Tina Shih and the conference participants for helpful comments and suggestions. Research for this study was supported by grant number 1 R01 AA10817 from the National Institute on Alcohol Abuse and Alcoholism (NIAAA) to the National Bureau of Economic Research (NBER). This chapter has not undergone the review accorded official NBER publications; in particular, it has not been submitted for approval by the Board of Directors. Any opinions expressed are those of the authors and not that of the NIAAA or the NBER.

1 From an economics standpoint, this second theory translates into using alcohol as a way of lowering the probability of facing penalties. Becker (1968) shows that the criminal's choice level of crime is determined by weighting the probable costs and benefits of crime. Alcohol use may decrease the probability of facing

penalties if the victim or the courts are less willing to impose costs on criminals who drink. This may occur if the criminal's behavior is deemed to be out of his or her control and is a result of being under the influence of alcohol. See Markowitz and Grossman (1998b) for a complete derivation of a model in which alcohol affects the probability of facing penalties. Note that this last argument may only hold for violent criminals. Criminals who commit property crimes may be more likely to be caught and face penalties when drinking if the drinking causes them to be more careless while committing the crime (Cordilia 1985).

2 Law enforcement variables are omitted from the models presented in this chapter because comparable cross-country data on police and other criminal justice measures are not available. In addition, including law enforcement measures would lead to biased estimates because these measures would be endogenous in the violence equation. The fixed-effect models presented below do help account for such unmeasured variables.

3 There may be an offsetting effect in that in areas with low crime rates, victims may have less incentive to protect themselves against crimes. In this situation, an increase in the price would still lower both parties' consumption, but the fall in violence would allow victims to be less defensive and perhaps consume more. This situation would only serve to weaken the negative price effect.

4 'The purchasing power parities (PPPs) are rates of currency conversion that enable the expression of the purchasing power of different currencies in a common unit. In other words, a given sum of money, when converted at the PPP rates, will buy the same basket of goods and services in all countries. Thus PPPs are the rates of currency conversion which eliminate differences in price levels among countries' (OECD 1993, p. 8). Prices deflated by the PPP are real prices expressed in US dollars at a moment in time. These must be deflated by the US GDP deflator in order to make comparisons over time. To spell this out in more detail, let p_{jt} be the price of alcohol in country j in year t expressed in country j's currency. Let e_{jt} be the nominal exchange rate expressed as country j's currency per US dollar. Then p_{jt}/e_{jt} is the nominal price of alcohol in country j in US dollars. Let r_{jt} be purchasing power parity expressed as country j's currency per US dollars. Then r_{jt}/e_{jt} is a cost of living index that reflects differences in the cost of living between the two countries at a moment in time. Hence the real price of alcohol (π_{jt}) at a moment in time in US dollars is

$$\pi_{jt} = [(p_{jt}/e_{jt})]/[(r_{jt}/e_{jt})] = p_{jt}/r_{jt}.$$

Note that the nominal exchange rate drops out of the above formula. With data for only a single year, no other computations would be required. But cross-sections of countries in two different years are employed. Hence the real price that reflects variations over time within countries as well as variations at a moment in time among countries (z_{jt}) is

$z_{jt} = p_{jt}/r_{jt}c_{ut}$,

where c_{ut} is the US GDP deflator in year t relative to year 0 since the real price at a moment in time is in US dollars.

5 Models were tested that include a separate variable indicating that 75 percent or more of a country's consumption comes from beer or wine. Including this variable did not alter the results.

6 All countries that ban beer and wine advertisements on radio and television also ban liquor advertisements. The converse is not always true.

7 Models were tested that limit the set of countries to only those that are in both years of the survey, but omit the country fixed effects. Results were very similar to those for the full set of countries presented in Tables 13.2–4. The United States is the omitted country category.

8 A comparison of the calculated price of alcohol for the United States to a similar price created from the American Chamber of Commerce Research Association's *Inter-city Cost of Living Index* shows the prices are fairly close in magnitude. ($0.61 and $0.72 versus $0.72 and $0.79 for 1988 and 1991, respectively.)

9 Statistical significance refers to a two-tailed test at the 5 percent level.

REFERENCES

American Chamber of Commerce Research Association (various years), *Inter-city Cost of Living Index*, Louisville, KY: ACCRA.

Becker, Gary S. (1968), 'Crime and punishment: an economic approach', *Journal of Political Economy*, **76**(2), March/April: 169–217.

Brewers Association of Canada (1997), *Alcoholic Beverage Taxation and Control Policies*, Ottawa, Canada: Brewer's Association of Canada.

Bureau of Justice Statistics (BJS), US Department of Justice (1988), *Report to the Nation on Crime and Justice*, 2nd edn, NCJ-105506, March.

Chaloupka, Frank J. and Henry Saffer (1992), 'Alcohol, illegal drugs, public policy and crime', Presented at the annual meeting of the Western Economic Association, San Francisco, CA, July.

Cook, Philip J. and Moore, Michael J. (1993), 'Economic perspectives on reducing alcohol-related violence', in Susan E. Martin (ed.), *Alcohol and Interpersonal Violence: Fostering Multidisciplinary Perspectives*, National Institute on Alcohol Abuse and Alcoholism Research Monograph 24, NIH Publication No. 93-3469, Washington, DC: US Government Printing Office, pp. 193–211.

Cordilia, A. (1985), 'Alcohol and property crime: explaining the causal nexus', *Journal of Studies on Alcohol*, **46**(2), March: 161–71.

Dolan, Ronald E. and Robert L. Worden (eds) (1994), *Japan, A Country Study*, Washington, DC: Federal Research Division, Library of Congress, January.

Fagan, Jeffrey (1990), 'Intoxication and aggression', in Michael Tonry and James Q. Wilson (eds), *Drugs and Crime: Crime and Justice, A Review of Research*, Vol. 13, Chicago: University of Chicago Press, pp. 241–320.

Fagan, Jeffrey (1993), 'Interactions among drugs, alcohol and violence', *Health Affairs*, **12**(4), Winter: 65–79.

Grossman, Michael, Frank J. Chaloupka and Ismail Sirtalan (1998), 'An empirical analysis of alcohol addiction: results from the Monitoring the Future panels', *Economic Inquiry*, **36**(1), January: 39–48.

Grossman, Michael and Sara Markowitz (1999), 'Alcohol regulation and violence on college campuses', Presented at the Taipei International Conference on Health Economics, Taipei, Taiwan, March 25–6.

Johnson, S.D., L. Gibson and R. Linden (1978), 'Alcohol and rape in Winnipeg, 1966–1975', *Journal of Studies on Alcohol*, **39**(11): 1887–94.

Kenkel, Donald S. (1993), 'Drinking, driving, and deterrence: the effectiveness and social costs of alternative policies', *Journal of Law and Economics*, October: 877–913.

Lenke, L. (1975), 'Valdbrott och alkohol: En studie I misshandelsbrottslighentens utvekling' (Violent crime and alcohol: a study of the developments in assaultive crime), Stockholm: Department of Criminology, University of Stockholm.

Leung, Siu Fai and Charles E. Phelps (1993), '"My Kingdom for a Drink....?" A Review of the Price Sensitivity of Demand for Alcoholic Beverages', in Gregory Bloss and Michael Hilton (eds), *Economic and Socioeconomic Issues in the Prevention of Alcohol-related Problems*, Washington, DC: US Government Printing Office, pp. 1–31.

Lindqvist, P. (1986), 'Criminal homicide in northern Sweden 1970–1981: alcohol intoxication, alcohol abuse and mental disease', *International Journal of Law and Psychiatry*, **8**: 19–37.

Manning, Willard G., Linda Blumberg and Lawrence H. Moulton (1995), 'The demand for alcohol: the differential response to price', *Journal of Health Economics*, **14**(2), June: 123–48.

Markowitz, Sara (2000), 'The price of alcohol, wife abuse and husband abuse', *Southern Economic Journal*, **67**(2): 279–303.

Markowitz, Sara and Michael Grossman (1998a), 'Alcohol regulation and domestic violence towards children', *Contemporary Economic Policy*, **16**: 309–20.

Markowitz, Sara and Michael Grossman (1998b), 'The effects of alcohol regulation on physical child abuse', National Bureau of Economic Research Working Paper No. 6629, July.

Markowitz, Sara and Michael Grossman (2000), 'The effects of beer taxes on physical child abuse', *Journal of Health Economics*, **19**(2): 271–82.

Miczek, K.A., J.F. DeBold, M. Haney, J.Tidey, J. Vivian and E.M. Weerts (1994), 'Alcohol, drugs of abuse, aggression, and violence', in Albert J. Reiss and Jeffery A. Roth (eds), *Understanding and Preventing Violence*, Vol. 3, Washington, DC: National Academy Press, pp. 377–570.

Myers, T. (1982), 'Alcohol and violent crime re-examined: self-reports from two sub-groups of Scottish male prisoners', *British Journal of Addiction*, **77**: 399–413.

Myers, T. (1986), 'An analysis of context and alcohol consumption in a group of criminal events', *Alcohol and Alcoholism*, **21**: 389–95.

National Research Council (1993), *Understanding and Preventing Violence*, edited by Albert J. Reiss and Jeffery A. Roth, Washington, DC: National Academy Press.

Organization for Economic Cooperation and Development (OECD) (1993), *OECD Health Systems: The Socio-economic Environment Statistical References*, Paris: OECD.

Organization for Economic Cooperation and Development (OECD) (1997), Health Data [Computer data file].

Pernanen, Kai (1981), 'Theoretical aspects of the relationship between alcohol use and crime', in James J. Collins Jr. (ed.), *Drinking and Crime: Perspectives on the Relationships between Alcohol Consumption and Criminal Behavior*, New York: Guilford Press.

Roslund, B. and C.A. Larson (1979), 'Crimes of violence and alcohol abuse in Sweden', *International Journal of the Addictions*, **14**(8): 1103–15.

Saffer, Henry (1991), 'Alcohol advertising bans and alcohol abuse: an international perspective', *Journal of Health Economics*, **10**(1): 65–79.

Sampson, Robert J. and Janet L. Lauritsen (1994), 'Violent victimization and offending: individual- situational- and community-level risk factors', in Albert J. Reiss and Jeffery A. Roth (eds), *Understanding and Preventing Violence*, Vol. 3, Washington, DC: National Academy Press, pp. 1–114.

Takala, H. (1973), 'Alkoholstrejkens inverkan pa uppdagad brottslighet' (The effect of the alcohol strike on reported crime), *Alkoholpolitik*, **36**: 14–16.

Virkkunen, M. (1974), 'Alcohol as a factor precipitating aggression and conflict of behaviour leading to homicide', *British Journal of Addiction*, **69**: 149–54.

PART V

Demand Analysis

14. Determinants of smoking cessation: an analysis of young adult men and women

John A. Tauras and Frank J. Chaloupka*

1 INTRODUCTION

Since the publication of the first Surgeon General's report on the health consequences of cigarette smoking in 1964, the government has been involved in a sporadic and often unsynchronized campaign to reduce the use of cigarettes in the United States. This campaign has included such elements as: widespread dissemination of information on the risks of smoking, anti-smoking advertisements, limits on cigarette manufacturer's advertisements, restrictions on smoking in private workplaces and public places, increases in cigarette excise taxes, restrictions on minors' access, and various others (USDHHS 1991). Throughout the 25 years following the onset of the government's anti-smoking effort, substantial progress was made in decreasing the prevalence of cigarette smoking among adults and youth alike. However, recent data suggests that the decades of steady decline have not been sustained. The prevalence of smoking among adults declined very slightly in the 1990s. According to the National Health Interview Surveys (NHIS), 25.5 percent of US adults were current smokers in 1990 as compared to 24.7 percent in 1995.[1] Even more troubling however is the increased prevalence of cigarette smoking among youth and young adults in the 1990s. According to the Monitoring the Future (MTF) Surveys, the prevalence of cigarette smoking among 8th, 10th, and 12th graders has increased for the better part of a decade (University of Michigan News and Information Services UMNIS 1998).

The upward trend in smoking among American teenagers in the 1990s has led to increased efforts to prevent the consumption of cigarettes by youth and young adults. The use of economic incentives to discourage cigarette smoking among America's young people has reached the national spotlight. One of President Bill Clinton's top domestic priorities for the past three years (1996–98) has been to pass legislation containing strong tobacco control provisions, including a significant increase in the price of cigarettes. On February 7, 2000, President Clinton unveiled his proposed budget for fiscal year 2001 which contained several important tobacco-related initiatives including a 25-cent excise tax increase on cigarettes.[2]

This chapter investigates the determinants of the decision to quit smoking by young adults. In particular, we examine the impact cigarette prices, clean indoor air laws, and other socioeconomic determinants have on smoking cessation by males and females separately. Semi-parametric Cox duration models are estimated employing panels formed from the nationally representative cross-sectional surveys of high school seniors conducted by the Institute for Social Research at the University of Michigan as part of the Monitoring the Future project. While preventing youth and young adults from initiating smoking is an extremely important approach to tobacco control, according to the 1990 Surgeon General's report, smoking cessation represents the single most important step that smokers can take to enhance the quality and length of their lives. In fact, many researchers consider smoking cessation as the 'gold standard' of healthcare cost effectiveness, producing higher quality and length of life at costs that are well below other healthcare interventions (Warner 1997).

2 BRIEF REVIEW OF ECONOMETRIC STUDIES OF CIGARETTE DEMAND

Over the past three decades, numerous econometric studies of the determinants of cigarette demand have been published.[3] Substantial econometric efforts have been devoted to examining the impact price has on an individual's consumption of cigarettes. One general conclusion emerges from these studies – the demand for cigarettes is responsive to the price of cigarettes.

Many of these studies employ aggregate-level data. Price elasticity estimates obtained using aggregate data ranged from –0.14 to –1.23, with a majority of the estimates falling within a narrower range of –0.20 to –0.50 (USDHHS 1994). Differences in the price elasticity estimates can be attributed to the use of diverse data, theoretical modeling, and estimation techniques.

A growing number of recent studies use micro-level data (individual or group level) to measure the impact price and other tobacco control policies have on the demand for cigarettes. The price elasticity estimates that are obtained from these studies are comparable to those using aggregate-level data. However, the use of micro-level data has several advantages over using aggregate-level data. First, simultaneity problems are lessened when using micro-level data. That is, no one person can smoke enough cigarettes to affect the market price. Second, the use of micro-level data allows researchers to analyse the effects of price on the probability that an individual smokes and on average cigarette consumption among smokers, and not just per capita cigarette consumption, which is the primary focus of studies that use aggregate data. Finally, micro-level data can be used to evaluate the differential effects of price on alternative demographic groups (such as by age, by gender, by race, and so on).

Although many econometric studies of cigarette demand have been published over the past 30 years, economists have given very little attention to estimating the determinants of the decisions to start or quit smoking in either empirical or theoretical work. The main reason why economists have neglected examining smoking initiation and cessation is due to the lack of appropriate data. In order to investigate the pathways and trajectories of cigarette smoking, the use of longitudinal data that tracks individuals' smoking behaviors and other covariates over time is required. Determining why people start smoking and what factors cause smoking cessation should be a central focus in formulating appropriate anti-smoking policies. Only one published econometric study and two unpublished studies have examined the impact economic factors such as cigarette prices and excise taxes have on smoking cessation.

Douglas (1998) used the 1987 National Health Interview Survey: Cancer Risk Factor Supplement to investigate the determinants of the decisions to start and quit smoking in the context of an economic model of addiction. Douglas uses several different functional forms (log-logistic, Weibull, and Schmidt and Witte Split Population) to model the starting and quitting hazard functions. He concluded that current, future, and past prices of cigarettes have a statistically insignificant effect on the probability of initiation. Likewise, current and past prices were found to be statistically insignificant in the probability of quitting. However, the duration estimates suggest that increases in future cigarette prices will significantly increase quitting rates. Douglas estimates a quitting hazard elasticity of 1.07 to 1.30 with respect to future price. This suggests that a 10 percent permanent increase in the future price of cigarettes will reduce the average duration of smoking by 11–13 percent. In addition, the study indicated that information dissemination regarding the adverse health consequences of smoking, bans on cigarette advertising, and state-level regulations significantly increase the probability of quitting.

While the study by Douglas (1998) made significant contributions to the investigation of the determinants of the decision to start and quit smoking, many of his findings, particularly those that deal with prices, are at odds with a majority of the research on the determinants of cigarette smoking conducted over the past several decades. One possible explanation why Douglas finds insignificant current and past price effects may be due to the fact that he uses one year of cross-sectional data. The application of duration methods in the econometric analysis of cigarette smoking requires relatively high-quality longitudinal data that can accurately measure cigarette consumption, cigarette prices, government-enacted policy variables, income, and sociodemographic variables over a relatively long time period. Indeed, Douglas's study employs cross-sectional data with retrospective information on smoking initiation and cessation. Therefore, incorrect recall by participants can dramatically influence any results obtained. A second possible explanation stems from the error in matching prices to respondents' previous states of residence. Douglas bases all previous prices that a respondent would have paid for cigarettes on the respondent's current state of residence. Therefore, if a respondent lived in a different state in the past, significant errors in price matching would be likely. As Douglas notes, the panel data requirements needed to use duration modeling are not met in this study, and future investigation is needed using true longitudinal data.

In a more recent study, Forster and Jones (1999) use both parametric and semi-parametric techniques to investigate the determinants of smoking initiation and cessation. As did Douglas, Forster and Jones use cross-sectional data (British Health and Lifestyle Survey) with retrospective information on cigarette smoking to approximate the length of time each individual smokes and abstains from smoking. Furthermore, in line with Douglas's work, they allow cigarette tax to act as a time-varying covariate.[4] They find cigarette taxes to be an insignificant determinant of smoking initiation. In addition, they find that the estimated elasticity of the number of years smoked before quitting with respect to tax falls in a range of –0.40 to –0.63, suggesting that a 5 percent increase in tax would lead to a reduction in smoking of approximately 6 to 9.5 months. However, the authors find strong evidence of 5-and 10-year recall bias in their quitting models. To control for the effect of recall bias, they include dummy variables equal to one for individuals who recall quitting either 5 or 10 years ago and zero otherwise. The authors conclude that recall bias had limited impact on the parameter estimates.

Finally, Tauras (1999) uses longitudinal data from the MTF Surveys to estimate the impact prices and clean indoor air laws have on smoking cessation decisions of young adults. He models multiple quit attempts of young adults and concludes that price has a positive and significant impact on smoking cessation. In addition, Tauras finds some evidence that stronger restriction on smoking in private worksites and other public places can increase the number of young adults who quit smoking.

Several recent econometric studies have examined the impact clean indoor air laws have on cigarette demand. Chaloupka and Grossman (1996) concluded that strong restrictions on smoking significantly reduce both the propensity and intensity with which youth smoke. Chaloupka and Wechsler (1997), and Tauras and Chaloupka (1999) concluded that strong smoking restrictions significantly reduce both smoking prevalence and average daily cigarette consumption among young adults. After accounting for the potential endogeneity of smoking restrictions, Ohsfeldt et al. (1998) concluded that the strongest restrictions on cigarette smoking lead to significant decreases in smoking prevalence. Finally, after accounting for the potential self-selection of workers, Evans et al. (1999) concluded that workplace smoking bans reduce the probability of adult smoking by 5 percent and reduce the average daily cigarette consumption of smokers by 10 percent.

To summarize, much has been learned over the past 30 years about the effects of cigarette prices on smoking – increased cigarette prices are expected to decrease cigarette consumption in all segments of the US population. Similarly, strong clean indoor air laws have been found to decrease both the propensity to smoke and the intensity with which smokers smoke. However, not much is known about how price, smoking restrictions, and other influences impact smoking cessation. A better understanding of what causes smoking cessation is of utmost importance in the efforts to decrease the burden that smoking causes. Our research proposes to address these issues by providing an analysis of the impact prices, clean indoor air laws, and other socioeconomic factors have on smoking cessation, using models based on duration, employing nationally representative longitudinal data.

3 DATA AND METHODS

The empirical models that are estimated in this study employ panels formed from the nationally representative cross-sectional surveys of high school seniors conducted by the Institute for Social Research (ISR) at the University of Michigan. Each year since 1975, ISR has conducted a nationally representative random sample of between 15,000 and 19,000 high school seniors as part of a national research program entitled Monitoring the Future: A Continuing Study of American Youth (MTF).[5] These surveys focus on the use of cigarettes, alcohol, and illegal drugs and provide an accurate cross-sectional representation of United States high school seniors.

The senior year of high school is an extremely interesting and relevant point in time to start tracking individuals. According to the 1994 Surgeon General's report, nearly all first use of cigarettes occurs before high school graduation, and most adults who regularly smoke are addicted to cigarettes by the time they are 20 years old. In addition, the completion of high school, for many, means the end of living under parental supervision and undergoing a transition into a different social environment.

One limitation that exists in the MTF data is that the survey includes only high school seniors who have not dropped out of high school or who were present the day the questionnaires were administered. Johnston et al. (1996) have argued that dropouts in general have substantially higher smoking prevalence rates than do in-school students, and that students who are consistently absent from school have similar smoking patterns to dropouts. DeCicca et al. (1999) take the argument one step further and conclude that students who drop out of high school have higher smoking prevalence rates years before they actually drop out of high school. Several recent studies have concluded that social economic status and cigarette price responsiveness are inversely related. For example, Chaloupka (1991) concluded that less-educated people are more price sensitive than are more-educated individuals; Farrelly and Bray (1998) concluded that individuals with lower income are more price elastic than are wealthier individuals; Townsend et al. (1994) concluded that individuals in the highest social class in Britain exhibit very little price sensitivity to cigarettes, whereas individuals in the lowest social class have elasticities close to –1.0. This suggests that the exclusion of dropouts from the analysis is likely to underestimate the true impact price has on young adult smoking.

Starting with the class of 1976, approximately 2400 individuals from each senior class are chosen to participate in follow-up surveys. The 2400 selected respondents are divided into two groups of 1200 individuals each. One group is surveyed on even-numbered calendar years, while the other group is surveyed on odd-numbered calendar years. As a result, one group is resurveyed for the first time one year after baseline (senior year in high school), while the other group is resurveyed for the first time two years after the baseline year. Subsequent follow-ups are conducted at two-year intervals for both groups for up to seven follow-ups and then less frequently.

The questionnaires used in the follow-up surveys are very similar to those used in the baseline. Respondents are mailed the same form of the questionnaire that they received in the baseline year in all subsequent follow-ups. Many of the questions that were asked in the baseline are also asked in all the subsequent follow-up questionnaires so that changes in behaviors and experiences can be measured. High school specific questions are dropped from the follow-ups and relevant post-high school questions are added such as college education, employment status, marital status, and so on.

As with any longitudinal survey, the retention rate declines over time. However, the panel retention rates from the MTF surveys have been very high. According to Johnston et al. (1996), an average of 80 percent of those selected for inclusion in the first follow-up have returned questionnaires. The 1995 panel retention from the class of 1981 (where individuals had reached a modal age of 32) was 60 percent. In general, the individuals who could not be reached or chose not to participate in follow-up surveys were very similar to those individuals that completed all the follow-up surveys. Nevertheless, the panel attrition did create a small degree of bias. First, individuals who had poorer grades in high school were slightly less likely to participate in follow-up surveys. Not surprisingly, those with better grades also had greater expectations about attending college. Given that education and price responsiveness to cigarettes are likely to be inversely related (Chaloupka 1991), the exclusion of bad students is likely to bias the price coefficients down toward zero in absolute value. Second, young adult males were slightly less likely to participate in follow-up surveys than were young adult females. Also, African Americans were less likely to participate in follow-up surveys than were Caucasians. This type of attrition is also likely to bias the price coefficients down toward zero in absolute value given that recent research conducted by Chaloupka and Pacula (1998) concluded that young men are much more responsive to changes in the price of cigarettes than are young women. They also conclude that young African American men are significantly more sensitive to price changes than are young Caucasian men.

The most prominent advantage of using the MTF data is that it is the only longitudinal data set that tracks individuals' smoking habits as they age from teenagers through early adulthood. This is an extremely important time to analyse, because for many, a transition from initiation/experimentation to regular smoking or to cessation takes place during this period.

A variety of cigarette consumption, socioeconomic, and demographic variables was constructed from the survey data for all respondents. Of particular importance for this research was the information collected on each individual's monthly cigarette consumption. In the baseline year and all subsequent follow-ups, all respondents were asked the frequency with which they smoked cigarettes during the past 30 days. The response to this question was used to construct two dichotomous smoking participation indicators. The first is equal to one if the respondent indicated that they had smoked any cigarettes in the 30 days prior to the survey, and equal to zero otherwise. In addition, since many young adults may occasionally experiment with cigarettes, and classifying an individual as a current smoker based on youthful experimentation is inappropriate, a second dichotomous participation indicator is constructed. The second indicator is equal to one if the respondent indicated smoking on average at least one to five cigarettes each day in the previous 30 days, and equal to zero otherwise. In the first follow-up that an individual responds that he or she has not smoked in the past 30 days, that person is considered to have stopped smoking. Since follow-ups are conducted at two-year intervals, cessation based on past month use may not imply long-term cessation because there is no way to assess whether or not an individual has stopped smoking for 30 days or two years. Furthermore, reinitiation of smoking is not looked at and therefore no conclusions on permanent smoking cessation can be drawn.

In addition to the cigarette consumption variables, a variety of independent variables was constructed from the surveys to control for other factors affecting cigarette demand. These include: the age of the respondent, in years; average real yearly income from employment[6] (deflated by national consumer price index (CPI) 1982–84 = 100); number of years of formal schooling, in years; average number of hours worked weekly; race/ethnicity (white, Black – omitted); indicators of college student status (full time, half time, less than half time, no college – omitted); indicators of frequency of participation in religious services (never – omitted, infrequent participation, moderate participation, and frequent participation); indicators of marital status (married, engaged, separated or divorced, and single – omitted); indicators of family structure (live alone, live with parents, live with spouse, live with child); and indicators of type of city/town (urban – omitted, suburban, and rural).

In addition, indicators of region according to the Bureau of Labor Statistics (Northeast, South, Midwest, and West – omitted) and variables capturing the year the questionnaires were administered (year and year squared) were constructed from the surveys to control for region and time trends.

Based on the site identifiers, cigarette prices were added to the surveys. The price data were obtained from the Tobacco Institute's annual *Tax Burden on Tobacco*. Each year, the Tobacco Institute publishes state-level cigarette prices as of November 1. These prices are weighted averages for a pack of 20 cigarettes based on the prices of single packs, cartons, and vending machine sales where the weights are the national proportions of each type of sale. These prices are inclusive of state-level sales taxes applied to cigarettes, but are exclusive of local cigarette taxes. Since the price published is as of November 1, and the survey is conducted between mid-February and early June and the dependent variables are based on past month smoking, a weighted average price for the first six months of the year is computed. The average price for the first six months of every year is computed by subtracting state and federal excise taxes from the current year's price and the previous year's price and weighting the pre-tax prices accordingly (7/12 previous year and 5/12 current year). Then the average federal tax and average state tax for the first six months of the year are added to the first six month's average pretax price. To account for changes in the relative price of cigarettes over time, all cigarette prices are deflated by the national CPI published by the Bureau of Labor Statistics (1982–84 = 100).

Based on state identifiers, a set of variables reflecting the presence and magnitude of state clean indoor air laws was added to the data. These data were obtained through special agreement with the Centers for Disease Control from an unpublished database. The data were used to construct three dichotomous indicators for state-level restrictions on smoking in private worksites, restaurants, and any other public place.

In an attempt to capture the magnitude of each state's clean indoor air laws, a clean indoor air index variable was created. The construction of this variable is similar to the classification scheme presented in various Surgeon General reports (USDHHS 1986 and 1989). The index variable is defined as follows: it takes on a value of 4 if the state has 'extensive' restrictions on cigarette smoking, that is, if it regulates smoking in private workplaces; it takes on a value of 3 if the state has 'moderate' restrictions, that is, if it regulates smoking in restaurants but not in private worksites; it takes on a value of 2 if the state has 'basic' restrictions, that is, if it limits smoking in healthcare facilities, grocery stores, or government worksites and not in restaurants or private worksites; it takes on a value of 1 if the state has 'nominal' restrictions, that is, if it limits smoking in public places other than healthcare facilities, grocery stores, restaurants, government worksites, and private worksites; and finally, it takes on a value of 0 if the state has no restrictions on cigarette smoking, that is, if it does not restrict cigarette smoking in private worksites, restaurants, healthcare facilities, grocery stores, government worksites, or any other public place.

Table 14.1 contains variable definitions and descriptive statistics of key variables employed in the smoking cessation equations. Duration modeling is the appropriate statistical tool to investigate the structural determinants of making a transition from one discrete state to another. A semi-parametric Cox regression is used to assess the probability of making a transition from the smoking state to the non-smoking state.[7] The Cox model allows changes in exogenous covariates to affect the quitting hazard (probability of cessation conditional on being a continuous smoker) while assuming no specific functional form for the underlying hazard function.[8]

4 RESULTS

Historical differences in patterns of smoking exist between men and women. Smoking prevalence rates for men increased dramatically during the first few decades of the century. Smoking prevalence rates among women however did not begin to rise rapidly until a few decades later. Consequently, by 1965, one year after the release of the first Surgeon General's report, 51.9 percent of men currently smoked, whereas only 33.9 percent of women currently smoked (NHIS, 1965). Since that time, cigarette smoking among both sexes has declined, but the rate of decline has been slower among women than men. In 1994, 28.2 percent of men were smokers, as compared to 23.1 percent of women. In order to explore the differences in smoking patterns, smoking cessation equations are estimated for males and females separately.

In addition, given the prevalence of teenage experimentation and the addiction associated with cigarette smoking, young smokers may react substantially differently to changes in exogenous covariates than do more established smokers. Therefore, classification of smoker versus non-smoker is established at two separate ages – age 18 and age 23.

Table 14.2 contains the estimates from the smoking cessation equations for females who are classified as smokers at age 18, whereas Table 14.3 contains comparable estimates for male smokers. Table 14.4 contains the estimates from the smoking cessation equations for females who are classified as smokers at age 23, whereas Table 14.5 contains comparable estimates for male smokers. Six alternative models are estimated. Model 1 of each table controls for the real price of cigarettes, race, income, religiosity, type of community, average work hours, marital status, family structure, formal years of schooling, college student status, region, and two time-trend variables (year and year squared). In addition, with the exception of price, time trend, region, and the indicators of family structure, which were not mutually exclusive, indicators for respondents with missing data for all of the above variables are included in the models. These missing value indicators were created to prevent the loss of a large number of observations. For example, if frequency of participation at

Table 14.1 Definition of variables

Variables	Definition, Male Mean Age 18+ (μ_{m18+}); Female Mean Age 18+ (μ_{f18+}); Male Mean Age 23+ (μ_{m23+}); Female Mean Age 23+(μ_{f23+})
Price	Average price of a pack of 20 for the first two quarters of the year, deflated by the national CPI, 1982–84 = 100. $\mu_{m18+} = 1.07$ $\mu_{f18+} = 1.08$ $\mu_{m23+} = 1.14$ $\mu_{f23+} = 1.15$
Clean indoor air index	Index of state restrictions on smoking in public places and private workplaces. The index is equal to: 4 if the state restricts smoking in private worksites; 3 if the state restricts smoking in restaurants and not private worksites; 2 if the state restricts smoking in healthcare facilities, grocery stores, or government worksites and not restaurants or private worksites; 1 if state restricts smoking in other public places excluding private worksites, restaurants, grocery stores, healthcare facilities and government worksites; zero if the state does not restrict smoking in any public place or private workplace. $\mu_{m18+} = 1.57$ $\mu_{f18+} = 1.56$ $\mu_{m23+} = 1.84$ $\mu_{f23+} = 1.83$
Private workplace restriction	Dichotomous indicator equal to 1 if respondent resides in a state that restricts cigarette smoking in private worksites and 0 otherwise. $\mu_{m18+} = 0.244$ $\mu_{f18+} = 0.241$ $\mu_{m23+} = 0.292$ $\mu_{f23+} = 0.289$
Restaurant restriction	Dichotomous indicator equal to 1 if respondent resides in a state that restricts cigarette smoking in restaurants and 0 otherwise. $\mu_{m18+} = 0.333$ $\mu_{f18+} = 0.328$ $\mu_{m23+} = 0.389$ $\mu_{f23+} = 0.383$
Other indoor restriction	Dichotomous indicator equal to 1 if respondent resides in a state that restricts cigarette smoking in government worksites, healthcare facilities, grocery stores, or any other public place. $\mu_{m18+} = 0.496$ $\mu_{f18+} = 0.491$ $\mu_{m23+} = 0.569$ $\mu_{f23+} = 0.565$
White	Dichotomous indicator equal to 1 if White or Caucasian and 0 otherwise. $\mu_{m18+} = 0.839$ $\mu_{f18+} = 0.822$ $\mu_{m23+} = 0.858$ $\mu_{f23+} = 0.840$
Yearly income	Average real yearly income from employment sources only (in dollars), deflated by the national CPI, 1982–84=100. $\mu_{m18+} = 90.94$ $\mu_{f18+} = 63.21$ $\mu_{m23+} = 143.15$ $\mu_{f23+} = 97.22$
Infrequent religion	Dichotomous indicator equal to 1 for individuals who attend religious services infrequently and 0 otherwise. $\mu_{m18+} = 0.461$ $\mu_{f18+} = 0.420$ $\mu_{m23+} = 0.490$ $\mu_{f23+} = 0.440$
Moderate religion	Dichotomous indicator equal to 1 for individuals who attend religious services occasionally and 0 otherwise. $\mu_{m18+} = 0.155$ $\mu_{f18+} = 0.185$ $\mu_{m23+} = 0.149$ $\mu_{f23+} = 0.183$
Frequent religion	Dichotomous indicator equal to 1 for individuals who attend religious services frequently and 0 otherwise. $\mu_{m18+} = 0.213$ $\mu_{f18+} = 0.274$ $\mu_{m23+} = 0.181$ $\mu_{f23+} = 0.251$

Table 14.1 Definition of variables (cont.)

Suburban	Dichotomous indicator equal to 1 for individuals who live in a suburban community and 0 otherwise. $\mu_{m18+} = 0.647$ $\mu_{f18+} = 0.666$ $\mu_{m23+} = 0.646$ $\mu_{f23+} = 0.666$
Rural	Dichotomous indicator equal to 1 for individuals who live in a rural community and 0 otherwise. $\mu_{m18+} = 0.150$ $\mu_{f18+} = 0.134$ $\mu_{m23+} = 0.140$ $\mu_{f23+} = 0.130$
Work hours	$\mu_{m18+} = 29.7$ $\mu_{f18+} = 24.6$ $\mu_{m23+} = 39.0$ $\mu_{f23+} = 31.1$
Married	Dichotomous indicator equal to 1 for individuals who are married, and 0 otherwise. $\mu_{m18+} = 0.228$ $\mu_{f18+} = 0.300$ $\mu_{m23+} = 0.417$ $\mu_{f23+} = 0.513$
Engaged	Dichotomous indicator equal to 1 for individuals who are engaged, and 0 otherwise. $\mu_{m18+} = 0.063$ $\mu_{f18+} = 0.090$ $\mu_{m23+} = 0.067$ $\mu_{f23+} = 0.070$
Separated / Divorced	Dichotomous indicator equal to 1 for individuals who are separated or divorced, and 0 otherwise. $\mu_{m18+} = 0.026$ $\mu_{f18+} = 0.038$ $\mu_{m23+} = 0.046$ $\mu_{f23+} = 0.068$
Live alone	Dichotomous indicator equal to 1 for individuals who live alone, and 0 otherwise. $\mu_{m18+} = 0.083$ $\mu_{f18+} = 0.060$ $\mu_{m23+} = 0.126$ $\mu_{f23+} = 0.088$
Live parents	Dichotomous indicator equal to 1 for individuals who live with their parents, and 0 otherwise. $\mu_{m18+} = 0.442$ $\mu_{f18+} = 0.407$ $\mu_{m23+} = 0.206$ $\mu_{f23+} = 0.169$
Live spouse	Dichotomous indicator equal to 1 for individuals who live with their spouse, and 0 otherwise. $\mu_{m18+} = 0.216$ $\mu_{f18+} = 0.290$ $\mu_{m23+} = 0.405$ $\mu_{f23+} = 0.504$
Live child	Dichotomous indicator equal to 1 for individuals who live with their child or children, and 0 otherwise. $\mu_{m18+} = 0.127$ $\mu_{f18+} = 0.216$ $\mu_{m23+} = 0.245$ $\mu_{f23+} = 0.386$
School years	Number of formal school years completed. $\mu_{m18+} = 13.06$ $\mu_{f18+} = 13.06$ $\mu_{m23+} = 14.04$ $\mu_{f23+} = 13.97$
College less than half time	Dichotomous indicator equal to 1 for individuals who are attending college less than half time, and 0 otherwise. $\mu_{m18+} = 0.044$ $\mu_{f18+} = 0.046$ $\mu_{m23+} = 0.064$ $\mu_{f23+} = 0.067$
College half time	Dichotomous indicator equal to 1 for individuals who are attending college half time, and 0 otherwise. $\mu_{m18+} = 0.030$ $\mu_{f18+} = 0.031$ $\mu_{m23+} = 0.034$ $\mu_{f23+} = 0.033$
College full time	Dichotomous indicator equal to 1 for individuals who are attending college full time, and 0 otherwise. $\mu_{m18+} = 0.200$ $\mu_{f18+} = 0.191$ $\mu_{m23+} = 0.111$ $\mu_{f23+} = 0.087$

Table 14.2 Estimates from female (age 18) cessation models

Independent variables	Any smoking past 30 days			Average at least 1–5 cigarettes per day		
	Model 1	Model 2	Model 3	Model 4	Model 5	Model 6
Real cigarette price	0.312	0.293	0.294	0.584	0.572	0.570
	(1.81)	(1.69)	(1.70)	(2.42)	(2.36)	(2.36)
Clean air index		0.015			0.012	
		(1.24)			(0.75)	
Other clean indoor air laws			0.066			0.056
			(1.23)			(0.77)
Private worksite			0.014			0.016
			(0.22)			(0.20)
Restaurant			−0.028			−0.023
			(−0.42)			(−0.26)
White	0.164	0.165	0.165	0.399	0.400	0.399
	(2.23)	(2.25)	(2.25)	(3.58)	(3.58)	(3.58)
Real income	0.000	0.000	0.000	0.000	0.000	0.000
	(1.08)	(1.08)	(1.08)	(0.00)	(0.00)	(0.00)
Suburb	0.036	0.036	0.036	0.011	0.011	0.011
	(0.80)	(0.79)	(0.80)	(0.18)	(0.18)	(0.19)
Rural	0.025	0.025	0.026	−0.006	−0.005	−0.005
	(0.41)	(0.43)	(0.43)	(−0.07)	(−0.07)	(−0.06)
Married	−0.149	−0.150	−0.150	−0.035	−0.036	−0.036
	(−1.20)	(−1.20)	(−1.20)	(−0.22)	(−0.23)	(−0.23)
Engaged	−0.088	−0.088	−0.089	0.007	0.007	0.007
	(−1.73)	(−1.73)	(−1.75)	(0.11)	(0.11)	(0.10)
Separated/Divorced	−0.333	−0.334	−0.335	−0.292	−0.293	−0.293
	(−3.07)	(−3.08)	(−3.08)	(−2.26)	(−2.27)	(−2.27)
Live alone	0.045	0.044	0.044	−0.018	−0.019	−0.019
	(0.54)	(0.53)	(0.53)	(−0.17)	(−0.18)	(−0.18)
Live with parents	0.140	0.140	0.141	0.134	0.134	0.135
	(3.29)	(3.29)	(3.30)	(2.38)	(2.37)	(2.38)
Live with spouse	0.044	0.044	0.043	0.031	0.031	0.031
	(0.34)	(0.34)	(0.34)	(0.19)	(0.19)	(0.19)
Live with child	−0.532	−0.533	−0.534	−0.426	−0.427	−0.428
	(−7.65)	(−7.66)	(−7.67)	(−5.31)	(−5.32)	(−5.32)

Table 14.2 Estimates from female (age 18) cessation models (cont.)

Independent variables	**Any smoking past 30 days**			**Average at least 1–5 cigarettes per day**		
	Model 1	**Model 2**	**Model 3**	**Model 4**	**Model 5**	**Model 6**
Infrequent religious attendance	0.107	0.107	0.106	0.076	0.076	0.075
	(2.07)	(2.07)	(2.06)	(1.17)	(1.18)	(1.17)
Moderate religious attendance	0.351	0.352	0.351	0.256	0.257	0.257
	(5.99)	(5.99)	(5.99)	(3.31)	(3.32)	(3.32)
Frequent religious attendance	0.523	0.523	0.523	0.355	0.356	0.355
	(9.13)	(9.13)	(9.13)	(4.53)	(4.53)	(4.53)
Hours worked	–0.015	–0.015	–0.015	–0.013	–0.013	–0.013
	(–10.49)	(–10.49)	(–10.49)	(–6.84)	(–6.84)	(–6.84)
Formal school years	–0.070	–0.071	–0.070	–0.056	–0.056	–0.056
	(–3.99)	(–4.01)	(–3.99)	(–2.57)	(–2.58)	(–2.57)
College less than half time	–0.080	–0.082	–0.080	–0.044	–0.045	–0.044
	(–0.89)	(–0.90)	(–0.89)	(–0.39)	(–0.39)	(–0.39)
College half time	–0.091	–0.093	–0.091	0.037	0.035	0.037
	(–0.90)	(–0.93)	(–0.90)	(0.30)	(0.28)	(0.30)
College full time	0.013	0.014	0.014	0.124	0.124	0.124
	(0.25)	(0.25)	(0.26)	(1.70)	(1.71)	(1.71)
North East	–0.319	–0.291	–0.283	–0.190	–0.169	–0.159
	(–6.33)	(–5.30)	(–4.96)	(–2.76)	(–2.26)	(–2.06)
Midwest	–0.244	–0.221	–0.212	–0.195	–0.177	–0.166
	(–4.97)	(–4.20)	(–3.72)	(–2.80)	(–2.41)	(–2.10)
South	–0.198	–0.167	–0.168	–0.174	–0.149	–0.145
	(–3.81)	(–2.90)	(–2.83)	(–2.33)	(–1.84)	(–1.75)
Year	0.482	0.501	0.502	0.572	0.593	0.595
	(3.27)	(3.38)	(3.38)	(2.74)	(2.80)	(2.81)
Year squared	–0.003	–0.003	–0.003	–0.003	–0.004	–0.004
	(–3.10)	(–3.21)	(–3.21)	(–2.70)	(–2.77)	(–2.78)
Price elasticity of cessation	0.367	0.392	0.343	0.794	0.772	0.769

Note: All equations also include missing indicators for income, age, religiosity, type of community, average work hours, marital status, and family structure. Asymptotic *t*-ratios are in parentheses. The critical values for the *t*-ratios are 2.58 (2.33), 1.96 (1.64), and 1.64 (1.28) at the 1, 5, and 10 percent significance levels, respectively, based on a two-tailed (one-tailed) test. All equations based on chi-square tests are significant at better than the 1 percent significance level.

Table 14.3 Estimates from male (age 18) cessation models

Independent variables	Any smoking past 30 days			Average at least 1–5 cigarettes per day		
	Model 1	Model 2	Model 3	Model 4	Model 5	Model 6
Real cigarette price	0.237	0.246	0.268	–0.108	–0.062	–0.053
	(1.19)	(1.24)	(1.34)	(–0.38)	(–0.22)	(–0.19)
Clean air index		–0.007			–0.034	
		(–0.51)			(–1.69)	
Other clean indoor air laws			–0.101			–0.137
			(–1.66)			(–1.59)
Private worksite			0.046			0.065
			(0.61)			(0.60)
Restaurant			0.051			–0.021
			(0.64)			(–0.18)
White	0.123	0.123	0.122	0.113	0.112	0.112
	(1.40)	(1.40)	(1.38)	(0.84)	(0.84)	(0.84)
Real income	–0.001	–0.001	–0.001	–0.001	–0.001	–0.001
	(–1.42)	(–1.41)	(–1.39)	(–1.13)	(–1.07)	(–1.05)
Suburb	–0.026	–0.026	–0.026	0.005	0.003	0.003
	(–0.48)	(–0.49)	(–0.48)	(0.07)	(0.04)	(0.04)
Rural	–0.015	–0.015	–0.016	0.029	0.027	0.026
	(–0.22)	(–0.23)	(–0.24)	(0.31)	(0.29)	(0.28)
Married	0.017	0.018	0.015	0.059	0.060	0.057
	(0.12)	(0.12)	(0.11)	(0.31)	(0.31)	(0.30)
Engaged	–0.192	–0.193	–0.191	–0.032	–0.034	–0.032
	(–2.33)	(–2.34)	(–2.32)	(–0.32)	(–0.34)	(–0.32)
Separated/Divorced	–0.600	–0.599	–0.592	–0.539	–0.538	–0.536
	(–3.36)	(–3.36)	(–3.31)	(–2.55)	(–2.55)	(–2.54)
Live alone	0.010	0.010	0.013	0.003	0.005	0.009
	(0.10)	(0.11)	(0.14)	(0.02)	(0.05)	(0.08)
Live with parents	0.149	0.149	0.148	0.023	0.023	0.023
	(2.89)	(2.89)	(2.87)	(0.34)	(0.34)	(0.34)
Live with spouse	0.101	0.100	0.102	0.098	0.095	0.097
	(0.62)	(0.61)	(0.63)	(0.47)	(0.46)	(0.47)
Live with child	–0.582	–0.583	–0.581	–0.540	–0.542	–0.540
	(–5.09)	(–5.09)	(–5.07)	(–4.15)	(–4.17)	(–4.15)

Table 14.3 Estimates from male (age 18) cessation models (cont.)

Independent variables	**Any smoking past 30 days**			**Average at least 1–5 cigarettes per day**		
	Model 1	**Model 2**	**Model 3**	**Model 4**	**Model 5**	**Model 6**
Infrequent religious attendance	0.059 (1.13)	0.059 (1.13)	0.058 (1.11)	–0.052 (–0.76)	–0.051 (–0.75)	–0.051 (–0.76)
Moderate religious attendance	0.308 (4.86)	0.308 (4.86)	0.307 (4.85)	0.119 (1.33)	0.117 (1.31)	0.116 (1.30)
Frequent religious attendance	0.522 (8.67)	0.522 (8.68)	0.521 (8.66)	0.448 (5.34)	0.447 (5.34)	0.447 (5.33)
Hours worked	–0.014 (–9.23)	–0.014 (–9.23)	–0.014 (–9.24)	–0.011 (–5.38)	–0.011 (–5.38)	–0.011 (–5.39)
Formal school years	–0.086 (–3.80)	–0.086 (–3.79)	–0.087 (–3.84)	–0.025 (–0.90)	–0.025 (–0.89)	–0.025 (0.91)
College less than half time	–0.151 (–1.21)	–0.150 (–1.20)	–0.146 (–1.17)	–0.115 (–0.77)	–0.111 (–0.75)	–0.107 (0.72)
College half time	0.148 (1.21)	0.149 (1.22)	0.146 (1.20)	0.133 (0.86)	0.139 (0.90)	0.133 (0.86)
College full time	0.051 (0.72)	0.052 (0.72)	0.052 (0.72)	0.022 (0.23)	0.023 (0.24)	0.023 (0.23)
North East	–0.221 (–3.72)	–0.232 (–3.70)	–0.254 (–3.86)	–0.071 (–0.83)	–0.122 (–1.36)	–0.141 (–1.52)
Midwest	–0.313 (–5.45)	–0.322 (–5.37)	–0.335 (–5.18)	–0.318 (–3.72)	–0.362 (–4.02)	–0.364 (–3.82)
South	–0.206 (–3.41)	–0.218 (–3.36)	–0.214 (–3.17)	–0.175 (–1.97)	–0.233 (–2.45)	–0.225 (–2.29)
Year	0.248 (1.49)	0.241 (1.44)	0.249 (1.48)	0.043 (0.18)	0.003 (0.01)	0.012 (0.05)
Year squared	–0.001 (–1.39)	–0.001 (–1.34)	–0.001 (–1.38)	0.000 (0.10)	0.000 (0.07)	0.000 (0.04)
Price elasticity of cessation	0.266	0.278	0.306	–0.101	–0.06	–0.05

Note: All equations also include missing indicators for income, age, religiosity, type of community, average work hours, marital status, and family structure. Asymptotic *t*-ratios are in parentheses. The critical values for the *t*-ratios are 2.58 (2.33), 1.96 (1.64), and 1.64 (1.28) at the 1, 5, and 10 percent significance levels, respectively, based on a two-tailed (one-tailed) test. All equations based on chi-square tests are significant at better than the 1 percent significance level.

Table 14.4 Estimates from female (age 23) cessation models

Independent variables	Any smoking past 30 days			Average at least 1–5 cigarettes per day		
	Model 1	Model 2	Model 3	Model 4	Model 5	Model 6
Real cigarette price	0.504 (1.93)	0.450 (1.71)	0.476 (1.80)	0.664 (2.03)	0.631 (1.92)	0.648 (1.95)
Clean air index		0.038 (2.18)			0.022 (1.01)	
Other clean indoor air laws			0.060 (0.77)			0.048 (0.50)
Private worksite			−0.066 (−0.72)			−0.151 (−1.37)
Restaurant			0.114 (1.17)			0.149 (1.28)
White	0.245 (2.32)	0.247 (2.34)	0.246 (2.34)	0.250 (1.93)	0.252 (1.94)	0.251 (1.94)
Real income	−0.001 (−2.04)	−0.001 (−2.03)	−0.001 (−2.07)	0.000 (0.41)	0.000 (0.41)	0.000 (0.45)
Suburb	−0.101 (−1.70)	−0.102 (−1.72)	−0.105 (−1.76)	−0.051 (−0.66)	−0.052 (−0.67)	−0.056 (−0.71)
Rural	−0.200 (−2.16)	−0.201 (−2.18)	−0.204 (−2.21)	−0.185 (−1.60)	−0.186 (−1.61)	−0.190 (−1.65)
Married	0.143 (0.96)	0.142 (0.95)	0.145 (0.97)	0.209 (1.06)	0.208 (1.05)	0.210 (1.07)
Engaged	0.077 (0.90)	0.078 (0.92)	0.077 (0.90)	0.065 (0.57)	0.066 (0.58)	0.065 (0.57)
Separated/Divorced	−0.129 (−1.28)	−0.130 (−1.29)	−0.127 (−1.26)	−0.107 (−0.89)	−0.108 (−0.89)	−0.102 (−0.84)
Live alone	−0.107 (−1.20)	−0.108 (−1.21)	−0.107 (−1.20)	−0.063 (−0.55)	−0.064 (0.56)	−0.062 (−0.54)
Live with parents	−0.009 (−0.13)	−0.008 (−0.12)	−0.011 (−0.17)	0.000 (0.00)	0.000 (0.00)	−0.003 (−0.04)
Live with spouse	−0.105 (−0.71)	−0.104 (−0.70)	−0.105 (−0.71)	−0.083 (−0.43)	−0.083 (−0.43)	−0.084 (−0.44)
Live with child	−0.238 (−3.48)	−0.237 (−3.48)	−0.239 (−3.51)	−0.199 (−2.48)	−0.199 (−2.48)	−0.203 (−2.52)

Table 14.4 Estimates from female (age 23) cessation models (cont.)

Independent variables	Any smoking past 30 days			Average at least 1–5 cigarettes per day		
	Model 1	Model 2	Model 3	Model 4	Model 5	Model 6
Infrequent religious attendance	0.203	0.201	0.203	0.124	0.124	0.127
	(2.57)	(2.55)	(2.57)	(1.34)	(1.34)	(1.37)
Moderate religious attendance	0.419	0.418	0.419	0.226	0.227	0.229
	(4.61)	(4.61)	(4.61)	(2.01)	(2.01)	(2.03)
Frequent religious attendance	0.578	0.581	0.582	0.449	0.453	0.455
	(6.21)	(6.24)	(6.24)	(3.92)	(3.94)	(3.96)
Hours worked	−0.001	−0.001	−0.001	−0.001	−0.001	−0.001
	(−0.35)	(−0.35)	(−0.34)	(−0.39)	(−0.39)	(−0.38)
Formal school years	0.101	0.101	0.102	0.101	0.101	0.103
	(6.65)	(6.65)	(6.67)	(5.15)	(5.15)	(5.20)
College less than half time	−0.036	−0.038	−0.039	0.056	0.055	0.051
	(−0.38)	(−0.40)	(−0.41)	(0.48)	(0.47)	(0.44)
College half time	0.039	0.032	0.032	0.104	0.101	0.097
	(0.31)	(0.25)	(0.25)	(0.62)	(0.60)	(0.57)
College full time	0.217	0.220	0.221	0.072	0.073	0.074
	(2.43)	(2.46)	(2.48)	(0.57)	(0.58)	(0.58)
North East	−0.220	−0.164	−0.168	−0.284	−0.252	−0.247
	(−2.82)	(−2.01)	(−2.00)	(−2.88)	(−2.45)	(−2.35)
Midwest	−0.196	−0.143	−0.170	−0.196	−0.166	−0.199
	(−2.48)	(−1.75)	(−2.00)	(−1.97)	(−1.61)	(−1.87)
South	−0.177	−0.103	−0.121	−0.202	−0.160	−0.177
	(−2.13)	(−1.15)	(−1.35)	(−1.91)	(−1.43)	(−1.57)
Year	−0.412	−0.292	−0.322	−0.739	−0.668	−0.698
	(−1.04)	(−0.73)	(−0.80)	(−1.43)	(−1.28)	(−1.34)
Year squared	0.002	0.001	0.002	0.004	0.003	0.004
	(0.91)	(0.59)	(0.66)	(1.29)	(1.13)	(1.19)
Price elasticity of cessation	0.707	0.611	0.654	1.00	0.942	0.975

Note: All equations also include missing indicators for income, age, religiosity, type of community, average work hours, marital status, and family structure. Asymptotic *t*-ratios are in parentheses. The critical values for the *t*-ratios are 2.58 (2.33), 1.96 (1.64), and 1.64 (1.28) at the 1, 5, and 10 percent significance levels, respectively, based on a two-tailed (one-tailed) test. All equations based on chi-square tests are significant at better than the 1 percent significance level.

religious services is unknown for a given time period, each of the religion participation variables takes on a value of zero for that time period, while an additional indicator, unknown religious service participation, takes on a value of one. This missing value indicator takes on a value of zero for all respondents whose religious participation is known. Model 2 of each table is identical to model 1, except model 2 adds a clean indoor air index variable. Model 3 of each table is identical to model 2, except the clean indoor air index variable is replaced by three dichotomous indicators for smoking in private worksites, restaurants, and any other public place restriction. Models 4 to 6 of each table are identical to models 1 to 3, except models 4 to 6 use a higher threshold of cigarette consumption in order to classify individuals as current smokers.[9]

To control for the possibility that unobserved state-level sentiment toward smoking is both causing the excise taxes to increase as well as increasing the probability that individuals quit smoking, alternative models were run that replaced the region fixed effects with state fixed effects. These models are not presented because there was not enough variation in cigarette prices within states over time to justify their inclusion. Estimates from these models are available upon request.

The real price of cigarettes is found to have a positive and significant impact on the probability of young adult female smoking cessation in all the models that are estimated. The price elasticity of cessation for females ranges from 0.243 to 1.000. This suggests that a 10 percent increase in the price of cigarettes will increase the probability of smoking cessation among young adult females by approximately 2.4–10.0 percent depending on the model specification. Price has a larger impact on females who are classified as smokers later in life (age 23) than on individuals who are classified as smokers younger in life (age 18). The average price elasticities of cessation are 0.573 and 0.815 for younger and older smokers, respectively. In addition, price has a larger impact on females who smoke more on average than on smokers who smoke less frequently. The average price elasticity of cessation for females who smoked at least one cigarette in the previous 30 days is 0.512 as compared to 0.875 for females who smoke at least 1–5 cigarettes per day on average during the past 30 days.

Price has a positive and significant impact on male smoking cessation in every model estimated for individuals who are classified as smokers later in life (age 23). Among these individuals, price has a larger impact on the probability of smoking cessation for individuals who smoke more on average than less-frequent smokers. The average price elasticity of cessation for males who smoke any cigarettes in the previous 30 days is 0.887 as compared to 1.227 for males who smoke at least 1–5 cigarettes

Table 14.5 Estimates from male (age 23) cessation models

Independent variables	Any smoking past 30 days			Average at least 1–5 cigarettes per day		
	Model 1	Model 2	Model 3	Model 4	Model 5	Model 6
Real cigarette price	0.582 (1.94)	0.617 (2.05)	0.620 (2.06)	0.724 (1.88)	0.780 (2.01)	0.800 (2.08)
Clean air index		−0.024 (−1.16)			−0.037 (−1.45)	
Other clean indoor air laws			−0.079 (−0.91)			−0.161 (−1.45)
Private worksite			0.038 (0.37)			0.085 (0.64)
Restaurant			−0.034 (−0.31)			−0.035 (−0.25)
White	−0.016 (−0.14)	−0.015 (−0.13)	−0.016 (−0.14)	0.060 (0.37)	0.059 (0.36)	0.056 (0.35)
Real income	0.000 (0.24)	0.000 (0.25)	0.000 (0.26)	0.000 (0.23)	0.000 (0.25)	0.000 (0.27)
Suburb	−0.102 (−1.50)	−0.105 (−1.54)	−0.106 (−1.56)	0.063 (0.67)	0.056 (0.60)	0.054 (0.58)
Rural	−0.080 (−0.81)	−0.082 (−0.83)	−0.083 (−0.84)	0.063 (0.49)	0.058 (0.45)	0.055 (0.43)
Married	−0.013 (−0.07)	−0.010 (−0.06)	−0.009 (−0.05)	0.093 (0.41)	0.096 (0.42)	0.101 (0.44)
Engaged	0.236 (2.46)	0.235 (2.45)	0.237 (2.47)	0.397 (3.28)	0.394 (3.25)	0.399 (3.29)
Separated/Divorced	−0.321 (−2.31)	−0.320 (−2.30)	−0.317 (−2.28)	−0.315 (−1.91)	−0.314 (−1.91)	−0.305 (−1.85)
Live alone	0.158 (1.86)	0.158 (1.87)	0.158 (1.87)	0.262 (2.37)	0.264 (2.39)	0.265 (2.39)
Live with parents	−0.052 (−0.69)	−0.053 (−0.70)	−0.053 (−0.70)	0.018 (0.19)	0.017 (0.17)	0.017 (0.17)
Live with spouse	0.154 (0.82)	0.150 (0.80)	0.149 (0.79)	0.247 (1.06)	0.244 (1.04)	0.238 (1.01)
Live with child	−0.398 (−4.35)	−0.399 (−4.35)	−0.397 (−4.34)	−0.491 (−4.57)	−0.494 (−4.58)	−0.490 (−4.55)

Table 14.5 Estimates from male (age 23) cessation models (cont.)

Independent variables	**Any smoking past 30 days**			**Average at least 1–5 cigarettes per day**		
	Model 1	**Model 2**	**Model 3**	**Model 4**	**Model 5**	**Model 6**
Infrequent religious attendance	0.020	0.019	0.021	–0.016	–0.017	–0.015
	(0.28)	(0.27)	(0.28)	(–0.18)	(–0.19)	(–0.17)
Moderate religious attendance	0.221	0.219	0.221	0.252	0.250	0.253
	(2.36)	(2.34)	(2.36)	(2.14)	(2.13)	(2.16)
Frequent religious attendance	0.498	0.498	0.500	0.418	0.420	0.422
	(4.92)	(4.93)	(4.94)	(3.12)	(3.15)	(3.16)
Hours worked	0.004	0.004	0.004	0.006	0.006	0.006
	(1.31)	(1.32)	(1.34)	(1.58)	(1.58)	(1.62)
Formal school years	0.096	0.096	0.096	0.065	0.064	0.064
	(5.86)	(5.86)	(5.86)	(2.98)	(2.95)	(2.95)
College less than half time	–0.030	–0.028	–0.028	0.055	0.058	0.057
	(–0.26)	(–0.25)	(–0.25)	(0.40)	(0.42)	(0.41)
College half time	0.210	0.210	0.210	0.107	0.107	0.106
	(1.50)	(1.50)	(1.51)	(0.54)	(0.54)	(0.54)
College full time	0.401	0.398	0.400	0.444	0.440	0.442
	(4.38)	(4.35)	(4.36)	(3.54)	(3.51)	(3.52)
North East	–0.097	–0.129	–0.141	–0.040	–0.088	–0.121
	(–1.07)	(–1.38)	(–1.46)	(–0.35)	(–0.74)	(–0.98)
Midwest	–0.213	–0.245	–0.244	–0.191	–0.239	–0.246
	(–2.41)	(–2.64)	(–2.53)	(–1.66)	(–2.01)	(–2.00)
South	–0.068	–0.111	–0.105	–0.072	–0.139	–0.133
	(–0.72)	(–1.10)	(–1.03)	(–0.59)	(–1.07)	(–1.01)
Year	–0.755	–0.829	–0.823	–0.524	–0.649	–0.635
	(–1.79)	(–1.95)	(–1.93)	(–0.94)	(–1.15)	(–1.13)
Year squared	0.004	0.005	0.005	0.003	0.003	0.003
	(1.69)	(1.86)	(1.84)	(0.83)	(1.05)	(1.02)
Price elasticity of cessation	0.841	0.905	0.916	1.130	1.250	1.300

Note: All equations also include missing indicators for income, age, religiosity, type of community, average work hours, marital status, and family structure. Asymptotic *t*-ratios are in parentheses. The critical values for the *t*-ratios are 2.58 (2.33), 1.96 (1.64), and 1.64 (1.28) at the 1, 5, and 10 percent significance levels, respectively, based on a two-tailed (one-tailed) test. All equations based on chi-square tests are significant at better than the 1 percent significance level.

per day on average during the previous 30 days. Price is found to have a positive and significant impact, at at least the 12 percent significance level, on smoking cessation among males who were classified as smokers at age 18 according to any positive consumption in the previous 30 days. However, price is found to have an insignificant impact on smoking cessation decisions of males who were classified as smokers at age 18 by smoking at least 1–5 cigarettes per day on average in the previous 30 days.

In general, state-level policies restricting smoking in private worksites and other public places seem to have little impact on young adult smoking cessation decisions,[10] although the estimates do indicate that stronger clean indoor air restrictions, as measured by the clean indoor air index variable, will increase the probability of cessation among young adult females. However, this relationship is only significant at the 5 percent level for females classified as smokers at age 23 by smoking any cigarettes in the previous 30 days.

Briefly reviewing the estimates for the other independent variables: in general, income is an insignificant determinant of smoking cessation with the exception of males classified as smokers at age 18 and females classified as smokers at age 23 based on any smoking in the past 30 days where income has a negative and significant impact on smoking cessation. With respect to race and ethnicity, the probability of cessation for female Caucasians is significantly higher than that of Blacks. In addition, white males classified as smokers at age 18 based on any positive smoking have a higher probability of smoking cessation than do black males. Both males and females with strong attachments to religion, as measured by religious service attendance, are more likely to quit smoking than individuals with less religious attachment.

With respect to the type of community individuals reside in, both males and females who live in the suburbs and are classified as smokers at age 23 based on any smoking in the previous 30 days are less likely to quit smoking than individuals who live in urban settings. In addition, females classified as smokers at age 23 who live in rural neighborhoods are significantly less likely to quit smoking than those who live in an urban setting. The number of hours worked has a negative impact on the probability of cessation for both males and females classified as smokers at age 18. However, when individuals are classified as smokers at age 23, the number of hours worked is positively related to male smoking cessation and insignificantly related to female smoking cessation decisions. Being married has an insignificant impact on smoking cessation decisions among both males and females. Both males and females who are separated or divorced have a lower probability of smoking cessation than individuals who are single. Both males and females who are engaged and classified as smokers at age 18 based on any smoking in the previous 30 days have a lower probability of cessation than are individuals who are single. However, males classified as smokers at age 23 that are engaged are significantly more likely to quit smoking than males that are single.

Males classified as smokers at age 23 who live alone are more likely to quit smoking than are males that live with others. Both males and females classified as smokers at age 18 who live with their parents are more likely to quit smoking than individuals who do not live with their parents. Both males and females who live with a child are significantly less likely to quit smoking than are individuals who do not live with a child. No significant differences are observed between any of the other variables capturing living arrangements and the probability of smoking cessation.

The probability of smoking cessation among both males and females classified as smokers at age 18 and education, as measured by the number of formal years of schooling completed, is negatively related. However, the probability of smoking cessation among both males and females classified as smokers at age 23 and education, as measured by the number of formal years of schooling completed, is positively related. Both males and females classified as smokers at age 23 and who attend college full time are more likely to quit smoking than individuals who do not attend college. However, the significance drops below conventional levels for women who smoke at least 1–5 cigarettes per day on average. Finally, individuals who live in the Northeast, Midwest, and South are less likely to quit smoking than those who live in the West region of the United States.

5 DISCUSSION

A significant number of previous studies have concluded that price and smoking participation are inversely related. However, these studies were unable to distinguish whether this decrease in participation, associated with a cigarette price increase, was a result of decreased initiation or increased cessation. This chapter concludes that price is positively related to the probability of smoking cessation for both young adult males and females. The price elasticity of smoking cessation is found to be positively related to the age at which individuals are classified as smokers. Similarly, the price elasticity of cessation is positively related to the quantity of cigarettes individuals are required to smoke in order to be classified as a current smoker, with the exception of males classified as smokers at age 18. These estimates indicate that large increases in cigarette excise taxes, as proposed in President Clinton's budget for fiscal year 2001, would lead a significant number of young adults to quit smoking.

Although President Clinton's proposal to increase the excise tax on cigarettes is aimed at preventing youth from initiating smoking until they are capable of making a mature and informed decision, according to the results described above, higher cigarette prices (which would result from higher excise taxes) will also increase the probability of cessation among young adults of both gender.

According to the 1994 Surgeon General's report, almost all first use of cigarettes occurs before high school graduation. Much like adults, many adolescents readily become addicted to cigarettes and find it very difficult to quit. Given the estimates above and the well-documented benefits of smoking cessation (USDHHS 1990), a significant increase in the excise tax will result in substantial reductions in tobacco causing disease and other harms caused by tobacco.

NOTES

* This chapter was prepared for the Taipei International Conference on Health Economics, March 25–27, 1999, Taipei, Taiwan. Support for this research has been provided by the Robert Wood Johnson Foundation and the Centers for Disease Control and Prevention. We are indebted to Patrick O'Malley and Timothy J. Perry for providing the Monitoring the Future data. Finally, we would like to thank Chee-Ruey Hsieh and conference participants for helpful comments on this chapter.

1. The definition used to assess smoking prevalence changed in 1992. As of 1992, some-day smoking was included in the definition of current smoking. The inclusion of intermittent smokers in the new definition will increase the prevalence estimates by approximately 1 percentage point over the previous definition (CDC 1994).

2. Other tobacco initiatives included: increasing the prices of smokeless tobacco and cigars; moving the already legislated 5 cent per pack excise tax increase slated for January 1, 2002 to October 1, 2000; imposing assessments on tobacco companies for underage smoking; ensuring Medicaid patients have access to medication that aids in smoking cessation; provide $39 million to the Food and Drug Administration to help enforce youth access laws; provide funds to pay for legal costs associated with the Department of Justice's litigation to recover federal expenditures on smoking; and various others.

3. For a comprehensive review of these studies, see USDHHS (1989, 1994), and

Chaloupka and Warner (2000).

4 Although Douglas allowed price to vary at the state level over time, whereas Forster and Jones allow tax to vary solely at the national level over time.

5 In the past, the Monitoring the Future Study was sometimes called the National High School Senior Survey.

6 Ideally, a measure of total disposable income would be used as a determinant of smoking cessation. However, data on other sources of income are not asked in any of the follow-up questionnaires. Therefore, we employ income from employment in our models because it is the only consistent measure of income across data waves. Income from employment for many is likely to significantly underestimate the total resources available to young adults because many young adults receive monetary allowances from family members such as parents and/or spouse. Given our ability to control for the number of hours worked and our inability to control for total disposable income, it is not surprising that income from employment has an insignificant impact on smoking cessation in some of the model specifications.

7 Cox (1972) was the first to propose a semi-parametric hazard model with time-dependent covariates. For a detailed description of the Cox regression, see Kalbfleisch and Prentice (1980), Hosmer and Lemeshow (1999), or Altman (1991).

Unlike standard regression methods that can calculate a measure analogous to R^2 to assess a model's overall goodness of fit, there does not exist a comparable easy to interpret measure for duration modeling. Instead, Cox–Snell residuals are used to assess the overall fit of the semi-parametric Cox model. If the Cox model fits the data, then the Cox–Snell residuals will have a standard censored exponential distribution with a hazard ratio of approximately 1. The graphical assessment of the cumulative hazard versus the Cox–Snell residuals suggests that the Cox model fits the data adequately. However not surprisingly, the right-hand tail of the distribution deviates further from 1 than the left-hand tail given the reduced sample caused by censoring.

8 Age of the respondent in each wave of data is treated as a time variable. That is, age measures how time is recorded in the data. Therefore, explicit control of age as a covariate is not feasible given its perfectly collinear relationship with the time variable.

9 Models 4 to 6 classify a current smoker as smoking at least one to five cigarettes per day on average during the previous 30 days, whereas models 1 to 3 classify a current smoker as smoking any cigarettes during the previous 30 days.

10 The state-level clean indoor air measures used in this analysis may underestimate the full impact smoking restrictions have on smoking cessation because they cannot account for local-level policies or employer initiated policies that may play an important role in smoking cessation.

REFERENCES

Altman, D.G. (1991), *Practical Statistics Medical Research*, London: Chapman and Hall.

Centers for Disease Control and Prevention (CDC) (1994), 'Cigarette smoking among adults – United States, 1992, and changes in the definition of current cigarette smoking', *Morbidity and Mortality Weekly Report*, **43**(19), Atlanta, GA: Centers for Disease Control and Prevention.

Chaloupka, F.J. (1991), 'Rational addictive behavior and cigarette smoking', *Journal of Political Economy*, **99**(4): 722B42.

Chaloupka, F.J. and M. Grossman (1996), 'Price, tobacco control policies, and youth smoking', National Bureau of Economic Research Working Paper No. 5740.

Chaloupka, F.J. and R.L. Pacula (1998), 'An examination of gender and race differences in youth smoking responsiveness to price and tobacco control policies', National Bureau of Economic Research Working Paper No. 6541.

Chaloupka, F.J. and K.E. Warner (2000), 'The economics of smoking', in Joseph P. Newhouse and Anthony Culyer (eds), *The Handbook of Health Economics*, Amsterdam: Elsevier Science, pp. 1539–627.

Chaloupka, F.J. and H. Wechsler (1997), 'Price tobacco control policies and smoking among young adults', *Journal of Health Economics*, **16**: 359–73.

Cox, D.R. (1972), 'Regression models and life tables (with discussion)', *Journal of Royal Statistical Society*: Series B, **34**: 187–220.

DeCicca, P., D. Kenkel and A. Mathios (1999), 'Putting out the fires: will higher taxes reduce youth smoking?', Cornell University Working Paper, June.

Douglas, S. M. (1998), 'The Duration of the Smoking Habit', *Economic Inquiry*, **36**(1): 49–64.

Evans, W. N., M.C. Farrelly and E. Montgomery (1999), 'Do workplace smoking bans reduce smoking?', *American Economic Review*, **89**(4): 728–47.

Farrelly, M.F. and J.W. Bray (1998), 'Response to increases in cigarette prices by race/ethnicity, income, and age groups – United States, 1976–1993', *Morbidity and Mortality Weekly Report*, July 31, **47**(29): 605–9.

Forster, M. and A. M. Jones (1999), 'The role of tobacco taxes in starting and quitting smoking: duration analysis of British data', Working Paper, University of York, September 3.

Hosmer, D.W. and S. Lemeshow (1999), *Applied Survival Analysis*

Regression Modeling of Time to Event Data, New York: John Wiley & Sons, Inc.

Johnston, L.D., P.M. O'Malley and J.G. Bachman (1996), 'National survey results on drug use from the Monitoring the Future Study, 1975–1995', US Department of Health and Human Services, Public Health Service, National Institutes of Health.

Kalbfleisch, J.D. and R.L. Prentice (1980), *The Statistical Analysis of Failure Time Data*, New York: John Wiley & Sons, Inc.

National Health Interview Survey (NHIS) (1965–99), US Department of Health and Human Services, Centers for Disease Control and Prevention, National Center for Health Statistics, Division of Data Services, Hyattsville, MD.

Ohsfeldt R.L., R.G. Boyle and E.I. Capilouto (1998), 'Tobacco taxes, smoking restrictions, and tobacco use', National Bureau of Economic Research Working Paper No. 6486.

Tauras, J.A. (1999), 'The transition to smoking cessation: evidence from multiple failure duration analysis', National Bureau of Economic Research Working Paper No. 7412.

Tauras, J.A. and F.J. Chaloupka (1999), 'Price, clean indoor air laws, and cigarette smoking: evidence from longitudinal data for young adults', National Bureau of Economic Research Working Paper No. 6937.

Tobacco Institute (1997), *The Tax Burden on Tobacco*, Historic Compilation, Vol. 32, Washington, DC: Tobacco Institute.

Townsend, J.L., P. Roderick and J. Cooper (1994), 'Cigarette smoking by socioeconomic group, sex, and age: effects of price, income, and health publicity', *British Medical Journal*, **309**(6959): 923B6.

University of Michigan News and Information Services (UMNIS) (1998), 'Monitoring the Future Study press release, December 18, 1998', Ann Arbor: University of Michigan News and Information Services.

US Department of Health and Human Services (USDHHS) (1986), *The Health Consequences of Involuntary Smoking. A Report of the Surgeon General*, Washington, DC: Office on Smoking and Health.

US Department of Health and Human Services (USDHHS) (1989), *Reducing the Health Consequences of Smoking: 25 Years of Progress. A Report of the Surgeon General*, Rockville, MD: US Department of Health and Human Services, Public Health Service, Centers for Disease Control, Center for Chronic Disease Prevention and Health Promotion, Office on Smoking and Health.

US Department of Health and Human Services (USDHHS) (1990), *The Health Benefits of Smoking Cessation. A Report of the Surgeon General*, Rockville, MD: US Department of Health and Human Services, Public Health Service, Center for Disease Control, Center for

Chronic Disease Prevention and Health Promotion, Office on Smoking and Health.

US Department of Health and Human Services (USDHHS) (1991), *Strategies to Control Tobacco Use in the United States: A Blueprint for Public Health Action in the 1990's*, Smoking and Tobacco Control Monographs: US Department of Health and Human Services, Public Health Service, National Institutes of Health, National Cancer Institute.

US Department of Health and Human Services (USDHHS) (1994), *Preventing Tobacco Use Among Young People: A Report of the Surgeon General*, Atlanta GA: Public Health Service, Center for Disease Control and Prevention, National Center for Chronic Disease Prevention and Health Promotion, Office on Smoking and Health.

Warner, K.E. (1997), 'Cost effectiveness of smoking – cessation therapies interpretation of the evidence and implications for coverage', *Pharmacoeconomics*, **11**(6): 538–49.

15. The relationship between the presence of children and men's cigarette consumption

Likwang Chen and Matthew Farrelly

1 INTRODUCTION

Since 1964, dissemination of information about the personal health consequences of smoking has significantly increased the public's awareness of such risks in the United States. According to the Adult Use of Tobacco Survey, 81 percent of all adults and 70 percent of current smokers in the United States agreed that cigarette smoking is harmful to health in 1964. Results from the same survey in 1975 showed that the percentage of all adults with this belief increased to 90 percent, and that of current smokers with this view increased to 81 percent (US Department of Health and Human Services 1989). The percentage of smokers in the US adult population has also significantly decreased since 1964 (Centers for Disease Control and Prevention 1999).

Because the personal health consequences of smoking had already been well documented in the early 1980s, research has continued to investigate the effects of involuntary smoking.[1] The 1986 report of the Surgeon General was the first governmental report to identify a health risk of secondhand smoke. As more information about the health consequences of involuntary smoking is released by the government and media, more and more people recognize the health risks of involuntary smoking in addition to the personal health consequences of smoking.

Dissemination of knowledge regarding the personal health consequences of smoking and the health effects of secondhand smoke may effectively change people's beliefs about these issues. It has been shown that the percentage of smokers in the US adult population has decreased significantly since 1964, when the landmark report of the Surgeon General was published (Centers for Disease Control and Prevention 1999). It has also been demonstrated that knowledge or health publicity about the personal health consequences of cigarette smoking reduces cigarette consumption in the United States (Kenkel 1991; Blaine and Reed 1994).

However, there has been little research on whether knowledge regarding the harmful effects of secondhand smoke on a non-smoker's health affects an individual's cigarette consumption. Since the negative effect of secondhand smoke on young children's health appears to be more serious and receives more attention in the United States, investigation of the relationship between the presence of children and parental smoking can shed light on the influence of such health information. If people believe that their secondhand smoke affects children's health, the presence of children should have an impact on parental smoking. This is because children's health (or quality) and happiness (or welfare) are generally factors influencing parents' own happiness or utility. There are two major reasons why children's outcomes influence parental utility. First, a child's quality is one kind of consumption commodity to parents. Children with good qualities (talents, health and so on) can bring satisfaction to parents. Second, parents, in general, care about their children, and are altruistic toward their children. In other words, children's happiness increases parental utility. Therefore, if parents are aware of and believe in the possible negative effects of secondhand smoke on children's health, they may internalize the risks of their secondhand smoke and adjust cigarette consumption because of the presence of children. On the other hand, smokers can also choose to not smoke around their children to avoid exposing their children to secondhand smoke.

In this chapter we investigate the relationship between the number of children and men's cigarette consumption in the United States from the early 1980s to the early 1990s, the period when information about secondhand smoke became widespread in the United States. The study does not include women in the sample for the analysis, and focuses on exploring the relationship between the presence of children and men's smoking decision because men and women tend to have differences in health decisions (Kenkel 1991). The relationship between the presence of children and women's cigarette consumption has been analysed in Chen and Kenkel (1999). They find that the presence of children at home is negatively associated with women's cigarette consumption and the negative association of the presence of young children with women's cigarette consumption has grown stronger over time. To shed light on the influence of information about secondhand smoke on men's cigarette consumption, we examine whether any change in the association of the presence of children with men's cigarette consumption occurred from the early 1980s to the early 1990s. If other factors influencing men's smoking were relatively stable during this period, any change in the association of the presence of children with men's cigarette consumption is probably related to knowledge about secondhand smoke and children's health.

In addition to examining the association of the presence of children with men's cigarette consumption over this period, this chapter also tries to explore whether socioeconomic differences in the association of the presence of children with men's cigarette consumption exist. There are a few reasons for examining such differences. First, people with different socioeconomic backgrounds may have different access to and unequal costs of health information. Previous research has documented that education enhances acquisition of health information and improves utilization of health information (Nayga 1996; Variyam et al. 1998). As a result, socioeconomic differences in health information levels may exist. Second, socioeconomic factors may influence the impact of health information because of socioeconomic differences in beliefs and attitudes related to health behaviors. Previous studies have shown that people with different socioeconomic status have different beliefs and perceptions regarding the health consequences of tobacco use and secondhand smoke (Brownson et al. 1992; de Vries 1995). Third, people with different socioeconomic backgrounds, such as education, tend to have different assessment of and acceptability of risks (Osei et al. 1997). Fourth, people with different socioeconomic status tend to have different levels of demand for children's quality. This implies socioeconomic difference in demand for children's health, which is a component of children's quality. Finally, because tobacco use and secondhand smoke are related to future health status, people's time preference is also likely to affect the impact of health information regarding cigarette consumption. Socioeconomic status is associated with people's time preference. Therefore, socioeconomic factors are likely to influence the effect of health information about smoking. All the socioeconomic differences discussed above are likely to cause socioeconomic differences in the association of the presence of children with men's cigarette consumption. Because most previous research indicates that education is an important factor influencing acquisition of, utilization of and beliefs in health information, this chapter focuses on exploring whether differences in the association of the presence of children with cigarette consumption exist between men with different educational attainment.

The remainder of this chapter is organized as follows. Section 2 presents a brief review of background for the dissemination of health knowledge regarding involuntary smoking in the United States. Section 3 describes the data and illustrates the statistical methods. Section 4 reports the results. Finally, Section 5 summarizes and discusses the findings and provides policy implications.

2 BACKGROUND

Involuntary smoking has gradually attracted attention since the early 1970s. However, while the personal health consequences of smoking had already been well recognized in the 1970s, the consequences of involuntary smoking had not been confirmed until the early 1980s. Although five Surgeon General's reports warned the public of potential health risks of secondhand smoke before the mid-1980s, none of them confirmed a causal relationship between involuntary smoking and non-smokers' health.

In 1986 the Surgeon General's report concluded that involuntary smoking causes diseases, including lung cancer, in non-smokers. It was the first time that the US government announced a causal relationship between involuntary smoking and human diseases. This report included many findings pertaining to parental smoking and children's health. Some examples are that parental smoking increases frequency of hospitalization for bronchitis and pneumonia for children during their first year of life; children with smoking parents have a higher frequency of various acute respiratory diseases, such as chest illnesses before two years old, and physician-diagnosed bronchitis, tracheitis, and laryngitis; children with smoking parents are more likely to have chronic cough and phlegm; young children with smoking parents may have a higher probability of getting chronic middle ear effusions; children with smoking parents appear to have slightly worse pulmonary function than children with non-smoking parents.

In 1992 another noticeable and probably more controversial governmental report, entitled 'Respiratory health effects of passive smoking: lung cancer and other disorders', was released by the US Environmental Protection Agency (EPA).[2] This is a more comprehensive report than the 1986 Surgeon General's report. It noted that secondhand smoke appears to be more detrimental to young children's health than older children or adults. According to this report, secondhand smoke aggravates asthma attacks in children and contributes to 150,000 to 300,000 lower respiratory tract infections in children less than 18 months old per year. It also concluded that parental smoking is a risk factor for Sudden Infant Death Syndrome (SIDS), which is the most frequent cause of death in infants aged one month to one year and is thought to be related to some sort of respiratory failure. Furthermore, various studies have discovered additional risks of secondhand smoke to children. For example, secondhand smoke exposure in the home causes 6 percent of cancers in children and 18 percent of children leukemia (Moorby 1995).

Health publicity regarding involuntary smoking has significantly increased public awareness of the health risks of secondhand smoke. For example, only 46 percent of all adults in the United States thought that involuntary smoking is probably hazardous to non-smokers' health in 1974, while 81 percent of all adults in the United States agreed that secondhand smoke is harmful to non-smokers' health in 1986, and the percentage of all adults with this view in the United States increased to 87 percent in 1992 (see Table 15.1). Along with health publicity regarding

Table 15.1 Trends in public knowledge about the health risks of secondhand smoke

Year	Source of data	% of all adults in USA who believe in a health risk from secondhand smoke
1974	Roper Survey	46
1976	Roper Survey	52
1978	Roper Survey	58
1986	Adult Use of Tobacco Survey (AUTS)	81
1987	Gallup Survey	81
1987	National Health Interview Survey (NHIS)	83
1992	National Health Interview Survey (NHIS)	87

Notes

1. Actual questions

1974, 1976, and 1978 Roper surveys Is smoking hazardous to non-smokers' health? (probably is hazardous, probably doesn't have any real effect, don't know).

1986 AUTS Think now for a moment about a non-smoker who lives or works with smokers … Do you think that exposure to tobacco smoke is harmful or not harmful to the non-smoker's health?

1987 Gallup survey If people smoke, do you think that it is harmful or is not harmful to people who are near them? (yes, harmful; no, not harmful; can't say/no opinion).

1987 NHIS The smoke from someone else's cigarette is harmful to you. (strongly agree, agree, disagree, strongly disagree). (Percentages include those who 'strongly agree' or 'agree'.)

1992 NHIS Other people's smoke is harmful. (agree/yes, disagree/no, not ascertained or no opinion/don't know).

2. Both Roper and Gallup are private organizations that conduct nationally representative surveys in the USA.

Sources: US Department of Health and Human Services (1989) and the authors' calculations using the 1987 and the 1992 National Health Interview Surveys.

secondhand smoke, parental smoking has become a concern in child custody disputes in the United States since the late 1980s (Cordes 1993; Sachs 1993; Schwartz 1993; Hall 1994; McCarthy 1994; Glassman 1994; Moorby 1995; Zgrodnik 1995; Butler 1996; Johnson 1997; Sobie 1997). Parental smoking is particularly a big issue in child custody battles involving asthmatic or otherwise medically vulnerable children. As a rule in this kind of cases, courts have issued orders prohibiting parental smoking in the presence of children. In some cases, judges have taken child custody from smoking parents. Some legal experts also advocate the extension of legal restriction of parental smoking around children to protect children in the marital home from health risks of parental smoking (Moorby 1995; Butler 1996; Johnson 1997).

In all, public knowledge with respect to the health risks of secondhand smoke has greatly improved over the past two decades. Such improvement of health information has brought about many disputes over non-smokers' and smokers' rights. Parental right to smoke and children's right to be in a smoke free home appear to be controversial issues.

3 DATA AND METHODS

Because improvement of public knowledge about involuntary smoking mainly occurred in the 1980s and the early 1990s, we decided to use this period for our analysis. Most of the data in our analysis are from the National Health Interview Survey of the United States (NHIS). The NHIS is a continuing series of cross-sectional surveys of the adult civilian non-institutionalized population of the United States. In some years, supplements to the NHIS provide information on smoking habits. We use the 1983 Alcohol/Health Practices Supplement, the 1985 Health Promotion and Disease Prevention Supplement, the 1987 Cancer Control Supplement, the 1990 Health Promotion and Disease Prevention Supplement, and the 1993 Year 2000 Objectives Supplement.

We restrict our sample to men aged 23–59 because men over 60 years old have very few children at home and men over 23 years old are more likely to report complete education.[3] Because only the numbers and the ages of children of reference persons or reference persons' spouses can be accurately identified, the sample for this study consists of male reference persons and female reference persons' husbands aged 23–59. Male respondents in these surveys are pooled to construct the sample for this study. Data in the person files of the NHIS for these years are used to compute the numbers of children in various age ranges in a family. Table 15.2 presents the weighted NHIS sample means of selected research

Table 15.2 Selected weighted NHIS sample means – men aged 23–59

Year	1983	1985	1987	1990	1993
Continuous variables					
Number of cigarettes smoked a day	9.05	8.26	7.37	6.55	5.75
Number of cigarettes a smoker smokes a day	23.58	23.33	23.10	21.48	19.35
Age (in years)	38.75	38.93	38.90	39.10	39.74
Median family income (1990 constant dollars)	36,086.85	33,403.81	37,392.17	37,500.00	33,918.69
Number of children aged 0–5 at home	0.34	0.35	0.34	0.36	0.32
Number of children aged 6–11 at home	0.32	0.32	0.34	0.33	0.33
Number of children aged 12–17 at home	0.33	0.33	0.30	0.27	0.29
Dummy variables (in percentage)					
Smoking status – smoker	38.4	35.4	31.9	30.5	29.7
Race					
White	89.1	88.4	88.0	87.1	85.9
Black	8.8	9.0	8.8	9.1	9.6
Other race	2.1	2.6	3.2	3.8	4.5
Marital status					
Married	80.3	80.9	80.0	80.0	79.5
Widowed	0.8	0.6	0.5	0.4	0.5
Divorced or separated	8.8	8.0	8.5	8.7	8.1
Single	10.1	10.5	11.0	10.9	11.9
Education level					
No more than elementary school	8.3	6.8	6.4	5.4	3.7
Some high school	10.8	9.9	8.7	8.6	8.7
High school graduate	35.3	35.3	35.2	34.7	35.5
Some college	19.5	20.1	21.1	21.8	22.7
College graduate	14.4	13.9	15.1	15.6	16.3
Graduate school	11.7	13.9	13.4	13.9	13.1
Employment status					
Working	85.1	88.7	89.4	89.4	87.1
Not working in the past two weeks but employed	1.5	1.7	1.5	1.4	1.8
Unemployed	6.4	3.6	3.3	3.0	3.5
Not in labor force	7.0	6.0	5.8	6.2	7.6
Veteran status – being a veteran	40.5	37.7	33.7	29.9	27.1
Living region					
Northeast	20.7	20.7	19.5	19.6	19.6
Midwest	28.0	25.7	26.0	25.4	26.8
South	30.9	32.5	32.3	32.0	30.0
West	20.3	21.2	22.2	23.0	23.6
Urbanization of living location – in an SMSA	67.9	77.4	79.0	79.9	79.1
Family income > 2 times of poverty threshold	72.7	77.0	77.6	78.9	74.2
With children at home					
With children aged 0–5 at home	24.5	25.3	25.0	25.6	23.6
With children aged 6–11 at home	24.3	23.5	25.0	24.1	23.9
With children aged 12–17 at home	23.4	24.0	22.5	20.3	21.1

variables.[4]

Because the NHIS does not contain cigarette price data, in our analysis we use price data reported in *The Tax Burden on Tobacco* (Tobacco Institute 1996) and assign cigarette prices to individuals by referring to information on primary sampling units (PSUs) reported in the NHIS.[5] Due to confidentiality, we further exclude some observations in very small PSUs from the study sample. Finally we obtain a sample comprising 31,326 men aged 23–59. Of these, 10,467 were current smokers, 15,950 of them had at least some college education and 15,376 had no more than high school education.[6]

This study utilizes a two-part model. The first part pertains to 'smoking participation', and the second part pertains to 'smoking intensity'. In this chapter, smoking participation denotes a status of being a person who has smoked at least 100 cigarettes and currently has a smoking habit, and smoking intensity is the average number of cigarettes a current smoker consumes a day. Therefore, the first part is a model for the probability of smoking, using the sample composed of both current smokers and non-smokers, and the second part is another model for a current smoker's daily consumption, using the sample comprising of only current smokers. The probit model is utilized to estimate smoking participation, and the ordinary least squares (OLS) model is used to estimate smoking intensity. The two-part model approach has been used in prior studies on cigarette consumption and regarded as an appropriate method (Wasserman et al. 1991; Leung and Yu 1996).

The dependent variable in the model for the probability of smoking is a binary variable indicating smoking status (1 = being a current smoker). The dependent variable in the model for a current smoker's daily consumption is the average number of cigarettes smoked a day.[7] The explanatory factors in the base models of men's smoking participation and intensity include year, age, age squared, race, marital status, education, employment status, veteran status, living region in the United States, urbanization of living location, annual family income, and the numbers of children aged 0–5, aged 6–11, and aged 12–17.[8]

To explore whether the association of the presence of children with men's cigarette consumption varied over time during the period from the early 1980s to the early 1990s, we estimate an alternative two-part model for each of the two groups of men of different educational attainment. In the alternative models of men's smoking participation and intensity, 12 additional variables are constructed to measure changes in the association of the presence of children with men's cigarette consumption over time. These 12 variables are constructed by interacting the three child variables with the four-year dummy variables. No restriction is imposed regarding the trend of the association of the presence of children with men's cigarette consumption.

Because not all of the five supplements provide information on a man's knowledge about personal risks from smoking, knowledge regarding personal health consequences is not included as an explanatory factor. Health knowledge about a man's knowledge with respect to the health consequences of secondhand smoke is also not included as an explanatory factor because only the 1987 Cancer Control Supplement offers information on such knowledge. Although health knowledge is a factor influencing a man's cigarette consumption, a model omitting health knowledge for all observations from the five supplements should still yield results for a fair comparison of the relationship between the presence of children and men's cigarette consumption for various years.

4 RESULTS

Table 15.3 provides the results of the two-part models without interaction terms with respect to year and the number of children, and Table 15.4 reports the results of the two-part models with interaction terms. Results from the probit model and the OLS model without interaction show that the number of children in each category is associated with a decrease in smoking participation for highly educated men. However, only the number of young children (aged 0–5) is associated with a reduction in smoking intensity for highly educated male current smokers. Results from models without interaction also indicate that the number of children aged 0–5 has a significant association with a decrease in smoking participation for less-educated men. The coefficients of the numbers of children aged 6–11 and 12–17 suggest that the presence of children in these age ranges may also correlate with a decrease in smoking participation for less-educated men. Nevertheless, results from the OLS model without interaction do not indicate any significant relationship between the presence of children and less-educated male current smokers' smoking intensity.

Results from the models with interaction terms suggest that the number of children in each category is negatively related to smoking participation for highly educated men, but this relationship is not growing stronger. On the other hand, the presence of children was not significantly associated with highly educated male current smokers' smoking intensity before 1990, but the number of young children is estimated to have a significantly stronger association with a reduction in smoking intensity for this group of men in 1993. In 1983, the presence of children younger

Table 15.3 Results of two-part model without interaction

Variable	Model for men with more than high school education		Model for men with no more than high school education	
	Probit model for smoking participation	OLS model for smoking intensity	Probit model for smoking participation	OLS model for smoking intensity
Real cigarette price in 1997 constant dollars	−0.0872	−2.0472 *	−0.2264 ***	−3.7429 ***
	(1.005)	(1.342)	(2.850)	(3.270)
Year dummy for 1985 (omitted = 1983)	−0.0796 **	0.2277	−0.0117	0.8371 *
	(−1.888)	(0.331)	(−0.297)	(1.524)
Year dummy for 1987	−0.1733 ***	−0.9024	−0.0797 **	0.7978
	(−3.605)	(−1.135)	(−1.769)	(1.258)
Year dummy for 1990	−0.2056 ***	−1.9443 **	−0.0106	0.1726
	(−3.542)	(−1.976)	(−0.200)	(0.236)
Year dummy for 1993	−0.2120 ***	−3.3239 **	0.0001	−0.1777
	(−2.701)	(−2.411)	(0.002)	(−0.179)
Age in years	0.1275 ***	1.0265 ***	0.0557 ***	1.1233 ***
	(11.316)	(5.233)	(5.865)	(8.532)
Square of age	−0.0015 ***	−0.0094 ***	−0.0009 ***	−0.0125 ***
	(−10.988)	(−3.854)	(−7.415)	(−7.670)
Black (omitted = white)	−0.0025	−7.8685 ***	−0.0606 **	−9.0961 ***
	(−0.059)	(−14.472)	(−1.884)	(−23.780)
Other race	0.1243 **	−4.1757 ***	−0.0160	−4.6077 ***
	(2.189)	(−5.599)	(−0.220)	(−4.397)
Married (omitted = single)	−0.0620 **	−0.3185	0.0916 **	−0.0009
	(−1.743)	(−0.523)	(2.493)	(−0.002)
Widowed	0.2620 **	3.7031 *	0.3497 ***	1.5850
	(2.036)	(1.394)	(3.243)	(1.116)
Divorced or separated	0.1677 ***	0.6837	0.3257 ***	1.5074 ***
	(4.097)	(1.004)	(7.970)	(2.718)
College graduate (omitted = some college)	−0.3527 ***	−2.2476 ***	0.1698 ***	0.3853
	(−13.124)	(−4.598)	(4.735)	(0.686)
Graduate school	−0.5528 ***	−3.8627 ***	0.3313 ***	1.4806 ***
	(−18.399)	(−6.931)	(11.967)	(3.943)
Working (omitted = not in labor force)	−0.1504 ***	−1.3467 *	−0.1536 ***	−0.9858 **
	(−2.955)	(−1.507)	(−4.015)	(−1.686)
Not working in the past 2 weeks but employed	0.0172	1.7017	−0.1248 *	−1.2461
	(0.166)	(1.050)	(−1.440)	(−1.105)
Unemployed	0.1255 *	−2.0664 **	0.1338 **	−0.4983
	(1.563)	(−1.739)	(2.323)	(−0.641)

Table 15.3 Results of two-part model without interaction (cont.)

Variable	Model for men with more than high school education		Model for men with no more than high school education	
	Probit model for smoking participation	OLS model for smoking intensity	Probit model for smoking participation	OLS model for smoking intensity
Being a veteran	0.1933 ***	0.9414 **	0.2050 ***	1.9754 ***
	(7.224)	(2.083)	(8.545)	(5.821)
Living in Midwest	0.0333	0.9524 *	0.0976 ***	0.6377 *
(omitted = living in northeast)	(0.943)	(1.574)	(3.114)	(1.407)
Living in south	0.0437	1.1827 **	0.0936 ***	0.7957 **
	(1.240)	(1.976)	(2.954)	(1.744)
Living in west	−0.0978 ***	−1.7144 ***	−0.0261	−1.5894 ***
	(−2.907)	(−2.988)	(−0.776)	(−3.155)
Living in an SMSA	0.0775 **	0.3246	0.0501 **	−0.2180
	(2.390)	(0.579)	(2.029)	(−0.611)
Annual family income in 1990	−0.000005 ***	0.00004 ***	−0.00001 ***	0.00003 ***
constant dollars	(−6.848)	(2.964)	(−8.836)	(2.948)
Number of children aged 0–5	−0.0804 ***	−0.9518 ***	−0.0643 ***	−0.3278
	(−3.753)	(−2.672)	(−3.451)	(−1.242)
Number of children aged 6–11	−0.0859 ***	0.1655	−0.0280 *	0.0624
	(−4.097)	(0.425)	(−1.621)	(0.238)
Number of children aged 12–17	−0.0664 ***	0.0252	−0.0253 *	−0.0047
	(−3.053)	(0.062)	(−1.414)	(−0.018)
Intercept	−2.4112 ***	2.1536	−0.5714 ***	4.7775 *
	(−9.721)	(0.494)	(−2.612)	(1.583)
Observations	15,950	3929	15,376	6538
Log likelihood	−8361.202		−10,091.616	
Chi-squared	1046.12		752.43	
R^2		0.129		0.113
F-statistic		24.96		38.38
Degree of freedom	26	[26, 3902]	26	[26, 6511]
Significance level	0.0000	0.0000	0.0000	0.0000

Notes

1. ** indicates significance at the 10 percent level, and *** indicates significance at the 1 percent level in a two-tailed test. * indicates significance at the 10 percent level in a one-tailed test.
2. *z*-statistics and *t*-statistics are in parentheses.
3. The White estimator of the covariance matrix is used in the OLS model.

Table 15.4 Results of two-part model with interaction terms

Variable	Model for men with more than high school education		Model for men with no more than high school education	
	Probit model for smoking participation	OLS model for smoking intensity	Probit model for smoking participation	OLS model for smoking intensity
Real cigarette price in 1997 constant dollars	−0.0905	−1.9260	−0.2309 ***	−3.7733 ***
	(−1.043)	(−1.268)	(−2.903)	(−3.291)
Year dummy for 1985 (omitted = 1983)	−0.1096 **	0.1400	−0.0223	0.3116
	(−2.102)	(0.167)	(−0.450)	(0.450)
Year dummy for 1987	−0.1988 ***	−1.3647 *	−0.1336 **	0.0401
	(−3.439)	(−1.432)	(−2.396)	(0.051)
Year dummy for 1990	−0.2137 ***	−2.0754 **	−0.0706	−0.2410
	(−3.271)	(−1.956)	(−1.161)	(−0.286)
Year dummy for 1993	−0.1937 **	−2.8085 **	−0.0447	−0.3266
	(−2.277)	(−1.925)	(−0.566)	(−0.301)
Age in years	0.1275 ***	1.0330 ***	0.0560 ***	1.1223 ***
	(11.316)	(5.241)	(5.889)	(8.511)
Square of age	−0.0015 ***	−0.0095 ***	−0.0009 ***	−0.0125 ***
	(−10.990)	(−3.867)	(−7.438)	(−7.654)
Black (omitted = white)	−0.0029	−7.8898 ***	−0.0601 **	−9.0996 ***
	(−0.069)	(−14.432)	(−1.866)	(−23.787)
Other race	0.1232 **	−4.2088 ***	−0.0119	−4.5813 ***
	(2.171)	(−5.597)	(−0.164)	(−4.329)
Married (omitted = single)	−0.0611 **	−0.2848	0.0881 **	−0.0257
	(−1.719)	(−0.467)	(2.392)	(−0.050)
Widowed	0.2617 **	3.5897 *	0.3466 ***	1.5834
	(2.032)	(1.348)	(3.210)	(1.117)
Divorced or separated	0.1685 ***	0.7287	0.3258 ***	1.5292 ***
	(4.118)	(1.068)	(7.965)	(2.757)
No more than elementary school (Omitted = high school graduate)	−0.3530 ***	−2.2401 ***	0.1696 ***	0.4317
	(−13.129)	(−4.578)	(4.724)	(0.770)
Some high school	−0.5530 ***	−3.8836 ***	0.3298 ***	1.4874 ***
	(−18.404)	(−6.989)	(11.905)	(3.961)
Working (omitted = not in labor force)	−0.1511 ***	−1.3263 *	−0.1524 ***	−0.9821 **
	(−2.967)	(−1.482)	(−3.980)	(−1.683)

Table 15.4 Results of two-part model with interaction terms (cont.)

Variable	Model for men with more than high school education		Model for men with no more than high school education	
	Probit model for smoking participation	OLS model for smoking intensity	Probit model for smoking participation	OLS model for smoking intensity
Not working in the past 2 weeks but	0.0151	1.6870	−0.1230 *	−1.2511
employed	(0.146)	(1.031)	(−1.420)	(−1.116)
Unemployed	0.1262 *	−0.0973 **	0.1337 **	−0.4819
	(1.572)	(−1.769)	(2.316)	(−0.620)
Being a veteran	0.1918 ***	0.9204 **	0.2049 ***	1.9995 ***
	(7.169)	(2.032)	(8.526)	(5.899)
Living in Midwest	0.0311	0.9420 *	0.0960 ***	0.6365 *
(omitted = living in northeast)	(0.880)	(1.553)	(3.060)	(1.401)
Living in south	0.0428	1.1768 **	0.0921 ***	0.7974 **
	(1.215)	(1.967)	(2.904)	(1.751)
Living in west	−0.0986 ***	−1.7439 ***	−0.0277	−1.5889 ***
	(−2.929)	(−3.029)	(−0.823)	(−3.157)
Living in an SMSA	0.0782 **	0.3672	0.0497 **	−0.1771
	(2.413)	(0.655)	(2.011)	(−0.496)
Annual family income in 1990	−0.000005 ***	0.00004 ***	−0.00001 ***	0.00003 ***
constant dollars	(−6.861)	(2.913)	(−8.860)	(2.920)
Number of children aged 0–5	−0.0993 **	−0.5447	−0.1258 ***	−0.9036 *
	(−1.753)	(−0.650)	(−2.645)	(−1.369)
Number of children aged 6–11	−0.0976 *	−0.5414	−0.0519	−1.5134 **
	(−1.608)	(−0.592)	(−1.024)	(−2.546)
Number of children aged 12–17	−0.0812 *	0.1880	−0.0481	0.8218
	(−1.437)	(0.180)	(−1.042)	(1.210)
(# Children aged 0–5)*(1985 year	0.0528	−0.6105	0.0312	1.0259 *
dummy)	(0.790)	(−0.601)	(0.551)	(1.288)
(# Children aged 0–5)*(1987 year	0.0552	1.2724	0.0584	1.8343 **
dummy)	(0.758)	(1.074)	(0.922)	(2.086)
(# Children aged 0–5)*(1990 year	−0.0070	−0.6637	0.1010 **	0.1986
dummy)	(−0.107)	(−0.653)	(1.820)	(0.257)
(# Children aged 0–5)*(1993 year	−0.0250	−2.2488 **	0.0922 *	−0.1740
dummy)	(−0.321)	(−2.002)	(1.454)	(−0.198)
(# Children aged 6–11)*(1985 year	0.0450	1.6511 *	0.0414	1.6022 **
dummy)	(0.626)	(1.406)	(0.696)	(1.976)
(# Children aged 6–11)*(1987 year	−0.0014	−0.0803	0.0073	1.2886 *
dummy)	(−0.018)	(−0.062)	(0.115)	(1.537)

Table 15.4 Results of two-part model with interaction terms (cont.)

Variable	Model for men with more than high school education		Model for men with no more than high school education	
	Probit model for smoking participation	OLS model for smoking intensity	Probit model for smoking participation	OLS model for smoking intensity
(# children aged 6–11)*(1990 year dummy)	0.0065	1.1211	0.0411	2.4278 ***
	(0.092)	(0.961)	(0.703)	(3.416)
(# children aged 6–11)*(1993 year dummy)	−0.0078	−0.3175	−0.0080	1.1904 *
	(−0.101)	(−0.263)	(−0.122)	(1.326)
(# children aged 12–17)*(1985 year dummy)	0.0142	−0.6629	−0.0477	−0.9177
	(0.206)	(−0.534)	(−0.875)	(−1.107)
(# children aged 12–17)*(1987 year dummy)	0.0457	0.7177	0.1076 **	−0.5433
	(0.610)	(0.515)	(1.746)	(−0.618)
(# children aged 12–17)*(1990 year dummy)	0.0377	−0.1092	0.0455	−1.3926 **
	(0.559)	(−0.084)	(0.807)	(−1.689)
(# children aged 12–17)*(1993 year dummy)	−0.0466	−0.5002	0.0663	−0.5156
	(−0.619)	(−0.359)	(1.032)	(−0.555)
Intercept	−2.3918 ***	1.8354	−0.5290 **	5.2418 **
	(−9.595)	(0.418)	(−2.400)	(1.727)
Observations	15,950	3929	15,376	6538
Log likelihood	−8357.975		−10,083.031	
Chi-squared	1054.33		767.36	
R^2		0.132		0.115
F-statistic		17.61		26.84
Degree of freedom	38	[38, 3890]	38	[38, 6499]
Significance level	0.0000	0.0000	0.0000	0.0000

Notes

1. ** indicates significance at the 10 percent level, and *** indicates significance at the 1 percent level in a two-tailed test. * indicates significance at the 10 percent level in a one-tailed test.
2. *z*-statistics and *t*-statistics are in parentheses.
3. The White estimator of the covariance matrix is used in the OLS model.

than six years old did not have a significant association with daily consumption for highly educated male current smokers. In 1993, the presence of a child younger than six years old is associated with a decrease of more than two cigarettes in daily consumption for highly educated male current smokers. Overall, the presence of young children appears to have a stronger association with cigarette consumption than the presence of older children.[9]

Results from models with interaction terms reveal some unexpected patterns of less-educated men's cigarette consumption. The presence of children under six years old appeared to be associated with a decrease in cigarette consumption for men with no more than high school education in 1983. However, this negative relationship between the presence of young children and cigarette consumption was weaker during the mid-1980s to the early 1990s. The presence of older children, generally speaking, had a weaker negative relationship with cigarette consumption for less-educated men during the mid-1980s to the early 1990s than in earlier years. The only exception is that the presence of children aged 12–17 might have a stronger negative correlation with smoking intensity for less-educated male current smokers in later years than in 1983.

The results of the other explanatory variables in the models for highly educated men do not show particularly unexpected patterns. The coefficients of year dummy variables suggest that highly educated men reduced cigarette consumption over time regardless of whether they have children or not, although the presence of children might further reduce their cigarette consumption. Older age results in higher cigarette consumption, but the increasing rate declines as age increases. Cigarette consumption among current black smokers is less than that of whites, although smoking participation is similar for the two groups. Highly educated men of other races have a higher smoking participation rate than their white counterparts, but smoke less, conditional on being a smoker. Married highly educated men smoke less than their single counterparts. On the other hand, widowhood, divorce and separation are associated with an increase in cigarette consumption. The coefficients of education variables suggest that even within men with at least some college education, higher education is associated with lower cigarette consumption. Compared to being out of the labor force, working has a negative relationship with both smoking participation and smoking intensity, while unemployment has a positive relationship with smoking participation but a negative relationship with smoking intensity for highly educated men. Veterans smoke more. Compared to men living in the northeast, men living in the Midwest and in the south smoke more, but men living in the west smoke less. Men living in statistical metropolitan sampling areas (SMSAs) smoke more than those living in a more rural area. Higher family income is associated with a decrease in smoking participation but an increase in male current smokers' smoking intensity.

Most of the results of the other explanatory variables in the models for less-educated men are qualitatively similar to those for highly educated men. An important difference between men with different educational attainment is that the time trend of highly educated men's cigarette consumption is downward while less-educated men's cigarette consumption in the early 1990s did not appear to be lower than that in the

1980s. It is somewhat surprising that less-educated men did not appear to be responsive to health publicity in the early 1990s even though the US government and media devoted much effort to anti-smoking campaigns in this period.

Some other differences between men with different educational attainment are as follows. Among less-educated men, blacks and those of other races smoke less. On the other hand, black highly educated men do not have a lower smoking participation than their white counterparts, and highly educated men of other races have a higher smoking participation than their white counterparts. While marriage is associated with a decrease in cigarette consumption for highly educated men, it has a positive relationship with cigarette consumption for less-educated men. Although higher education negatively correlates with cigarette consumption in general, men with some high school education not only smoke more than men with more education but also smoke more than men with less education. For highly educated men, unemployment positively correlates with smoking participation but negatively correlates with smoking intensity. In contrast, unemployment is associated with an increase in smoking participation and has no significant correlation with smoking intensity for less-educated men.

To provide a further comparison of the association of the presence of children with cigarette consumption between men with different educational attainment, we calculate elasticity estimates of cigarette consumption with respect to the presence of children under six years old. Although we report the coefficient estimate of the number of children in each age category in Tables 15.3 and 15.4, we decide to report only elasticity estimates with respect to the presence of young children. This is mainly because the presence of young children had a stronger association with men's cigarette consumption during the period from the early 1980s to the early 1990s. It is hard to explain the weak and unstable relationship between the presence of older children and men's cigarette consumption, and the association of the presence of young children with men's cigarette consumption appears to be more direct and significant. Therefore, we focus on discussing the association of the presence of young children with men's cigarette consumption in the remainder of this chapter.

Table 15.5 reports elasticity estimates of cigarette consumption with respect to the presence of children under six years old. This table presents three kinds of elasticity estimates: elasticity associated with smoking participation, elasticity associated with smoking intensity and elasticity associated with overall demand for cigarettes. These elasticity estimates are calculated with the explanatory variables evaluated at their weighted sample means. We only report the average elasticity for two time groups:

years in the 1980s and those in the 1990s. We adopt such a categorization of time in order to present a clear contrast of the association of the presence of children with men's cigarette consumption between the two decades.

As shown in Table 15.5, the elasticity estimate in its absolute value for highly educated men in the early 1990s is significantly larger than that in the 1980s. The change in the association of young children with highly educated male current smokers' smoking intensity is particularly dramatic. In contrast, the elasticity estimate in its absolute value for less-educated men in the early 1990s is very close to that in the 1980s.

The elasticity estimate for highly educated men in the early 1990s is –0.082. Since the mean number of children under six years old in the early 1990s is slightly larger than 0.3 for highly educated men, the presence of a child under six years old is associated with a reduction of almost 30 percent for highly educated men's overall cigarette demand. Although the number of children, strictly speaking, is not continuous, these elasticity estimates are suggestive. They suggest that the presence of young children may have a strong impact on highly educated men's cigarette consumption in the 1990s. To highly educated men, the effect of the presence of a child under six years old may be equivalent to the effect of a large increase in cigarette price in the 1990s. Most estimates of price elasticity of demand for cigarettes are between –0.4 and –0.6 (Wasserman et al. 1991). Suppose the price elasticity is –0.5, the effect of the presence of a child under six years old may be equivalent to the effect of an increase of 60 percent in cigarette price to a highly educated man in the early 1990s.

In the 1980s, no significant difference in the relationship between the presence of young children and cigarette consumption existed between highly educated and less-educated men. However, the association of the presence of young children with cigarette consumption is much weaker

Table 15.5 Estimated elasticity of cigarette consumption with respect to children under six years old

Time	Men with high education			Men with less education		
	Smoking participation	Smoking intensity	Total	Smoking participation	Smoking intensity	Total
1983–87	–0.025	–0.005	–0.030	–0.027	0.001	–0.026
1990–93	–0.049	–0.034	–0.082	–0.009	–0.014	–0.024

for less-educated men than for highly educated men in the 1990s. The presence of young children had a significantly stronger association with a reduction in cigarette consumption for highly educated men in the early 1990s than in the early 1980s. In contrast, the association of the presence of young children with a decrease in cigarette consumption was actually weaker in the early 1990s than in the early 1980s for less-educated men. The patterns of less-educated men's cigarette demand may be puzzling and troubling because information about the impact of secondhand smoke on young children's health was much more widespread in the 1990s than in the early 1980s. Particularly, to advocates of protecting children from secondhand smoke at home, this may exhibit a problem.

To provide another piece of evidence on the existence of difference between men with different educational attainment, we report the proportion of men in the United States who believe in a health risk from secondhand smoke by socioeconomic status. As shown in Table 15.6, men with high education and a high family income level are more likely to believe that secondhand smoke is harmful to health. The difference between men with different educational attainment is especially remarkable. While about 90 percent of men with at least some college education believed in a health risk from secondhand smoke in 1992, only

Table 15.6 Men's beliefs about the health consequences of secondhand smoke by socioeconomic status

Year	% of men in USA who believe in a health risk from secondhand smoke[1]				
	All men	High education[2]	Less education[2]	High income[3]	Lower income[3]
1987	81.7	85.9	78.4	82.5	79.7
1992	84.9	89.7	80.5	86.8	80.5

Notes

1. Actual questions
   1987 NHIS The smoke from someone else's cigarette is harmful to you. (strongly agree, agree, disagree, strongly disagree). (Percentages include those who 'strongly agree' or 'agree'.)
   1992 NHIS Other people's smoke is harmful. (agree/yes, disagree/no, not ascertained or no opinion/don't know).
2. High education is defined as 'having at least some college education'; less education is defined as 'having no more than high school education'.
3. High income is defined as 'a family income more than twice the poverty threshold of a family of the same size'; lower income is defined as 'a family income no more than twice the poverty threshold of a family of the same size'.

Sources: The authors' calculations using the 1987 and the 1992 National Health Interview Surveys.

80 percent of men with less education did. These statistics also indicate that the difference between men with different educational attainment expanded rather than decreased from 1987 to 1992.

5 DISCUSSION

This study finds that the presence of children in the household is associated with declines in smoking among men with greater than a high school degree. In addition, this effect was larger in the 1990s than in the 1980s. This finding is driven primarily by an increase in the effect of the presence of children on smoking intensity. The presence of children younger than six years old had no effect on smoking intensity for this group prior to 1990, but is associated with a drop in daily cigarette consumption of two cigarettes in 1993.

Our results also indicate that the association between the presence of children and decreased consumption differs significantly for men with and without more than a high school degree. In contrast to men with more than a high school degree for whom the effect of children on smoking grew over time, this effect diminished over time for men with less education. Therefore, the children of men with a high school degree or less not only face other disadvantageous influences of lower socioeconomic status on health, but also benefit less from the recent public education campaigns of the risks of secondhand smoke.

We interpret the change in the relationship between the presence of young children and highly educated men's cigarette consumption as a piece of evidence that men may decrease cigarette consumption out of a concern over young children's health. We also think that the difference in the effect of the presence of young children on cigarette consumption between men with different educational attainment in the 1990s may partly result from different beliefs about secondhand smoke of men with different socioeconomic status. In addition to information diffusion, other developments, such as stricter regulation for merchandising and consuming cigarettes, should also influence the effect of the presence of young children on men's cigarette consumption. Therefore, differences in response to various health policies and regulations related to tobacco use among men with different socioeconomic status can also cause differences in the effect of the presence of children on cigarette consumption among men from different social classes.

While it is likely that some other unobserved factors also influence the effect of the presence of young children on men's cigarette consumption, it seems plausible to us that information about secondhand smoke and parental concern over children's health play a role in men's smoking decision. At least to some men, such as those who are highly educated, dissemination of health knowledge about secondhand smoke is very like to enhance the effect of the presence of young children on their smoking decision. However, our results suggest that the presence of young children had an increasing effect on reducing highly educated male current smokers' smoking intensity, but might not also have an increasing effect on reducing highly educated men's smoking participation during the period from the 1980s to the early 1990s. Furthermore, the pattern of less-educated men's cigarette consumption seems troubling. Therefore, it should be recognized that information dissemination does not necessarily have impacts on the entire population. How to design policies that effectively affect all current and potential smokers' propensity to consume tobacco remains a tough task.

More studies are needed to better understand why the presence of young children does not significantly affect less-educated men's cigarette consumption. It is likely that men with lower socioeconomic status do not perceive personal relevance even when this group of men are aware of information about the harmful effects of involuntary smoking and recognize a general risk. More research is needed to help in understanding how men assimilate health knowledge and whether men with different socioeconomic status differently perceive health risks from secondhand smoke.

Socioeconomic differences in health knowledge and smoking behavior have policy implications regarding health education and advocacy efforts.[10] Men with low education are at a higher risk for smoking. The presence of children is also less influential on their cigarette consumption. Such patterns suggest that public health education and advocacy efforts should be particularly targeted to men with low socioeconomic status. Health promotion that can effectively convey messages to less-educated and poor men and change such populations' perceptions and beliefs about smoking is important to enhance the impact of health information.

If increasing health knowledge about secondhand smoke is not sufficient to further reduce cigarette consumption of men with lower socioeconomic status, policies other than disseminating relevant information are needed to help reduce cigarette consumption of men with lower socioeconomic status and protect children of the less educated and poor. For instance, imposing larger taxes on cigarette consumption, which discourages smoking, can have the additional benefit of reducing children's exposure to secondhand smoke. The government can also encourage families to establish home smoking rules that protect children from the harmful effects of secondhand smoke, and these are becoming prevalent according to the 1996 Current Population Survey. Furthermore, the government can enforce some legal restrictions on parental smoking around children. Such legal restrictions can also convey the idea that parental smoking is detrimental for children's health and to some extent socially unacceptable. However, without question such legal restrictions are controversial. The issue of reconciling parental right to smoke and children's welfare can be a difficult matter. Nevertheless, if society has a stronger agreement on protecting children from the health risks of involuntary smoking, opposition to such legal restrictions should be weaker. For example, according to a Gallup poll in 1991, 48 percent of people agreed that a woman should be held liable for any adverse health consequences suffered by her baby because of her smoking during pregnancy (Johnson 1997). This shows that a considerable proportion of people think that parents should control their smoking behaviors in order to protect their children's health. If social acceptability of parental smoking in the presence of children continues to decline, objection to legal restrictions on parental smoking should also fade.

In fact, ordering parents to refrain from smoking in the presence of children is not a new idea in courts. As mentioned in the second section, parental smoking is an issue in child custody disputes. The majority of legal experts agree that parental smoking should be a factor in the decision in child custody/visitation cases involving children medically vulnerable to secondhand smoke and that parents should not smoke around children. Some legal experts even propose the use of child abuse and neglect statutes to help in restricting parental smoking around children and protecting children's health (Moorby 1995; Butler 1996; Johnson 1997).[11] In addition, some legal experts advocate prevention and training programs similar to those for physical, sexual, drug or alcohol abuse to help parents with nicotine addiction (Butler 1996).

In short, our findings suggest that as information on the health consequences of secondhand smoke emerges over time, men with high education may reduce cigarette consumption out of a concern over their young children's health. Significant differences in beliefs about health risks from secondhand smoke and in the association of the presence of young children with cigarette consumption between men with different education levels demonstrate a need for more effective health promotion in order to further reduce cigarette consumption of men with lower socioeconomic status. Our findings also suggest that at least some men may internalize risks of their secondhand smoke to their children. In other words, secondhand smoke at home is not a pure externality. This also implies that cigarettes should not be regarded as a kind of adult good, which is thought to be demographically separable from children, and cigarette consumption should not be used to help calculate child costs and adult welfare.

Finally, comparison of our results regarding men's cigarette consumption with those about women's cigarette consumption reported by Chen and Kenkel (1999) reveals some interesting contrasts. Chen and Kenkel's estimates show that the presence of a child aged 0–5 was associated with a reduction of 9 percent in women's overall demand for cigarettes in 1983 and one of about 20 percent in 1993. Women might decrease cigarette consumption because of the presence of young children to a larger extent than less-educated men in the early 1990s, regardless of their educational attainment. Nevertheless, compared to women, highly educated men's cigarette consumption appeared to be more negatively correlated with the presence of young children. Chen and Kenkel's results also suggest that the time trend is particularly strong for women with no more than high school education while the presence of young children had already been strongly associated with a decrease in cigarette consumption for highly educated women in the early 1980s. They find that the disparity in knowledge about the health risks of secondhand smoke between women with different educational attainment got narrower from the 1980s to the early 1990s, too. Contrary to diminishing informational advantage to highly educated women from the early 1980s to the 1990s, the differences in health knowledge and smoking behavior between men with different educational attainment expanded in the same period. This is consistent with the argument that men and women may have differences in health behavior. This also again suggests a need for more effective health promotion to influence less-educated men's smoking behavior.

NOTES

1. The term 'involuntary smoking' means non-smokers' exposure to environmental tobacco smoke. Occasionally, involuntary smoking is also referred to as passive smoking. Environmental tobacco smoke is also referred to as passive smoke, secondary smoke, and secondhand smoke. This chapter uses the term 'involuntary smoking' to describe this exposure, and the term 'secondhand smoke' for environmental tobacco smoke.
2. The EPA has encountered court challenges because of this report.
3. We also try an alternative sample composed of men aged 25–59. The results for these two samples are very similar. Because a sizable proportion of men aged 23–24 have young children, we finally decide to use the sample composed of men aged 23–59.
4. To convert categorical income data reported in the NHIS to continuous income

data, we use family income data from the Current Population Survey (CPS), which reports income continuously and has a sampling frame similar to that of the NHIS, to calculate point estimates of income categories in the NHIS.

5 The cigarette price we adopt is the price of a pack of 20 cigarettes and it is measured in 1997 constant dollars. Cigarette prices were merged at the state level using clusters of PSUs associated with states.

6 In this chapter we address whether differences in the association of the presence of children with cigarette consumption exist between men with different educational attainment. We categorize men into two groups: men with at least some college education (defined as high education) and those with no more than high school education (defined as less education). Separate models are estimated for these two groups. Previously, we have tried a pooling model for these two groups of men, and utilized the chi-squared test and the F test to test whether the association of the presence of young children with cigarette consumption is different for men with different educational attainment. According to our calculation, the chi-squared test statistic is 28.75 with 9 degrees of freedom; the F test statistic is distributed as F [(9, 10416)] and its value is 1.58. The results suggest that the relationship between the presence of young children and cigarette consumption is different for these two groups. Therefore, we estimate separate models for these two groups.

7 An OLS model using the log of daily consumption as the dependent variable is also estimated for comparison purposes. It generates similar conclusions.

8 Refer to Table 15.2 for more detailed definitions of these explanatory factors. Variables pertaining to 'year' are not listed in Table 15.2. These variables are created as follows. A binary variable is generated for each of the five years except 1983 to capture the time trend of men's cigarette consumption in the United States. Family income is measured in constant 1990 dollars. This study does not consider adult children or other adults in the household, and just focuses on the effect of non-adult children at home. A model including only the number of non-adult children rather than three child-age categories is also estimated. The former model has significantly less explanatory power. The result suggests that the magnitudes of the effects of children in various age ranges are different. We also try models including the square terms of the numbers of children to test whether the extra effect due to an additional child diminishes quickly. In most cases, the coefficients of the square terms are not statistically significant. Therefore, we decide to exclude the square terms from the explanatory variables and keep simpler models.

9 There are several possible explanations for the weaker effect of older children. For example, compared to younger children, older children may cause more parental stress, which is associated with higher cigarette consumption; men may think that secondhand smoke is more harmful to young children and reduce cigarette consumption more significantly because of young children. Another

possible reason for the weaker effect of older children pertains to a cohort effect. Children at home may affect their father's cigarette consumption to the same extent, regardless of their ages. However, because children of a younger birth cohort, compared to older cohorts, have a stronger effect on their father's cigarette consumption, we observe a stronger effect of the presence of young children. Regarding the possible cohort effect, Chen (1998) examines the effects of children of several birth cohorts on their parents' cigarette consumption by using cross-sectional data. Her results do not provide support to the hypothesis that children of a cohort affect their parental cigarette consumption to a constant extent over time. The reasons why children of different ages have different effects on parental cigarette consumption appear to be complicated. Therefore, it is difficult to ascertain the real reasons for the weaker effect of older children using cross-sectional data. Panel data are useful for clarifying this problem.

10 In addition to our study, some other research also finds differences in health knowledge about secondhand smoke between persons with different socioeconomic status. For instance, according to a survey in 1990 by Brownson et al. (1992), people with low education are less likely to agree that secondhand smoke is harmful to young children's health.

11 Some legal experts have doubts about the effectiveness of legal restrictions on in-home smoking behavior due to enforcement problems. Nevertheless, other legal experts suggest that there are available efficient ways to monitor smoking at home, such as asking physicians to report episodes of children's exposure to parental smoking in the same way they report episodes of physical abuse on children.

REFERENCES

Blaine, T.W. and M.R. Reed (1994), 'U.S. cigarette smoking and health warnings: new evidence from post World War II data', *Journal of Agricultural and Applied Economics*, **26**(2): 535–44.

Brownson, R.C., J. Jackson-Thompson, J.C. Wilkerson, J.R. Davis, N.W. Owens and E.B. Fisher (1992), 'Demographic and socioeconomic differences in beliefs about the health effects of smoking', *American Journal of Public Health*, **82**(1): 99–102.

Butler, M.O. (1996), 'Parental autonomy versus children's health rights: should parents be prohibited from smoking in the presence of their children?', *Washington University Law Quarterly*, **74**: 223–52.

Centers for Disease Control and Prevention (1999), 'Tobacco use – United States, 1900–1999', *Morbidity and Mortality Weekly Report*, **48**(43): 986–93.

Chen, L. (1998), 'The effect of the presence of children on parental smoking', PhD Dissertation, Cornell University, Ithaca, NY.

Chen, L. and D. Kenkel (1999), '"Externalities" within the family: children and women's smoking decisions', unpublished manuscript.

Cordes, R. (1993), 'Smoking adds new fire to custody disputes', *Trial*, **29**(2): 95–6.

de Vries, H. (1995), 'Socio-economic differences in smoking: Dutch adolescents' beliefs and behaviors', *Social Science Medicine*, **41**(3): 419–24.

Glassman, A.J. (1994), 'Parental rights going up in smoke: cigarette smoking in the home as a factor in making custody awards', *Journal of Juvenile Law*, **15**: 168–77.

Greene, W.H. (1995), *Limdep Version 7.0 User's Manual*, Plainview, NY: Econometric Software, Inc.

Hall, J.L. (1994), 'Secondhand smoke as an issue in child custody/visitation disputes', *West Virginia Law Review*, **97**: 115–39.

Johnson, K.L. (1997), 'An argument for consideration of parental smoking in neglect and abuse determinations', *Emory Law Journal*, **46**(4): 1661–996.

Kenkel, D.S. (1991), 'Health behavior, health knowledge, and schooling', *Journal of Political Economy*, **99**(2): 287–305.

Leung, S.F. and S. Yu (1996), 'On the choice between sample selection and two-part models', *Journal of Econometrics*, **72**: 197–229.

McCarthy, L.F. (1994), 'Smoking and child custody', *Parenting*, **8**(3): 21.

Moorby, M.S. (1995), 'Smoking parents, their children, and the home: do the courts have the authority to clear the air?', *Pace Environmental Law Review*, **12**(2): 827–58.

Nayga, R.M., Jr. (1996), 'Determinants of consumers' use of nutritional information on food packages', *Journal of Agricultural and Applied Economics*, **28**(2): 303–12.

Osei, E.K., G.E. Amoh and C. Schandorf (1997), 'Risk ranking by perception', *Health Physics*, **72**(2): 195–203.

Sachs, A. (1993), 'Home smoke-free home', *Time*, **142**(17): 56.

Schwartz, A.D. (1993), 'Environmental tobacco smoke and its effect on children: controlling smoking in the home', *Boston College Environmental Affairs Law Review*, **20**: 135–71.

Sobie, M. (1997), 'Second hand smoke and child custody determinations – a relevant factor or a smoke screen?', *Pace Law Review*, **18**(1): 41–9.

Tobacco Institute (various years), *The Tax Burden on Tobacco*, Washington, DC: Tobacco Institute.

US Department of Health and Human Services (1989), *Reducing the Health Consequences of Smoking. 25 Years of Progress. A Report of the Surgeon General, 1989*, US Department of Health and Human Service, Public Health Service, Centers for Disease Control, Center for Chronic Disease Prevention and Health Promotion, Office on Smoking and Health.

Variyam, J.N., J. Blaylock and D. Smallwood (1998), 'Information effects of nutrient intake determinants on cholesterol consumption', *Journal of Agricultural and Resource Economics*, **23**(1): 110–25.

Wasserman, J., W.G. Manning, J.P. Newhouse and J.D. Winkler (1991), 'The effects of excise taxes and regulations on cigarette smoking', *Journal of Health Economics*, **10**: 43–64.

Zgrodnik, A.H. (1995), 'Smoking discrimination: invading an individual's right to privacy in the home and outside the workplace?', *Ohio Northern University Law Review*, **21**: 1227–55.

16. Gender and race differences in youth alcohol demand

Rima Nair, Frank J. Chaloupka, Michael Grossman and Henry Saffer*

1 INTRODUCTION

Youth alcohol use has been of some concern to state and federal policymakers for at least 25 years. Starting with Minnesota in 1976, a number of states began raising minimum legal purchase ages for alcoholic beverages in response to concerns about youth drinking and its consequences, reversing a downward trend that began in 1970. This concern culminated in the Federal Uniform Drinking Age Act of 1984 (Public Law 98–363). This act accelerated the upward trend in drinking ages by withholding federal highway funds from states that failed to raise drinking ages on all alcoholic beverages to 21 years by October 1, 1986. By 1987, all states had complied, although grandfather clauses in some states kept the effective age below 21 years until 1989. From the economist's perspective, increases in the legal drinking age are expected to significantly raise the full price of alcoholic beverages to youth by reducing availability and increasing the expected legal costs associated with drinking.

In contrast, policymakers have generally ignored using higher alcoholic beverage excise taxes as a way to discourage youth alcohol use and its consequences. Federal excise taxes on beer and wine, for example, were last raised in January 1991, the first time these taxes had been increased in nearly 40 years. While there is some evidence that Congress may have been persuaded by the public health benefits of higher alcohol taxes (Cook and Moore 1993), these increases were largely intended to generate new revenues for deficit reduction and were well below the increases recommended by numerous public health organizations. Like the federal government, state and local governments have raised taxes on alcohol modestly and infrequently, almost always with the intent of increasing tax revenues rather than discouraging alcohol use and abuse. In large part due to the stability of these taxes, the real prices of alcoholic beverages have declined considerably over time. If alcohol abuse among youth and adults is sensitive to price, as economists have argued, then allowing the real value of alcoholic beverage taxes and, consequently, prices to decline will exacerbate the problems resulting from alcohol use and abuse.

Of particular concern to the public health community is the stubbornly high level of alcohol use among youth. According to the estimates from the Monitoring the Future (MTF) study, although illegal for most, experience with alcohol is almost universal among secondary school students and college students, with the vast majority of them reporting at least one drinking occasion in the previous year throughout the study. Similarly, after declining relatively steadily from the early 1980s through the early 1990s, the prevalence of drinking in the past month among high school seniors has leveled off at just over 50 percent in the 1990s.

While trends in drinking prevalence in different youth population subgroups are generally similar over time, there are a few notable differences. Past month drinking prevalence for young whites, for example, was relatively flat in the early to mid-1980s, while that among young blacks was falling more consistently. In the late 1980s and into the early 1990s, however, past month drinking prevalence fell more sharply among young whites than it did among young blacks. In the 1990s, the opposite has been observed, with drinking prevalence among young blacks rising until recently, while prevalence among young whites was relatively flat. This is seen in Figure 16.1.

Of greater concern, heavy drinking among youth is relatively widespread, with 15 percent of eighth graders, one-quarter of tenth graders and nearly one-third of high school seniors reporting having had at least five or more drinks on a single occasion at least once in the prior two-week period. More disturbingly, after falling throughout the late 1980s, heavy drinking among youth has been on the rise throughout the 1990s. This is seen in Figure 16.2. Again, somewhat different patterns emerge for different youth population subgroups as is seen from Figures 16.1–3.

Drinking and heavy drinking by youth have been shown to increase the likelihood of fatal and non-fatal motor-vehicle accidents, youth suicide attempts, and other violence, and lead to earlier initiation of and more frequent sexual activity and less frequent condom use. Drinking is also related to poor school performance, poorly developed social skills and relationships and results in a number of other problems. Moreover, heavy drinking during the teenage years significantly increases the risk of alcohol use and abuse during adulthood. Thus, policies that discourage

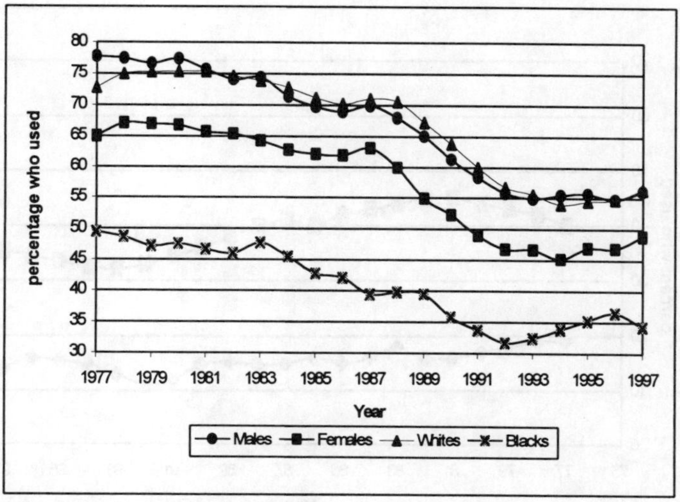

Source: Monitoring the Future Historical Data (1977–97).

Figure 16.1 Trends in thirty-day prevalence of use by subgroups for 12th graders

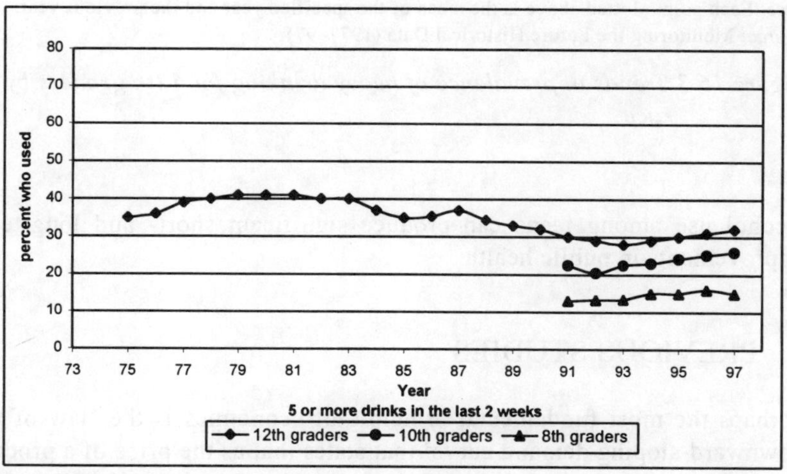

Source: Monitoring the Future Historical Data (1975–97).

Figure 16.2 Trends in two-week prevalence of heavy drinking by grade

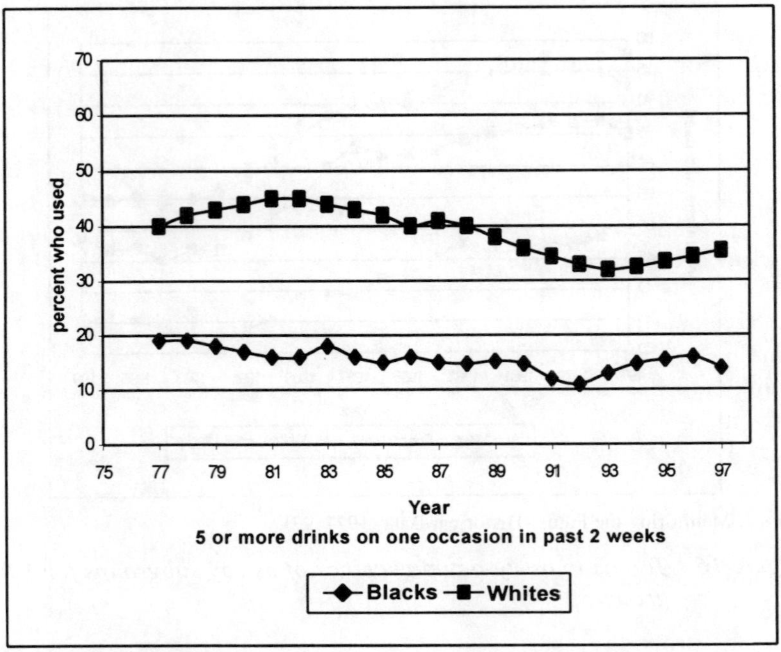

Note: Each point plotted above is the mean of the specified year and the previous year.
Source: Monitoring the Future Historical Data (1977–97).

Figure 16.3 Trends in prevalence of heavy drinking for 12th graders by race

alcohol use among teens can produce significant short- and long-term improvements in public health.

2 PREVIOUS STUDIES

Perhaps the most fundamental principle of economics is the 'law of the downward-sloping demand curve' that states that as the price of a product rises, the quantity demanded of that product falls. An extensive literature in economics clearly demonstrates the inverse relationship between alcohol use and abuse and the full price of alcoholic beverages (see Chaloupka et al. 1998 and forthcoming, for reviews of this literature). In one of the first empirical studies of the impact of prices and alcohol control policies on youth drinking, Coate and Grossman (1988) found that raising the minimum drinking age significantly reduces the frequency of youth alcohol consumption. They also found that as the drinking age rises, the fractions of youth who are frequent and fairly frequent drinkers fall more in absolute or percentage terms than does the fraction of infrequent drinkers. This finding is of import because frequent and fairly frequent drinkers are likely to be responsible for many of the health and other consequences of alcohol use. This conclusion was confirmed by Saffer and Grossman (1987), for example, who found that increases in minimum legal drinking ages and state beer taxes would lead to significant reductions in youth motor-vehicle accident fatality rates.

Laixuthai and Chaloupka (1993) investigate the effects of a uniform drinking age of 21 on youth price sensitivity and also the effects of minimum legal drinking ages and alcoholic beverage prices on youth drinking. They find that price sensitivity of youth drinking falls after the federal mandate that all states raise their minimum legal drinking age to 21. However, this is only part of the 'full price' of consuming alcohol so that when the minimum legal drinking age is below 21, an increase in the money price of alcohol will have a larger impact on the full price of alcohol than when the minimum age is relatively high at 21. Further, they find that increasing the tax on alcohol in 1989 is more effective in reducing drinking frequency and heavy drinking than raising the uniform drinking age from 18 to 21 in 1982. Chaloupka (1993) compare the relative efficacy of all major drunk-driving legislation, beer taxes and the minimum legal drinking age on motor-vehicle fatalities. They find that the beer tax and a severe one-year administrative license penalty are the most effective policies in reducing fatalities from drinking and driving. The next most effective are a minimum legal drinking age of 21, preliminary breath-test law and high mandatory minimum fines.

Studies have also examined the price sensitivity of alcohol consumption and related outcomes. According to Kenkel (1993), the price elasticity of total alcohol use for men was estimated at –1.95 and for women at –2.19. Grossman et al. (1987) estimated beer and spirits price elasticities for youth at –3.05 and –3.83, respectively. Kenkel (1993) estimated higher alcohol price elasticities for women than for men. Women and youth seem to have a more elastic demand for alcohol than the general population. However, little research has been done on the differential impact of the full price of alcohol such as alcohol taxes, minimum legal drinking age, and other aspects on drinking among various youth population subgroups.

This chapter examines differences in youth responsiveness to the different aspects of the full price of alcohol, including tax and the minimum legal drinking age. Results show that significant differences exist among the various population subgroups.

3 METHODS

Data on youth alcohol use come from the 1982 and 1989 Monitoring the Future surveys of high school seniors conducted by the Institute for Social Research (ISR) at the University of Michigan. Every year since 1975, ISR has collected data on alcohol, tobacco, and other drug use from a nationally representative sample of approximately 17,000 public and private high school seniors. The surveys are conducted in school and address issues such as youths' attitudes, perceptions and use of legal and illicit drugs. On account of the sensitive nature of the subject matter, care is taken to ensure the reliability and validity of responses.

From the survey responses, various indicators of alcohol use were constructed. The indicators used in this analysis include: a measure of the frequency of drinking in the past year with four categories: 0 for no drinking occasions, 1 for 1–9 drinking occasions, 2 for 10–39 drinking occasions and 3 for 40 or more drinking occasions. A second indicator of drinking in the past month is defined as: 0 for no drinking occasions, 1 for 1–5 drinking occasions, 2 for 6–9 drinking occasions, and 3 for ten or more drinking occasions. Finally, a dichotomous indicator was used that is set equal to 1 if at least one drinking occasion in the past two weeks occurred where five or more drinks were consumed and 0 otherwise.

The other variables used in this analysis were: dichotomous variables for socioeconomic and demographic factors such as for year, 1 if 1982 and 0 otherwise, gender (male or female), race (white, black or other race),[1] area of residence (rural, urban or suburban area), marital status (single or married, divorced, engaged, separated), family structure (live alone, live with father only, live with mother only, live with both parents or live with someone else), mother's work status (work full time, part time or unemployed), importance of religion (not important, of little importance, somewhat important or very important), and a dichotomous border-age variable that is set equal to 1 if there is a lower drinking age for low alcohol beer within 25 miles of the youth's county of residence and 0 otherwise.

Continuous variables included: age, the minimum legal drinking age for low-alcohol beer, real weekly income from all sources, and the real beer tax calculated as the average of the federal and state taxes during the first two quarters of the survey year. Real measures reflect differences in prices over time and are based on the national consumer price index (CPI) and a local cost-of-living index taken from the American Chamber of

Commerce Researchers' Association.

Descriptive statistics for variables of interest by race and gender are provided in Appendix Tables 16A.1 (a and b). The mean age of the sample is 18.27 years while the minimum legal drinking age for low-alcohol beer is 20.33 years. The mean real beer tax is 97 cents.[2] Of the sample, 37.35 percent report at least one incident of heavy drinking in the past two weeks; 12 percent are black while 73 percent are white, with 14 percent from other races; 91 percent are single and 50.77 percent are male. As shown in Table 16A.1a, 46 percent of all males report at least one recent heavy drinking incident as opposed to 28 percent of all females. Only 15 percent of the black sample report heavy drinking. From Table 16A.1b, we see that 89.66 percent of white males report any drinking in the past year. Approximately 25 percent of the white male sample report frequent drinking in the past year as compared with 18 percent of the same sample who report frequent drinking in the past month.

4 RESULTS

Using as controls the variables described above, the probability of consuming alcohol was estimated for males, females, blacks, whites, black males, black females, white males and white females using probit and ordered probit specifications.[3] In all, three different measures of alcohol consumption were used. Each specification includes a measure of the minimum legal drinking age along with the border-age variable. Real beer tax is the policy variable used and provides a measure of the price of beer. Therefore, each of the eight gender/race-specific specifications was estimated separately for each indicator of alcohol use. (See Appendix Tables 16A.2–4 (a and b).)

Marginal effects for the above equations were also calculated. Appendix Tables 16A.5–7 (a and b) report the marginal effects for certain variables obtained from each of the eight gender/race-specific regressions. These separate regressions were run for all three dependent variables. For the dichotomous independent variables, the marginal effects are calculated for a discrete change in the variable value from 0 to 1 but for the continuous independent variables, the marginal effects are calculated at the means.

In general, estimates showed that the real beer tax has a strong negative effect on drinking probability for all subgroups for almost all measures of alcohol use except among African–American males. Religiosity is also significant across all subgroups.[4] Considering religion to be of little or no importance in one's life increases the probability of drinking across the board. In contrast, youths for whom religion is a very important factor are significantly less likely to drink. Income is positive and significant for all subgroups indicating that alcohol use increases as income rises. Based on the year indicator, alcohol consumption in all groups fell between 1982 and 1989, except among black males.

The minimum legal drinking age has a significantly negative effect on drinking among females, whites and black males for two of the three measures of drinking. The border-age variable indicating the existence of a lower drinking age within 25 miles of one's county of residence positively affects drinking probability of all subgroups for at least one measure of drinking, except among black females.

Comparing genders for each measure of alcohol use, results showed that being white or of other race significantly increases the probability of drinking for both males and females. Income also has a positive and significant effect for both. Although religion is important to both sexes, its effect is found to be stronger for females in two of the indicators of alcohol consumption. Differences between drinking probability of the sexes showed up strongly with regard to the beer tax and the border-age variable. Results showed that the beer tax affects female drinking probability more than it does male drinking probability. The existence of a lower drinking age within 25 miles of one's county of residence also significantly increases drinking probability. Mother's working status significantly increases drinking probability, affecting females more than males. Being single also affects females positively but seems unimportant for males. We also found that whether or not race-specific estimates are obtained, male binge drinking effect exceeds female effect. This last result is striking because binge drinking is the most important indicator of alcohol abuse examined and its incidence among males is 50 to 60 percent higher than among females.

The marginal effects calculated echo the above results and provide a quantification of effects as seen from the coefficients. Except for the dichotomous indicator of heavy drinking, an increase in real beer tax reduces the probability of drinking for females more than it does for males. Specifically, a $1 increase in the tax reduces the probability of male heavy drinking by 2.35 percent, other things constant. As is shown in Table 16A.6a, for the categorical indicator of drinking in the past month, when the real beer tax is increased, the probability of being in the first category (0 drinking occasions) increases while the probability of being in the highest category (over 10 drinking occasions) decreases. For the two in-between categories, the effect is a decrease. In other words, more people move into the lowest drinking category from the higher drinking categories when the beer tax is increased. Similarly, for the categorical indicator of drinking in the past year, for both males and females, an increase in the tax increases the probability of being in the first category and reduces the probability of being in the last category. However, the effects differ for the two in-between categories. Changes in real income affect both sexes by approximately the same degree as seen from the marginal effects. For both categorical indicators, an increase in real income reduces the probability of being in the first category and increases the probability of being in the last category for both sexes. However, an increase in real income reduces the probability of being in the second category (Y=1) for males but has the opposite effect for females. The border-age indicator affects females more strongly than males.

Examining differences in the likelihood of youth drinking by race, results showed that being male and an increase in real income significantly increase the likelihood of drinking for both whites and African–Americans. Further, being male increases the probability of drinking for whites more than it does for African–Americans. The beer tax also affects drinking probability for whites more than it does for African–Americans. While the minimum legal drinking age significantly affects all measures of drinking by young whites, it affects only one measure of drinking by young blacks. Similarly, the border-age indicator significantly affects whites more than it does blacks. Mother's working status affects neither whites nor blacks as compared to other races.

Tables 16A.6a and 16A.7a show that changes in the real beer tax increase the probability of being in the lowest drinking category (0 drinking occasions) and reduce the probability of being in the highest category (over 10/40 drinking occasions in past month/past year) for both, whites and blacks. The effects are mixed for the two in-between categories. A change in the border-age variable value from 0 to 1 reduces the probability of being in the lowest category and increases the probability of being in the highest category for both whites and blacks. The in-between categories show mixed effects.

Further examination of the differences by racial subgroup reveals interesting information. Comparing white males and females, an increase in real income significantly increases the likelihood of drinking by both. Religiosity significantly reduces drinking probability for white females more than it does for white males. The beer tax affects white male drinking for all measures of drinking. The border-age variable has a greater effect on white females than on white males. Interestingly, living with the mother only has a significant positive effect on white female drinking probability for two of the indicators of alcohol use. In general, living with the father only has a positive effect on drinking probability. However, compared to living with both parents, this is reasonable. A significant variable for full-time employment by the mother in those equations might be another explanation.

Comparing African–American males and females, the beer tax has no effect on male drinking probability while it does on female drinking probability but for only one of the measures of alcohol use. While the minimum legal drinking age and the border-age variable have no effect on black female drinking probability, they do affect black male drinking.

For the gender and racial subgroups, we find that an increase in real beer tax significantly affects drinking probability of white males, white females and black females. Tables 16A.6b and 16A.7b show that an increase in the real beer tax increases the probability of being in the lowest category for all of the above subgroups and reduces the probability of being in the highest category. In general, family structure and religiosity affect all measures of drinking for almost all demographic groups and subgroups. From Table 16A.6b, we see that the effects of an increase in the real beer tax on the different measures of drinking are negative for all gender and racial subgroups except for black males.[5]

A change in the border-age variable value from 0 to 1 reduces the probability of being in the lowest drinking category but increases the probability of being in the highest category for all subsamples, for both categorical indicators of drinking. Weaker religiosity reduces the probability of being in the lowest category but increases the probability of being in the highest category across the board although effects on the two in-between categories are mixed for the various subgroups.

5 DISCUSSION

When drinking in the youth population is broken down by race and gender, one striking finding is that some policies have significantly different effects on some population subgroups. A comparison of males and females showed that beer tax is a stronger policy for females than for males. Minimum legal drinking ages similarly have a more significant effect on females than on males. Drinking among young whites is more tax responsive than among young blacks. Similarly, the minimum legal drinking age affects drinking by young whites more than it does young blacks. Drinking by young black males seems to be the least responsive to a tax policy although the minimum legal drinking age does affect black males. Black females are not responsive to the lower border-age indicator but black males are. While white females are responsive to minimum legal drinking age as a policy, black females are not.

The beer tax is a significant determinant of alcohol consumption decisions made by white males and white females. It also is a significant determinant of the frequency of consumption in the past year for black females. Excise tax hikes have their largest impacts on the probability of binge drinking and frequent drinking by white males and on the probability of abstention from drinking by white females. The drinking age is a significant determinant of binge drinking, the frequency of consumption in the past month, and the frequency of consumption in the past year for black males. The drinking age also has significant effects in the case of binge drinking for white males, the frequency of consumption in the past month for white males and white females, and the frequency of consumption in the past year for white females. Drinking age increases have their largest impacts on the probabilities of binge drinking, frequent drinking, and abstention by black males.

Discouraging drinking among all youth is not an easy goal when significant differences exist among gender and racial subgroups. A blanket policy for all youth would be inappropriate, as some subgroups would be more responsive to the policy and some less. One must also bear in mind that the policies discussed here only measure the existence of a policy and not its enforcement. Strict enforcement of these policies is more likely to change youth behavior than merely enacting them. If reducing youth male drinking is the goal then as the results above have shown, a policy that increases beer tax alone will not be as effective as one might anticipate based on estimates from the total youth population. A mix of policies is almost certainly needed to reduce drinking in all youth population subgroups.

NOTES

* This chapter was prepared for the Taipei International Conference on Health Economics organized by the Institute of Economics, Academia Sinica, March 25–27, 1999, Nankang, Taipei, Taiwan. Support for this research was provided by Grant RO1 AA09435 from the National Institute on Alcohol Abuse and Alcoholism to the University of Illinois at Chicago. The authors are grateful to Patrick M. O'Malley and Jerome J. Hiniker of the University of Michigan's Institute for Social Research for providing restricted data sets from the Monitoring the Future Project.

1 We examine only two races – whites and blacks. The category for comparison is all other races, grouped together.

2 For a case of 24 12-oz cans.

3 Likelihood ratio tests were carried out to examine whether significant differences in coefficients exist across the subsamples. In all cases, the chi-

squared test statistic showed that there is a significant difference between the pooled sample and the subsamples, rejecting the pooled sample in favor of the subgroups.

4 Significance level examined here is at 95 percent level.

5 In the regressions for black males, the variable real beer tax is insignificant.

REFERENCES

Chaloupka, F.J., M. Grossman and H. Saffer (1998), 'The effects of price on the consequences of alcohol use and abuse', in M. Galanter (ed.), *Recent Developments in Alcoholism, Volume 14: The Consequences of Alcoholism – Medical, Neuropsychiatric, Economic, Cross-Cultural*, New York: Plenum Press, pp. 331–46.

Chaloupka, F.J., M. Grossman and H. Saffer (forthcoming), 'The effects of price on alcohol consumption', *Alcohol Research & Health*.

Chaloupka, F.J., H. Saffer and M. Grossman (1993), 'Alcohol-control policies and motor-vehicle fatalities', *Journal of Legal Studies*, **22**(1): 161–86.

Coate, D. and M. Grossman (1988), 'The effect of alcoholic beverage prices and legal drinking ages on youth alcohol use', *Journal of Law and Economics*, **31**(1): 145–71.

Cook, P.J. and M.J. Moore (1993), 'Taxation of alcoholic beverages', in M. Hilton and G. Bloss (eds), *Economic Research on the Prevention of Alcohol-Related Problems*, NIH Publication No. 93-3513, Rockville, MD: National Institute on Alcohol Abuse and Alcoholism, pp. 33–58.

Grossman, M., D. Coate and G.M. Arluck (1987), 'Price sensitivity of alcoholic beverages in the United States: youth alcohol consumption', in H. Holder (ed.), *Control Issues in Alcohol Abuse Prevention: Strategies for States and Communities*, Greenwich: JAI Press, pp. 169–98.

Kenkel, D. (1993), 'Drinking, driving, and deterrence: the effectiveness and social costs of alternative policies', *Journal of Law and Economics*, **36**(2): 877–913.

Laixuthai, A. and F.J. Chaloupka (1993), 'Youth alcohol use and public policy', *Contemporary Policy Issues*, **11**(4): 70–81.

Saffer, H. and M. Grossman (1987), 'Beer taxes, the legal drinking age and youth motor vehicle fatalities', *Journal of Legal Studies*, **16**(2): 351–74.

APPENDIX

Table 16A.1 Descriptive statistics

(a) By gender and race

	Males $N = 17{,}366$	**Females** $N = 16{,}833$	**Whites** $N = 25{,}988$	**Blacks** $N = 4277$
Drinking in the past year	0.8742	0.8478	0.8946	0.7325
Frequent drinking in the past year	0.2294	0.1109	0.1997	0.0547
Drinking in the past month	0.7173	0.6285	0.7189	0.4900
Frequent drinking in the past month	0.1676	0.0917	0.1495	0.0526
Heavy drinking	0.4605	0.2816	0.4179	0.1569

(b) By racial subgroup

	Whites		**Blacks**	
	Males $N = 13{,}276$	**Females** $N = 12{,}712$	**Males** $N = 1884$	**Females** $N = 2393$
Drinking in the past year	0.8966	0.8951	0.7675	0.7124
Frequent drinking in the past year	0.2578	0.1332	0.0992	0.0192
Drinking in the past month	0.7484	0.6950	0.5621	0.4504
Frequent drinking in the past month	0.1843	0.1080	0.0944	0.0192
Heavy drinking	0.5017	0.3274	0.2323	0.1001

Notes: Missing responses for some questions account for errors in subsample size, causing numbers to be slightly inflated. Although 'heavy drinking' is the only originally dichotomous variable, drinking in the past year and drinking in the past month are viewed here as dichotomous for ease in calculations, that is, proportions are calculated for any drinking reported in the past year and any drinking reported in the past month.

Percentages for frequent drinking in the past year and past month refer to category $Y = 3$ for the respective categorical variables.

Source: The 1982 and 1989 Monitoring the Future surveys, Institute for Social Research, University of Michigan.

Table 16A.2 Dichotomous measure of heavy drinking

(a) Probit specification for each demographic group

	Males	**Females**	**Whites**	**Blacks**
Real beer tax	–5.9274 (–2.266)	–1.3067 (–0.486)	–7.8100 (–3.474)	6.1621 (1.472)
Real income	0.2805 (11.988)	0.3333 (11.869)	0.3069 (14.167)	0.1345 (2.564)
Min. legal drinking age	–0.0110 (–0.851)	–0.0115 (–0.842)	–0.0203 (–1.928)	–0.0475 (–1.316)
Border age	0.0620 (1.681)	0.1394 (3.585)	0.1104 (3.768)	0.2185 (1.870)
Year (1982)	0.1905 (6.642)	0.1614 (5.035)	0.1909 (7.937)	–0.0667 (–0.720)

(b) Probit specification for each subgroup

	Whites		**Blacks**	
	Males	**Females**	**Males**	**Females**
Real beer tax	–11.179 (–3.616)	–4.6840 (–1.477)	5.9435 (1.031)	7.0985 (1.184)
Real income	0.2824 (10.222)	0.3608 (10.745)	0.1329 (1.932)	0.1714 (2.141)
Min. legal drinking age	–0.0219 (–1.524)	–0.0188 (–1.249)	–0.0897 (–1.792)	–0.0172 (–0.336)
Border age	0.0718 (1.801)	0.1364 (3.228)	0.3831 (2.308)	0.0415 (0.253)
Year (1982)	0.2211 (6.919)	0.1665 (4.678)	–0.2733 (–2.151)	0.1135 (0.848)

Notes: The above are probit coefficients with z-scores in parentheses. Also included are an intercept, age, religiosity, residence, living arrangements, maternal work status and marital status. Significance level examined is at the 95% level.

Table 16A.3 Categorical measure of drinking in the past month

(a) Ordered probit specification for each demographic group

	Males	**Females**	**Whites**	**Blacks**
Real beer tax	–6.9269 (–3.154)	–8.4376 (–3.923)	–11.041 (–5.862)	–2.1544 (–0.674)
Real income	0.3216 (16.234)	0.3522 (15.060)	0.3601 (19.654)	0.1556 (3.832)
Min. legal drinking age	–0.0171 (–1.567)	–0.0337 (–3.022)	–0.0314 (–3.553)	–0.0222 (–0.846)
Border age	0.0266 (0.858)	0.1872 (5.834)	0.1066 (4.337)	0.1876 (2.162)
Year (1982)	0.2189 (8.993)	0.1891 (7.222)	0.2222 (10.971)	0.1126 (1.682)

(b) Ordered probit specification for each subgroup

	Whites		**Blacks**	
	Males	**Females**	**Males**	**Females**
Real beer tax	–12.200 (–4.647)	–11.226 (–4.261)	1.2427 (0.266)	–3.7477 (–0.870)
Real income	0.3393 (14.465)	0.3794 (13.445)	0.1403 (2.494)	0.2067 (3.580)
Min. legal drinking age	–0.0229 (–1.883)	–0.0450 (–3.574)	–0.0801 (–2.057)	0.0275 (0.786)
Border age	0.0176 (0.525)	0.1889 (5.345)	0.3324 (2.503)	0.0438 (0.386)
Year (1982)	0.2446 (8.991)	0.1902 (6.419)	–0.1140 (–1.160)	0.3225 (3.589)

Notes: See Table 16A.2. The above are ordered probit coefficients. The above specification does not include an intercept.

Table 16A.4 Categorical measure of drinking in the past year

(a) Ordered probit specification for each demographic group

	Males	**Females**	**Whites**	**Blacks**
Real beer tax	–9.9613 (–4.645)	–10.867 (–5.342)	–13.945 (–7.614)	–5.9069 (–1.981)
Real income	0.3039 (15.408)	0.3623 (15.911)	0.3560 (19.530)	0.1250 (3.242)
Min. legal drinking age	–0.0111 (–1.026)	–0.0244 (–2.233)	–0.0194 (–2.216)	–0.0535 (–2.143)
Border age	0.0647 (2.090)	0.2069 (6.545)	0.1346 (5.495)	0.2141 (2.595)
Year (1982)	0.2241 (9.303)	0.1711 (6.729)	0.2237 (11.196)	–0.0046 (–0.074)

(b) Ordered probit specification for each subgroup

	Whites		**Blacks**	
	Males	**Females**	**Males**	**Females**
Real beer tax	–15.813 (–6.118)	–13.023 (–5.142)	–1.9888 (–0.445)	–9.3745 (–2.364)
Real income	0.3231 (13.742)	0.4024 (14.456)	0.0741 (1.364)	0.1813 (3.345)
Min. legal drinking age	–0.0105 (–0.867)	–0.0315 (–2.536)	–0.0957 (–2.566)	–0.0088 (–0.265)
Border age	0.0660 (1.963)	0.2072 (5.912)	0.2906 (2.287)	0.1193 (1.105)
Year (1982)	0.2581 (9.540)	0.2033 (6.863)	–0.1498 (–1.604)	0.1907 (2.249)

Notes: See Table 16A.3.

Table 16A.5 Dichotomous measure of heavy drinking

(a) Marginal effects for each demographic group

	Males	Females	Whites	Blacks
Real beer tax	–2.3500 (–2.27)	–0.4260 (–0.49)	–3.0257 (–3.47)	1.3502 (1.47)
Real income	0.1112 (11.99)	0.1087 (11.69)	0.1189 (14.17)	0.0294 (2.56)
Min. legal drinking age	–0.0043 (–0.85)	–0.0037 (–0.84)	–0.0078 (–1.93)	–0.0104 (–1.32)
Border age	0.0246 (1.68)	0.0469 (3.58)	0.0431 (3.77)	0.0527 (1.87)

(b) Marginal effects for each subgroup

	Whites		Blacks	
	Males	Females	Males	Females
Real beer tax	–4.4597 (–3.62)	–1.6653 (–1.48)	1.7742 (1.03)	1.1248 (1.18)
Real income	0.1126 (10.22)	0.1282 (10.75)	0.0396 (1.93)	0.0271 (2.14)
Min. legal drinking age	–0.0087 (–1.52)	–0.0067 (–1.25)	–0.0268 (–1.79)	–0.0027 (–0.34)
Border age	0.0286 (1.80)	0.0495 (3.23)	0.1274 (2.31)	0.0067 (0.25)

Notes: *z* scores are in parentheses. *dF*/*dx* is for discrete change of dummy variable from 0 to 1. Also included are an intercept, age, year, religiosity, residence, living arrangements, maternal work status and marital status.

Table 16A.6a Categorical measure of drinking in the past month: marginal effects for each demographic group

	Y = 0	Y = 1	Y = 2	Y = 3
Males				
Real beer tax	2.3736	0.0196	–0.6944	–1.6988
Real income	–0.1102	–0.0009	0.0322	0.0789
Min. legal age	0.0059	0.0000	–0.0017	–0.0042
Border age	–0.0091	–0.0001	0.0027	0.0065
Females				
Real beer tax	3.2250	–1.0872	–0.9026	–1.2353
Real income	–0.1346	0.0454	0.0377	0.0516
Min. legal age	0.0219	–0.0044	–0.0036	–0.0044
Border age	–0.0716	0.0241	0.0200	0.0274
Whites				
Real beer tax	3.7619	–0.1238	–1.2158	–2.4223
Real income	–0.1227	0.0040	0.0397	0.0790
Min. legal age	0.0107	–0.0004	–0.0035	–0.0069
Border age	–0.0363	0.0012	0.0117	0.0234
Blacks				
Real beer tax	0.8409	–0.4889	–0.1341	–0.2179
Real income	–0.0607	0.0353	0.0097	0.0157
Min. legal age	0.0087	–0.0051	–0.0014	–0.0023
Border age	–0.0732	0.0426	0.0117	0.0190

Notes: Y = 0, 1, 2 and 3 represent the categories – 0 for no drinking occasions, 1 for 1–5 drinking occasions, 2 for 6–9 drinking occasions, and 3 for over 10 drinking occasions. The *z*-scores for the above are the same as in the tables presenting the respective coefficients.

Table 16A.6b Categorical measure of drinking in the past month: marginal effects for each subgroup

	Y = 0	**Y = 1**	**Y = 2**	**Y = 3**
White males				
Real beer tax	3.9432	0.4434	–1.2110	–3.1756
Real income	–0.1097	–0.0123	0.0337	0.0883
Min. legal age	0.0074	0.0008	–0.0023	–0.0060
Border age	–0.0057	–0.0006	0.0018	0.0046
White females				
Real beer tax	4.0249	–0.7713	–0.2767	–1.9769
Real income	–0.1361	0.0261	0.0432	0.0668
Min. legal age	0.0162	–0.0031	–0.0051	–0.0079
Border age	–0.0677	0.0130	0.0215	0.0333
Black males				
Real beer tax	–0.4958	0.1972	0.0879	0.2107
Real income	–0.0560	0.0223	0.0099	0.0238
Min. legal age	0.0320	–0.0127	–0.0057	–0.0136
Border age	–0.1326	0.0527	0.0235	0.0564
Black females				
Real beer tax	1.3922	–1.0268	–0.1849	–0.1805
Real income	–0.0768	0.0566	0.0102	0.0100
Min. legal age	–0.0102	0.0075	0.0014	0.0013
Border age	–0.0163	0.0120	0.0022	0.0021

Notes: See Table 16A.6a.

Table 16A.7a Categorical measure of drinking in the past year: marginal effects for each demographic group

	Y = 0	*Y* = 1	*Y* = 2	*Y* = 3
Males				
Real beer tax	1.9426	2.0199	–0.9815	–0.9810
Real income	–0.0593	–0.0616	0.0300	0.0910
Min. legal age	0.0022	0.0023	–0.0011	–0.0033
Border age	–0.0126	–0.0131	0.0064	0.0194
Females				
Real beer tax	2.3460	1.7619	–2.2856	–1.8224
Real income	–0.0782	–0.0587	0.0762	0.0608
Min. legal age	0.0053	0.0040	–0.0051	–0.0041
Border age	–0.0447	–0.0335	0.0435	0.0347
Whites				
Real beer tax	2.4077	3.1514	–1.8103	–3.7489
Real income	–0.0615	–0.0805	0.0462	0.0957
Min. legal age	0.0034	0.0044	–0.0025	–0.0052
Border age	–0.0232	–0.0304	0.0175	0.0362
Blacks				
Real beer tax	2.0222	–0.4908	–0.9261	–0.6052
Real income	–0.0428	0.0104	0.0196	0.0128
Min. legal age	0.0183	–0.0045	–0.0084	–0.0055
Border age	–0.0733	0.0178	0.0336	0.0219

Notes: *Y* = 0, 1, 2 and 3 represent the categories – 0 for no drinking occasions, 1 for 1–9 drinking occasions, 2 for 10–39 drinking occasions and 3 for over 40 drinking occasions.

Table 16A.7b Categorical measure of drinking in the past year: marginal effects for each subgroup

	Y = 0	*Y* = 1	*Y* = 2	*Y* = 3
White males				
Real beer tax	2.7339	3.4573	–1.1575	–5.0337
Real income	–0.0559	–0.0707	0.0237	0.1029
Min. legal age	0.0018	0.0023	–0.0008	–0.0034
Border age	–0.0114	–0.0144	0.0048	0.0210
White females				
Real beer tax	2.2982	2.8543	–2.4494	–2.7032
Real income	–0.0710	–0.0882	0.0757	0.0835
Min. legal age	0.0056	0.0069	–0.0059	–0.0065
Border age	–0.0366	–0.0454	0.0390	0.0430
Black males				
Real beer tax	0.6358	0.0155	–0.2943	–0.3570
Real income	–0.0237	–0.0006	0.0110	0.0133
Min. legal age	0.0306	0.0007	–0.0142	–0.0172
Border age	–0.0929	–0.0023	0.0430	0.0522
Black females				
Real beer tax	3.3630	–1.6222	–1.3620	–0.3788
Real income	–0.0650	0.0314	0.0263	0.0073
Min. legal age	0.0032	–0.0015	–0.0013	–0.0004
Border age	–0.0428	0.0207	0.0173	0.0048

Notes: See Table 16A.7a.

17. The impact of trade liberalization on alcohol consumption in Taiwan

Chee-Ruey Hsieh, Mau-Shan Shi and Chien-Fu Jeff Lin*

1 INTRODUCTION

In recent years, economists have become increasingly interested in the consumption of alcoholic beverages. Although there is some evidence to suggest that moderate levels of alcohol consumption may be beneficial, it is now generally acknowledged that alcohol abuse leads to at least four harmful outcomes. First, drunk driving is the major cause of motor-vehicle fatalities in many countries. For example, several studies pointed out that alcohol has been involved in half or more of the traffic fatalities in the US (Saffer and Grossman 1987; Kenkel 1993; Mullahy and Sindelar 1994; Sloan et al. 1995). Second, heavy drinking also leads to a number of adverse health effects, such as cirrhosis of the liver, which in turn impose medical and other costs to individual users, their families, and society as a whole. Third, heavy drinking may also influence the return and investment of human capital. For example, French and Zarkin (1995) indicate that heavy drinkers have lower wages than light to moderate drinkers. Hamilton and Hamilton (1997) suggest that heavy drinkers attain lower return for higher education than non- and moderate drinkers. Cook and Moore (1993) also find that heavy drinking in high school has a significantly negative impact on the average number of years of schooling completed following high school. Finally, there is a strong link between alcohol consumption and violence, according to the literature in the field of biology, psychology, sociology, and epidemiology (Markowitz and Grossman 1998). The significant costs of alcohol-related violence, such as emotional and physical harm as well as the criminal justice costs, are also costly to both individuals and society.

The existing economic research on alcohol is largely based on data from developed countries. Currently, there is little work that pays attention to the analysis of alcohol consumption in developing countries. As shown in economic literature, the income elasticities for alcoholic beverages are positive, which imply that alcohol consumption is a normal good (Selvanathan 1988; Clements and Selvanathan 1991; Goel and Morey 1995; Manning et al. 1995). This result suggests that economic growth in developing countries will lead to an increase in the demand for alcohol. Furthermore, the recent development of trade liberalization has significantly promoted a worldwide increase in alcohol marketing efforts. For example, as a result of trade negotiation, the alcohol market in Taiwan was opened to alcoholic beverages produced by foreign countries, first to the United States in 1987, and then to other developed countries. Given the evidence that alcohol consumption is responsive to price, the decrease in alcohol prices resulting from trade liberalization will lead to an increase in alcohol consumption and alcohol abuse.

The objective of this chapter is to examine the effect of the opening-up of an alcohol market on alcohol consumption, focusing specifically on Taiwan. We also estimate the price and income elasticities of alcohol demand in Taiwan. The data set used in this study is annual time-series data for Taiwan for the years 1966 through 1996. This chapter proceeds as follows. We first review the institutional history of the alcohol market in Taiwan. Based on the Taiwanese market structure, we then present a conceptual framework to analyse the impact of trade liberalization on alcohol consumption. Thereafter, we provide an empirical model to test the theoretical prediction and then describe the data. In Section 5, we analyse the empirical findings. The final section provides the summary and conclusion.

2 AN OVERVIEW OF THE ALCOHOL MARKET IN TAIWAN

As in the tobacco industry, Taiwan's alcohol industry was controlled by a government-run monopoly. The monopolistic system for alcoholic beverages was established by the Japanese colonial government in 1922, and was reorganized under its present name, the Taiwan Tobacco and Wine Monopoly Bureau (TTWMB) after the Second World War (Zhou 1980). The major advantage of the monopolistic system is that the government can earn the monopolistic profit from selling alcoholic beverages. Clearly, the monopolistic profit is an implicit form of an indirect tax and represents a major source of government revenue, especially at the early stage of economic development. In 1951 the monopolistic profit from alcoholic beverages was NT$90 million, contributing approximately 6 percent to Taiwan's total tax revenues. The monopolistic profit from alcoholic beverages reached a peak percentage of 10 percent of total government tax revenue in 1962, and then declined to about 6 percent in 1986, one year before the market opened up to imports. In recent years, alcohol taxes have contributed only about 3 percent to total government tax revenue. For instance, the total government tax revenue for 1996 was NT$1197 billion; the alcohol tax revenue that same year was NT$34 billion (TTWMB 1997).

In addition to the contribution to government revenue, the monopolistic system imposes several regulations upon Taiwan's alcohol market. First, TTWMB controls the number of retailers by license and also the retail prices of alcoholic beverages. Second, prior to 1987, TTWMB was protected by high tariffs and quotas on imported alcohol. As a result of this protection, imports comprised less than 1 percent of total alcohol consumption prior to the opening-up of the market (see Figure 17.1). Third, TTWMB also restricts the advertising of domestic and imported alcohol. Prior to 1987, alcohol advertising could only be seen in the case of new product announcements and on billboards near the TTWMB's branch offices and distribution centers. This was because the price rigidity due to regulation and the restriction on imported alcohol made market competition almost non-existent. Therefore, alcohol advertising was considered unnecessary by TTWMB.

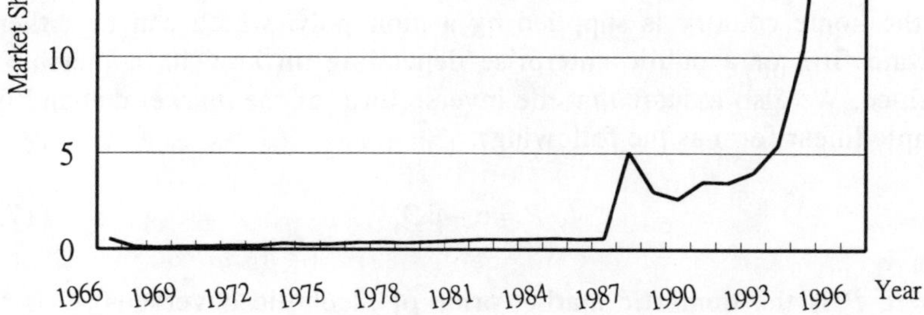

Figure 17.1 Market share of imported alcohol in Taiwan

The limited market access to imported alcohol resulting from high tariffs and quotas, in combination with the unfavorable balance of trade between the United States and Taiwan, caused the US Trade Representative to initiate a Section 301 case against Taiwan in late 1986 (Chaloupka and Laixuthai 1996). Under the threat of trade sanctions, and in conformity with the international policy trend towards trade liberalization, Taiwan agreed to open its alcohol market (and its cigarette market) to US producers in 1987. The agreement to open the alcohol market applied to other countries subsequently.

After the alcohol market opened to imports, the monopolistic system remained unchanged for domestic alcohol. However, the open policy led to three major changes in the Taiwanese alcohol market. First, the government abolished the quota and imposed an excise tax on imported alcohol. Second, the market share of imported alcohol increased rapidly once the alcohol market was opened to imports. As shown in Figure 17.1, the market share of imported alcohol rapidly increased to 5 percent in the first year (1987) the alcohol market was opened. This share grew further to about 20 percent by 1996. Finally, the open policy introduced competition into Taiwan's alcohol market. As a result, advertising and other promotional activities have become a pervasive phenomenon in Taiwan. Whether the market competition between national monopoly (TTWMB) and foreign alcohol manufacturers will increase the overall alcohol consumption is an important question that will be discussed below.

3 THEORETICAL FRAMEWORK

In this section we provide a theoretical framework to analyse the effect of opening up the alcohol market on the consumption of alcoholic beverages. Before the market opens up to imports, we assume that the alcohol market in the home country is supplied by a monopoly, which can be either a private firm or a public enterprise depending on how its ownership is defined. We also assume that the inverse form of the market demand is a simple linear form as the following:

$$P = \alpha - \beta Q, \tag{17.1}$$

where P is the domestic market price of alcoholic beverages, Q is the market demand for alcohol, and α is a demand shifter which captures the other determinants of alcohol demand, such as income and alcohol advertising. For simplicity, we assume α is a constant and $\alpha > 0$. Similarly, based on the law of demand, $\beta > 0$.

Assume that the production technology of alcohol is a constant return to scale so that the cost function is represented by a simple linear function as the following:

$$C_h = r_h q_h , \tag{17.2}$$

where r_h is the constant marginal cost, and q_h is the production of alcohol provided by the monopolistic firm. As in an 'autarky' situation, $Q = q_h$. The profit function of the firm is then

$$\pi_h = P q_h - r_h q_h . \tag{17.3}$$

Differentiating (17.3) with respect to q_h and solving the first-order condition, we obtain the profit-maximizing production under a monopoly:

$$q^{pre} = \frac{\alpha - r_h}{2\beta} , \tag{17.4}$$

where superscript 'pre' stands for the situation prior to market opening. Technically speaking, the scale of the domestic market for alcohol needs to be adequately defined so as to ensure that $q_h > 0$ for all levels of production. Here we just pass away that problem by assuming that $\alpha > r_h$.

Now assume that there is a foreign rival firm knocking at the door of the domestic alcohol market. Its cost function, analogous to (17.2), is defined as:

$$C_f = r_f q_f , \tag{17.5}$$

where subscript 'f' stands for the foreign rival firm. The two competing firms produce homogeneous goods but with different cost, so that $Q = q_h + q_f$. To assure that the open policy is effective, we assume that $r_h > r_f$ for all levels of production quantity. In other words, we assume that the domestic firm is a high-cost firm and the foreign firm is a low-cost firm.

The opening of the domestic alcohol market is not free to the foreign firm. It pays an alcohol tax for each unit (in specific form) of its product in the home country. However, the tax level is far below the trade-prohibited level so that $q_h, q_f > 0$ is always the case to be considered. With an alcohol tax levied, the profit function of the foreign firm is

$$\pi_f = Pq_f - r_f q_f - tq_f . \qquad (17.6)$$

We are now faced with a two-stage game at hand. At the first stage, the government of the home country determines what level of alcohol taxes is levied; at the second stage, given the level of alcohol taxes, both firms determine what quantity to produce so as to maximize their own profit. The two rival firms play quantity competition in the market while treating the government tax as exogenously given to them. The equilibrium is a subgame perfect, and is solved by backward induction. That is, we solve the second stage first, and then take the reaction functions of the firms to solve for the first stage. Based on the above framework, the solution of the second stage yields the reaction functions of the two firms as:

$$q_h^{post} = \frac{\alpha - 2r_h + r_f + t}{3\beta}, \qquad (17.7)$$

$$q_f^{post} = \frac{\alpha + r_h - 2r_f - 2t}{3\beta}, \qquad (17.8)$$

$$Q^{post} = q_h^{post} + q_f^{post} = \frac{2\alpha - r_h - r_f - t}{3\beta}, \qquad (17.9)$$

where superscript 'post' stands for the situation after the market was opened to imports. To assure that $q_{h,} q_f > 0$, we need to assume that t has to fall into the interval of 0 and $\bar{t}$, where $\bar{t} = (\alpha - 2r_f + r_h)/2$. This is because if $t \geq \bar{t}$, the foreign firm will exit the domestic market as a result of $\pi_f \leq 0$.

Comparing equations (17.4) and (17.9), we obtain the effect of opening the market on alcohol consumption as follows:

$$\Delta Q = Q^{post} - q_h^{pre} = \frac{\alpha + r_h - 2r_f - 2t}{6\beta} > 0 \quad \forall t \in [0, \bar{t}). \qquad (17.10)$$

Equation (17.10) indicates that trade liberalization will lead to an increase in alcohol demand. As shown in equation (17.10), the magnitude of the demand expansion effect of opening the market depends on three factors: (i) cost advantage of the foreign firm; (ii) tax rate imposed on imported alcohol; and (iii) demand shifter. The expansion effect of alcohol demand will clearly be seen if the cost advantage of the foreign firm is higher. This is because opening up the domestic market to a low-cost foreign firm reduces the equilibrium price in the domestic market and hence increases the domestic demand for alcohol. The effect of demand expansion is also higher, the lower the tax rate imposed on imported alcohol. Finally, it has been shown in most literature that alcohol demand increases with income and alcohol advertising (for example, Saffer 1991). This result suggests that the expansion of alcohol demand resulting from trade liberalization will be more significant in higher-income developing countries. The demand expansion effect will be further strengthened if the foreign firm spends more advertising expenditures to influence the overall demand for alcohol.

4 EMPIRICAL FRAMEWORK

4.1 Empirical Specification

Based on the analytical result of equation (17.10), we formulate a testable hypothesis that trade liberalization leads to an increase in alcohol consumption. To test this hypothesis, we construct an empirical model for alcohol demand as follows:

$$Q_t = a_0 + a_1 P_t + a_2 Y_t + a_3 X_t + \varepsilon_t. \qquad (17.11)$$

Term Q_t is the quantity of alcohol demand at period t, P_t is the price of alcohol, Y_t is the income variable, X_t is a measure of trade policy toward the alcohol market, and ε_t is a random error term. Equation (17.11) states that alcohol consumption depends on the price of alcohol, income, and trade policy. Based on economic theory, plus evidence from previous studies, we predict that the parameter a_1 is negative, and parameter a_2 is positive if alcoholic beverages are normal goods. Our theoretical analysis also predicts that a_3 is positive because market demand will expand as the two firms compete against each other.

As mentioned, the research employs annual time-series data to estimate equation (17.11). For time-series data, stationarity is an important issue. A variable is referred to as I(1) category if the variable in level is non-stationary but becomes stationary after its first difference.[1] In general if one I(1) variable is regressed on other I(1) variables, the residual is I(1) and the *t*-statistic is significant. This dubious ordinary least squares (OLS) result is called 'spurious regression' in Granger and Newbold (1974). However, they have identified a situation in which this does not happen. If the residuals become stationary after a linear combination of the variables, the variables are cointegrated. The idea of cointegration analysis captures the property of long-run equilibrium because the variables have a common trend and move together, showing a close link. Therefore, we should conduct the unit root test first to investigate whether the variables we considered are stationary. The methods of unit root test employed in this study include the augmented Dickey–Fuller (ADF) test and the non-parametric test developed by Phillips and Perron (P&P) (1988). If the result of the unit root test shows that all the variables are stationary, the traditional OLS method can be employed to estimate equation (17.11).[2] If the testing results show that variables are I(1) then we shall employ cointegration analysis to estimate equation (17.11). This choice is based on the assumption that each individual variable has a drift (constant) term that makes the trend embedded, but the long-run equilibrium conditions does not have trends, which is common for most economic time series. A test for cointegration can be thought of as a pre-test to avoid 'spurious regression' results (Granger 1986).

4.2 Data and the Variables

The data set employed in this study is annual time-series data from Taiwan covering the years from 1966 to 1996. The dependent variable used in the regressions is per capita annual consumption of alcoholic beverages in liters, which is computed by adding together the quantities of sales for all types of alcoholic beverages, including beer, wine, and spirits, and then dividing by annual population data on mid-year estimates.[3] These data come from the *Taiwan Tobacco and Wine Statistical Yearbook* published by the Taiwan Tobacco and Wine Monopoly Bureau (TTWMB 1997), and the Ministry of the Interior (1996). Figure 17.2 shows the total quantity consumed per capita for all types of alcoholic beverages in Taiwan from 1966 through 1996. It reveals that annual alcohol consumption per capita grew steadily during the past three decades, from about 10 liters in 1966 to nearly 40 liters in recent years.

The real alcohol price is computed by dividing the consumer price index for alcoholic beverages (ACPI) by the consumer price index for all goods (CPI). The price indices data are taken from the survey report by the Directorate-General of Budget, Accounting and Statistics (DGBAS 1997a). As Figure 17.3 indicates, the nominal price index of alcoholic beverages increased over time. However, the real price index declined steadily. If we set 1966 as the base year and let the 1966 real price index equal 100, then the real price index in 1996 is only 37.23. This result suggests that price inflation is lower for alcoholic beverages than for the

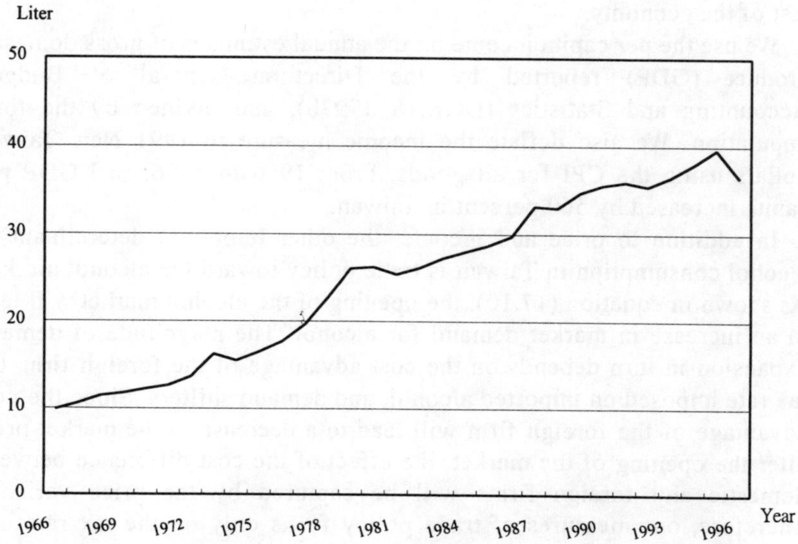

Figure 17.2 Annual per capita consumption of alcoholic beverages in Taiwan

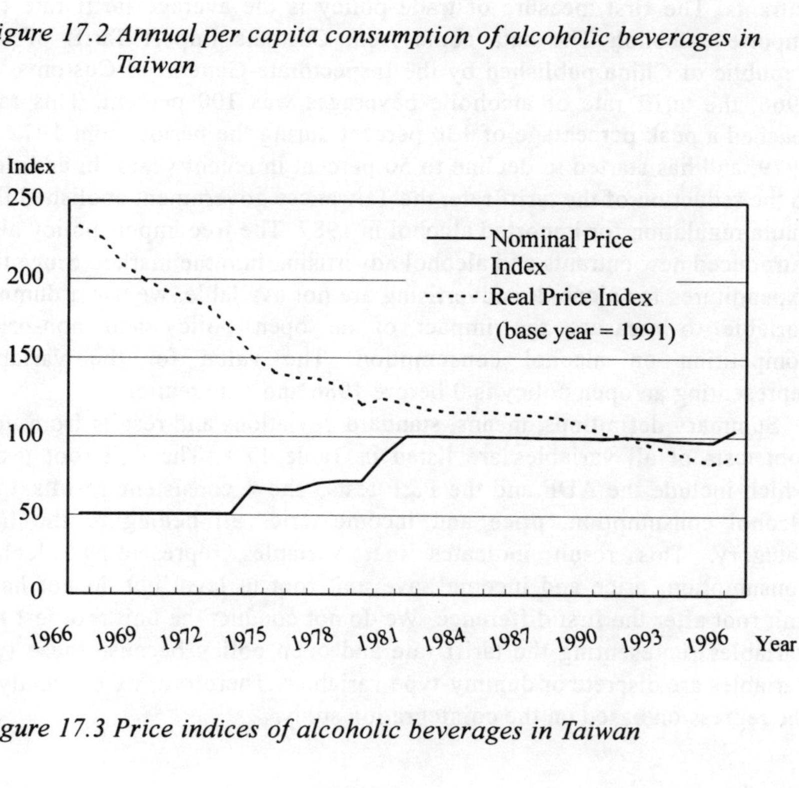

Figure 17.3 Price indices of alcoholic beverages in Taiwan

rest of the economy.

We use the per capita income on the annual estimates of gross domestic product (GDP) reported by the Directorate-General of Budget, Accounting and Statistics (DGBAS 1997b), and divided by the total population. We also deflate the income measure to 1991 New Taiwan dollars using the CPI for all goods. From 1966 to 1996, real GDP per capita increased by 560 percent in Taiwan.

In addition to price and income, the other important determinant of alcohol consumption in Taiwan is trade policy toward the alcohol market. As shown in equation (17.10), the opening of the alcohol market will lead to an increase in market demand for alcohol. The magnitude of demand expansion in turn depends on the cost advantage of the foreign firm, the tax rate imposed on imported alcohol, and demand shifters. Since the cost advantage of the foreign firm will lead to a decrease in the market price after the opening of the market, the effect of the cost difference between domestic and foreign firms will be captured by the price variable. Therefore, our measures of trade policy focus only on the tax rate and demand shifter resulting from competition, such as advertising of new entrants. The first measure of trade policy is the average tariff rate for imported alcohol. The data come from Customs Import Tariff of the Republic of China published by the Inspectorate-General of Customs. In 1966, the tariff rate of alcoholic beverages was 100 percent. This rate reached a peak percentage of 130 percent during the period from 1972 to 1979, and has started to decline to 50 percent in recent years. In addition to the reduction of the tariff rate, the Taiwanese government abolished the quota regulation for imported alcohol in 1987. The free import policy also introduced new entrants and alcohol advertising into the market. Since the expenditures for alcoholic advertising are not available, we use a dummy variable to measure the impact of an open policy and non-price competition on alcohol consumption. The value for the variable representing an open policy is 0 before 1986 and 1 thereafter.

Summary definitions, means, standard deviations and results from unit root tests of all variables are listed in Table 17.1. The unit root tests, which include the ADF and the P&P tests, show consistent results that alcohol consumption, price and income series all belong to the I(1) category. This result indicates that variables representing alcohol consumption, price and income have unit root in level but do not have unit root after the first difference. We do not conduct the unit root test for variables representing the tariff rate and open policy because these two variables are discrete or dummy-type variables. Therefore, we can analyse the regression based on the cointegration study.

Table 17.1 Variable definitions and descriptive characteristics

Variable	Definition	Mean (standard deviation)	ADF test	P&P test
Alcohol consumption	Annual per capita consumption of alcoholic beverages (including beer, wine and spirits), in liters	24.74 (9.72)	L −1.73 D −3.39*	L −1.73 D −3.85**
Price	Real consumer price index of alcohol, 1991 as a base year (=100)	136.27 (42.78)	L −1.68 D −3.58**	L −2.57 D −3.83**
Income	Real GDP per capita, in 1991 New Taiwan dollars	142,210.61 (77,709.60)	L −1.15 D −3.90**	L −1.06 D −4.22**
Tariff rate	Tariff rate for alcoholic beverages (%)	86.47 (33.12)	NA	NA
Open	A dummy variable representing the opening of the alcohol market in Taiwan, zero before 1986 and one thereafter	0.32 (0.47)	NA	NA

Notes

1. The exchange rate (NT$/US$) was 25.75 in December 1991.
2. L = level, D = difference of the series. ** means significant under 5 percent critical value, * indicates 10 percent level. The unit root test is based on test with constant term and time trend. The ADF test uses 1 lag difference and the P&P test used three truncation lags in the test. The null hypothesis in both tests is unit root.
3. Tariff rate and open variables are discrete or dummy-type variables. The unit root test on these two variables is not appropriate.

5 EMPIRICAL RESULTS

Because of the integrated property of the variables, we have to consider whether the cointegration relationship among alcohol consumption, price and income exists to avoid the possibility of spurious regression. The cointegration test statistics of these three variables by Johansen's likelihood ratio test is 36.229 for non-cointegration, 14.018 for at most one cointegrating vector, 0.484 for at most two cointegrating vectors. Comparing with the critical value, we can reject the null hypothesis of no cointegration at the 1 percent significance level, but cannot reject the hypothesis of more than one cointegrating vectors at the 5 percent level.[4] This shows that the likelihood ratio test suggests only one cointegrating vector. This is a good result as it enables us to analyse the relation without encountering the difficulty we may have had in identifying the true relationship if there were more than one cointegrating vector (Wickens 1996). In the following, we first estimate equation (17.11) using OLS.[5] In different models, we also include the tariff rate and open variables to capture the effect of trade liberalization. Adding dummy variables cannot change the cointegration relationship and the estimation result of cointegrating regression is still valid. However, the residuals from the regression may have a strong serial correlation. To correct for possible serial correlation, we also consider the transfer function by including an AR(1) in the residual.[6] After the model is estimated we conduct several residual diagnostic tests to examine whether the model is adequate. The diagnostic tests include the Jarque-Bera statistic test for normality, the Ljung-Box Q statistic test for serial correlation, the Lagrange multiplier statistic test for ARCH, and the White test for heteroskedasticity.

Table 17.2 presents four alternative specifications that represent different estimations of the alcohol demand equation. Several summary statistics to judge the general performance of the estimated models are also reported in Table 17.2. The Durbin–Watson test statistics are less than 1 in all specifications, indicating that the residuals in the models are serially correlated. Therefore, we estimate the model with first-order autocorrelation and the results are reported in Table 17.3. The estimated coefficients of AR(1) are positive and significant, suggesting a positive autocorrelation of the residual errors. After the adjustment of AR(1), the diagnostic tests on the residual show that no systematic information is left on the fitted model.

As predicted, the real price has a significantly negative effect on the demand for alcohol beverages. This is quite robust because the coefficient estimates remain significantly negative in all specifications. The empirical results produce estimates for the price elasticity of alcohol demand (measured at sample means) in a relatively narrow range, from –0.54 to –0.68, centered on –0.60. These estimates imply that a 10 percent decrease in alcohol prices will lead to a 6 percent increase in the per capita consumption of alcoholic beverages. As suggested in Manning et al. (1995), the price elasticity estimates for overall alcohol demand from aggregate data fall within the relatively wide range from –0.5 to –1.6. Thus, our findings for price elasticities suggest that the demand of Taiwan's alcohol consumers is at least as responsive to changes in prices as that of their counterparts in developed countries.

Tables 17.2 and 17.3 also show a significantly positive effect of income on alcohol consumption. The results produce estimates of the income elasticity of alcohol demand, calculated at the means of the variables, in a relatively narrow range centered on 0.3. The elasticity estimates suggest that a 10 percent growth in income will lead to an increase in per capita alcohol consumption by 3 percent, implying that alcoholic beverages are normal goods. Our income elasticity of 0.3 for all types of alcoholic beverages is within the range (0.18 to 1.75) of estimates for the US data (Goel and Morey 1995; Manning et al. 1995).

Table 17.2 Estimated coefficients of the alcohol demand equations

	Model 1	Model 2	Model 3	Model 4
Estimation results				
Price	–0.098***	–0.116***	–0.105***	–0.124***
	(–6.254)	(–8.830)	(–5.417)	(–7.806)
	[–0.54]	[–0.64]	[–0.58]	[–0.68]
Income	0.00007***	0.00004***	0.00006***	0.00003*
	(8.475)	(4.239)	(3.429)	(1.870)
	[0.42]	[0.23]	[0.34]	[0.17]
Tariff rate	–	–0.064***	–	–0.065***
		(–4.202)		(–4.213)
Open	–	–	1.260	1.445
			(0.629)	(0.918)
Intercept	27.710***	40.075***	29.712***	42.447***
	(8.461)	(10.216)	(6.467)	(9.017)
Summary statistics				
R^2	0.964	0.978	0.965	0.979
Adjusted R^2	0.961	0.976	0.961	0.976
DW	0.393	0.901	0.367	0.877
SE of regression	1.908	1.511	1.929	1.515
J-B	0.382	0.762	0.256	0.773
L-B Q(2)	0	0.023	0	0.106
B-G(2)	0	0.004	0	0.001
ARCH(2)	0.449	0.009	0.104	0.003
White	0.215	0.13	0.197	0.005

Notes

1. Asymptotic t-statistics are in parentheses.
2. Price and income elasticities calculated at their means are reported in square brackets.
3. J-B denotes Jarque-Bera statistic test for normality, L-B Q(2) denotes 2 lags included in the Ljung-Box Q statistic test for serial correlation, and ARCH(2) denotes 2 lags included in the Lagrange multiplier statistic test for autoregressive conditional heteroskedasticity (ARCH). All the numbers reported are p-values of the test statistics.
4. ***, **, and * denote coefficients that are statistically significant at the 1, 5, and 10 percent levels, respectively (two-tailed test).

Table 17.3 Estimated coefficients of the alcohol demand equations, with AR(1) adjustment

	Model 5	Model 6	Model 7
Estimation results			
Price	–0.110**	–0.107**	–0.114**
	(–2.214)	(–2.025)	(–2.306)
	[–0.58]	[–0.56]	[–0.60]
Income	0.00006***	0.00007***	0.00005***
	(3.928)	(3.778)	(2.840)
	[0.39]	[0.40]	[0.31]
Tariff rate	–	0.004	–
		(0.121)	
Open	–	–	2.216*
			(1.658)
AR(1)	0.826***	0.839***	0.840***
	(6.221)	(5.245)	(6.522)
Intercept	29.062***	28.110***	30.940***
	(3.779)	(3.403)	(4.092)
Summary statistics			
R^2	0.986	0.986	0.987
Adjusted R^2	0.984	0.984	0.985
SE of regression	1.190	1.213	1.151
J-B	0.047	0.04	0.025
L-B Q(2)	0.343	0.312	0.222
B-G(2)	0.404	0.352	0.266
ARCH(2)	0.643	0.654	0.663
White	0.118	0.275	0.071

Notes

1. Asymptotic *t*-statistics are in parentheses.
2. Price and income elasticities calculated at their means are reported in square brackets.
3. J-B denotes Jarque-Bera statistic test for normality, L-B Q(2) denotes 2 lags included in the Ljung-Box Q statistic test for serial correlation, and ARCH(2) denotes 2 lags included in the Lagrange multiplier statistic test for autoregressive conditional heteroskedasticity (ARCH). All the numbers reported are *p*-values of the test statistics.
4. ***, **, and * denote coefficients that are statistically significant at the 1, 5, and 10 percent levels, respectively (two-tailed test).

Results of the effects of trade policy are consistent with prior expectations. As shown in Table 17.2, the estimated coefficients of the tariff rate variable are negative and statistically significant at the 1 percent level. This result suggests that reducing the tariff rate of imported alcohol leads to an increase in overall consumption of alcoholic beverages. However, as shown in Table 17.3, the above effect becomes insignificant after the adjustment of serial correlation. A plausible explanation for this result is that the effect of tariff reduction was captured by the decrease in alcohol prices after controlling for the effect of first-order autocorrelation.

In addition to the direct effect on price reduction, the opening of the alcohol market has other indirect effects, such as the increase in non-price competition and alcohol advertising, which may have a positive impact on alcohol consumption. This indirect effect is captured by the dummy variable representing the opening of the alcohol market (*OPEN*). Table 17.3 shows that the coefficient of the *OPEN* variable is positive and statistically significant at the 10 percent level. The estimated coefficient indicates that opening the market to alcohol imports led to a 2.2-liter increase in annual per capita consumption of alcoholic beverages, after accounting for price and other variables. The increment of 2.2 liters represents 7.38 percent of the per capita alcohol consumption (29.79 liters) in 1986, the year before trade liberalization for alcohol. This result suggests, albeit moderately, that opening up the alcohol market to foreign competition will lead to an increase in alcohol demand.

During the study period, the per capita alcohol consumption in Taiwan increased by 269 percent, from 9.87 liters in 1966 to 36.46 liters in 1996. Our results also provide an empirical basis to account for the driving forces of the rise in alcohol consumption. The estimates indicate that alcohol is a normal good, thus growth in income is an important source to drive up demand for alcoholic beverages. As noted in the previous section, real GDP per capita increased by 560 percent in Taiwan during the period from 1966 to 1996. Using our estimate of income elasticity of 0.3, income growth could account for a 168 percent increase in per capita alcohol consumption, about 62 percent of the 269 percent actual increase.

The second source that drives up demand for alcoholic beverages is the drop in the real alcohol price. As mentioned, the real alcohol price decreased by 63 percent in Taiwan during the study period. Based on our estimate of price elasticity of –0.6, the drop in real price should have caused about a 38 percent increase in alcohol demand from 1966 to 1996. There are three plausible reasons for the sustained decline in the real price of alcohol. First, productivity gains are higher for the production of alcohol than in the rest of the economy. Thus, relative alcohol prices would decline over time. Second, the tariff rate imposed on imported alcohol has decreased steadily during the study period. The reduction of the tariff rate, in turn, has led to a decrease in the market price of alcohol. Third, the opening up of imported alcohol introduced competition into the market, and hence provided another driving force to lower the market price. Our data indicate that the real alcohol price has decreased by 24 percent in Taiwan from 1986 to 1996. Therefore, we can conclude that some effects of trade liberalization were captured by the decrease in the real alcohol price, and this, in turn, led to an increase in alcohol consumption. This result, in combination with the finding that the opening up of the alcohol market also has a positive effect on alcohol consumption, provides strong evidence to support our theoretical prediction that trade liberalization has a positive impact on the per capita consumption of alcoholic beverages.

6 CONCLUSIONS

In this study, we use aggregate time-series data to estimate the demand function for alcoholic beverages in Taiwan. This estimation provides an empirical basis to test the impact of trade liberalization on alcohol consumption. Our results indicate that alcohol consumption is responsive to price, with a price elasticity of –0.6. This result suggests that the reduction of alcohol price resulting from trade liberalization, such as the reduction of the tariff rate for imported alcohol, will lead to an increase in per capita alcohol consumption. In addition to the effect on price, the trade liberalization introduces non-price competition between domestic and foreign firms, such as an increase in alcohol advertising. Our results find that the non-price competition resulting from the opening of the alcohol market also leads to an increase in alcohol consumption. Therefore, our empirical results provide evidence to support the prediction that trade liberalization has resulted in significant increases in per capita alcohol consumption. Furthermore, our analysis reinforces the conventional wisdom that alcoholic beverages are normal goods. Based on the estimates of income elasticity of 0.3, we find that income growth is the most important driving force for the increase in alcohol consumption in Taiwan during the past three decades.

The estimated results presented above suggest that the global trends of economic growth and trade liberalization will increase the overall alcohol consumption in developing countries. Given the evidence that alcohol abuse problems, such as drunk driving, adverse health effects, and violence, are likely to be closely related to average consumption levels, the potential adverse impact of increasing alcohol consumption resulting from economic growth and trade liberalization is an important health policy issue in developing countries. Many developed countries have long used various types of alcohol control policies to reduce the adverse health effects of alcohol abuse (Chaloupka et al. 1991). Among them, alcohol tax has been recognized as an effective policy tool to control the consumption of alcohol as well as the problems of alcohol abuse (Grossman et al. 1993). Our analysis also sheds light on the potential effectiveness of such a policy in Taiwan. Our results indicate that a tax increase could have a strong effect on alcohol consumption in Taiwan, while still being financially beneficial to the government. According to our estimates, a 10 percent increase in the price of alcohol as a result of a tax increase would lead to a 6 percent reduction in overall alcohol consumption.

NOTES

* This is a revised version of a paper presented at the Taipei International Conference on Health Economics organized by the Institute of Economics, Academia Sinica in Taipei, Taiwan, March 25–26, 1999. Research for this study was supported by a grant from the ROC National Science Council (Grant number: NSC 88-2415-H-001-014). We are grateful to Matthew C. Farrelly, Michael Grossman and anonymous referees for their valuable advice and comments on earlier drafts. The authors take full responsibility for any remaining errors.

1 The I(1) category corresponds to the idea of random walk in the stock or exchange rate market, which states that the markets are efficient or lack arbitrage opportunity, or consumption is a random walk derived from the Euler equation based on the permanent income hypothesis and rational expectations (Hall 1978).

2 In this case, researchers often include a time trend in the regression model to capture the long-run effect.

3 An alternative measure of alcohol consumption is to express the quantity of consumption in terms of pure alcohol by adjusting the percentage of alcohol in each alcoholic beverage. However, the disaggregated data by types of alcoholic beverages are not available for imported alcohol.

4 We ran the cointegration test with one lag in the levels. The cointegration test we applied here was the Johansen test (Johansen 1991). Johansen's framework considers five combinations of these ingredients: (i) series have means but the cointegrating equations do not have intercepts; (ii) series have means and the cointegrating equations have intercepts; (iii) series have means and linear trends but the cointegrating equations have only intercepts; (iv) series have means and linear trends and the cointegrating equations have intercepts and linear trends; or

(v) series have means, linear, and quadratic trends but the cointegrating equations have only intercepts and linear trends. These five cases are nested from the most restrictive to the least restrictive, given any particular cointegrating rank. The testing result reported is from the third model since most of the economic discussions relate to this case.

5 When even only one cointegrating vector exists in the model, the OLS approach has been criticized because the second-order bias in the regression remains even after an increase in the sample size. Phillips suggests using a fully modified estimator to correct this problem. However, the fully modified estimation result is similar to the OLS result obtained here.

6 As mentioned, the cointegration analysis simply uses the feature that individual economic time series are I(1) but become stationary after linear combination. The linear combination cancels out the embedded trends that I(1) variables created. Since this framework has captured the property of long-run equilibrium, we do not need to include a time trend in the cointegration analysis.

REFERENCES

Chaloupka, Frank J. and Adit Laixuthai (1996), 'U.S. trade policy and cigarette smoking in Asia', National Bureau of Economic Research, Working Paper No. 5543.

Chaloupka, Frank J., Henry Saffer and Michael Grossman (1991), 'Alcohol control policies and motor vehicle fatalities', National Bureau of Economic Research, Working Paper No. 3831, September.

Clements, Kenneth W. and Saroja Selvanathan (1991), 'The economic determinants of alcohol consumption', *Australian Journal of Agricultural Economics*, **35**(2), August: 209–31.

Cook, Philip J. and Michael J. Moore (1993), 'Drinking and schooling', *Journal of Health Economics*, **12**(4), December: 411–29.

Directorate-General of Budget, Accounting and Statistics (1997a), *Commodity-price Statistics Monthly in Taiwan Area, ROC*, Taipei: DGBAS (in Chinese).

Directorate-General of Budget, Accounting and Statistics (DGBAS) (1997b), *National Income in Taiwan, ROC*, Taipei: DGBAS (in Chinese).

French, Michael T. and Gary A. Zarkin (1995), 'Is moderate alcohol use related to wages? Evidence from four worksites', *Journal of Health Economics*, **14**(3), August: 319–44.

Goel, Rajeev K. and Mathew J. Morey (1995), 'The interdependence of cigarette and liquor demand', *Southern Economic Journal*, **10**(2), October: 451–9.

Granger, Clive W.J. (1986), 'Developments in the study of co-integrated economic variables', *Oxford Bulletin of Economics and Statistics*, **48**: 283–307.

Granger, Clive W.J. and Paul Newbold (1974), 'Spurious regressions in econometrics', *Journal of Econometrics*, **2**: 111–20.

Grossman, Michael, Jody L. Sindelar, John Mullahy and Richard Anderson (1993), 'Policy watch: alcohol and cigarette taxes', *Journal of Economic Perspectives*, **7**(4), Fall: 211–22.

Hall, R.E. (1978), 'Stochastic implications of the life cycle-permanent income hypothesis: theory and evidence', *Journal of Political Economy*, **86**: 971–87.

Hamilton, Vivian and Barton H. Hamilton (1997), 'Alcohol and earnings: does drinking yield a wage premium?', *Canadian Journal of Economics*, **30**(1), February: 135–51.

Johansen, S. (1991), 'Estimation and hypothesis testing of cointegration vectors in Gaussian vector autoregressive models', *Econometrica*, **59**(6): 1551–80.

Kenkel, Donald S. (1993), 'Drinking, driving, and deterrence: the effectiveness and social costs of alternative policies', *Journal of Law and Economics,* **36**(2), October: 877–913.

Manning, Willard G., Linda Blumberg and Lawrence H. Moulton (1995), 'The demand for alcohol: the differential response to price', *Journal of Health Economics*, **14**(2), June: 123–48.

Markowitz, Sara, and Michael Grossman (1998), 'Alcohol regulation and domestic violence towards children', *Contemporary Economic Policy*, **16**(3), July: 309–20.

Ministry of the Interior (1996), *Taiwan-Fukien Demographic Fact Book, ROC*, Taipei: Ministry of the Interior (in Chinese).

Mullahy, John and Jody L. Sindelar (1994), 'Do drinkers know when to say when? An empirical analysis of drunk driving', *Economic Inquiry*, **32**(3), July: 383–94.

Phillips, P.C.B. and P. Perron (1988), 'Testing for unit root in time series regression', *Biometrica*, **75**: 335–46.

Saffer, Henry (1991), 'Alcohol advertising bans and alcohol abuse: an international perspective', *Journal of Health Economics*, **10**(1), May: 65–79.

Saffer, Henry and Michael Grossman (1987), 'Drinking age laws and highway mortality rates: cause and effect', *Economic Inquiry*, **25**(3), July: 403–17.

Selvanathan, Antony E. (1988), 'Alcohol consumption in the UK, 1955–85: a system-wide analysis', *Applied Economics*, **20(8)**, August: 1071–86.

Sloan, Frank A., Bridget A. Reilly and Christoph Schenzler (1995), 'Effects of tort liability and insurance on heavy drinking and drinking and driving', *Journal of Law and Economics*, **38**(1), April: 49–77.

Taiwan Tobacco and Wine Monopoly Bureau (TTWMB) (1997), *Taiwan Tobacco and Wine Statistical Yearbook*, Taipei: TTWMB (in Chinese).

Wickens, M.R. (1996), 'Interpreting cointegrating vectors and common stochastic trends', *Journal of Econometrics*, **74**(2): 255–71.

Zhou, Xian-Wen (1980), *Economic History of Taiwan*, Taipei: Kai-Ming Publishing (in Chinese).

Index